Catholics and Communists in Twentieth-Century Italy

Catholics and Communists in Twentieth-Century Italy

Between Conflict and Dialogue

Daniela Saresella

BLOOMSBURY ACADEMIC
LONDON · NEW YORK · OXFORD · NEW DELHI · SYDNEY

BLOOMSBURY ACADEMIC
Bloomsbury Publishing Plc
50 Bedford Square, London, WC1B 3DP, UK
1385 Broadway, New York, NY 10018, USA
29 Earlsfort Terrace, Dublin 2, Ireland

BLOOMSBURY, BLOOMSBURY ACADEMIC and the Diana logo
are trademarks of Bloomsbury Publishing Plc

First published in Great Britain 2020
Paperback edition first published 2021

Copyright © Daniela Saresella, 2020

Daniela Saresella has asserted her right under the Copyright,
Designs and Patents Act, 1988, to be identified as Author of this work.

For legal purposes the Acknowledgements on p. vii constitute
an extension of this copyright page.

Cover image: Aldo Moro, Prisoner of The Red Brigades in Italy in February, 1979.
(© Francois LOCHON/Getty Images)

All rights reserved. No part of this publication may be reproduced or
transmitted in any form or by any means, electronic or mechanical,
including photocopying, recording, or any information storage or retrieval
system, without prior permission in writing from the publishers.

Bloomsbury Publishing Plc does not have any control over, or responsibility for,
any third-party websites referred to or in this book. All internet addresses given
in this book were correct at the time of going to press. The author and publisher
regret any inconvenience caused if addresses have changed or sites have
ceased to exist, but can accept no responsibility for any such changes.

A catalogue record for this book is available from the British Library.

A catalog record for this book is available from the Library of Congress.

ISBN: HB: 978-1-3500-6142-2
PB: 978-1-3502-4505-1
ePDF: 978-1-3500-6143-9
eBook: 978-1-3500-6144-6

Typeset by Integra Software Services Pvt. Ltd.

To find out more about our authors and books visit
www.bloomsbury.com and sign up for our newsletters.

Contents

Acronyms	vi
Introduction	1
1 Christianity and Socialism in Italy: The First Period	7
2 Catholic Anti-Fascists and Their Relationship with the Left-Wing World	23
3 From Catholic Communists to the New Openness to Centre-Left Governments	59
4 Changing Times	85
5 The Long Seventies	107
6 The Political System Heads towards Crisis	119
7 On the End of the First and Second Millennium	149
Conclusion	175
Notes	179
Bibliography	225
Index	254

Acronyms

AC	Azione Cattolica (Italian Catholic Action)
ACLI	Associazione Cattolica Lavoratori Italiani (Catholic Association of Italian Workers)
AN	Alleanza Nazionale (National Alliance)
BR	Brigate Rosse (Red Brigades)
CAI	Concentrazione Antifascista Italiana (Italian Antifascist Concentration)
CCD	Centro Cristiano Democratico (Christian Democratic Centre)
CEI	Conferenza Episcopale Italiana (Italian Episcopal Commettee)
CISL	Confederazione Italiana Sindacati Lavoratori (Italian Confederation of Trade Unions)
CL	Comunione e Liberazione (Communion and liberation)
CLN	Comitato di Liberazione Nazionale (National Liberation Committee)
CPS	Cristianos por el Socialismo (Christians for Socialism)
DC	Democrazia Cristiana (Christian Democratic Party)
DP	Democrazia Proletaria (Proletarian Democracy)
DS	Democrarici di Sinistra (Democrats of the Left)
FIM-CISL	Unione Lavoratori Metalmeccanici (Metalworkers' Union)
FOCSIV	Federazione Organismi Cristiani Servizio Internazionale Volontario (Federation of Christian International Voluntary Service Organisations)
FUCI	Federazione Universitaria Cattolici Italiani (Italian Catholic University Association)
GIAC	Gioventù Italiana di Azione Cattolica (Catholic Action Italian Youth)
GSF	Forum Sociale di Genova (Genoa Social Forum)

IDOC	Centro Internazionale di Documentazione e Comunicazione (International Centre of Documentation and Communication)
INSMLI	Istituto Nazionale per la Storia del Movimento di Liberazione in Italia (National Institute for the history of the liberation movement in Italy)
IRI	Istituto per la Ricostruzione Industriale (Institute for Industrial Reconstruction)
LD	Lega Democratica (Democratic League)
LDN	Lega Democratica Nazionale (Democratic National League)
MCC	Movimento dei Cattolici Comunisti (Movement of Communist Catholics)
MCP	Movimento Cristiano per la Pace (Christian Movement for Peace)
MPL	Movimento Politico dei Lavoratori (Workers' Political Movement)
MSI	Movimento Sociale Italiano (Italian Social Movement)
PCI	Partito Comunista Italiano (Communist Party)
PCS	Partito Cristiano Sociale (Social Christian Party)
PD	Partito Democratico (Democratic Party)
PdA	Partito d'Azione (Action Party)
PDS	Partito Democratico della Sinistra (Democratic Party of the Left)
PDSC	Partito della Sinistra Cristiana (Party of the Christian Left)
PLI	Partito Liberale Italiano (Liberal Party)
PPI	Partito Popolare Italiano (Italian Popular Party)
PRC	Partito della Rifondazione Comunista (Communist Refoundation Party)
PRI	Partito Repubblicano Italiano (Republican Party)
PSC	Partito Sociale Cristiano (Christian Social Party)
PSDI	Partito Socialdemocratico (Social Democratic Party)
PSI	Partito Socialista Italiano (Socialist Party)
RSI	Repubblica Sociale Italiana (Italian Social Republic)

Introduction

This book tackles the twentieth century, a period in Italian history that has been much studied. There is extensive historiography on the subject, mostly written in Italian but also in English. Some British historians – Christopher Duggan, Donald Sassoon, Jonathan Dunnage, John Foot – have gone more deeply into aspects of twentieth-century Italy, for example, with studies on specific events, whilst others have provided general histories of Italy intended for a non-specialist but curious audience.

There are also equally important works in Italian and English dealing with political Catholicism (John Pollard, Guido Formigoni, Agostino Giovagnoli) and significant international literature on the Catholic left in Europe (Gerd-Rainer Horn, Hugh McLeod, Jay Carrin, Yvon Tranvouez, Denis Pelletier), but there are none on a key aspect of twentieth-century Italian history: the relationship between Catholic and Marxist culture, between Catholics and Communists, and on the real dilemma of those Catholics who, throughout the twentieth century, identified with the political left. This book – and the wide range of sources that it deploys – offers readers new insights, interpretations and re-considerations of this vital part of Italian history.

The book analyses the fundamental impact of modernist ideas throughout the twentieth century, in the belief that Catholic culture has been deeply influenced by the legacy of Modernism. The relationship with modernity has always been a crucial issue in Italian history, as evidenced by Rosario Forlenza and Bjørn Thomassen's *Italian Modernities*: unlike the majority who say that Italy was 'a latecomer to modernity', the authors claim that the country was in fact a 'first-comer'.[1] Italy has certainly been, for very evident reasons, a 'crucial reference point' in terms of thinking about religion, secularity and modernity,[2] and the intention of this book is to shine a torch down the path – often fraught with obstacles and difficulties – of the Italian Catholic world towards modernity.

The author's objective is to offer a reconstruction of the past that will be of use in order to understand the peculiarities of today's world; what becomes evident is that the direction taken by Western culture (from the French Revolution onwards) towards the separation of the political and religious spheres has lately met with a crisis, so much so that in recent times Christianity has been used by populist groups and parties to legitimize their political identity.[3] This is an on-going process that future historians will be able to analyse and will probably place in the context of the epochal watershed that Western political culture is experiencing.

An outline of the book

The relationship between Catholics and socialists emerged at the beginning of the twentieth century, when, with the start of industrialization, Italy experienced the phenomenon of mass mobilization. Though a Catholic country, Italy has always been distinguished by the presence of a deeply rooted Socialist Party. The Italian left has always shown an interest in the Catholic world: the Vatican city state's presence within the national territory, and the strong religious traditions amongst its population, led important members of the Italian Socialist Party (PSI) to develop a tolerant and open attitude towards Catholics from the party's foundation (1892) onwards. The majority of PSI members were strongly anticlerical and saw the Church as part of Italy's retrograde power structure; but, unlike the German Social Democratic Party, the PSI was rooted in the countryside, and country people were profoundly under the influence of Catholicism. This was the origin of 'evangelical socialism' in Italy, something that was especially typical of the Emilia Romagna area.

At the same time, encouraged by the economic and social changes taking place, as well as by a new and growing awareness of social issues, a number of Catholics made the decision to initiate a dialogue with the socialist world. Some, such as Father Romolo Murri, saw in PSI a possible partner for debate and discussion, convinced that the programmes of democratic Catholics and socialists had many elements in common, both being intent on improving conditions for the poor. It is worth pointing out, as the socialist philosopher Giuseppe Rensi did in a letter to Murri, that the proposal served to acknowledge that, for Murri, 'it was not the religious criterion but the criterion of social, economic etc. issues (to sum up, earthly ones) that were the only ones capable of forming the cement for building a political party'.[4] So Murri, in a period of strong religious conservatism, placed emphasis on his lay conception of politics; he also challenged the idea that Christ's message could or should be interpreted in only one way from a social and political point of view, and interrogated the unity of the faithful in the face of Pius X's conservative directives.

Others, particularly those within intellectual circles, who were sensitive to modernist issues, believed that Christianity at its origins and early forms of socialism shared the same basic identity. Thus some scholars (including Father Ernesto Buonaiuti) chose to focus on the origins of the Church, convinced that examples could be found there of how the world could be changed according to Christian ethics.

These experiences of 'Christian socialism' were strongly opposed by the Church and almost disappeared after the Great War. The world of the left also underwent great changes in the aftermath of the First World War: the Italian Communist Party (PCI) was founded in Livorno in 1921 and, throughout the years of Mussolini's dictatorship, represented the most organized force in the fight against fascism. Pius XI, on the other hand, was keen to sign the Lateran Pacts in 1929 with the fascist leader, an event that put an end to the conflict between church and state in Italy that had begun in 1870, with the occupation of Rome by Italian troops. Relations between the Holy See and the Italian government were good until Mussolini began to draw increasingly close to Hitler, when the Vatican showed obvious concerns regarding the pagan nature of Nazism.

It was this period that gave rise to the Catholic-communist experience (1937–1945) in Italy. It took root in an intellectual environment: the movement joined the Comitato di Liberazione Nazionale (the National Liberation Committee, CLN) in January 1944 and was very active in the defence of Rome against German troops; it also included a partisan unit, known as the banda Ossicini which was active in Lazio and Umbria as well as in Rome.

The group developed significant philosophical and cultural ideas, since Catholic communists sought out new cultural horizons and were interested in exploring both Catholic and Marxist cultures. Franco Rodano, one of the keenest members of the Catholic Communist group, was interested in theoretical issues and set out to undertake a double de-ideologization. On the one hand, he tried to reduce Marxism to political science, while, on the other, he saw the risks of an ideologized religion with links to political and economic forces. Culturally alien to a 'simplified' interpretation of Marxism, one that promoted a mechanical view of the relationship between structure and superstructure and unaware of Antonio Gramsci's historicist and liberal interpretation, Rodano considered historical materialism as a scientific methodology operating within Marxism that was able to transform it into political science. An enthusiastic reader of Benedetto Croce's *Materialismo storico ed economia marxistica*[5] ('Historical materialism and a Marxist economy') and acquainted with Antonio Labriola's Marxism, Rodano did not embrace the materialist and immanentist vision of the Marxist model. And yet he supported the thesis that viewed Marxism as 'historiographical canon', and it encouraged him to consider economic factors. The influence of neoidealism is evident in Rodano's thought and led him to promote a new foundation of both secular and Catholic culture in order to achieve an ultimate synthesis between the two.

For a long time, it has been maintained that the principal conviction of Catholic Communists was that dogma should not be historicized and religion should not meet the demands of a society undergoing transformation. In his famous *Questione democristiana e compromesso storico*[6] ('The Christian-Democratic Question and the Historical Compromise'), the book that contains the synthesis of his religious and political thought, Rodano, inspired by Hugues-Félicité Robert de Lamennais, maintained that a correct interpretation of the scriptures could only take place within the Catholic Church, since only there did Revelation take on a universal character. The Church was identified with the pope, and it was therefore up to the latter to guarantee the conditions for the biblical message to be uniformally received and translated into social practice. Like his Breton fellow-thinker, Rodano did not believe in the necessity of ecclesiastical reform, deeming it possible for Catholics to have an open attitude towards modern politics. He was not interested in a version of Christianity that, excluding the evangelical category of a kingdom promised to the poor, raised objections to the current state of things. In the same way, he criticized those believers who were tempted to project transcendence into history.

Rodano remained in the PCI until his death: he was a valuable advisor to Palmiro Togliatti on Catholic matters and is considered to have inspired the famous proposal of the 'Compromesso storico' (historic compromise). This was formulated in 1973 by the communist leader Enrico Berlinguer and comprised a great alliance that – in times of unrest due to the subversive force of neo-fascist extremism – was designed to bring together the large parties, mainly the PCI and the Democrazia Cristiana (Democratic Catholic Party, DC).

Unlike Rodano, Adriano Ossicini, another member of the Catholic communist group, had always harboured doubts in relation to religion and, above all, did not feel in line with ecclesiastical authority. An avid reader of French philosophy, especially Maritain and Mounier, he also looked with interest at the ideas that developed within modernist culture at the beginning of the twentieth century and believed it was necessary to reform the Church.

The conviction that action for social justice could not be separated from profound Church reform had already been expressed by Buonaiuti, who had pointed out the political-administrative degeneration that had afflicted the Church from Constantine onwards. After the Second World War, believers came to the fore who envisaged a Church that was both poor itself and close to the poor: these included Don Primo Mazzolari, the Servants of Mary David Maria Turoldo and Camillo De Piaz, the Piarist Ernesto Balducci, together with Giuseppe Dossetti, Giorgio La Pira and Giuseppe Lazzati. Many of them were important figures in the renewal years of the Council and the post-Council, when the belief was established that the Church should deal with the problems of humanity and cease all compromise with political power.

The question of Catholic political unity, which had been an issue since the beginning of the century, still remained unresolved in the sixties and seventies. After the Second World War, the majority of Italian Catholics, supported by the ecclesiastical hierarchy, gave their votes to the Christian Democrats, who, within the Italian context, assumed the role of an anti-communist force. The question of Catholic political unity had been a crucial issue since Vatican II, when a significant number of Catholics advocated freedom of choice in politics. In the aftermath of the Council, many Catholic organizations decided to stop giving electoral support to the DC, thus making a religious choice, and some believers, involved in helping the poor, tried to find a new direction through a cultural dialogue with the left. In the 1970s, the Christians for Socialism group was founded and in the 1976 elections many Christians decided to vote for the Communist Party.

The most interesting occurrence, however, was that, shaken by the crisis of 1956, a number of Italian communist intellectuals began to distinguish between their own positions and those of the USSR. Many turned their attention towards Marxist scholars, such as Adams Schaff and Roger Garaudy, who were developing independent lines of research in the direction of 'Marxist humanism'. Marxists were in fact engaging in the rediscovery of subjectivity and the importance of human action in history. These intellectuals played important roles in a dialogue with a Catholic world, which, in the wake of Vatican II, was also involved in reassessing its core convictions. The post-Conciliar emphasis on the difference between the communist movement, which followed erroneous doctrines, and the doctrines themselves was an innovation, and this facilitated relations between these two very different cultures. On the Catholic side, the dialogue was grounded in the intention to separate Marxism, which represented an abstraction, from Marxists; to separate communism, a doctrine founded on error, from the workers' movement, which represented the healthy backbone of society. While Marxists and Christians could, and did, come together on the basis of their shared interest in the values of human dignity and social justice, not all of their differences could be resolved. But Italy's particular circumstances, with both a strong Catholic presence in society and firmly rooted communist intellectual circles, produced a fruitful exchange of views at a theoretical level which could not have taken place in other national contexts.

In the early 1990s, the Italian political system, strongly conditioned by the events of the Cold War, collapsed. The Communist Party changed its name and abandoned Marxist ideology, and parties (the DC and PSI) that had been in government for decades were overwhelmed by investigations into corruption. The relationship between Catholic and Marxist culture, between Catholics and Communists, which had been at the centre of debate throughout the twentieth century, came to an end. The dilemma of those Catholics who identified themselves with the political left remained a crucial topic but took on a different character. At the end of the 'century of ideologies', the Italian political system split into two parts, progressives and conservatives, with Catholics dividing along these two fronts.

Following the dissolution of the Christian Democrat Party (1994), and thus the conclusion of the experience of a national Catholic party, the Italian Church continued to condition political parties with regard to ethical issues such as abortion, assisted procreation and euthanasia. Special treatment, however, especially in the years of the Wojtyla and Ratzinger pontificates, was given to the centre-right and to conservative and populist parties. Progressive Catholics tried to put a stop to this kind of interference, and one significant gesture in this direction was Romano Prodi's statement that it was necessary to confront the Church hierarchies as 'adult Catholics', who were willing and able to express their dissent. Prodi was one of the founders, in 2007, of the Partito Democratico (Democratic Party, PD), a new political grouping that brought together members of the left and progressive Catholics and which, despite various scissions and difficulties, is still a significant force in Italian political life.

1

Christianity and Socialism in Italy: The First Period

The contest

The break between conservative and democratic Catholicism coincided with the French Revolution. Between 1789 and 1792, the world of the Church was divided into those who wished to bring back the ideals of the *Ancien Régime* and those who were ready to face up to the issues of 'modernity' raised by the revolution and accept the positive elements that it had introduced. Whether Jansenist or anti-Jansenist, despite the different theological choices that marked their point of departure, democratic Catholics shared the need to forge an agreement between religion and democracy.[1] More significantly, these believers, spurred on by the new myths of radical renovation, concentrated on rediscovering the experiences of the first Christian communities: convinced that models and inspiration could be found there, they devoted themselves to re-reading the Bible and the gospels.

In this context, the interest in social issues was not the prerogative of a single line of thought. While it remained true that the French Revolution, and François-Noël Babeuf in particular, directed its attention towards the problems of the poorer classes, it was just as true that certain conservative Catholics did not hesitate to stress that many contradictions stemmed from the affirmation of the capitalist system, which had upset long-established social relations. The confrontation between the Catholic and the socialist worlds initially took place in Germany, Belgium and France.[2] In France, it was primarily Frédéric Ozanam, founder of the Société de Saint Vincent de Paul, who committed himself to helping the poor. A firm believer in the need for an understanding between Catholicism and democracy, he thought that the church should accept the new political and social developments emerging from the French Revolution. In Germany, too, in the early nineteenth century, certain Christians, such as Franz von Baader and Adam Heinrich Müller, were fierce critics of capitalism, emphasizing the inhuman exploitation suffered by workers in modern factories. At the same time as publication of Marx and Engels's *Communist Party Manifesto*, the Catholic bishop Wilhelm Emmanuel von Ketteler, in his sermons in Mainz Cathedral, was thundering against the egoistic concept underlying the relations between factory owners and proletarians. A critic of unbridled capitalism, Ketteler did not wish to abolish the market economy but hoped that it might be transformed in the interests of social well-being.[3] This awareness that it was necessary to take action in the world also changed the character of the Catholic movement, so much so that during the 1800s the work of religious congregations assumed an important role in the fields of education and social assistance. In particular, many religious men and women moved from a cloistered life of contemplation to more active participation, distinguishing themselves in the field of social commitment.[4]

The utopian socialist movement was, as is well known, suffused with strong religious feeling.[5] However, this link between Christianity and the Left was hard put to overcome the affirmation of Marx's concept of materialism and his conviction that it was not only the exploitation induced by the capitalist economic system that had to be eliminated, religion, too, which formed the system's social basis and was regarded as the 'opium of the people', must go the same way. This Marxist philosophy, with its aspects of atheism and materialism, triggered the Church's reaction, together with its concern that as a doctrine it would erode Christian sentiments in Western culture. Above all, alarm was raised by its subversive view of social equilibrium, which the ecclesiastical institutions – possessors of enormous wealth – could not tolerate.

Engels, on the other hand, who had a religious education, dealt with the question of religion rather differently from Marx. He showed interest in the original Christian Church and emphasized the considerable ground shared by early Christian experience and the modern workers' movement: in both cases, groups of the poor and oppressed were persecuted by those in power, who were desperate to maintain the status quo. Unlike Marx, who considered religion mainly a tool of the ruling class for controlling the lower social levels, Engels did not express a negative view of Christianity, believing that it might assume a positive function in the evolution of the lower classes – this had happened, for example, in Germany at the beginning of the 1500s during the peasant uprisings. Karl Kautsky took the same line and in 1902 wrote that the socialist movement had many features in common with early Christianity, since its origins, like the latter's, were proletarian.[6]

The first official condemnation of socialism by the church came in the encyclical *Qui plurius* of 9 December 1846 and the concept was reinforced by Pius IX in December 1864 in the encyclical *Quanta cura* and the *Sillabus errorum*, in which, whilst stigmatizing the century's ills, emphasis was placed on the 'deadly error of communism and socialism'. Leo XIII, who had already inspired a doctrinal analysis of socialism, dealt systematically with the problem in the *Rerum novarum*, which was published in May 1891.[7] The intention of the first part of the encyclical was to confute the theory of socialism, while in the second part alternative solutions were put forward, dictated by general ideals of solidarity between classes and a corporative model that was little suited to the industrial society of the late nineteenth century.[8]

Italy's singularity

Italy was constituted as a national state in 1861, incorporating within its territory regions that were part of the Vatican State. The break between the Holy See and the new state took place with the occupation of Rome in 1870. Pius IX, shutting himself away behind the Vatican walls, refused to recognize the Italian state and issued the *Non Expedit* decree in order to prevent Italian Catholics from participating in political elections. Thus Italy, led by liberal-inspired forces, was created with a certain inherent fragility and, in the Catholic Church, had to deal with a powerful and hostile entity within its own borders. The Jesuit journal *La Civiltà Cattolica* (founded in 1850) resolutely maintained that in Italy, while the government represented 'legal power', the church represented 'real power' and this was a fair picture of the true state of things, given the strong roots of Catholicism in the country and the elitist policies of the liberal forces.

Catholic aversion to the Italian state was not only due to the accusation that it was a 'usurpatory state', guilty of confiscating lands from the Holy See: Italy was also an expression of those liberal and secular ideas that the church had been inveighing strongly against since the time of the French Revolution. Criticism of economic conditions in Italy, driven by the emergence of new and modern systems of production and the development of the church's social doctrine, was encompassed in this more general context of cultural conflict.

In the last decade of the nineteenth century, Italy was still a backward country. Characterized by deep economic differences between north and south, it began the process of industrialization very late (after the protectionist shift of 1887). While in Germany the Sozialdemokratische Partei was founded in 1875, the PSI emerged many years later, in 1892, when the main organizations linked to the Second International had already been founded.

The majority of PSI members were anticlerical, but the party, unlike the German SPD, had roots both in industrial areas (Milan, Turin, Genoa) and in the countryside (especially in the Emilia Romagna region), and the peasantry were profoundly influenced by Catholicism. This gave rise to the creation of 'evangelical socialism' in Italy and the appearance, at the beginning of the twentieth century, of the figure of Camillo Prampolini in the Emilia area. Prampolini argued that socialism was the accomplishment of the ideals of the first Christians, and his ideas were echoed by Francesco Paoloni, founder of the magazine *Il seme*, who advocated a pedagogical project based on evangelical notions for farmers in the Lazio region.[9]

In Italy, due to the slow pace of economic development, contact between the Catholic and socialist worlds began late compared to other European countries. They shared a common interest in their aversion to the policies of the liberal state and their concern for the 'marginalized' elements of society and the victims of the economic transformations brought about by the new methods of production.

In 1885, the first attempts by a Catholic to deal with the challenges introduced by socialism were made by Father Carlo Maria Curci, the Jesuit author of *Di un socialismo cristiano nella questione operaia* ('On Christian Socialism with regard to the issue of the workers'), who revealed a strong sensitivity to social issues. After arguing that the aim of socialism was to find remedies for a system marked by 'an economic disorder that is not temporary and accidental', but alters the very fabric of society, with effects that are 'pernicious for most of society itself', he suggested the need to unite the terms 'Christian' and 'socialism'. Moreover, Curci pointed out how, according to the apostle Paul, Christ had intended to encourage the renewal of humankind and that the task of this 'new creature' would be to create a 'new society'.[10] Ideas along the same lines came from the Unione Cattolica per gli Studi Sociali (Catholic Union for Social Studies), founded in Padua by Giuseppe Toniolo. In 1894, the latter drew up the *Programma dei cattolici di fronte al socialismo* ('Catholic programme with regard to socialism') in which he argued the need to adopt a Catholic social doctrine in order to solve the problems of contemporary society.[11]

From the 1890s onwards, the Protestant minority in Italy, mostly Waldensian, also showed an interest in the fate of the workers' movement. While still expressing reservations with respect to Marxist materialism, the Protestants considered the criticisms of the capitalist economic system formulated by the Socialists to have some justification.[12] The debate on social issues was tackled mainly in the journal *Il Rinnovamento*, published in Rome between 1903 and

1907 by the Comitato di Evangelizzazione (Committee for Evangelization). The discussion was subsequently continued in the journals *La Luce* and *L'Avanguardia*, the latter being a monthly publication by Italian-speaking Social Christians, founded and edited by Giovanni Enrico Meille and published between 1908 and 1910. *La Rivista Cristiana, Bilychnis, Fede e vita* and *Lumen de lumine* also took part in the debate. The Protestant intellectuals were rarely in agreement with socialist arguments, preferring the prospect of Social Christianity, but they still considered dialogue and exchange with the cultural and political proposals of the left to be possible.[13] Amongst these socialist-leaning evangelists, it is worth remembering Pastor Enrico Meynier, author of two small volumes, one published in 1894, *Il socialismo e il cristianesimo di fronte alla questione sociale* ('Socialism and Christianity and the challenge of the social issue') and the other in 1902, *Problemi sociali contemporanei* ('Contemporary social problems').[14]

From the end of the nineteenth century onwards, Catholics in Italy had to deal with the sort of socialism that was rooted in society, and this particular feature created the conditions for possible collaboration. Be that as it may, in practice there was often a shared attempt to improve the living conditions of workers. In Milan, Don Umberto Benigni (who was to become one of the fiercest opponents of Modernism), together with Angelo Mauri and Filippo Meda, founded the journal *La Rassegna sociale*. They challenged the bases both of the liberal and the Marxist schools of thought and considered the *Camere del Lavoro* (official workers' centres), once Christianized, as useful tools for solving the problems of both workers and farm labourers.[15] Some Catholics even decided to cooperate with the socialists: Aristide Tagliabue, representing the Catholic workers' mutual aid society, was on the organizing committee of the *Camera del Lavoro* in Monza in 1893; Don Anastasio Rossi (who was to become Bishop of Udine) collaborated with the *Camera del Lavoro* of Pavia and Don Luigi Cazzamali[16] with the *Camera* in Lodi. Although the intention of these Catholic figures was to tackle the spread of socialist theories amongst the proletariat, their contact with the problems of the poor led them, in contrast to the corporative theories put forward by the *Rerum novarum*, to accept the strike as a means of defence by the workers and the idea of class war.[17]

The watershed at the end of the nineteenth century

The turning point in relations between Catholics and Socialists took place at the end of the nineteenth century. In May 1898, when the population of Milan organized strongly supported demonstrations to protest against food shortages, the part of the Catholic world which, since the French Revolution, had tended to condemn the nineteenth century's modern, bourgeois, liberal civilization started to realize that another, far more serious problem was appearing in Italian politics: the rise of socialism.

The Italian government, headed by the Marquis Antonio Starabba Di Rudinì, reacted forcefully to the peoples' uprisings, a policy largely supported by the Catholics. A gradual reconciliation between the Catholics and the state took place, united by their main concern of social subversion, the extremely serious problems between Italy and the Vatican were forgotten. For example, when Mother Francesca Saverio Cabrini was in Milan during the uprising, although sensitive to the needs of the 'poorest of the poor' through her work with her sisters alongside Italian emigrants in the United States in the last decade of the nineteenth century, she took up a firm position in favour of repression and military action against the strikers, clearly demonstrating the proliferating Catholic concern with regard to the spread of socialist ideas.[18]

However, not everyone in the Catholic universe restrained their animosity towards the liberal government: Don Davide Albertario[19] and Don Romolo Murri[20] intensified their criticism of a political class that had upset the old equilibrium of traditional society, depriving the people of the chance to make a decent living. Some figures from traditional Catholicism thus found themselves sharing their support of the popular uprisings with the Socialists and at times, as happened with Albertario, even sharing a prison (the priest was put in the same cell as Filippo Turati, leader of the Socialist Party).[21] On that occasion, as the historian Pietro Scoppola points out, 'the basic uniformity of the Catholic ranks' was broken,[22] and while the Jesuit journal *La Civiltà Cattolica* expressed concern at the violent solutions proposed, which aimed to overthrow established power, Murri sided with those who were fighting on the barricades.

Murri went to the heart of the matter when, in June 1898, in the journal *Cultura sociale*, the voice of the Christian Democratic movement and which he had founded, he stressed that the bourgeoisie were interested in conserving the privileges they had acquired: the ideas they had professed in the past were now denied 'egoistically and crudely and they forbade their adversaries freedom of association, limiting their political rights, attacking the freedom of the press, creating special laws, with military tribunes and penal colonies for political prisoners'.[23] Of the freedom they had once boasted of, all that remained was economic freedom. The only two parties able to fight to 'free us from the awful burden that is crushing us', were, according to Murri, 'the two opposites in recent Italian politics, social radicalism and Catholicism, which has become a basis for a legal and honest national party that is also valid and vigorous'.[24] Murri's intention to include the religious inspiration of the Catholics amongst the progressive forces of liberal Italy thus became clear.[25]

It was obviously the direct experience of poverty that came with the work of the parish priests, as well as evidence of the contradictions of capitalism, that opened up the possibility of an alliance of Catholics and Socialists. It was an alliance that was especially favourable in Italy, since both groups had grievances against the Italian state and the liberal bourgeoisie (which had promoted national unification and change in the economic structure).

It is already well known that Murri, who in 1893 to 1894 attended courses on historical materialism held at the La Sapienza University in Rome by the philosopher Antonio Labriola,[26] had started out along a path that would lead him away from the cultural beliefs prevalent in Catholicism from 1789 onwards, with their outright condemnation of the modern, contemporary world.[27] He soon declared that he felt himself to be no part of this culture and stated forcefully that he considered the social contradictions introduced by capitalism to be far more serious than the unresolved territorial bickering between the two states. He began to work on drawing up a project for a peoples' Catholic party – the Democrazia Cristiana – that would be capable of fighting alongside the poorer classes, and he openly declared that he wished to make use of the socialist organizational model for the party's constitution. What is more interesting to note, however, is his respect for Marxist organization, envisaged as a bulwark against those who attempted to compromise democracy in Italy.

In 1905 a surprising and provocative proposal came to Turati that the Christian Democrat movement, founded by Murri, and the Socialist Party should come to an agreement on a political programme. Murri did not underestimate the differences between the two movements, particularly as regards the interpretation of religious issues, but he believed that it was possible to fight together for the implementation of the 'basic programme' proposed by the PSI and based on a project for social reform which he had declared himself in favour of for years. The Catholic leader argued that the political affinity between democratic Catholics and those reformist socialists who had abandoned the revolutionary standpoint[28] was no less important than the religious aspect that linked democratic Catholics and moderates: he thus challenged the idea that Christ's message could or should be interpreted in one way only from a social and political point of view, as well as challenging the unity of the faithful faced with Pius X's conservative directives.[29]

In addition, Murri, a careful reader of Marx's texts and Marxist imitators, encouraged by the ideas of Antonio Labriola and Benedetto Croce,[30] suggested a distinction between historical materialism and dialectic materialism, believing it possible to accept the analysis of contemporary society provided by the former and thus opening up the way to an exchange between Marxist philosophy and the Catholic world which would be useful to many believers in the years to come.[31]

Hope of an agreement was put into perspective by a derisive and ironic reply from Turati. Influenced by a positivist cultural and philosophical outlook, and probably aware of the split that a move towards dialogue would create with Arturo Labriola's revolutionary union wing of the party (close to George Sorel and decidedly anticlerical), he stressed the differences between the Catholic and the socialist movements: 'We are the firstborn of the devil – that is, of free thought [...] and no fear of election derision would persuade us to give up our Satanic primogeniture.' Turati further accused the Catholics of not supporting the strikes, of wanting Sunday to be a day of rest so as to make Mass obligatory and of 'talking about the proletariat but supporting the conservatives'. Murri's proposal thus came to nothing. It is, however, interesting to stress, as the socialist philosopher Giuseppe Rensi did in a letter to Murri, that the proposal served to acknowledge that, for Murri, 'it was not the religious criterion but the criterion of social, economic etc. issues (to sum up, earthly ones) that were the only ones capable of forming the cement for building a political party.'[32]

Most of the Catholic world reacted with disagreement or perplexity to Murri's proposal, to the extent that the priest would state that a sort of 'holy war' had been declared against him. He counter-attacked by remarking on the strange alliance that had formed between Turati and the more conservative of the faithful, since both agreed that the church could not be reformed and was politically aligned with the conservatives.[33] However, the position of the Bologna Curia's official journal, *L'Avvenire d'Italia*, which had already distinguished itself in the past for its sympathy towards Murri's movement, should not be neglected. The publication commented that Murri's initiative in itself had 'nothing unorthodox' about it, since 'what was and is acceptable elsewhere is acceptable for Italian Catholics, too' (the situation elsewhere was referring to events in Belgium, where Catholics and Socialists had been working together for years).[34]

The group of believers that gathered around Murri wished to put an end to electoral abstention and intended to present its own programme in Italy, one that was designed to help the people but offer an alternative to the Socialists. Pius X's policies proved quite different, involving Catholics who were abandoning their isolated position not by forming their own party but through an alliance between the clergy and conservatives. This programme took shape for the first time in the 1904 elections. Catholics who had not voted since 1874, given their lack of recognition of the Italian liberal state, started to channel their votes – with tacit permission from the Holy See – towards the conservative candidates. Once all hope had been lost of involving the whole of the Catholic movement in his project, Murri decided to lead a minority campaign against clerical-moderates and, in November 1905, in Bologna, founded the Lega Democratica Nazionale (Democratic National League, LDN), thus taking a stand against the policy of the ecclesiastical hierarchy.[35]

The LDN, founded as a contrast to Pius X's conservative position, included the division between spiritual and temporal realms amongst the main points on its agenda and criticized the clerics for their inability to come up with a social and economic programme that would meet the needs of the masses. Concerned with the need to distinguish themselves from socialist ideas, whose influence in the rural world they intended to challenge, the LDN did not accept the concepts of collective property and worker management of industries, but supported the peaceful expropriation of landed property when the latter failed to carry out its social function.[36] Adopting as its aims the defence of workers' interests and their political education, the LDN nonetheless allowed its members to take part in socialist unions, believing the principle of the unity and non-religious nature of the union organizations to be important.[37] Thus, some of its members came into contact with exponents of reformist socialism and tried to find agreement on the basis of their mutual aversion to the position of clerical moderates.[38] In a political system squeezed between two blocks, with radical socialism on one side and moderate clerics on the other, the LDN preferred systematic dialogue with progressive groups, hoping to modify extreme anticlericalism.

The organization moved on two levels, the political and the religious: on the political level with the intention of bringing about profound innovation and on the religious level with the objective of reclaiming the freedom of Catholics to act according to their own consciences, with the religious level supported by Tommaso Gallarati Scotti in particular.[39] Pius X reacted harshly to these new ideas, and in his encyclical *Pieni l'animo* he denied that Catholics could act independently in the political and social fields and forbade priests to become party members. The LDN, which stood alone in the Catholic world and was not even properly understood by a progressive world overly conditioned by preconceived anticlericalism, did not enjoy much room for manoeuvre in Giolitti's Italy.[40]

Because of the stand Murri had taken, on 14 April 1907, Pius X had him suspended *a divinis* and in September of the same year, in the encyclical *Pascendi dominici gregis*, the priest's line of thought was associated with that of the modernists.⁴¹ In March 1909, he was excommunicated *ad personam* for accepting to stand as a candidate for the Radical Party. In his programme, Murri, who had based his election campaign primarily on anticlerical issues and holding the clerical-moderate agreement to be the country's worst ill, envisaged the creation of a radical left, which would also include the socialists. He believed the clerical-moderate movement should be countered by a project in support of the non-religious nature of the state, freedom of teaching, the banning of catechism in primary schools and the inclusion of the history of religions in secondary schools.⁴²

Murri was in favour of Italy's entrance into the Great War and, in its aftermath, drew close to fascism, under the illusion – one now difficult to comprehend – that Mussolini's policies might make some of the hopes he had professed in his youth come true. Married with children, he became a journalist with the Bolognese daily newspaper *Il Resto del Carlino*. The hostility of the ecclesiastical hierarchy towards him continued to be ferocious, even though in November 1943, only a few months before Murri's death, Pius XII revoked his excommunication.

The *Plebei* of Reggio Emilia

Even more radical than Murri's position was that taken up by the group of socialist priests known as the *Plebei* (Plebeians), who gathered around the newspaper *La Plebe* in Reggio Emilia (near Bologna) from 1904 onwards.⁴³ Historians point out that in this agricultural area there was no tradition of small property owners.⁴⁴ There were large estates, owned by a few capitalists, which meant that farm labourers were working in the same conditions as factory workers: a capitalist employed farmhands who did not own the means of production. It was no coincidence that the *Plebei*, living in the Emilia countryside, where the socialist movement was particularly strong amongst farm labourers and peasants, had become convinced of the need to unite socialism and Christianity. They had abandoned the more embittered characteristics of anticlericalism to support instead the idea of 'evangelical socialism'. Those socialists who were active propagandists amongst the peasants, had, indeed, given up the materialism and positivism of the Second International, thinking it better to deploy the values of the Catholic tradition, which had particularly strong roots in the Italian countryside.

The objective of the newspaper, which merged with the Macerata journal *Giovane Italia* on 1 November 1905, was to christianize socialists and socialize Christians in the name of the gospel.[45] In 1905, *La Plebe* even invited some Socialists to join its editorial board. The *Plebei* thus increasingly tended to approach the position of the Socialist Party, 'trying to bring respect for the Church and the observation of Christian principles to the masses'.[46] They clearly stated that they considered themselves simultaneously socialists and Christians, holding there to be no lack of compatibility between the two programmes, 'at least in theory, nor any barriers dividing them'.[47]

If the equating of early Christianity and socialism separated the *Plebei* from Murri, the former shared this interpretation with the evangelical Socialists, who were a strong presence in the countryside of Reggio Emilia. The *Plebei*, like the socialist Camillo Prampolini,[48] believed that over the centuries the message of Christ had encouraged the struggle for greater social equality and even went as far as to state that Jesus had been history's 'first socialist'. For them, however, unlike the socialist leader of Emilia, the teachings of the gospel did not stop there, and they refuted any secular transformation of the Christian experience, insisting on the need to safeguard its transcendent aspect.

The 'good priests' (as Prampolini called them) were also in disagreement with Murri over the perplexity he had expressed towards collectivism. In an open letter to the leader of the Christian democrats, they wrote:

> You say that collectivism is a Utopia. That may be. We ourselves believe it to be possible. In any case, if the people wish for it, why oppose it? Who stops you from becoming a socialist? Is it necessary to accept the entire philosophical basis of Marx's *Capital* to encourage and help prepare a collective régime? If this were so, there would be very few socialists indeed. Instead there are thousands, millions, and this is because [...] the Socialist Party is not a party of philosophers and even less of theologians, but simply a party that supports the interests of the proletariat.[49]

In his reply to the letter, Murri admitted that the Christian democrats had at times been 'too anti-socialist' but he insisted on his belief that it was right to fight collectivism, because it was 'a bad dream, a false mirage'. Murri declared that he had no problem with the class struggle, and he feared it not in itself but because often 'hatred and greed wormed their way in'. He concluded by repeating that he could not totally 'be with the *Plebei*', although they were inspired by 'many principles and criteria that had been too neglected on our side and that the social movement should assimilate and put into practice', because their extreme ideas could spark off a reaction and thus a further change in the attitude of Catholics towards the moderates. Murri thus confirmed the reasons for his perplexity towards the positions assumed by the *Plebei*, criticizing them mainly for having completely abandoned all Christian social principles in order to adhere to the socialist idea. Despite this, the leader of the Christian Democrats did declare that, 'my warmest sympathies are with the *plebei* and I am following the development of their generous and precarious attempt with keen interest.'[50]

Like Murri himself, the *Plebei* stated that it was the reformist spirit within the socialist movement that they were attracted to. In this they were reassured by a direct knowledge of Prampolini's work,[51] while proving to be even more intransigent than the Marche priest in their judgements of revolutionary unionists: the latter were accused of sympathizing with 'the egoistic instincts of the masses', being devoid of 'humanitarian and altruistic ideals' and encouraging clashes between workers.[52]

The church institutions looked on the propagation of these ideas with concern and, in August 1906, Don Rodrigo Levoni, one of the priests belonging to the group, was suspended *a divinis*. The following year *La Plebe* was obliged to close down because of growing economic difficulties, and Levoni and other 'plebeian priests' decided to join the socialist organization and to embrace Marxist philosophy.

During 1905, the Reggio Emilia experience aroused interest in other regions and the geography of dissidence became extensive. A group of socialist priests started up in Umbria, in Val Tiberina, taking the side of the peasants and supporting their claims, trying to coordinate the struggle in order to obtain agricultural agreements that were more favourable to the labourers. In this case, too, it was a journal, *La Rivendicazione*, that acted as an instrument for spreading the thoughts of these Christians. The priest Urbano Segapeli argued in the journal that the socialist message was a contemporary projection of the demand for justice and truth that existed in the gospels.[53] During the early years of the century, in Mantua, the weekly journal *Il destino della plebe*, close to the position of the Christian Socialists, was published.[54] In Naples, the demands of the Catholic Socialists were spread, thanks to the journals *Battaglie d'oggi* and the *Nuova Riforma*, both the fruits of Giovanni Avolio's militancy. Avolio believed that socialism had to deal with the whole nature of humankind, in other words, its material needs as well as its spiritual ones, and that materialist premises should thus be abandoned. Believers and non-believers – all those working towards greater social justice[55] – should, he said, support Turati's party, which stood out for its political programme in favour of the people. Avolio's ideas found expression in groups such as the Associazione dei Preti Lavoratori (Association of worker-priests) and the Avanguardia dei Cristiano-Sociali d'Italia (Christian-Social Vanguard in Italy), the latter led by the Protestant Giovanni Enrico Meille and the Piedmontese Mario Tortonese.[56]

The radical group in Rome and Ernesto Buonaiuti

In the first decade of the twentieth century in Rome, the Gruppo Radicale Romano (Radical group of Rome) was founded,[57] with Ernesto Buonaiuti as its most prominent member.[58] Buonaiuti was an exponent of the modernist movement and supporter of the need to return to the values of early Christianity which he himself, as a historian of the church, had studied in detail.[59] He arrived at the conclusion that the experiences of the early Christian communities were based on principles and values not far removed from those of contemporary socialism.

In *Rivista storico-critica delle scienze teologiche* (Journal historical-critical of theological sciences), published in 1905, Buonaiuti praised the eschatological interpretation of Christian origins, and this position led him to argue a 'perfect likeness' between the Christian message and the hopes of modern socialism.[60] In the same way, in the work published in Rome in 1908 *Perché siamo socialisti e cristiani* ('Why we are Socialists and Christians') he states: 'We say to our companions in religious faith: be truly Christian and you will be socialist and anti-clerical. And to our companions in social faith: be truly socialist and you will be Christians.'[61]

Buonaiuti was one of the founders of the journal *Nova et Vetera*, published in Rome in 1908 on the initiative of a group of believers, including Manlio Mario Rossi and Nicola Turchi.[62] According to Buonaiuti, the journal was designed to be a space for comparing and exchanging views and open to all the innovative currents in modern Christianity.[63] As to the closeness of Christianity to socialism, the journal emphasized that both had as their objective a fairer distribution of wealth and the establishment of an earthly world where there was also room for joy. It should be noted, however, that, in the same journal, George Tyrell, the leading exponent of English Modernism, made no bones about the fact that he had little truck with such theories, and the group from the journal *Il Rinnovamento*, directed by the aristocrats Tommaso Gallarati Scotti, Alessandro Casati and Stefano Jacini, expressed their bewilderment with regard to the equivalence between early Christianity and socialism.[64] Only a few months after the publication of *Pascendi*, Buonaiuti independently published *Il programma dei modernisti* ('The modernist programme') and in 1908 *Lettere di un prete modernista* ('Letters from a Modernist priest'), in which he confirmed his convictions.[65]

Buoniauti's thoughts were shared by some young people from the Lega Democratica Nazionale, supporters of an innovative socialist strategy and the need to work simultaneously for political and religious innovation. In July 1908, two members of the group, Felice Perroni and Guglielmo Quadrotta, who also contributed to *Nova et vetera*, went as far as to ask for membership of the Socialist Party by reason of their faith,[66] writing an open letter that was published in *Avanti!*, the newspaper of the Socialist Party. The request was refused by Turati's party: still characterized by a positivist culture, the party considered it impossible to unite religious belief with a political project for social transformation.[67]

Unlike Murri, who had limited himself to suggesting an electoral alliance with the socialists, Felice Perroni and Guglielmo Quadrotta stated their faith in the socialist programme and declared that they accepted its methods with regard to pressing the demands of the proletariat. The two young men thought a radical reform of economic and political institutions was needed, so that all people were in a position to express their own spiritual resources. Moreover, recalling the Christian precept of love and the hope in a kingdom of heaven on earth, they were convinced that historically the Christian experience was an inspiration for social progress, therefore siding with socialism was the necessary and natural outlet for their religious faith.[68]

It was Buonaiuti who pointed out the differences between Perroni and Quadrotta's political perspective and that of Murri, stressing how the Christian democrat, who had always criticized socialism and been averse to its political and social policies, hardly proved credible in his attempt to approach the party. In contrast to this, the young Romans insisted that it was not the objective but the principles of their socialism that were different. They also 're-evoke the great hope in a Kingdom of Heaven on Earth, which in every troubled age of history has shaken the ecclesiastical Christian masses and led them to change, like new yeast; they acknowledge the social aspect of religion'.[69]

Though it is true that the Socialists refused to let them join the party, it is nonetheless interesting to note that their request opened up a debate inside the organization and the socialists Ivanoe Bonomi[70] and Giuseppe Rensi expressed themselves in favour. Bonomi in particular, by then critical of the party majority, refused the idea that the socialist movement should remain entirely in 'the Marxist rut' and therefore believed that it was inopportune to refuse Christians who, despite different cultural premises, sustained the political ideas in question.[71]

For his part, the philosopher Rensi believed that the only 'eternal foundation of socialism' was a spiritual one, which he judged to be superior to 'any vicissitudes in doctrine or any scientific confusion'. In his opinion, therefore, professing a religious belief, unless it adhered to an authoritarian and papist line of thought, could not be considered to be in contradiction with any adhesion to socialism.[72]

Critica sociale (the theoretical journal of the Italian Socialist Party) published an article by Domenico Spadoni, in which he recognized that the preaching of Christ emanated 'a spirit of brotherly equality which, together with the utmost disdain for riches, led to communism as a natural consequence'.[73] Links between socialism and communism were also inferred by Angelo Crespi, initially a socialist and a contributor to *Critica Sociale*, who subsequently came to the conclusion that any real reform of society should contemplate a renewal of the spirit; he had thus come to sustain a renovated religion close to modernist positions.[74] Crespi wrote: 'I began to distinguish between the degeneration of religion as a phenomenon and its essence as manifest in religious genius and I felt that this was an immense power, capable of enormous good in the world'.[75]

Angelica Balabanoff[76] declared herself sceptical of these suggestions. Writing in the Socialist Party newspaper *Avanti!*, she argued that being a socialist implied embracing Marxism and she wondered how Perroni and Quadrotta could remain in the Italian Socialist Party, which professed the materialist 'philosophical concept': Marx's merit was to have 'thoroughly investigated Feuerbach's materialism and transferred Hegel's dialectic method onto materialistic terrain'. The Ukrainian revolutionary also argued against Rensi, declaring that Marxism was 'poles apart from idealism'.[77]

The debate in the Socialist Party newspaper was also joined by Alberto Malatesta who claimed that 'a profound contrast' existed between socialism and Christianity and, above all, that the action taken by Catholics was 'conservative and manipulative'. He added that in its long history the church had always persecuted those it considered to be 'the enemies of religion', organizing wars and legitimizing the practice of the Inquisition. He concluded: 'In that they advocate and spread the word of Christ, there is no possibility of an understanding with the Christians'.[78] The radical nature of these affirmations led Quadrotta to intervene in *Avanti!*, making it clear that Christianity was 'an eminently social movement', or 'the preparation of humankind for an earthly kingdom of love and justice, through inner renewal'. Quadrotta urged socialists to consider the gospels as a historical document and thus, in the wake of the studies carried out by Alfred Loisy,[79] to realize that 'Jesus' preaching had been altered by the theological concerns 'of certain great advocates of Christianity, such as Saint

Paul.' This is what gave rise to his conviction that only socialism could bring about 'the great, human hope that the word of Christ had announced twenty centuries previously'.[80]

These statements led the editorial board of *Avanti!* to intervene in the debate, declaring that they agreed with Quadrotta when he maintained that 'the theological interpretation of Christianity' was a distortion of Christ's words but adding that until the movement for the revision of the Bible had managed to substitute the notion of original Christianity for its theological version in people's minds, it was impossible to consider Christianity as an element of progress for society.[81]

The demand for greater social justice and for religious renewal also appeared in the journal *Coenobium*, founded in Lugano in 1906 by the socialist Enrico Bignami[82] and the republican Arcangelo Ghisleri.[83] Particularly in its early months, it assumed a 'philosophical and pro-modernist' standpoint, so much so that it numbered amongst its contributors Romolo Murri, Domenico Battaini, Arnaldo Cervesato, Angelo Crespi and Friedrich von Hügel. The journal attempted to integrate two value systems, the Christian and the socialist, which were held to be akin and complementary in terms of ethics, with a view to a 'revolution in morals'. It was in the pages of this journal that Rensi coined the expression 'idealist socialism', meant as a sort of socialism that tended to 'attribute greater importance to spiritual values rather than to material goods'.[84]

The 'cenobitic approach' was followed by *Bilychnis* (1912–1931), the newspaper of the Battista Theology Faculty in Rome which, like the Swiss journal, took up a strong position against the Great War, and by Giuseppe Gangale's *Conscientia* (1922–1927). Both shared with *Coenobium* the prospect of evangelical inspiration as a spur to the inner experience of faith, the aversion to religious dogma and the need for a new search by the individual: they were convinced that without a new individual conscience any project for political renewal was impossible.[85]

2

Catholic Anti-Fascists and Their Relationship with the Left-Wing World

The 'left' in the Partito Popolare

While Italy, which entered the war in May 1915 alongside Great Britain and France, emerged victorious from the conflict, many problems remained unresolved: social conflict, in the wake of the Russian Revolution, shook the country, and strikes and disputes were organized by workers and peasants. It seemed to many that the results of the peace treaties were far from satisfactory for a people who had paid the price of half a million dead, and while Trento and Trieste were assigned to Italy, the city of Fiume was not. The rhetoric of 'vittoria mutilata' (a mutilated victory) spread amongst the ex-combatants and was widely exploited by the poet Gabriele D'Annunzio in his political ascent, soon becoming a breeding ground for right-wing movements and fascism.

The liberal governments that had led the country since 1861 were weak due to the emergence of parties representing the masses, a phenomenon legitimized by universal male suffrage (introduced in Italy for the first time in the 1913 elections). The Socialist Party (PSI), headed by the maximalist policies of Giacinto Serrati, was particularly successful in the 1919 elections, with 30 per cent of the votes, but fragmentation soon followed. In January 1921, Antonio Gramsci, Palmiro Togliatti and Amedeo Bordiga founded the Italian Communist Party (PCI), and then, in October 1922, a few days before the March on Rome organized by Benito Mussolini, reformist elements split from the PSI, including such prestigious figures as Filippo Turati and Giacomo Matteotti.

In the aftermath of the First World War, the radical political and religious experiences that had characterized some Christian minorities in the early twentieth century ended up being repressed by a Catholic Church that had declared war on Modernism and established a 'witch hunt' to identify any 'critics' or 'innovators' within it. This led to a new movement with the birth of the Partito Popolare

(Italian People's Party, PPI), founded in 1919 by the priest Don Luigi Sturzo. This represented the first political experience of the Italian Catholics, who had remained largely detached from the process of the Risorgimento and had long been reluctant to collaborate with the Italian state.

The PPI was immediately determined to differentiate itself from both the Socialists and the Liberals, and claim for itself its own political project based on Christian principles.[1] Sturzo wanted it to be a reformist party, aimed at valorizing local autonomy, reducing the role of the state, and supporting a pacifist and internationalist foreign policy. Its heterogeneous composition, however, was both a distinctive feature and element of limitation for the PPI, bringing together as it did figures from very different social and cultural backgrounds.[2] Exponents of the Azione Cattolica (Italian Catholic Action, AC) and conservatives, such as Count Giovanni Grosoli Pironi and Stefano Cavazzoni, coexisted alongside the president of the Textile Union, Achille Grandi, and union organizer Giovanni Longinotti. The party was also joined by a group of former followers of Romolo Murri, such as Giovanni Bertini and Angelo Mauri,[3] as well as Guido Miglioli, a lawyer and left-wing leader. Division came to this heterogeneous party when, on 31 October 1922, the decision was made regarding whether or not to give support to Mussolini's government. Despite the opposition of Sturzo and the majority of the party, many members of PPI decided to back the fascist undertaking.

Miglioli was undoubtedly one of the most significant figures in the sphere of Catholic anti-fascism. He had started out his career at the beginning of the century as part of the Murri initiative but, realizing the danger that could be involved in the excessive radicalization of the conflict with ecclesiastical hierarchies, he did not approve of requests for Church reform.[4] Instead, he channelled his efforts into helping the trade unions, beginning with the area of Soresina and Castelleone, in the province of Cremona. In 1907, he launched a campaign to improve the contracts of the rural workers, organizing 'white' leagues as an alternative to the socialist 'red' ones. He believed he had to fight the Socialists on their own ground, creating agrarian pacts more favourable to the peasants and introducing a policy of reforms that could be truly competitive with respect to what was being offered by the Left.[5]

Firmly against the Libyan war, he entered parliament in 1913 with an overwhelming victory in the first round of votes; in 1915, he also opposed Italy's participation in the First World War. Miglioli was also elected deputy for the PPI in the 1919 elections, but he remained in the minority in the party because of his left-wing ideas, favouring as he did the expropriation and division of land. A supporter of the motto 'the land for the peasants', he worked on achieving a collaboration between agrarian capitalists and farmers, with the aim of gradually obtaining land ownership for the workers. The agitation in the Cremona countryside organized by Miglioli was a worry to the landowners, and, from the spring of 1921, violent attacks began to be carried out on the workers by the fascist squads led by Roberto Farinacci. Up until the first months of 1921, Miglioli was mistrustful with regard to the Socialist Party, so much so that the newspaper *L'Azione*, which supported him, interpreted the fascist attacks as 'a violent reaction' to the harassment of 'red tyranny'.[6] The assassination of the socialist Attilio Boldori by a group of Fascists in December 1921 represented a turning point and initiated a process of understanding between popular and socialist forces, which in March 1922 resulted in the signing of a pact of unity to oppose fascist violence. A significant moment for this new alliance was the great demonstration in support of unity organized in Soresina on 1 May 1922.

The need for an agreement with the PSI was supported by the left-wing members of the PPI in the Venice congress of October 1921, with fascist violence a major concern; then, during the Turin congress of April 1923, pressure was applied by the left to force the PPI ministers who were part of Mussolini's government to resign. After Mussolini's takeover, Miglioli remembered, meetings were also organized in Milan at the unions' *Camera del lavoro* to create a 'unitary organisation, long dreamt of and now imposed by current events'. Meetings subsequently continued to be held at a religious institute. What was certain was that, from the end of 1922, the climate in Italy had changed, and a united effort was urgently required to stem fascist violence. As Miglioli later noted: 'The clandestine work in that first phase of anti-Fascism was anything but easy and fruitless.'[7]

In 1924, following a chance meeting on a train with Antonio Gramsci, during which they discussed the possible union of all workers, Christians and non-Christians, Miglioli was interviewed in the pages of the Communist Party newspaper *l'Unità*. Here, he stressed the urgency of achieving union collaboration, overcoming the anticlerical spirit in the socialist world and the anti-socialist spirit in the world of Catholicism, in order to guarantee the 'progress of the workers'. Miglioli noted with concern that 'the parties that say they represent the thought [of the workers] split and divide into ever smaller factions' and hoped that union collaboration would represent a stepping stone towards political cohesion.[8] These ideas provoked a harsh reaction in the PPI and at the January 1925 National Council, where the ideas were declared 'outwith the directives of the party' and the trade unionist expelled. Some weeks later, Miglioli accepted an invitation from Moscow to participate in the first assembly of the Krestintern, the General Assembly of International Peasantry, inaugurating a relationship with Moscow that would last until the end of the Second World War. During the Christmas of 1926, Miglioli decided to permanently abandon Italy, spending the years of his exile in Switzerland, Germany, Belgium and France. In 1935, he published *La collectivisation des campagnes soviétiques*[9] and *Études historiques: Humanisme et réalisme dans la question agraire soviétique*.[10] In 1938, in order to escape fascist persecution, he moved to the Soviet Union. Returning to Paris, he was arrested by the Germans and handed over to the fascist authorities, and in 1941 he was condemned to internal exile, where he remained until July 1943. Arrested again by the police of the Repubblica Sociale Italiana (Italian Social Republic, RSI) at the beginning of 1944, he only regained his freedom in April 1945.[11]

The left-wing group in the PPI also included Romano Cocchi and Giuseppe Speranzini, who were expelled from the party because of their ideas. At the end of 1919, in Verona, Speranzini founded the journal *Conquista popolare*, to which Catholics from a variety of geographical areas contributed. These contributions prevented the possibility of any collaboration with the liberals, judging their positions to be irreconcilable with those of the Catholics, and proposed the possibility of agreements with the more progressive bourgeoisie and the Reformist Socialists.[12] Cocchi, after being ousted from the PPI, became involved with the parties of the Left, joining first the Socialist Party and then, in 1924, the Communist Party. A member of the Central Committee and supporter of the Popular Front line, he condemned the Molotov–Ribbentrop pact of 1939 and for this reason was expelled from the Italian Communist Party. He died in 1944 in Buchenwald concentration camp.

Other significant anti-fascist exponents in the party included Francesco Luigi Ferrari and Giuseppe Donati who, both originally from Emilia-Romagna, had dealings with Murri in the early part of the century and had joined the Lega Democratica Nazionale (Democratic National League, LDN).[13]

Ferrari, unlike the followers of Murri, and in a similar way to Miglioli, soon abandoned the idea of a religious renewal, and together with other Catholics from the Modena area focused on trade union organization, establishing the Ufficio del lavoro (the Labour Office) in 1909. The relationship between this institution and the Socialists was not an easy one, partly due to the fact that the goal of the Catholics was to protect smallholdings and not the collectivization of land.[14] An interventionist during the First World War, but respectful of the rights of other nationalities and a staunch opponent of imperialist ideas, Ferrari entered the PPI in 1919. The emergence of fascism in the Modena area, with its violence against both Socialists and Catholics involved in social issues, convinced him to ally himself with the left wing of the party. In December 1922, he founded the weekly *Il Domani di'Italia*, which became a reference point for the popular Left.[15]

The periodical's explicit intention was to reconnect with the democratic principles of Murri's original Democrazia Cristiana (Christian Democratic Party, DC) and it forcefully expressed the need for a great alliance of all the anti-fascist forces – though it was not shy in terms of being severely critical of the maximalist policies of certain elements in the Socialist Party.[16] The issues addressed by the journal were based on the development of Ferrari's own personal viewpoint and mirrored his particular focus on the political world and secular culture: so it is unsurprising to find an interview with Turati in the first issue[17] and subsequently with figures such as Gobetti, Salvemini, Salvatorelli, Nenni and Gramsci.[18]

In 1926, he left Italy to go to Belgium, where he joined the world of anti-fascist culture: in 1928 he published *Le régime fasciste italien* in Paris, a re-elaboration of his thesis, discussed the previous year at the Université de Louvain.[19] He also began a close collaboration with the socialist Gaetano Salvemini, whom Ferrari had known for years and with whom he shared democratic and reformist ideas as well as great moral rigour. In a letter addressed to Salvemini, and written after the signing of the 1929 *Patti Lateranensi* (Lateran Pacts), Ferrari responded to his friend's claim that it was not possible for Catholics to disobey hierarchies by countering that 'one can remain Catholic even though one does not adhere to the conservative politics of Pius XI, even though one opposes his system of centralisation to the bitter end.'[20] For Ferrari, therefore, first came fidelity to the gospel and then to the Church.[21] Ferrari died in Paris in 1933 due to pulmonary trauma, probably induced by the beatings he received during attacks by fascist squads in Italy. When he learned of the news, Salvemini wrote to Sturzo: 'It is truly a great loss, because that man was truly a man one could be certain of: one could foresee what he would do today, tomorrow, always: a very rare thing amongst men in general and Italians in particular.'[22]

The other popular representative from Romagna was Giuseppe Donati, who was also sympathetic to Murri and his movement in his youth. As a supporter of the need for collaboration between Catholics and Socialists to improve the working conditions of agricultural workers, he came into conflict with clerical and moderate circles. Already a member of the Lega democratica nazionale as early as 1905, Donati considered the distinction between the religious and civil spheres essential for the progress of the human spirit. This idea of separation was something he put forward forcefully during the administrative elections of 1908, when he fiercely criticized the practice of Catholics voting for moderate politicians.[23]

In contact with secular culture and a contributor to Giuseppe Prezzolini's journal *La Voce*, he was also close to Salvemini.[24] His was an interventionist during the First World War, and in the post-war period Donati decided to join the PPI. Like other exponents who had been influenced by Murri, he placed himself in the centre-left group, far from the conservative right but also from the left of Miglioli.[25] Sturzo regarded him as a valuable figure and entrusted him with delicate tasks; he was appointed a member of the party's National Council and then editor of the journal *Il Popolo*, which came out in April 1923 and became the reference point for anti-fascist Catholics. While sceptical with regard to certain aspects of Turati socialism, Donati, in the face of the spread of fascist violence, did not hesitate to propose a coalition that would involve collaboration between Socialists and Catholics.

In June 1925, in response to the insistence of party members, he agreed to leave Italy. He tried to form a core group of the PPI in exile, but his attempt to integrate the populist party with the Concentrazione Antifascista Italiana (CAI), an Italian coalition of anti-fascist groups, was a failure. He refused to accept the influence of the socialist faction on the CAI which, considering fascism as part of the capitalist reaction against the proletariat, was determined to equate anti-fascism with the struggle of the working class. Donati, in contrast, believed that resistance to fascism was something that every social class should contribute to, that it was an issue that involved all people, given that everyone had the right to justice and freedom.[26] Despite this, his collaboration in Paris with socialist figures was particularly close, especially with Turati, with whom he organized meetings and conferences. Unlike Ferrari, in 1929 Donati adopted a position in favour of the Lateran Pacts, judging them to be the conclusion of the 'Roman question', and this led to his marginalization in the world of anti-fascism. He, too, died young, in August 1931, at the age of 42.

During the years of his militancy in the PPI, Donati showed himself to have close links with Don Luigi Sturzo. The Sicilian priest, in his youth sympathetic to the ideas of Murri, hostile to any alliance with the liberals and radically anti-fascist, opposed both the right-wing of the party and the leftist faction, due to its extremism on social issues. Thus the party he founded, unlike Murri's Christian democratic leanings, was characterized by its rejection of the class struggle: even when he intervened in defence of the struggles of the peasantry, Don Sturzo never allowed himself to profess 'classist tendencies'.[27] Moreover, unlike the Socialists who excluded the ideas of the participation of workers in company profit and believed in the goal of collectivization, Sturzo thought that worker control had to pass through shared ownership, as a means of transforming company capitalist structure. The shareholding worker could encourage the better development of production, something which was of benefit to the workers and which did not damage employers.[28]

Don Sturzo also strongly opposed those within the party who were amenable to possible agreements with fascism and thus found himself in alliance with the party's left wing against the decision of the parliamentary group to allow some of its members to participate in Mussolini's first cabinet. He was, as early as July 1922,[29] already contemplating a parliamentary alliance between all the country's democratic forces, including Turati's Socialists. He was however hindered in this attempt by the pope, who had by then decided to come to an agreement with Mussolini in order to obtain privileges for the Church.[30] Thus, by direct order of the Secretary of State, Sturzo was forced to abandon the office of party secretary in July 1923 and the following year to leave Italy and take refuge in exile in London, as the guest of his friend Angelo Crespi. From abroad, he continued to encourage Catholics to keep the patrimony of democratic and anti-fascist ideals of populism intact and to refuse all mediation with fascism.[31]

Don Sturzo's successor as PPI secretary in May 1924 was Alcide De Gasperi. Resolutely anti-fascist, he showed an initial diffidence towards the 'red' organizations, still accused in 1920 of carrying out acts of violence around the country. However, his opinion underwent a transformation – assisted by the brutality of fascist violence and by a trip that he made to Weimar Germany with other party members, where he was able to observe first hand the political collaboration taking place between the Zentrum and the Sozialdemokratische Partei. Thus, when the question of agreements with the Socialists in Italy was raised at the 1921 Venice congress, De Gasperi, citing the German example, indicated that the possibility was a real one. The devastation in July 1922 of the residences of the parliamentary deputies Guido Miglioli and Giuseppe Garibotti, a socialist, outraged parliament and convinced De Gasperi even more strongly of the need for collaboration between the two parties in order to stem the fascist attacks.

After the 1924 elections and the kidnapping and murder of Giacomo Matteotti, the PPI – like the other anti-fascist parties – took part in the 'Aventine Secession' and withdrew from attending parliamentary sessions. The opposition of the Holy See to this decision was made very clear and the Vatican's hostility increased when Turati released an interview with Donati in *Il popolo* in which, while respecting their differences, he proposed a common path for the two parties. De Gasperi responded strongly to the Vatican rebukes, recalling the experience of the Belgian Catholics, the political centre in Germany, the Austrian Christian Social Party, the Swiss Catholic-conservatives and the Polish Catholics, all of which were allied with leftist forces.[32]

At the last PPI congress, held in Rome in June 1925, De Gasperi argued forcefully against fascism, declaring that the natural rights of people, family and society existed before the state, and reiterating that it was the duty of the people to defend democracy. In December 1925, he resigned as party secretary and in November of the following year he was dismissed from his position as a deputy, as the prefect of Rome proceeded to dissolve all the anti-fascist parties, including the PPI.

In 1927 he was arrested for 'attempted clandestine expatriation'[33] and condemned to four years in prison. In July 1928, through the intercession of the bishop of Trento, Celestino Endrici, he was pardoned, and from April 1929, thanks to Igino Giordani,[34] he began working as a cataloguer at the Vatican Library, where he remained until 1943.[35]

Giordani too, though of less importance than Sturzo and De Gasperi, was a significant figure both for his religious sensibility and his political commitment, first against intervention in the Great War, then in the PPI and then, after the end of fascism, in the Christian Democrats. Close to Sturzo politically, during the *biennio rosso* (two red years) Giordani was extremely critical of Socialists and Communists, who were responsible for violence and intimidation against Catholic militants.[36] After 1921, however, the Fascists became his main target, the language of his writings varying between seriousness and mockery. It was a stance that became more accentuated following the march on Rome, his voice taking on a graver and more preoccupied tone with the fate of the country and democratic institutions at stake. It was this concern with regard to fascist arrogance that led Giordani – who contributed to Donati's *Il Popolo* from April 1923 to November 1925 – to mitigate his attitude towards the Socialists, while continuing to reaffirm his perplexities in relation to Marxist materialism.[37] The year 1925 also saw the publication of his book *Rivolta cattolica* ('Catholic Revolt')[38] which represented a point of reference for Christian Democrats and which emphasized his hostility towards collusion between Catholics and the fascist regime. After a period of internal exile, Giordani, too, was employed by the Vatican Library.[39]

Following the dissolution of the PPI as part of the suppression of all anti-fascist political organizations in November 1926, Don Sturzo attempted to rebuild the party in exile. A faction of the party already existed abroad, in Paris, founded by Giuseppe Stragliati, and this became a point of reference and place of refuge for Catholics forced to leave Italy. Stragliati, however, soon abandoned the tenets of PPI in favour of socialism, in the belief that it was necessary to address the problem of the exploitation of man induced by capitalism. He wrote, in a letter to Sturzo in 1935: 'If humanity wants to advance in the direction of justice, then it must look to Russia, where the new political situation has abolished the privileges of a few pleasure-seekers and brought continuously developing improvement to an immense people, who will soon be at the head of social progress.'[40]

In exile, Sturzo attempted to promote a journal, open to the various elements of anti-fascism, that would go more deeply into the cultural and political aspects of the crisis in Italian democracy. Informed of this intention, the socialist Salvemini, convinced of the necessity of a close collaboration between democratic and Catholic emigrants, showed interest in the project. The journal, which was going to be called *Il Rinnovamento*, was scheduled to be published in Brussels in 1929: the editorial board was to include Sturzo, Salvemini, Turati, Carlo Sforza and Silvio Trentin, with management duties entrusted to Ferrari and Armando Zanetti. The hope was that the periodical, starting off as a cultural meeting place, would also become the cornerstone for the construction of a political design, a point of contact between democratic Catholicism and reformist socialism.

As it turned out, the journal never became a reality: the signing of the Lateran Pacts in February 1929 caused immense discord between Catholic and secular factions, and in particular between Ferrari and Zanetti. Both declared themselves critical of the agreement, but while Ferrari looked at things from a procedural point of view and did not say he was absolutely opposed to the possibility of a Concordat, Zanetti instead claimed that the separation between church and state was a constitutive element in a new political project.

The few Catholics who chose the path of anti-fascism and exile were, therefore, mainly in contact with Reformist Socialists, but the deaths of Ferrari and Donati prevented the relationship between these different political cultures from developing further. Moreover, as the historian Paolo Pombeni pointed out, from the Resistance onwards, while the Catholic world established a privileged dialogue mainly with the Communist Party, the Socialist Party assumed a marginal and subordinate role to that of the member organization of the Third International.[41]

Catholics against *Duce*

The period immediately after the First World War was characterized by a series of violent attacks, especially on left-wing militants, but members of the PPI and religious organizations were also targets for fascist aggression.[42] There is the well-known case of Don Giovanni Minzoni who, first as a chaplain in 1910 and then from 1915 as a parish priest, organized the young people and workers in Argenta, a district near Ferrara. Don Minzoni was convinced that Christianity should also be an engine of social change, and during his seminary years he dreamed of the possibility of bringing together socialism and Christianity. Direct contact with Enrico Ferri, however, a figure in the most radical wing of the PSI and elected to parliament for the constituency of Argenta, made him change his mind and led him to the conclusion that the socialist political perspective, imbued as it was with materialism and dogmatism, was in opposition to Christianity. His adherence to the principles of democracy, drawn from his youthful reading of Murri's writings,[43] encouraged his strong aversion to Mussolini in the post-war period. He decided to join the PPI in April 1923, after the Turin Congress had made its anti-fascist position quite clear; writing in his diary:

> As one day I offered all my young life for the salvation of the fatherland, happy that it might be of help, today I realise that a much harsher battle awaits me. We prepare ourselves tenaciously for the struggle and with a weapon that for us is sacred and divine, as it was for the first Christians: prayer and good hearts. To withdraw would be to renounce a mission of too sacred a kind. With open heart, with a prayer for my persecutors that I hope will never be dashed from my lips, I await storm, persecution, perhaps even death, for the triumph of Christ's cause.[44]

Determined to counter fascist insolence, he was targeted by fascist squads and, on the evening of 26 August 1923, he was beaten to death.[45] Fascist violence took place almost everywhere in the post-war period: a parish house in Turin was occupied by fascist agitators and the president of a Catholic group was attacked, as were several young PPI militants. But, in the city, the cradle of the workers' movement and a place in turmoil after the tensions of the biennio rosso, the Catholic movement refused to be intimidated. The review *Il Lavoratore* was launched in 1921, with contributions from some of the main representatives of Catholic trade unionism: Giuseppe Rapelli, Gioachino Quarello, Maria Luda and Rodolfo Aratasi. The periodical engaged in a reconsideration of the social thought of the Church, in order to create the possibility of collaboration between Catholic workers and those in Marxist parties.[46] Then, in 1924, again in Turin, the *Corriere* was published, one of the few newspapers, together with the *Popolo* of Donati, to support the positions of democratic Catholicism, and which Alessandro Cantono, already a follower of Murri's DC, worked on.[47]

One of the most significant figures in Catholic anti-fascism was Don Primo Mazzolari, a seminarian in Cremona during the episcopate of Geremia Bonomelli, with whose teaching he always remained linked. In the early part of the century, Don Mazzolari established contact with certain members of the radical Catholic intelligentsia, such as the Barnabite presbyter Pietro Gazzola, accused of 'Modernism'. An interventionist during the First World War and then, with the war's end, realizing his mistake in believing in the redemption of humanity through violence, Mazzolari decided to abandon teaching and to devote himself to pastoral duties, placing himself at the service of the poorest and most needy members of society. A parish priest in various small towns in the Cremona area, Mazzolari always declared his 'understanding' for those soldier-peasants who, returning from the front and yearning for greater social justice, had embraced socialist ideas.

Openly opposed to Mussolinian propaganda, in the autobiographical novel *La pieve sull'argine* ('The church on the river bank'), published in 1952, he expressed the disgust he felt for the Fascists, the armed representatives of the great landowners and for the most part characters with no moral or cultural depth. In the years of the fascist regime, he stood up for the poor and humble peasants, oppressed by violence and by the philosophy of the 'survival of the fittest'. His ideas led to repeated warnings from the political authorities and, in 1931, shots were fired one night outside the canonry in order to intimidate him.[48]

In 1937, on the front page on the *Vita cattolica*, the diocese of Cremona's weekly journal, Mazzolari published an article entitled 'I cattolici italiani e il comunismo' ('Italian Catholics and communism'), which caused the paper to be seized by order of the local prefect. After having established how, from the October Revolution onwards, communist thought had 'gradually increased, rather in the way of an avalanche, gaining enormously in impressiveness', he maintained that Catholic judgment with regard to communism could not be conditioned by conservative opinion: the reasons for the success of that particular political perspective had to be analysed, because 'when the honest and humble are in turmoil due to the almost inhuman conditions of life' answers are required. As an alternative to communism, it was necessary for the Church to envisage a new human society, because 'no one better than the Christian puts at such a high level the dignity of man, in whom we see, in addition to intelligence, a true son of God'.[49]

Mazzolari acknowledged that communism was responding to the need for justice that existed in society, even if he believed that transformation and change should find their motivations in the radicality of the gospel's message: in his view, Jesus was the one true and authentic liberator, a concept well expressed in his book published in 1945, *Il compagno Cristo* ('Comrade Christ').[50] Mazzolari said that he felt isolated from other priests because of his declared anti-fascism, something hardly surprising considering the relationship between the Church and the fascist regime. The Lateran Pacts of 11 February 1929 had in fact soothed the perplexities still hovering around certain Catholic circles, and Pius XI's description of Mussolini as the man 'sent to us by Providence'[51] seemed to many a legitimation of the fascist government. But there were also other religious figures who were openly against the regime. One of these was the bishop of Vicenza, Ferdinando Ridolfi, who, in a letter addressed to the Pontiff, on 26 June 1928, spoke sadly of the Church's acquiescence to fascism:

> When the new party came to power, established authority was accepted and the prevailing arrogance was endured; apologies were made, even with an attitude of deploration, for the crimes and violence (Don Minzoni, for example); hope was placed in the wisdom of the leader and in the future; the fitting benefits bestowed upon the clergy and the restitutions made to the Church and to the religious were exalted as providential, and in compensation all the banners, all the demonstrations, all the offices and buildings and all the hierarchies of the new regime were given blessing.[52]

Another figure worth mentioning is the bishop of Cremona, Giovanni Cazzani, who, as early as 1921, had aroused the protests of the landowners by refusing to condemn peasant agitation. The prelate, a friend of Don Mazzolari, also had problems with the fascist leader in Cremona, Roberto Farinacci, due to his critical stance towards Nazism and his conviction that the universality of Christianity meant that Catholics could not accept the superiority of one race over another.[53]

Anti-fascism therefore found roots in even the most official areas of the Catholic world, so much so that Gioacchino Malavasi recalled that in the 1920s 'the Catholic University of Milan was essentially a place where there was a general intolerance of Fascism'. The Azione Cattolica association, too – at least in Milan – adopted a position that, while certainly not openly political, certainly represented 'a motivated and unequivocal distance from Fascism'.[54] Moreover, after the dissolution of the PPI, many militants poured into the AC, swelling its ranks with members who had no truck with fascist rhetoric. The Catholic scout movement, too, adopted an attitude of non-involvement in relation to the regime; it was hardly unsurprising, therefore, that the organization decided to break up in 1928, due to fascist and Vatican pressure.[55]

The sensibility expressed by the Federazione Universitaria dei Cattolici Italiani (Italian Catholic University Association, FUCI) was also one that had nothing to do with the ideas of fascism. This was true during the period when it was led by Mgr. Luigi Piastrelli – who was forced to resign in 1925 – as well as when the federation was under the spiritual guidance of Giovanni Battista Montini. Unlike the majority of Italian Catholics who supported fascism in the name of a war against modernity, the federation declared that it was necessary to be open with regard to confronting the modern world.[56] After the crisis that occurred in 1931 between fascism and the Catholic Church, and the compromise that brought about a decline in importance in the role of the AC, less space was available even to moderate forms of anti-fascism, and Mgr. Montini, too, was removed from the FUCI.[57]

Other important Catholic exponents who worked against fascism included Gioacchino Malavasi and Piero Malvestiti, two young men from the AC who founded the Movimento guelfo (Guelph Movement) in 1928. Their opposition to fascism was rooted in the fact that they believed in and supported the Risorgimento process as a promoter – in their eyes – of the values of liberty and democracy. The conviction of these modern Guelphs was not only that democracy was compatible with Christianity but that the most profoundly fertile soil for its growth lay uniquely in Christian principles.[58] The movement began to take shape in the period following the dissolution of the PPI, especially amongst the young people who attended Milan's Catholic University of the Sacred Heart. The Guelphs made their appearance on the political scene in 1931, during the months of crisis in the relationship between the Church and fascism, with eye-catching initiatives, such as distributing thousands of leaflets with contents avowedly opposed to the dictatorship. *L'Osservatore Romano* intervened against the 'Guelfi' on 24 May 1931, condemning the movement and describing its members as 'provocateurs' and 'followers of Lenin', their ideas imbued with 'socialistoid heraldry'.[59]

In reality, their ideas were far from pro-socialist and the attention they showed towards social contradictions was absolutely in line with Church doctrine: the 'Guelfi' condemned fascism because they judged it to have fatal links with capitalism, economically sustained as it was by the wealthy and bourgeois and employed as an instrument of social intimidation in order to reaffirm their social power.

Between the end of 1932 and the beginning of 1933, the group began to establish contacts with secular anti-fascism, in particular with the Socialists and the group Giustizia e libertà (Justice and liberty). Malavasi, meanwhile, continued to maintain personal and professional relationships with Lelio Basso, Ugo La Malfa and Mario Paggi. The Guelphs were arrested in the spring of 1933, tried by a special tribunal and convicted, although the sentence was remitted. The movement ceased to exist on 25 July 1943, when it merged with the DC.[60]

Catholic 'heretic': Ernesto Buonaiuti

During the fascist period, the faint voices raised to hypothesize agreements, meetings or contacts between Catholics and the Left were progressively thinned out and marginalized. The pope, Achille Ratti, who succeeded Benedict XV in February 1922, immediately demonstrated an intense aversion towards communism: thus, while throughout Europe the revolutionary wave died down and conservative and authoritarian solutions came to the fore, Pius XI entrenched the Church in positions of religious, political and social conservatism, reaffirming its opposition to modern civilization.[61] The PPI, tolerated by Benedict XV, who had abolished the *Non expedit* in 1919, was disowned by the new pontiff, who thought it best to establish a direct relationship with political power.[62] The Church's attentiveness in relation to fascism came not only from the hope of concluding a favourable agreement that would shelve the 'Roman question' forever: they had in common, as the historian Giovanni Miccoli underlined, the 'need for order, discipline, authority, hierarchy, a substantial disdain and pessimism with regard to man as a social being, who must always be guided, corrected, restricted. There was a lack of trust therefore in every form of discussion and study, in every attitude that was not one of obedience and submission.'[63] The Church, in short, believed that fascism represented an opportunity for it to achieve its goal of reconquering Italian society.[64]

Pio XI's pontificate was a period when the international character of Catholic cultural life was scaled back and any hypothesis of renewal within the Church set aside: the belief imposed was that as an institution it should be preserved in its most traditional vestments. Thus in 1925 the Pope instituted the holiday of *Cristo Re* (Christ the King), with the intention of encouraging Catholics to act for the transformation of the structures of society on the basis of the teachings and principles of the Church.[65] It was a context well suited to the thought of the Franciscan friar Agostino Gemelli who, a strenuous opponent of the modern world, reproposed the model of the medieval world and subscribed to the prospect of the reconquest of society by Christian values.[66]

One of the intellectuals who expressed most strongly his estrangement from a perspective of this kind was Ernesto Buonaiuti, a Catholic priest and leading figure in the Modernist movement at the beginning of the century. He became professor of the History of Christianity at the University of Rome in 1915,[67] and in 1917 formed a Christian community, the so-called *Koinonìa*, which consisted of a group of disciples who met Buonaiuti every Sunday in Rome (and during the summer at the San Donato hermitage, near Subiaco). The group included, amongst others, Raffaello Morghen, Alberto Pincherle, Ambrogio Donini, Mario Niccoli, Giorgio Levi della Vida and Arturo Carlo Jemolo. Their meetings were based on study, conversation, the reading of the New Testament and ecclesiastical authors, and the discussion of contemporary thinkers and issues.[68]

Buonaiuti was excommunicated in 1926 for his 'heretical' positions (a *scomunica vitando*, which meant it was not permitted for a believer to approach him). The condemnation of the ecclesiastical authorities with regard to the priest soon developed into a form of persecution: as a result of the Concordat – and a clause that stated that excommunicates could not teach in public universities – he was also deprived of his university teaching post.[69] Assigned to extra-academic duties, as director of the National Edition of the Works of Gioacchino da Fiore, he lost his university professorship when he and ten other university professors refused to take an oath of loyalty to the regime in 1931.[70] The following year he published the work *La Chiesa romana* ('The Roman Church'),[71] which the Holy Office included on its list of proscribed books shortly after the title was issued. In the work, Buonaiuti maintained that religious life was essentially an associated existence; he also emphasized the millennarian tension of the primitive Church and judged that the expiration of Romanism was due to the ties contracted by the Church with national and capitalist establishments.[72]

In the following years, a period of hardship due to the suspension of his salary, Buonaiuti – constantly under the watchful eye of the fascist secret police – busied himself with life as a lecturer, especially to the Roman Methodist congregation. He was offered the chair of History of Christianity at the Faculty of Theology at the University of Lausanne, but he declined, since it required his official conversion to the Christian Reformed Church.

His persecution continued even after the fall of fascism: in August 1944, the Bonomi government decided to restore the state roles of all those who had been expelled during fascism and the Minister of Education, Guido De Ruggiero, intended to offer a university course to Buonaiuti. There was a hostile reaction from the ecclesiastical sphere, however, which pointed out that Article 5 of the Concordat provided for the exclusion of Buonaiuti from teaching.

In 1945, Buonaiuti founded the weekly journal *Il Risveglio*, which the communist Concetto Marchesi contributed to and where Ignazio Silone's novel *Fontamara* was published for the first time. The journal expressed the need, in that moment of the reconstruction of civil and democratic coexistence, to 'return to the Gospel and rediscover there ideals and duty'. The publication soon had to close down – due, Buonaiuti suspected, to Vatican pressure – but in June the ex-priest founded another weekly, *1945*, with contributions from important left-wing intellectuals, including Massimo Bontempelli, Giovanni Giudici, Corrado Alvaro, Corrado Barbagallo and Elio Vittorini.[73]

In 1937, Buonaiuti published an article on Christianity and communism, in which he harshly criticized the anti-religious policy advocated by the Soviet government, a policy that had its roots in hatred and envy: the message of Jesus, he said in the article, was one that grew out of love.[74] In May 1945, he published the book *La Chiesa e il comunismo* ('The Church and communism'), in which he opened with the statement: 'Christianity was born communist, and communism was born Christian. It is, of course, a matter of coming to an understanding with one another about the meaning of the word Christianity and the meaning of the word communism.' Buonaiuti immediately clarified that the differences between communism and Christianity were evident: while modern communism was based on 'an overestimation of economic assets', the communism of primitive Christians presupposed 'a capital devaluation of economic goods, in view of a super-valuation of spiritual values'. Buonaiuti emphasized, however, that there had always been a tendency towards communist life in the Church, most noticeably especially in the religious orders, which represented 'human aggregations that practice the fraternal communion of material goods and common administration of the daily economy'.[75] He would never return to university teaching,[76] though he never lost hope that he might,[77] and died on 20 April 1946.[78] Giorgio La Piana, who had shared Buonaiuti's passion for historical and religious research at the beginning of the 1900s and who had been obliged, like many 'Modernists', to leave Italy because of the climate that had developed under Pius X's pontificate, wrote of his friend, who had remained true to the ideas he had professed in his youth: 'When he was driven outside the Church, he found consolation in the idea that his expulsion decreed by ecclesiastical power had no value in the sight of God. Up to the end, Buonaiuti considered himself a member of the Church of God and an instrument chosen by the Spirit to communicate Divine law.'[79]

One student of Buonaiuti's was the Church historian and militant communist Ambrogio Donini, with regard to whom Buonaiuti had prophesied, as early as 1926: 'I have failed in my mission, but he will succeed.'[80] In his memoirs, too, Buonaiuti recalls his followers Ambrogio Donini, Alberto Pincherle and Mario Niccoli, called to carry out 'an activity that would represent, in different forms, but with a spirit not without comradeship and affinity, the continuation of my concerns and my aspirations'. Donini, in particular, was described as his 'intellectual disciple'[81] and, on his part, the future senator always felt a strong cultural debt towards his teacher: 'I was a student of Buonaiuti's for many years, from when I joined the Faculty of Letters of the university in Rome; student in an almost medieval sense, that is, a co-participant not only in his doctrine, but also in his way of living and thinking.'[82]

Donini, born in 1903 into a wealthy, very Catholic, Turin family, graduated under Buonaiuti in 1925 with a thesis on Hippolytus of Rome. The following year, he joined the Communist Party and obtained a lecturing post in the History of Christianity. The study of the history of religions led him, after his university years, to the abandonment 'of every devotional practice and of the Catholic faith itself'. In 1928, he emigrated to the USA with a scholarship obtained thanks to Giorgio La Piana, but in 1932 he returned to Europe, called back by the Foreign Section of the party, who asked him to manage the publishing house, the *Edizioni di Cultura Sociale*, in Brussels and to be the editor of the anti-fascist newspaper *La Voce degli italiani*. On a clandestine mission to Milan with the aim of making contact with intellectual circles, he met Buonaiuti at the end of a conference:

> I reminded him that in my work I was trying to realise some of the principles on which he had based his teaching: the necessity of daily risk in order to realize a program of understanding and the regeneration of society [...] similar to that of the first Christian groups, in total dissent with the structures of the ancient world.

Buonaiuti greeted his student's words with an air of detachment and did not appear at the appointment they had set for the following day: 'Evidently my presence in the guise of a Communist propagandist had only succeeded in shocking him and throwing him into a panic.'[83] Buonaiuti, in *Pellegrino di Roma*, gives a very different interpretation of the meeting, talking not of the unease and disappointment which Donini describes, but reporting certain of the reflections that he had formulated as a result of what he had been told: 'Should one have thought that there was some truth in what my young student, who presumed to carry out his communist propaganda in a Christian manner, had so suddenly said to me?' Buonaiuti seems to have been very struck by the words, and the meeting, in his eyes, appeared to 'enfold both a warning and a portent'.[84]

Following the Second World War, Donini paid the price of having been a student of Buonaiuti's. When Palmiro Togliatti, leader of the Communist Party, at the end of 1946, proposed him as undersecretary for the Foreign Office in a broad coalition government, De Gasperi responded: 'We do not want Buonaiuti's men in our ministerial team.' Donini's closeness to the teachings of his mentor was also made clear at a conference held on 15 December 1946, at the *Teatro Lirico* in Milan. The subject regarded the 'secular state and the freedom of conscience', on the occasion of the beginning of the discussion in the Constituent Assembly with respect to relations between state and church. On that occasion, the communist intellectual maintained the thesis of 'the absolute independence and freedom of the Catholic Church in the exercise of its spiritual mission and in the complete and utter separation of political life from the religious life of the Italian people'.[85]

An 'unusual' kind of Communist: Antonio Gramsci

Gramsci and Catholic policy

In the world of the Italian Left, the person that most stood out in the years between the two wars as an intellectual, and as a figure engaged in an attentive dialogue with the Catholic sphere, was undoubtedly Antonio Gramsci. Gramsci began as a member of the Socialist Party,[86] co-founding the Communist Party in January 1921.[87] Secretary and leader of the PCI from 1924 to 1927, he was arrested and imprisoned in 1926 in the prison of Turi, near Bari. In 1934, as his state of health became serious, he was conditionally released from custody and admitted to a clinic, where he died in April 1937.

Gramsci was the first Italian thinker, after the Marxist philosopher Antonio Labriola,[88] to deal with the religious question in an organic way, influenced by his reading of Engels and knowledge of Sorel's ideas. In fact, reflecting on the French revolutionary's thinking, in September 1920 he wrote that 'after Sorel, it became commonplace to refer to the first Christian communities when considering the contemporary proletarian movement'.[89]

There were three different phases in Gramsci's thinking with regard to this issue: the first coincided with his socialist militancy in Turin when, under the influence of Benedetto Croce, his ideas about the religious world were chiefly negative. He was opposed to any hypothesis of a relationship between Christianity and socialism, describing the latter as the new religion that was supposed to 'put Christianity to death'.[90] In the aftermath of the Great War, however, his attitude changed. With his anticlerical phase behind him, he broached the idea that Marxist Socialists 'even if they were not religious' should not be 'anti-religious'. He noted that

> Marxist socialists believe that religion is a transitory form of human culture that will be overcome by a higher form, the philosophical. They believe that religion is a mythological form of life and the world, a conception that will be superseded

and replaced by one based on historical materialism: a conception, that is, that locates, and investigates, the causes and forces that produce and create history in the very heart of human society and in the individual conscience.⁹¹

In his opinion, the labour movement had to arrive at a secular religiosity capable of promoting change not only in economic structures – and thus overcoming the capitalist system – but also to work to induce a profound change in humanity itself. This was the period of the foundation of the Communist Party, an organization Gramsci conceived as 'a religious faith, although a secularised one'. And to understand the genesis of this faith, notes Gabriele De Rosa, it is necessary not only to refer to the history of socialism but to hold up primitive Christianity as a term of fundamental comparison.⁹² Gramsci considered it a revolutionary element, in that it aimed to destroy the old existing social system in order to create a new and original one. He wrote: 'For Sorel, as for Marxist doctrine, Christianity represents a revolution in the fullness of its development, a revolution that has reached its extreme consequences, the creation of a new and original system of moral, juridical, philosophical and artistic relationships.'⁹³ However, he went on to explain that 'every historical phenomenon must be studied for its own specific characteristics, in the context of the real contemporary world', and, probably taking to task Camillo Prampolini – an exponent of socialist evangelism, who claimed Christ as the 'first socialist' in history – Gramsci reiterated that 'the finality, the institutions, the forms, of past historical phenomena' cannot be confused with the present.⁹⁴

Integrity and maturity of judgment came to Gramsci only with his *Quaderni dal carcere* ('Prison notebooks').⁹⁵ He began writing them in February 1929 – coinciding with the signing of the Lateran Pacts, which explains his constant interest in Vatican policy. He believed it was crucial to reflect on the history of the Church and to keep it's role clearly in mind when considering the causes of the defeat of democratic forces and the victory of fascism in Italy.

The goal of Italy's 'intellectual and moral reform' therefore had to take the vision of the Catholic world into account, deeply rooted as it was in the various social strata, and especially amongst those peasant masses that Gramsci, in the Lyon theses,⁹⁶ had identified as subjects of a possible alliance with the working class. Moreover, it is evident that there were political motivations at the basis of Gramsci's thoughts regarding the Catholic question and his objective of constructing 'an alternative bloc to that of the dominant bourgeoisie' in order to arrive at the 'hegemony of the proletariat'.⁹⁷

In the *Quaderni*, Gramsci addressed the history of Christianity from its origins, dwelling on the Edict of Constantine, the medieval church, the heretical sects, the Reformation and the Counter-Reformation, delineating a path and formulating interpretative hypotheses. In particular, speaking of the heretical movements, he noted how they had represented a reaction 'to the Church's politicking and to the scholastic philosophy' that were in its disposition: founded as an expression of the subordinate classes, after AD 313 the Church had in fact become the ideological apparatus of power and of the state, first imperial and then feudal. The strategy of the ecclesiastical establishment, faced with the popular, mystical and progressive ferments that were born within it, was to repress or reabsorb them, giving rise to religious orders based around strong personalities (Dominic, Francis, etc.). With the Counter-Reformation things changed: popular religious movements lost their vigour, while the new orders that were coming to the fore lacked eschatological fervour and had no sense of innovation. They were, rather, characterized by their 'disciplinary' function towards the faithful: fundamentally, it was a matter of being 'instruments of resistance to preserve the political positions acquired'.[98]

Gramsci saw no continuity between primitive Christianity and the Church of Rome, and divided the history of Christianity into three phases: first, primitive and 'communistic'; then, 'Constantinian'; and then, following the Counter-Reformation, a climate of conformism, of which the maximum expression was the Society of Jesus.[99] It is worth noting that these interpretations echoed those of certain exponents of Modernism in the early twentieth century and especially formed the basis of Buonaiuti's thinking, the reason for his excommunication.

With regard to the period following the French Revolution, the Azione Cattolica, as an expression of Vatican policy, was at the centre of Gramsci's reflections. In his view, the foundation of the AC was an indication that the Church had lost its totalitarian nature and needed an instrument that could spread through society in a ramified fashion. The Church was now on the defensive and found it difficult to deal with the new modern forces that were coming to the fore in society. Considering an essay by Ernesto Vercesi,[100] in which the Catholic thinker maintained that, despite the attacks on the Church that had characterized the entire nineteenth century, Roman Catholicism still remained a force to be reckoned with, Gramsci could only show his bewilderment when presented with an interpretation of this kind. He wrote in the *Quaderni*:

> Catholicism has become one party amongst others. It has passed from the uncontested enjoyment of certain rights, to the defence of them and to reclaiming them as having been lost. It is undoubtedly incontestable that, in some respects, the Church has strengthened certain of its organisations, that it is more concentrated, that it has tightened its ranks, that certain principles

and directives have been better established. But this is precisely why it has less influence on society and why it therefore needs to struggle and to have a more intrepid militia. It is also true that many states no longer contend with the Church, because they want to make use of it and subordinate it to their own ends.

And then, Gramsci wondered, 'in philosophy, what does the Church matter today? In what state is Thomism the prevailing philosophy amongst intellectuals? And, socially, where does the authority of the Church control and direct social activity?'[101]

In his studies following the Great War, Gramsci addressed the theme of the role of Catholics in Italian political and social life, formulating positive judgments with regard to the political experience, the innovative aspect of which he was keen to underline. In the period preceding the foundation of the PPI, when discussion and communication in the Catholic sphere were fervent, in *Avanti* the Marxist leader reflected on the disruptive significance that such a political organization would assume in his country's history. A Catholic party would, in fact, be 'the greatest event in Italian history since the Risorgimento' and would cause the 'bourgeois class cadres to be dismantled, because the domination of the state would be fiercely contested. And it could not be excluded that the Catholic party, thanks to a powerful national organisation centred in a few skilful hands, would emerge victorious in competing with the liberal classes and secular conservatives of the bourgeoisie.'[102]

Gramsci also considered the PPI in November 1919, again underlining the innovative dimension that it represented for Italy: 'The process of social renewal of the Italian people', he wrote, was embodied not only in a religious movement but in a historical action based on 'real, immanent and operative forces within the very heart of society'. It had spread widely throughout the masses, so that 'the constitution of the popular party was equivalent in importance to the Germanic Reformation, was the irresistible unconscious explosion of the Italian Reformation'.[103] Moreover, Gramsci noted, it was precisely because the new party was a mass movement, thanks to its entrenchment in Catholic associations, its mutual societies, its small cooperative credit banks, that political Catholicism did not enter into competition with the liberal world but, given that the same social interlocutors were in contention, with socialism. And he continued: 'The *Popolari* are a necessary stage in the development process of the Italian proletariat towards communism. They create associationism, create solidarity where socialism could not, because the objective conditions of the capitalist economy are lacking.'[104] In Gramsci's view, the PPI was born amongst the most backward classes, especially in the countryside, where the organizations on the Left struggled to impose themselves, envoys as they were of an undertaking that was too advanced in form. 'Democratic Catholicism', he added, 'does what socialism could not: it amalgamates, orders, vivifies and then vanishes from the scene'. Socialists, therefore, should not look with suspicion on the birth of a new political party, because eventually the Catholic 'masses' would merge together 'with the conscious socialist masses', and together they would work to overcome the contradictions of capitalism.[105]

Gramsci's thinking was not shared by other exponents of the secular and left-wing world of the period. Piero Gobetti, for example, was critical of the decision to found the PPI and only re-evaluated Sturzo's political vision when the latter's opposition to fascism was made clear.[106] There were also worried comments in *Critica sociale* about the influence that the PPI, a party linked to the Church, could have in parliamentary discussions on school and divorce.[107] Arguments were raised, moreover, regarding the popular party's defence of private property, with the contradiction being pointed out between this position and 'primitive evangelical socialism'.[108] In March 1920, the Gramsci-founded journal *L'Ordine nuovo* ('The New Order') published a letter from a reader from Bologna asking what the attitude of socialist militants should be towards workers and peasants who were politically close to the PPI. He went on to declare his bewilderment at statements that appeared in the Turin journal whereby 'if a friar, a priest, a nun performed a socially useful job, then they were, indeed, workers and they had the right to be treated like other workers'. Gramsci, in response, did not fail to criticize a certain maximalist and anticlerical socialism that did not realistically confront the problem of the Catholic movement's deep-rootedness in certain peasant areas of Italy and underestimated the fact that 'in Italy, in Rome, there *was* the Vatican, there *was* the Pope'. The liberal state, too, had to find a 'system of equilibrium' with the political power of the Church, and a future workers' state would have to do the same.[109] In particular, Gramsci referred to a worker from Turin who, although a 'devout Christian', recognized that the Socialist Party was the party for him. The Marxist leader declared that he appreciated the choice that this worker had made and said that convictions had to be respected: 'the religious idea was not a reason for division within the working class', and there was nothing outrageous in the fact that a worker should pray for Christ to punish those who employed violence against workers on strike.[110]

After the Livorno congress and the foundation of the new party, Gramsci wanted to reflect on the strategies to be adopted. In particular, he thought it appropriate that the PCI should establish roots amongst the peasant masses:

in Italy 'the industrial proletariat' represented only 'a minority of the working population'. As well as the southern peasants, therefore, he also focused his attention on those 'grouped in central and northern Italy, which were strictly organized by the *Azione Cattolica* and by the ecclesiastical apparatus in general'.[111] And again in 1922 Gramsci was careful to point out that the PPI was a 'party that was made up of, and represented, vast organized masses'.[112]

In particular, the Communist Party would have to try to foster 'left-wing formations' within the Catholic sphere, even if these were in competition with the Communists in the countryside. To win over the sympathies of the peasant masses, those on the Left had even clashed with landowners because they made 'statements of a programmatic nature that the landowners could not bear'.[113] This sort of political radicalism, localized in certain Italian areas, probably explained why the Popular Party had 'more luck in northern and central Italy than in the south'.[114] Gramsci's remark here undoubtedly refers to Miglioli's experience in Cremona, a situation that he was well aware of, and to which he would make more than one reference.

While Gramsci emphasized that 'the conflicts that were born in the field of religion' derived in fact from class conflict, he refrained from dealing with religious reform. It was evident that he preferred a trade union organizer such as Miglioli to the exponents of Catholic Modernism, but it was equally clear that he understood the disruptive character that religious renewal might have for 'the authority of the official religious organisation'.[115]

The roots of left-wing Catholicism, Gramsci noted, were to be found in the structural changes that the Italian economy and society had experienced in the early twentieth century. The birth of the agricultural proletariat and of movements involved in the struggle in the countryside forced 'the Vatican to react [...] with the foundation of a "social" movement that, in its extreme forms ... assumed the appearance of a religious reform'. At the same time, however, the Holy See stipulated an agreement with the ruling classes 'to give the state a more secure base'. In Gramsci's eyes, the PPI possessed characteristics that were decidedly contradictory: 'in its founding, it presumed to represent the economic interests and political aspirations of all the social stratas of the countryside, from landowning baron to middle holder, from smallholder to tenant farmer, from sharecropper to poor peasant'.[116]

The leaders of the popular party had worked to convince the masses to accept a 'reformist' program, making them believe that 'the fulfillment of their needs for economic and political liberation' could be achieved without replacing a bourgeois state with 'a state of workers and peasants'.[117] Their behaviour was, in other words, analogous to that of the Reformist Socialists,[118] and Gramsci's judgement was therefore that 'Don Sturzo and Turati were beginning to look strangely like old-man Giolitti', the advocate of a policy that was 'political gangsterism and wholly unscrupulous'.[119] The contradictions of the Popular Party were bound to explode in the near future because 'the large masses of small landowners and poor peasants no longer had any wish to be the passive reserve formation for the implementation of the interests of the medium and large landowners'.[120] The People's Party had split into a right wing, centre and left wing, and under pressure from the poor peasantry the 'extreme left' had begun to 'adopt a revolutionary stance', entering into competition with the parties of the Left that were also 'representatives of the vast peasant masses'. Thus, the parliamentary section of the party and the leadership no longer represented 'the interests and the acquired self-awareness of the electoral masses and the organised forces of the white – (i.e., non-communist) – unions', and the extremists who controlled them were 'led to resort to violent struggle'.[121] This was a belief that Gramsci also expressed during his parliamentary intervention in May 1925 against the Mussolini-Rocco bill.[122] While the fascist deputies hurled insults, he reiterated his appreciation of Catholic leaders such as Miglioli, who guided the masses 'towards revolutionary struggle'.[123]

With regard to the 'extreme right' of the PPI, Gramsci considered the occasion of this group's departure from the party in 1924, emphasizing that they were the descendants of the 'old reactionary Catholics' who had always had 'the preservation of the existing social order' as their objective. To avoid 'the revenge of the workers and peasants' against the ruling castes, they had entered into an agreement with Giolitti, thus succeeding in using the social entrenchment of the Catholic movement in defence of the state and against 'the parties of class'.[124] Gramsci was not convinced that the conservative group's exit from the party could be considered an important success on the part of Mussolini, as the fascist leader believed: while the extreme right remained an integral part of the Popular Party, he could easily exert his influence over the Catholic masses, but, with its departure and its constitution as an autonomous political group, confusion was created in the world of the faithful.[125] Thus Gramsci hoped for a 'clarifying solution' within the PPI, as well as acquisition of the awareness that 'the masses had need of freedom and legality' – things that could only be achieved 'by tearing down the Fascist dictatorship'.[126]

The historian Giuseppe Galasso argues that Gramsci, in his analyses carried out between 1924 and 1926, intended to highlight a 'distinction between Vatican policy and Italian political Catholicism'.[127] The communist leader pointed out that the majority of the PPI were quick to offer harsh criticism of the system of violence and intimidation established by Mussolini. In an article of December 1924, Gramsci referred to the initiative of Giuseppe Donati, who had courageously presented the Senate Presidency with a formal protest denouncing complicity in the murder of Giacomo Matteotti on the part of the ex-director of public safety, Emilio De Bono.[128] At the same time, however, he underlined how the Vatican was progressively drawing closer to fascism and, writing in *La Correspondance internationale*[129] of March 1924 with regard to the Holy See's politics, he judged the Vatican to be 'the greatest reactionary force existing in Italy, all the more to be feared given its insidious and elusive nature'. Even fascism, before carrying out its 'coup d'état', had to come to an agreement with the Church.[130] The Azione Cattolica, moreover, was now 'an integral part of Fascism' and tended, through religious ideology, 'to provide Fascism with the consensus of the large popular masses'; it was even intended, no less, 'to replace the Fascist Party itself in its function as a party of the masses and an organism of political control of the population'.[131]

Thus the Popular Party, with its attested anti-fascist positions, risked coming into 'open conflict with the Azione Cattolica', because unlike the latter, which was an expression of the politics of the ecclesiastical hierarchy and 'was in the hands of the aristocracy and great landowners', the PPI had become the organization 'of the low clergy and poor peasants'. Gramsci predicted that the ongoing struggle between the various elements of the Catholic world, which reflected 'the class conflicts of the rural Italian masses', would, given the 'reactionary' character of Pius XI Catholicism, have to be won by the conservative faction.[132]

Gramsci and the religious question

The attempt at renewal that pervaded Catholic culture between the nineteenth and twentieth centuries did not arouse great interest in the Italian and European socialist world, something that was acknowledged in the words of Emile Vandervelde, for whom socialism 'doit rester étranger aux questions purement religieuses et dogmatique, dont le royaume n'est pas de ce monde'.[133] Thus the exponents of socialism mainly focused their attention on the social and political manifestations of the Catholic movement, appreciating, for example, the innovatory nature of the birth of Christian Democracy in Belgium, France and Italy. An exception was represented by Sorel who, while grasping the importance of religious Modernism, shared with Croce – a regular correspondent of his in those years[134] – a substantially negative judgment with regard to the movement.

Gramsci, for his part, also gave religious reformism careful consideration, but unlike Sorel he did not criticize it; indeed, he judged Modernism to be an exception in terms of the manifestations of Christianity that followed the Counter-Reformation, given that it was not conservative in nature but demonstrated aspects in common with the medieval heretical movements. Unlike these movements, however, Modernism 'had not created "religious orders"' but a mass political party, the Christian Democrats.[135]

Gramsci did not seem to have any doubts with regard to the progressive character of Modernism: the problem was, rather, to define such a complex and heterogeneous phenomenon. The *Pascendi* encyclical had herded intellectuals, who in fact had little in common, into excommunication together. This provoked the polemical reaction of those who, like Murri – a Thomist opposed to religious immanentism – felt he had been unjustly grouped in with George Tyrrell, a Jesuit priest and the main exponent of English Modernism.

Gramsci was one of the first to identify a possible definition and differentiation between the various modernist elements, writing that:

> It is evident that there is no fixed and always easily identifiable model of 'modernism' and the 'modernist', something that does not exist for any '-ist' or '-ism'. It was a matter of a complex and multifaceted movement, with a variety of meanings: 1) one which the modernists gave themselves; 2) one which modernists were given by their adversaries; and the two did certainly not coincide. It might be said that modernism had a variety of different manifestations: 1) a social-political aspect, which intended to bring the Church closer to the working classes, and was therefore favourable towards reformist socialism and democracy [...]; 2) a 'scientific-religious' aspect, which supported a new attitude towards 'dogma' and 'historical criticism' compared to that of ecclesiastical tradition, and therefore a tendency towards the intellectual reform of the Church.[136]

What is interesting to note is that Gramsci related Modernism, analogously with the liberal Catholicism of the early nineteenth century and popularism, to contemporary culture, arguing that it was a phenomenon linked to the 'spontaneous attraction aroused by the modern historicism of the secular intellectuals of the upper classes on the one hand and by the practical movement of the philosophy of praxes on the other'.[137] Modernism was the fruit of the confrontation between the most vibrant aspects of Catholic culture and modern philosophy, at that time certainly a 'winning' topic. Gramsci, therefore, showed himself to be in disagreement with Sorel who, idealizing the 'mystical principle that had vivified' Catholic tradition, had stigmatized those who had proposed to 'elevate the Church to the level reached by the lay spirit'.[138] Sorel believed that the repression carried out by the ecclesiastical establishment against these religious reformers could 'render de grands service à la science comme à la théologie', and did not appear to think that the Modernists were the 'nouveaux Galilée', let alone 'rapresentants de l'eprit scientifique'.[139] An analogous opinion was expressed by Benedetto Croce, who judged that the attempt to equip a religion such as Catholicism with modern philosophy was something 'contradictory and absurd'.[140]

One of the few secular cultural spheres that gave credit to religious reformism was the journal *Critica sociale* which, unlike the other European socialist periodicals – *Mouvement socialiste, Neue Zeit, Avenir social* and *Social-democrat* – said that the main figures of Modernism were 'natural flowers' born to respond to 'the intellectual challenges of rationalistic and scientific criticism'.[141] It was a point of view that Gramsci shared, and he too interpreted Modernism as a reaction by the Catholic intelligentsia to the demands of the modern world. The Modernists, he emphasized, had called scholastic philosophy – the philosophy that Leo XIII, with the encyclical *Aeterni Patris* (1879), had reaffirmed as the only one accepted by the Church – into question and, through studies that had led them to a 'deviation from orthodoxy', had arrived at immanentism.[142] Gramsci did not go into the specifics of religious matters, and he confirmed the beliefs already expressed by other socialist thinkers – and which did not differ from the criticism of anti-modernist propaganda – that the final outcome of this intellectual research was atheism. In particular, he noted how the abbot Joseph Turmel had by now moved 'completely out of the religious field', while continuing as a priest: it was an outcome shared by other representatives of religious renewal and to prove this Gramsci cited Félix Sartiaux's work, *Joseph Turmel prêtre historien des dogmes*[143] and the *Memoire* by Alfred Loisy.[144]

Gramsci's interest was addressed not so much to the debate on religious reformism as to the social character that Modernism assumed. As the historian Lorenzo Bedeschi also noted, Modernism, in Italy especially, spread from the cultural to the political sphere, becoming an important movement for social renewal.[145] Gramsci pointed out that, in the area of the Po Valley at the turn of the nineteenth and twentieth centuries, the phenomenon of the day labourer became something commonplace. He stressed that there was a close relationship between the changes in the economic structure that took place in the region and the affirmation there of the democratic Catholic movement. In some areas, socialism had a large following, and leaders such as Andrea Costa, Enrico Ferri and Camillo Prampolini had managed to organize the protests of those who worked the land; but in the hilly region running to the left of the Via Emilia, from Cesena to Imola, where smallholders continued to persist, the democratic Catholic movement organized by Don Giovanni Ravaglia and Eligio Cacciaguerra, thanks to radical political proposals inspired by Murri's ideas, had succeeded in raising a following amongst the peasants.[146] Gramsci emphasized the aversion of fundamentalist Catholics towards this movement of social reform: while conservatives tolerated Modernists such as Turmel, who focused their attention on a 'scientific' sphere, they were opposed to the Christian Democratic movement, 'being closely linked to the most reactionary classes and especially to the landowning nobility and landowners in general'.[147]

Gramsci's political sensibility, which led him to interpret religious facts as inseparable from the dynamics of the struggle for land, is also to be found in his analysis of Croce's thoughts in relation to the modernist phenomenon. Gramsci set out to understand the reasons that had induced Croce, sensitive to the issues of liberal Catholicism in the early nineteenth century, to produce judgments that were highly critical of the religious reform movement at the beginning of the century and identified them in the Italian philosopher's political conservatism.

The official thesis supported by the idealist philosopher – 'between transcendental religion and immanentist philosophy there could not exist a *tertium quid ancipite ed equivoco*' – was something Gramsci thus considered to be far from convincing.[148] The true religion was, in Croce's opinion, of an idealistic nature, while for the uncultivated masses, for whom it was impossible to understand an elitist philosophy, the Catholic religion was fine as it was and required neither change nor modernization. Attempts, indeed, in such a direction only helped to erode the 'massive practical-ideological structure of the Church'.[149] Croce's opinion was based on a profoundly conservative vision of the world and the desire to 'reinforce reactionary currents'; and Gramsci went on to say:

> Modernists, given the mass character that was given to them by the contemporary birth of a rural Catholic democracy (linked to the technological revolution that took place in the Po valley with the disappearance of the figure of the *obbligato* or tenant farmer and the expanding role of the day labourer and of less servile forms of sharecropping) were religious reformers. Their appearance did not accord with pre-established intellectual schemes, dear to Hegelianism, but with the real and historical conditions of Italian religious life. It was a second wave of liberal Catholicism, far more extensive and more popular in character than that of neo-Guelphism before 1848 and the most outspoken Catholic liberalism following 1848.[150]

The reasons for the hostility towards Modernism of Croce, Giovanni Gentile[151] and Giuseppe Prezzolini[152] lay in the popular and progressive character of the movement, and the fact that it could make life difficult for the class and the economic and social interests that were dear to those with a conservative conception of politics. These secular intellectuals thus bear a heavy responsibility for the repression of Modernism: 'The stance of Croce and Gentile (with Prezzolini as altar boy) isolated Modernists in the world of culture and made their repression by the Vatican easier. Indeed, it seemed to hand the pope a victory over all modern philosophy: the anti-modernist encyclical,' Gramsci observed, 'was in reality against immanence and modern science and in this sense was commented upon in seminaries and religious circles'.[153]

Mario Missiroli,[154] too, distinguished himself for his 'anti-modernist and anti-*popolare*' attitude, stating that 'the people could not achieve the conception of political freedom and the idea of nation until after they had undergone a religious reform – that is, after having conquered the notion of freedom in religion'. He was 'fiercely' opposed to the attempt at reform supported by the Modernists. This happened, added Gramsci, 'because modernism, in political terms, meant Christian Democracy, which was politically strong in Emilia-Romagna and throughout the Po Valley and Missiroli and his liberals fought on the side of the landowners'.[155]

The Church, in order to combat Modernism, after the encyclical of condemnation of September 1907, also instituted an oath which all religious persons had to swear, undertaking not to follow interpretations or ideas considered heterodox with respect to traditional doctrine. This led some to abandon the church, but, as Gramsci acutely pointed out, 'not all the modernists were identified', and they continued to operate secretly in the seminaries and parishes.[156] The Vatican was 'impotent' in the face of individual conscience and 'the young clergy did not hesitate to pronounce the anti-modernist oath, while continuing to preserve their own opinions'.[157] Like an underground stream, the need for renewal of the Church in the political and religious sphere was never dormant in the conscience of many believers and would resurface in the sixties and seventies, encouraged by the reflections and solicitations of the Vatican II.

The struggle for liberation

Relations between Catholics and Marxists were few and far between until the Resistance, except for those of a personal nature,[158] but there was always very keen interest on the part of the ecclesiastical sphere in the world of the left.

In 1932, Pius XI started an investigation into world communism, his intention being to learn about the propaganda and diffusion of that doctrine in the various corners of the planet. The conviction of the Holy See, and of the Secretary of State Eugenio Pacelli, was that Moscow was planning a destabilizing move aimed at the destruction of religion and of the Catholic Church in particular. In 1936, Pacelli again sent a circular letter to all the Apostolic Nuncios with the idea of soliciting new information regarding the spread of Marxism: in particular, the Holy See showed concern both that the ideology could extend amongst the workers and that it seemed to be gaining ground amongst some Catholics as well.[159]

The danger of atheism and secularization was evident, and ecclesiastical authorities identified various Catholic states as a bulwark in the defence of this, such as Italy, Austria, Portugal and, later, Francoist Spain as well. Although dictatorial regimes, they guaranteed the influence of the Church in society and the state.[160] This 'Latin bloc' was given its official seal with the encyclical *Divini redemptoris* of 19 March 1937, conceived and written mainly by the Polish Jesuit Włodzimierz Ledóchowski. The intention was to outline the contours of a strategy aimed at curbing communism, countering it with a new Christian order based on Catholic doctrine.[161]

In the mid-1930s, in conjunction with the watershed of the 7th congress of the Communist International, the communist world, meanwhile, inaugurated a new relationship with religious believers. Eyebrows were raised by French Maurice Thorez's 'outstretched hand' to Catholics in a radio message of 17 April 1936, on the occasion of the elections that would see the victory of the Popular Front coalition. Similar steps were taken by the Communist Party in Italy, which was prompt to reaffirm its respect for all religious convictions and its readiness to uphold the values of family and morality. It was a strategy that featured, amongst others, figures such as Ambrogio Donini and Emilio Sereni, both students of Buonaiuti's,[162] who organized a meeting with Mariano Rampolla del Tindaro, undersecretary of the *Congregazione dei seminari* and close to the Deputy Secretary of State, Giovanni Battista Montini. The meeting took place in August 1938 and it is unclear whether Rampolla's initiative was a personal one or if the Secretary of State was aware of it; both sides, however, agreed on the gravity of the international situation and the danger posed by German foreign policy.[163]

The hostility that marked the attitude of the Holy See towards the forces of the Left provoked the isolation of Catholic anti-fascists, who were accused of connivance with Socialists and Communists. Moreover, the condemnation of Modernism prevented a generation of the faithful from conceiving of a relationship between believer and civil order that differed from the authoritarian and hierarchical one imposed by the Vatican. The consequence was that those who were not in agreement with the general stance of the Church were forced to retire to private life, while Catholic anti-fascism rarely dared to go beyond rebellion in terms of morals and principles.

In the second half of the 1930s, as Italy's bond with Germany became ever closer, and then with the promulgation of the racial laws, the situation began to change and relations between the two banks of the Tiber started to show their first cracks. Historiography has highlighted the concern of Pius XI for the spread in Germany, and progressively in Italy, of neo-pagan theories with their hymns to the 'people' and the 'nation' and that led to the idea of the superiority of one race over another; and the Vatican archives have produced the text of an encyclical written, at the pope's urging, to condemn Nazi and fascist ideologies. It was, however, never published – Pius XI died at the beginning of 1939 and his successor Pius XII had no wish to exacerbate relations with Hitler and Mussolini.[164] Italy's decision to enter the war in June 1940, and especially the inability shown by the political class in dealing with the problems of such a difficult period, created a split between fascism and Italian society: the terrible defeats on the battlefield marked the end of the illusion of an 'imperial' Italy, heir to the warrior traditions of ancient Rome.

It was in this context that, at the end of 1942, the foundation of the DC took place, after a series of meetings of Catholic exponents at the home of Giorgio Enrico Falck, an important Milanese businessman.[165] The constitution of the new party was an opportunity for lively debate, given the cultural and political heterogeneity of the various figures attracted to this political movement. Many came from the PPI, but others, for generational reasons, were formed in Catholic associations during the years of fascism or in classrooms at the Catholic University of Milan. The main figures in this political adventure drafted a document in July 1943 which passed into history as the *Codice di Camaldoli* ('Camaldoli code').[166] Here, they expressed their hope that the DC would carry on the best of the experience of the PPI but also take into account the ideas of democratic Catholicism from the early years of the twentieth century.[167] In June 1944, through the instigation of Giovanni Battista Montini, the Associazione Cattolica Lavoratori Italiani (Catholic Association of Italian Workers, ACLI) was founded, which had the task of coordinating worker demands on the basis of Church social doctrine.

During the Second World War, most Catholics opted for a line of obedience to established authority and a willingness to serve the homeland. Military chaplains followed the soldiers to the front, but the ecclesiastical authorities continued to reaffirm the traditional reading of the war as a form of divine punishment, due to contemporary's society moving away from the precepts and values of tradition. After the armistice signed by Italy on 8 September 1943, a more cautious tone was adopted by Catholics, even though the Cardinal of Milan, Ildefonso Schuster, at Christmas that same year, felt impelled to point out the 'error of centralising the destiny of an entire nation in the will of only one person'.[168]

During the difficult months of the Repubblica sociale italiana (Italian Social Republic, RSI; September 1943–April 1945), much of the country was controlled by German troops and military and political power were in German hands. Mussolini, stripped of his role as prime minister on 25 July 1943 at the behest of the king and placed at the head of the new RSI state by Hitler, seemed at the mercy of events, unable to cope with a situation that was obviously precipitating. In this period of political chaos and enormous difficulty for the Italian people, the Church worked to limit the iniquities of the German occupying forces, helping Jews to hide and flee to Switzerland and defending persecuted politicians. While 2,000 Jews were deported from the capital to concentration camps, around 20,000 managed to escape by hiding themselves in the city, thanks to the help of the Roman people. Convents, parishes and religious institutions were mobilized to protect Jews, wanted people and political opponents.[169] Something similar also took place in Milan, where Cardinal Ildefonso Schuster invited the attorney Giuseppe Sala, president of the Associazione San Vincenzo, to organize aid for members of the 'Semitic race' (for which Sala was arrested).[170] During the same months, the Cardinal – with a view of maintaining a certain equidistance from the parties in conflict – also went on to condemn both the *Crociata italica* (Italic crusade) movement, which was sympathetic to the fascist-inspired RSI,[171] and the groups of communist insurrectionists. Thus, faced with the collapse of civil institutions, the absence of the state and the disorientation of civil society, the Church became an important point of reference for the population.[172]

But there were also Catholics who adopted a clear stance in relation to the German occupation and the political experience of the RSI. In September 1943, the newspaper of the Milan curia *L'Italia* – directed by Don Mario Busti, who had been unpopular with the fascist authorities since 1938 to 1939 – took a stand, in an article by Piero Malvestiti, in the face of the tragic events in progress: 'Those who are partisan', wrote Malvestiti, 'are those who give meaning to freedom: it is they who define it, who reveal it, who sometimes sanctify it with their sacrifice.'[173] There were many Catholics who expressed their anti-fascist sentiments, laid claim to values such as freedom, democracy and peace, and who took a stand against nationalism, imperialism and totalitarianism. Teresio Olivelli, a member of the Catholic Resistance who died in prison in Hersbruck in January 1945, worked on a text in which he envisaged the need for profound social transformation, revealing an outlook that was both anti-capitalist and anti-bourgeois. He believed that the division of society into classes was 'anti-Christian' and criticized the principles of capitalism that reduced relationships between people 'to relations of things, of goods, of signs'. While his condemnation of the Soviet state was clear-cut, seeing it as a 'tyrant state', he held that land should be assigned only to those who worked it and companies given over to producers, technicians and workers.[174] Giuseppe Dossetti, a figure destined to have a long-lasting influence on the Catholic world of the second half of the twentieth century, thought along similar lines. With experience in the AC and having studied at the Catholic University in Milan,[175] Dossetti, in his *Lettera ai parroci della giunta per la montagna del movimento democratico cristiano* ('Letter to the parish priests of the mountain council of the Christian Democratic movement') wrote that anti-capitalist and communitary theories shared common elements with the values present in the Christian experience; antithetical to these, in his judgement, were the political praxis and ideology of capitalism.[176]

It is clear, therefore, that a significant part of the Catholic world played a primary role in the battle for liberation, as is demonstrated by the cases of the anti-fascist martyrs. These include, together with Olivelli, Giancarlo Puecher – who, coming from an upper-class Milanese family, was shot at the age of twenty[177] – and Ernesto Vercesi, who died in the Fossoli deportation camp. Neither should we forget the acts of solidarity performed towards partisans and the persecuted at the Catholic University of Milan.[178] Dossetti, too, participated actively in the Resistance, coming into contact with them through some childhood friends who were members of the Communist Party. The latter also proposed that he be made president of Reggio Emilia's Comitato di Liberazione Provinciale (Provincial Liberation Committee), a role which soon forced him to go into hiding. Another prominent figure was Giuseppe Lazzati: an officer in the *Alpini*, the Italian mountain troops, he was imprisoned in Nazi concentration camps after 8 September because he refused to collaborate with the Germans, only returning to Italy in August 1945.[179] Writing thirty years later, he described Fascists and Nazis as 'representatives, on a concrete historical level, of the negation of the ideals of liberty, justice, solidarity and peace'.[180]

There were many priests, well known and otherwise, who did not limit themselves to saving human lives but helped to hide the arms of the partisans, and some encouraged the organization of the first partisan groups. Some even made the choice – one stigmatized by the ecclesiastical authorities – to go with the young people into a clandestine life. Priests involved in helping the resistance included Don Mazzolari, who, in the spring of 1944, organized a partisan group composed mainly of Catholics[181]; Don Giovanni Ticozzi, invited by the Lecco Socialists to become president of the town's Comitato di Liberazione Nazionale (National Liberation Committee, CLN) and who was sent to prison for his anti-fascist commitment; and Don Luigi Rinaldini, from Brescia, of the *Oratorio della Pace* congregation, who came from a family involved in the Resistance.[182]

It is also worth remembering the figure of Don Lorenzo Bedeschi, a priest from Romagna, who, after the Second World War, was a journalist for *Avvenire*, a professor of History at the University of Urbino, a scholar of Modernism[183] and a leading figure in the encounters between Catholics and Marxists in the 1960s and 1970s. Already a declared anti-fascist in 1935, and removed from the diocese of Faenza because of his public stance against the war in Ethiopia, on 8 September he was a military chaplain in Montenegro. After a long and eventful journey, he returned to his hometown of Bagnocavallo, near Ravenna, organizing the first attempts at resistance together with the Communists. He then moved south, to the territory liberated by the Anglo-American forces, where he collaborated with Radio Napoli and volunteered for the Corpo Italiano di Liberazione (Italian Liberation Corps), actively participating in the armed struggle. Arrigo Boldrini, a communist partisan leader, presented the 'partisan priest' with a red handkerchief from the 28th Garibaldi Brigade (a notoriously communist group) and was keen to write the preface to Bedeschi's diary. In the notes he made between the end of 1943 and 1945, Bedeschi wrote:

> It is believed that we stand at the dawn of a century of a more human universal concord, in which all hatred and egoism are quieted in a just peace, in a climate of freedom. But first there will be a dark period of revolution. Those responsible for war and disorder must perish under the blows of the people's vendetta. Humanity will be purged. With blood, unfortunately. It is perhaps destined that only with blood can it find the path of justice: its path, given that persuasion, love and morality are silent voices that are lost in the desert.[184]

The last years of the conflict, due to the great difficulties experienced by the Italian people, lacerated by an internal war and occupied by a foreign power, represented a moment of encounter between those who shared a common anti-fascist feeling and placed their hopes in the construction of a new Italy – one based on the values of peace and liberty. It was these months that saw the birth of the social cohesion and positive political dialectic that in the post-war period would facilitate the relationship between Catholics and the Left, and which would find their highest form of expression in the Italian Constitution.[185]

3

From Catholic Communists to the New Openness to Centre-Left Governments

The Catholic communist movement during the fascist regime (1937–1945)

The emerge of Catholic Communists as a political force

Drawing mainly on sources from the Vatican Secret Archives, historians have recently investigated the relationships between the Holy See and the fascist regime, highlighting Pius XI's misgivings with regard to the latter after Italy's rapprochement with Germany in the middle of the 1930s. It was during this time that the pope decided to press for an encyclical that would articulate his critiques of Hitler's political project. The encyclical, written by American Jesuit John La Farge, was, however, never published, due to the pope's untimely death.[1] The Azione Cattolica (Italian Catholic Action, AC), meanwhile, had been suspicious in its stance towards fascism since the beginning of the thirties, mainly because of the aggressive competition in the educational field from organizations linked to the regime and in the socialization of younger generations, which had traditionally been a prerogative of the Church. When, following Italy's entente with Germany, 'neo-pagan myths' were progressively adopted by fascist ideology, Catholics began to raise objections to the regime, questioning nationalistic, racist and warmongering ideologies, as well as the exaltation of force and power.[2]

The regime's rejection of Christian civilization, which had influenced the development of European culture for centuries, caused deep unrest, especially in those people attracted by the ideas of Emmanuel Mounier and Jacques Maritain. Those very same intellectuals, however, were reluctant to translate their ideas into explicit political choices.

Between 1937 and 1938, when a group of Catholic communists began to take shape, it became evident that the times demanded political action. The origins of this new politicization can be found within the climate of opposition to fascism that prevailed in Rome, especially in former scout members and in the younger generations of families that had traditionally been close to the Partito Popolare (Italian People's Party, PPI). It was not, however, a cultural and religious environment to which all the organization's militants really belonged.[3]

Most of the movement's young militants attended the Pontificio ginnasio-liceo S. Apollinare and were members of the Circolo Dante e Leonardo, located in Piazza S. Agostino in Rome, opposite the seat of the Federazione Universitaria Cattolici Italiani (Italian Catholic University Association, FUCI). The Circolo Dante e Leonardo had been established at the beginning of the century by Egilberto Martire and a group of friends, under the aegis of Giovanni Pioli, a modernist priest.[4] Until the promulgation of the *Pascendi dominici gregis* encyclical (with which Pius X excommunicated modernists) the Circolo had been a meeting place for people seeking dialogue: they included Antonio Fogazzaro, Tommaso Gallarati Scotti and Antonio Rosmini's niece Antonietta Giacomelli, all members of the Modernist movement. After the PPI's disbandment in 1926, and during the years of dictatorship, the Circolo became the meeting place for all those who were critical of the collusion between the Church and the regime[5]: faithful to the lay and democratic tradition of the PPI, these young members were explicitly inspired by Catholic anti-fascists such as Giuseppe Donati and Francesco Luigi Ferrari: they thought that an alliance with the Left was the only way to defeat fascism.[6] Adriano Ossicini, a student at liceo S. Apollinare, close to Romolo Murri, who had convinced him of the 'impossibility of ignoring the issues raised by modernism', recounts how Father Stefano Bianchi advised him in those years to study Marxism: 'Among others, I remember Croce's and Labriola's writings on Marxism and Marx's *Capital* edited by Cafiero, the anarchist.'[7]

There were also other meeting places in the very heart of Rome devoted to anti-fascist ideas. The Liceo Visconti, for example, was known for offering an education that was less sympathetic to the regime than that of other schools. Catholic students from the school used to meet at the La Scaletta club, run by Jesuits and located close to the church of St. Ignatius. The members of the club included Franco Rodano and Paolo Moruzzi (son of the director of the Banco Ambrosiano).[8]

Those young people did not limit themselves to mere cultural proselytism: they felt it was necessary to tackle the Italian situation from a social and political point of view, convinced that Catholics would have to adopt a new stance once the regime was defeated. They thought, therefore, that Catholics had to work together with anti-fascist forces, and also establish a relationship with the proletarian world of the Roman suburbs and with their young working-class contemporaries. The parish of San Francesco a Ripa – home to the Azione Cattolica Sud (Rome Trastevere) – had traditionally been engaged in social work to the benefit of its members, who mainly came from working-class families. The president of the parochial council was Paolo Pecoraro, who had been a member of the Circolo Dante e Leonardo and would later become a priest.

Some of the young people who attended the parish soon adopted anti-fascist opinions and established contact with communist militants from working-class areas. This prompted a dialogue that featured harsh criticism both of the regime and also of the Church, for its secret dealings with fascism. They were thus able to overcome the anti-fascism of their parents, which followed a 'bourgeois' idea of democracy that exclusively advocated individual freedom as opposition to dictatorship, and develop the idea of a society based on social justice. In 1937, they drafted the first policy document of the Christian Left, written on 22 December at the 'Roma Sud' branch of the Azione Cattolica. The document stressed the need to establish a Catholic anti-fascist organization, abandoning the illusion of a united PPI, in order to promote a movement of the Catholic Left that would explicitly oppose fascism.[9] Abandoning the fashionable Crocean interpretation of fascism as 'moral disorder', as an 'irrational parenthesis' in Italian history, in the wake of Marxist interpretations the young Italians saw fascism as a 'class phenomenon'. Reading history in terms of a class struggle led them to envisage the Catholic role in those very terms: for promoting an inter-class perspective amongst workers actually meant endorsing conservative positions.[10] In their view, Catholic workers could claim their rights only if they sided with their fellow workers in the left-wing parties.[11]

In the first months of 1940, Ossicini's group made contact with the La Scaletta club, whose president was Franco Rodano. Out of this soon grew a unified political entity, involving frequent meetings and the exchange of ideas. Ossicini recalled his encounter with Rodano: 'I must say that he was one of the most brilliant and well-educated people I've ever met. He was keen on relationships, genuinely interested in other people, whom he tried hard to understand, in his attempt to communicate with them, to orient them, to guide them; he was clearly a leader.'[12] Besides Rodano and Ossicini, the group also included Filippo Sacconi, Tonino Tatò, Mario Vivaldi, Marisa Cinciari, Romualdo Chiesa (killed at the Fosse Ardeatine) and Ennio Severi (who died as a partisan in Yugoslavia). The group was later joined by Luciano Barca, Lele D'Amico and Giglia Tedesco and also spread to Milan, with Giorgio Sebregondi, and Turin, with the significant figure of Felice Balbo.[13]

Unlike the majority of Catholic Communists, Balbo had not been a member of the AC, the FUCI or the Catholic Alumni Association, nor had he ever joined any fascist youth association. His personal and intellectual growth had taken place in Turin's secular and anti-fascist circles, thanks especially to the liberal-democratic group of Piero Gobetti. His approach to Christianity had therefore been a belated one; it originated in his rational notion of faith, paradoxically something he had come to when he had chosen to join a Marxist party.[14] His political ideas revolved around St Thomas, Croce and Marx, eventually producing a Thomism that also took into account the thought of Teilhard de Chardin.[15]

From the Synarchic Cooperativist Party to the Movement of Communist Catholics

In July 1941 the groups founded the Partito Cooperatista Sinarchico (the Synarchic Cooperativist Party), whose programme manifesto was drafted by Rodano and Pecoraro. The very name of the party revealed the readiness to overcome capitalism through forms of cooperative production, returning to Catholic social doctrine. As believers, while rejecting the ideological premises of Marxism and of collectivization with regard to individuals, they did not deny its political implications.[16]

In the early forties, the movement made contact with the Communist Party in Rome and in particular with Lucio Lombardo Radice, Mario Alicata and Pietro Ingrao. In the summer of 1942, Rodano, and then, in January 1943, Ossicini, joined the party's executive in Rome.[17] Ossicini remembered the events as follows:

> Communists were not only, from prison, keeping the anti-Fascist school alive, but they also urged us to analyse the Fascist phenomenon scientifically and to take concrete action within a precise structure of alliances. Relationships with working-class people such as Pompilio Molinari, or with intellectuals such as Paolo Bufalini, Lucio Lombardo Radice or Pietro Ingrao were for us a crucial experience in our common struggle, one which went beyond friendship.[18]

In the summer of 1942, the organization changed its name to the Movimento dei cattolici comunisti (Movement of Communist Catholics, MCC). The change was brought about by the pleas coming from the rank and file of the movement that advocated close collaboration with communist militants and wished to prohibit ideological distinctions and sophisticated analyses. The movement's manifesto announced the necessity for a 'new social order based on control over means of production, the abolition of class and the foundation of a society which included neither exploiters nor exploited'. The document also declared that the Catholic religion should not necessarily be considered a conservative one and that it could in fact represent a spur to revolutionary action.[19]

The stances adopted by Catholics, therefore, did not necessarily coincide with those of the bourgeoisie, since working-class Catholics shared interests with the working class at large. Class took priority over religious affinity. Another document drafted by the movement read:

> The economic order of capitalism, founded on freedom of initiative, has actually resulted in the attribution of higher functions to restricted groups, not only at an economic, but also at a political and social, level; the remaining groups are therefore reduced to a state of economic and political subjection. The confrontation between the two classes is therefore inevitable, the former being in control of society thanks to its economic position, and the latter having no possibility at all of even achieving control.[20]

The article echoes Balbo's positions: unlike Rodano, who targeted the lower middle class and farmers, Balbo thought that the MCC had to establish a privileged dialogue with the Catholic working class, thus 'making Marxism come true within a Christian perspective'. Historical materialism was therefore considered as political science: that is, as an instrument to understand history. Theoretical debate was crucial to the movement's life. Ossicini did not hesitate to voice his perplexity regarding the use of the word 'Catholic' within the movement's name, since such a choice entailed a risk of 'clerical fall'.[21]

Catholic Communists chose to side with the Communist Party (PCI) because Togliatti's organization seemed to be the only one capable of building a new society after the moral and material disruption caused by fascism. Furthermore, the PCI was deeply committed to fighting fascism, which only added to its attractive potential.[22] In the aftermath of the movement's foundation, Rodano thought it right to ask for Balbo's philosophical support. In a letter he invited him to move from his home in Turin to Rome, to take an active part in the emerging political project.[23] Balbo did indeed arrive in Rome and contributed to the draft of the pamphlet *Il comunismo e i cattolici* ('Communism and Catholics'), printed in May 1944. The pamphlet stressed the acceptance of historical materialism and of the 'communist solution' that went with it. It further expressed the conviction that the foundation of a 'socialist society, that is, of a classless society' did not necessarily clash with the Catholic Church, since the actual goal of religion was the promotion of justice, in order to foster moral and material welfare. It was not for religion to decide what means were required to reach these ends. Religion had to set goals and people had to find the right means to achieve them.[24]

At that time, the movement's relationship with the Communist Party was a very close one. The arrest of Mario Alicata in January 1943 left the PCC exposed. Thus, in May, the party cadres were also arrested: this included Ossicini and Rodano. Luigi Maglione, the Cardinal Secretary of State, on behalf of the Pope, asked Mussolini if, as members of the AC, they might be released. This actually came about fairly quickly, since, by 25 July, when the regime fell, they were all out of prison.

The German occupation of Rome after 8 September 1943 was a turning point for these young men, and for the Italian people in general: for it became clear that the time for talk and theoretical musing was over. The only thing to do was to rally against the German troops. The movement joined the Comitato di Liberazione Nazionale (National Liberation Committee, CLN)[25] in January 1944 and was very active in the defence of Rome, collaborating both with the Democrazia Cristiana (Christian Democratic Party, DC) and left-wing parties. There was also a partisan unit known as the banda Ossicini, which, with its 744 members, was active throughout Rome, Lazio and Umbria.[26]

During the German occupation, help for the young opponents of fascism came from the Vatican, which allowed them to hide their weapons in the dormitory of the San Pietro club. In an article published in *Rinascita* in 1973, Ossicini mentioned the 'increasing sympathy for the group from a not irrelevant part of Catholic associations and the clergy'. In particular, he highlighted the role played by Father Felice Mirabilia, a vice chaplain of the prison who, during their custody, acted as liason between the Catholic Communists, the Secretary of State and the leaders of the AC.[27] The Catholic Communists paradoxically also enjoyed the protection of certain members of the Vatican right-wing (Alfredo Ottaviani and Domenico Tardini): the latter did not actually share their position, but they considered that the very existence of the group contributed to legitimize a cross-party Christian presence in political life. Giovanni Battisti Montini, instead, was opposed to the Catholic Communists, believing, like Alcide De Gasperi, that the lack of unity amongst Catholics would eventually favour the right-wing area of the Catholic world.[28]

In the struggle for liberation, the MCC definitely played an important role, partly because it did address Catholics, who had long been apathetic bystanders in Italian politics or, even worse, allies of the most conservative forces in society.

The Party of the Christian Left

On 23 July 1944, *L'Osservatore Romano* published an article by Dominican theologian Father Mariano Cordovani. An expert in economic and social issues, Cordovani refuted the theoretical foundations of the movement: 'They mean to remain Catholic and, as to communism, they refuse dialectical materialism, which they consider deeply unchristian. And yet, they accept historical materialism, since they consider politics to be a ruthless game of force.' The movement's members refused the official lesson of the Church, Cordovani went on, and their programmes resounded 'with doctrines and statements that bear the hallmark of socialism and communism rather than being informed by a Christian spirit'.[29]

Vatican perplexity led the group, in September 1944, to change its name to the Partito della Sinistra Cristiana (Party of the Christian Left, PDSC). This decision to switch from movement to party was induced by the need for a tighter organizational structure that was able to 'concretise politically Christian postulates of charity, liberty and justice and in which all categories of Catholic workers' could give life to a 'political practice inspired by democracy and progress'.[30]

The minutes of the meeting in which the change of name was decided read: 'Considering the misunderstandings and misgivings, all of them historically justifiable, that the word communism might generate in some strata of the Catholic working class, considering the pointless and harmful contrasts, at the present moment, that this could cause,' considering the perplexity many people had expressed with regard to the name MCC itself, since 'it could seem close to philosophies that go against our religion,' and 'further considering the deep mistrust created by the juxtaposition of Catholicism and communism in several religious circles, the movement of Catholic Communists has decided to change its name to the *Partito della Sinistra Cristiana*.'[31] The new party's statute stated that the PDSC was 'a political organisation of Catholic workers', their 'direct emanation and political expression, since it defended their interests, their needs, their aspirations and their ideals, acting as a guide towards the achievement of their immediate and ultimate goals'.[32]

The decision to drop any reference to communism was highly relevant: the new party intended to be democratic and progressive, originating in a deep religious experience and aiming to concretize postulates ideas of liberty, justice and charity that were essential to Christ's earthly experience. This was the sense of the party's critique of capitalism. The founding of this new party led to a merger with Gerardo Bruni's Partito Sociale Cristiano (Christian Social Party, PSC), a decision voted for by the majority of the party. In favour of this were Pio Montesi and Oreste Gasperini. Bruni himself, on the other hand, voted against the move and decided to found a new Christian social party, which led to great confusion amongst the rank and file. Those members of the former PSC who decided to join the new party shared with it the intention to win over Catholic workers and to drop any reference to communism: there was a need, they felt, to join forces with all progressive Catholic movements inspired by the principles of Christian ethics to defend the working class and to struggle against capitalist exploitation.[33]

Difficulties in the relationship with the Vatican increased dramatically: so much so that, with a note dated 2 January 1945, the Holy See took a stance against the Party of the Christian Left, denying its members the right to speak as representatives of Christian thought and to voice the needs of Catholic workers. Further, the Christian Left was accused of adopting positions that were not in line with the Magisterium. Such a charge, however, was not clearly formulated and the widespread feeling was that criticism concerned political matters rather than doctrinal ones.[34]

The party responded to those charges by stressing its allegiance to the Catholic Church and its values, inviting all the members of the PDSC to 'draw inspiration from the principles of their conscience as Catholics beyond any ideal, even the most precious, and any interest, even the most human'. Further, they underlined the political importance of the PDSC, 'the use of its function for the defence of supreme religious and moral values of which the Catholic Church is the eternal keeper'.[35]

One thing was clear, however: the Secretariat of State, Montini in particular, had eventually chosen Alcide De Gasperi as the figure with whom he wished to maintain a dialogue. Further, the idea of a united Catholic party had finally established itself. In fact, Father Sergio Pignedoli and Monsignor Adriano Bernareggi, Montini's closest collaborators, insisted that militants of the Christian Left join the DC.

On that occasion, communist leader Palmiro Togliatti, in an article published in the journal *Rinascita*, underlined that the 'Christian Left' was a political party and that its programmatic statements did not contain any indication as to its 'religious' nature. In fact, its positions concerned issues of domestic and foreign policies, which had nothing to do with religion. Further, the communist leader wrote, the Church was not entitled to evaluate political stances, adding: 'For those of us who want Catholic and non-Catholic workers to join together, the condemnation [...] of the Christian Left at a political level is regrettable.' He also declared that this was a 'direct intervention in the current political arena, which actually jeopardised the Church's prestige for good'. In fact, the Church would benefit from all parties respecting religious freedom, without interfering in its issues, and from Christian workers endorsing the positions more in line with their thought according to their conscience.[36]

Following the Church's official endorsement of De Gasperi, the PCI lost interest in the PDSC, now seen rather as something of a problem and no longer a link with the Catholic world. The DC, as the most successful party in the Catholic world (a fact confirmed by its 35 per cent share in the general elections on 2 June 1946), became the PCI's party of choice for political dialogue.

Vatican hostility and the position of the PCI provoked a debate within the PDSC regarding whether it was possible to continue with the party's political role. Ossicini stressed the AC's antipathy towards left-wing Catholics, who were seen as displeasing to the pope and, indeed, heretical. Cocchi and Montesi pointed out that disbanding the party would mean 'handing hegemony over the Catholic world to the DC', suggesting that Catholics would vote for De Gasperi's party and thus actually legitimize the political union of Catholics: the danger was a kind of 'Catholic totalitarianism', embodied by the DC.[37]

On 7 and 8 December 1945, an extraordinary party congress was therefore called, which took place in the assembly hall of the Liceo Mamiani in Rome. Mario Motta, one of the party's two secretaries (the other one being Ossicini), raised the issue of breaking up the party, maintaining that, since politics was the same for Catholic and non-Catholic workers, a Catholic workers' party had no reason to exist.[38] Rodano agreed with him, since he considered that the Christian Left was no longer useful in terms of the current goals the group intended to achieve: on a political level, it would be wiser to combine the PCI and the unions.[39] Balbo, remembering his first approach to politics – before making contact with the Movement of Communist Catholics, which had taken place within the PCI – maintained that, as a Christian he knew 'on which front of political history' he should fight and that 'positive forces originating in the contradictions of a collapsing bourgeois society' had a name: 'the working class'. Within the latter, believed Balbo, thrived the 'most natural men, spirited, close to the image of man as issued forth from the hands of God'.[40]

Ossicini was against breaking up the party and reiterated his perplexities regarding Christians going into the PCI, a highly ideologized party heavily influenced by the USSR. Joining it would 'subject political action to ideological motivation, which would affect its lay character'.[41] A majority of the congress voted for the party's disbandment, and, at the end of 1945, Rodano and Balbo joined the PCI, albeit for different reasons. Unlike Rodano, who based his choice on political grounds, Balbo thought that such a decision should come from a 'Christian attitude aimed at finding the best standpoint to contribute to social and civil progress', without any kind of tactical and strategic considerations.[42]

With the fifth party Congress (between the end of 1945 and the beginning of 1946) and the approval of Article 2 in the party's new statute, which stated that one could join the PCI regardless of 'race, religious faith and philosophical convictions', the conditions were created for members of the Christian Left to join the party. Catholics would be able to endorse communist policies and subscribe to the party's programmes even without embracing Marxist ideology in toto.[43] Togliatti, in the speech he gave at the session of the Constituent Assembly on 25 March 1947, praised the 'religious peace' that had reigned during the Resistance, when Catholic workers, military chaplains, priests and clergymen had joined forces with socialist and communist militants. Stressing the difference between the Italian party and ideological practices in Eastern Europe, he went on to state that the same kind of harmony also had to be achieved in the aftermath of the war in order to avert the risk of a 'war of religion'.[44]

This gave rise to the decision to approve Article 7 of the Constitution, which ratified the Lateran Treaty in the direction of a future agreement between communist and Catholic masses. The article was ideated and promoted by Giuseppe Dossetti who, in an interview given shortly before his death, denied that the Vatican had any influence on the drafting of the text. In fact, he mentioned a meeting with Togliatti, in which the communist leader suggested some revisions to the draft he had submitted to him.[45] At the end of the forties, former Catholic Communists went their separate ways: some, such as Rodano, remained in the PCI, while others, such as Balbo, left the party, pledging allegiance to the Church.[46]

Gerardo Bruni's Partito Cristiano Sociale (the Social Christian Party, PCS) had a longer life. Bruni, a past member of the PPI and a staunch opponent of fascism from its foundation, unlike the Christian Left, which always had a keen eye for the communist experience, preferred to draw inspiration from democratic socialism. Familiar with the thought of Mounier and Maritain, in 1939 Bruni began to publish the *Biblioteca cristiano-sociale* ('Christian-social library') a cyclostyled pamphlet which constituted the first point of reference for anti-Fascist Catholics who were willing to engage in the resistance to fascism.[47] The founding congress of the PCS took place in Rome on 27–28 March 1943, and involved about thirty militants from different regions. The programme included the reconstruction of the economy on a social basis and the socialization of sectors of industry where financial capital predominated. Nationalization was not excluded, but self-management was preferred through cooperative and consortium systems. It was also considered necessary for workers and management to work in partnership, sharing company profits, and eventual worker ownership of the companies themselves was also proposed.

The Social Christians presented themselves at the elections of June 1946 with very modest results, considering their action and commitment during the Resistance. The PCS were dedicated to positions of republican intransigence, were opposed the political unity of Catholics, supported socialism of a personalist kind and declared itself critical with regard to Marxism but were willing to establish contacts with left-wing parties. The Social Christians also maintained close relations with the Movimento Comunità (Community Movement), which was inspired by the ideas of Adriano Olivetti and in which the traces of French Catholic thought were evident. However, the collaboration was not destined to last long, as political differences and personal disagreements took over.[48]

At the end of 1947, the PCS joined the Popular Democratic Front (the electoral alliance formed by the PCI and PSI that presented itself at the April 1948 elections). Bruni was a candidate in the general elections, but, despite obtaining 70,000 votes, he was not elected.[49] In the sixties, Bruni kept an attentive eye on the changes introduced by Vatican II, and in September 1973 he took part in the national convention in Bologna which sanctioned the birth of the Christians for Socialism movement.[50]

Catholicism and communism during the Cold War

In the post-Liberation period, the secular and Marxist world underwent a very lively cultural development, intent on freeing Italy from the legacies of fascism and giving life to a political perspective based on the principles of social and economic justice. It was a time that saw the birth of several cultural journals including *Società* – founded in 1945 by Ranuccio Bianchi Bandinelli – which, while close to the PCI, did not represent the official party line, leaving space for free-ranging commentary from a variety of prestigious intellectuals. Also in 1945, at the behest of Piero Calamandrei, the journal *Il Ponte* was started in Florence. This featured a declared ethical and civil commitment and was culturally close to the political experience of the Partito d'Azione (Action Party, PdA). Other journals that came out at that time included *Belfagor, Mondo europeo, Cultura, Lo Stato moderno* and, most importantly, Elio Vittorini's *Il Politecnico*.[51] These journals were places of encounter and discussion for the cream of the Italian intelligentsia, and in some cases they were also open to Catholic culture. In the first issue of the *Politecnico* (January 1946), Vittorini launched an appeal for the creation of a new culture, which received a response from Nando Fabro, founder of the Catholic review *Il Gallo* in Genoa, declaring his 'spontaneous' and 'total' acceptance of the communist intellectual's proposals. It is worth recalling that Felice Balbo, too, discussed the new horizons of culture with Vittorini in the *Politecnico* and that the journal also featured articles from the Catholic intellectuals Carlo Bo and Carlo Arturo Jemolo.

In the Catholic world, the post-war period was a time of substantial immobility, due to the conservative positions in both the theological and political circles of Pius XII.[52] The Vatican continued to propose a model of society that was based on Catholic sociology as set down by Leo XIII, while the most innovative elements were marginalized and accused of collusion with the left. Catholics 'on the left' therefore found themselves in conflict with the Holy See's aversion to the world and to progressive culture, and Pasquale Colella – who in the seventies would become one of the main figures of 'Catholic dissent' – called this 'the period of silence'.[53] To be a left-wing Christian was a personal choice, one that was opposed and challenged by the Church and by the majority of Catholics, and one often rewarded with exclusion and marginalization. Only a few believers had the courage to give their support to innovative ideas and experiences, keeping alive the 'underground stream' that would emerge during the years of the Council.

The desire for 'normalization', after the years of the Resistance, soon gained the upper hand and its repercussions were felt in the political sphere. In the spring of 1947, as the Cold War grew more intense, the governmental collaboration between the DC and the left-wing parties, which had begun during the Resistance years and continued with the government of Ferruccio Parri and the first governments of De Gasperi, came to an end.[54] It was a break which also involved pressure from the Holy See being exerted on the Catholic party: behind Vatican walls, everyone shared the aversion to the left, an aversion that would become evident in the Catholic mobilization during the elections of 18 April 1948. The overwhelming electoral victory of the DC, winning 48.5 per cent of the votes, represented a real turning point: the Italians had chosen for themselves a place in the western bloc, and from that moment on the PCI and PSI were excluded from the country's government. The left-wing parties, united in the Popular Front coalition, obtained only 31 per cent of the votes, and their most militant members did not find it easy to accept the crushing defeat, partly because many still hoped that socialist revolution was still a possible goal.

Things became tense when, on 14 July 1948, Antonio Pallante, a member of the extreme right, shot and wounded Togliatti. The mobilization of communist supporters was immediate, with the occupation of Prefectures and strategic places, but the party secretary moved to quash any possible attempt at insurrection. Togliatti was aware that Italy was part of the western bloc and that had a 'proletarian revolution' taken place in the country, the Allies would have swiftly intervened, as had happened in Greece at the end of 1944.

The 1950s were characterized by an atmosphere of intense anti-communism, something emphasized in the Catholic world by the excommunication, imposed by the Holy Office decree of 1 July 1949, of those who 'professed the materialist and anti-Christian doctrine of communism'. The conservative climate was also fostered by the opinions of Cardinal Alfredo Ottaviani who, in 1953, in a speech to the Pontifical Lateran University, attacked the French philosopher Maritain, guilty of being an inspiration to Catholics who dared to support the autonomy of politics. In the same period, the Holy See made a point of stigmatizing the choice of those priests who, especially in France, had decided to work in factories alongside the workers; the Vatican fearing that they could be compromised by left-wing parties and unions.[55]

The conformist climate also influenced the communist militants: attracted by the myth of the USSR and convinced that in that country a regime of real social equality had been established, they dedicated their life to the party, in the hope that socialist revolution would soon occur in Italy as well. Their notions of Marxism and the history of communism were taught to their members: one of the suggested reading texts for years was the *The History of the Communist Party of the Soviet Union*, drafted and approved by Stalin in 1938 and disseminated in millions of copies all over the world.

What is evident is that, in a way rather similar to Catholic militants, organized in associations and frequent patrons of parishes and oratories, communist militants lived in a world apart. This was partly due to the fact that their political commitment was a totalizing experience that often ended up eradicating any form of private life. Members were also subjected to ideological control by higher authorities: the frequent request to write and revize their autobiographies made it possible for the supervisors to verify the evolution of the militants' convictions and ideas over time, and impede any ideological 'backsliding'.[56]

In the fifties, the PCI and the Catholic world also shared traditional ideas towards women and the family, and many militant communist women were marginalized by the party because they were considered to be too 'free' in their relations with men. Two of the top communist leaders, however, were involved in rather 'unorthodox' relationships: Togliatti left his wife, Rita Montagnana (who he had met in Turin in the early 1920s) to start a relationship with the young Reggio Emilia deputy Nilde Jotti; and Luigi Longo left his wife Teresa Noce. This created great embarrassment in the party, and in 1953 the National Secretariat of the PCI took action to verify the possibility of obtaining the annulment of the Togliatti and Longo marriages in San Marino. The initiative was a failure, but it revealed that even the largest opposition party needed to demonstrate a sense of 'regularity'.[57]

While many diverse elements existed between Catholic and communist militants, there were also common features, and these contradictions were particularly inspiring for the pen of journalist Giovannino Guareschi when he invented the figures of Peppone and Don Camillo. The stories – first published in the humorous weekly *Candido* and then later turned into hugely successful films – related the confrontational clash between a Christian Democrat priest and a communist mayor in a small town in the Po Valley. The relationship between Peppone and Don Camillo is one of disagreement, dispute and disparagement, but what emerges from the stories is the image of an Italy that shares a common desire for coexistence and human respect, something that not even the ideological aggravation of the Cold War years could manage to call into question.

The Christian avant-garde

If it is true, as historian Carlo Arturo Jemolo claimed, that the fifties were marked by a 'religious climate', it is also true that not all Catholics aligned themselves with the prevailing air of conformism. Primo Mazzolari, David Maria Turoldo, Camillo De Piaz, Don Zeno Saltini, Don Lorenzo Milani and the priest Ernesto Balducci, to name just a few,[58] testified to a different way of conceiving religion, shifting attention from the theological to the historical and claiming the possibility of interpreting and acting in history on the basis of their own evaluations. In doing so, they opened up Catholic culture to certain elements of modern thought that traditional theology stigmatized. This did not mean that they accepted secularization or the values of contemporary society: on the contrary, they emphasized the importance of criticism in relation to the world and held that Christians had to commit themselves to curbing its contradictions. Above all, they were uncomfortable with Pius XII's indications to accept the West because of its function as a barrier to communism and judged the Western world as something far from the true evangelical vocation. It was not, in their opinion, necessary to identify Christianity with the West, and it was necessary, on the other hand, to understand and support the struggles of those peoples who wanted to emancipate themselves from their European colonizers. What happened in the 'Christian avant-garde', said Lorenzo Bedeschi, was the 'reawakening of the secular sense of the political' and the revendication of the primacy of conscience.[59]

This form of religious sensibility was well expressed by Don Zeno Saltini, who, in Fossoli, near Modena, founded the community of *Nomadelfia* on a site that, during the war, had been a deportation, prisoner of war and concentration camp. The community consisted of a group of families, with no blood ties, who took care of abandoned children. Don Zeno proposed the need for a radical reform of the Church, criticizing the charity of wealthy Catholics and arguing that the poor should not aspire to crumbs from the tables of the rich but rather to a fair division of material goods.[60] This project, which represented an attempt to 'completely fulfill the carrying out of the ethics of the Gospel',[61] foundered due to the debts that the community accumulated. Saltini had, in 1951, been advised by the Holy Office to leave Nomadelfia, and was accused by the Catholic press of 'occult communist mysticism'.[62] Thus, in order not to involve the Church in economic problems, and assuming all responsibility for the disorder in the community's accounts, in 1953 he obtained a return to secular life; he did not resume his priestly duties until 1962.

In Milan, after Liberation, some professors at the Catholic University – including Mario Apollonio and Gustavo Bontadini, as well as the writer and politician Dino Del Bo – worked together on the periodical *L'Uomo*, which had been printed clandestinely during the Resistance as an expression of the 'spiritual movement for the unification of Italy'. Other founders were the priests David Maria Turoldo and Camillo de Piaz, who were in contact with the communist Eugenio Curiel and in charge of religious assistance to the politically persecuted and their families. The convent of San Carlo in Milan, a meeting place during the Resistance for Catholics and communists, hosted initiatives in favour of Nomadelfia after the war, while Turoldo and De Piaz, perplexed by the mobilization of the AC in the 1948 elections,[63] showed no desire to interrupt their personal and intellectual relations with the secular and left-wing world. In 1952, the two priests created the association Corsia dei Servi which, in addition to organizing meetings and debates on religious issues, also produced a newsletter. This publication, from 1955 on, represented an important opportunity for the dissemination and discussion of issues at the centre of the Church's attention during the years of Vatican II: liturgical reform, the relationship between the Church and the West, the role of missionaries in the context of the emancipation of the peoples of the Third World and the poor in contemporary society.[64] The ideas of Turoldo and De Piaz, however, aroused tension in their Order, and the former was sent away from Milan in 1954 and the latter in 1957.

The Gioventù Italiana di Azione Cattolica (Catholic Action Italian Youth, GIAC) had ideas about Catholicism similar to those in France. Soon, due to these different perspectives, which gave more attention to religious questions and to the needs of the lowest echelons of society rather than to militant faith, the association clashed with Luigi Gedda's centralistic vision of the AC (Gedda was general president of the AC from January 1952).[65] Thus, in October 1952, the GIAC president Carlo Carretto was forced to resign, to be replaced by Mario Rossi. Rossi, in continuity with Carretto's ideas, expressed his thoughts in a selection of writings collected in the 1954 book *La terra dei vivi* ('The land of the living'), in which he reiterated his aversion to fascism and gave his support to the concept of resistance as an ethical choice. He declared himself to be on the side of the poor, the biblical 'last', because it was with this rank of society that the Church had to seek a privileged dialogue.[66] Rossi's commitment in both the religious and social fields, as well as the attention he gave to issues of justice, were interpreted by the hierarchy as support for the Left; he was even accused of being a communist. *L'Osservatore Romano*, too, had some harsh words for 'certain dangerous tendencies in the GIAC' and declared that, given the 'doctrinal deviations', a change was required.[67] Forced to resign, Rossi returned to his profession as a doctor and continued his religious militancy by taking over direction of Mazzolari's review *Adesso*. In a letter from Mazzolari to Rossi dated 14 November 1954, the priest wrote: 'There is a limit to how far we can fall. We love the Church and that is how we wish to remain until the end. Sinners, not heretics.'[68]

One of the most significant figures in the post-war 'Catholic avant-garde', particularly in terms of his commitment to the dialogue between the Catholic and the communist world, was Guido Miglioli, who published the book *Con Roma e con Mosca* ('With Rome and with Moscow') at the end of 1945. In the introductory pages, the union activist wrote:

> The experience derived from several decades of battles, especially amongst the rural working classes, has led me, more than any doctrinal reflection, to this conclusion: whenever the Christian forces of labour move closer to those of other political movements, almost as a prelude to more acute struggles and vigorous assaults in social and economic areas, the Italian anti-clerical and clerical bourgeoisie have always tried to divide them, diverting their attention to other issues, especially those to do with religion, thus establishing a 'democratic' anticlericalism on the one hand and a 'conservative' clericalism on the other.[69]

The need to overcome the divisions among the workers had, for only a short period of time, led him to share the vision of the Christian Left. Then, in 1946,

Miglioli asked to join the DC, but, since the opinions he had espoused were regarded as too radical, he was denied membership.[70]

After the war, the return of Miglioli to political debate saw him involved in a controversy in which he was opposed by Mazzolari: the two confronted each other on the relationship between Christianity and communism and on the possibility of collaboration between Christians who were more sensitive to social and Marxist issues. The debate began with the publication of an article by Miglioli, written on the occasion of the 29th anniversary of the Soviet revolution, entitled *Civiltà cristiana e Rivoluzione d'ottobre* ('Christian civilization and October Revolution'), in which he repeated the thesis – already put forward in the book *Con Roma e con Mosca* – that the Bolshevik revolution was to be considered a sort of 'Christian revolution'. Mazzolari replied to the article, problematizing the relationship between Christianity and communism and contrasting 'communist materialism' with Christianity 'in its highest form of spirituality', in order to demonstrate the irreconcilability of the two beliefs. Mazzolari's idea – taken from his reading of Mounier[71] – was that at the root of every social transformation there should be a moral and religious conscience, and that the Christian should be on the side of the poor and oppressed because this 'choice of battlefield' derived from reading the gospel.[72] He wrote, in a 1948 letter to Carlo Bo: 'In Communism, a Christian can find positive suggestions that can lead him from a somewhat detached level to one of full human reality: in Christianity, a communist can find the reason and virtue to take to a successful conclusion that which, in a materialistic vision of man and the universe, is an absurd and inhuman utopia.'[73] Mazzolari recognized that both communists and Catholics wanted 'an end to injustice, and the happiness of all men', and that the differences between the two cultures lay in how to achieve this goal.[74]

Miglioli's ideas urged the need for a new unity between the forces that had fought together during the Resistance and criticized the DC for ending the collaboration with the Communists in 1947. This led to the founding of the Movimento Cristiano per la Pace (Christian Movement for Peace, MCP) between the end of 1947 and the the beginning of 1948 with the intention of working against the tension produced by the Cold War. The group included Ada Alessandrini, Maria Maggi and Mario Montesi – who had left the Rome DC following the breakup of the alliance with the Communists and Socialists – and former members of the Partito Sociale Cristiano and the Christian Left. The movement, with Alessandrini nominated as president, believed that the political battle for the unity of workers and democratic forces and the struggle for peace were to be understood as an expression of the teaching of the gospel.[75] The MCP came to an end in late 1948, its following too limited in a period marked by the unyielding nature of the confrontation brought about by the Cold War.

In the following period, there was also little luck in coordinating all the Catholics dissatisfied with the moderate politics of the DC through the constitution of a committee for the unity of left-wing Christians, chiefly involving Ada Alessandrini, Maria Maggi, Mario Montesi and Otello Sacchetti. The group then assumed the name of the Movimento unitario dei cristiani progressisti (Unitary Movement of Progressive Christians). The main features of their thinking can be summarized as follows: freedom of conscience; respect for all creeds, ideologies and religions; alliance with progressive and leftist movements; and the equation of the cause of democracy with that of peace. It was not a manifesto to convince the Holy See, which, through the words of the authoratitive *L'Osservatore Romano* of 15 January 1950, intended to dissuade Catholics from adopting such a point of view: 'As the Church has repeatedly declared, the principles and tendencies manifested by the promoters of movements of this kind and their alliances with groups of atheistic materialism do not conform to Catholic doctrine and the teachings of the Holy See'.[76] Miglioli continued to work with the Costituente della terra (Foundation of the land) association, supporting strikes for land reform; in the last years of his life (he died in 1954) he collaborated with Mazzolari's *Adesso*.

Adesso, 'a fortnightly review of Christian commitment', as the subtitle read, had been published in Modena since 1949. The periodical was characterized by obedience to the Church and emphasized the duty and commitment of Christians towards the 'last', the poorest of the earth.[77] These convictions meant that the review had a natural sympathy for progressive political forces – in particular for the Christian Democratic left and the socialists – as well as the awareness that only by detaching the Catholic party from its intimate embrace with powerful economic forces would it be possible to breach the following that communism had managed to secure for itself amongst the poorer classes. As he described in his book *Rivoluzione Cristiana* ('Christian Revolution'), written in 1943 while he was in hiding and hunted by the Germans – but published posthumously in 1967 – Mazzolari aspired to a 'true revolution', the revolution that had begun with Jesus Christ and that bound the Christian to a commitment to foster the values of peace and justice.

In the fifties, Mazzolari had problems with the ecclesiastical authorities: in 1951, priests were forbidden to write for *Adesso*, and Mazzolari was not allowed to publish his works without ecclesiastical revision. He continued to write anonymously for the journal, however, and it was this gesture that provoked a harsh reaction from the Holy Office when, on 28 June 1954, he was prevented from preaching outside his parish. Mazzolari died in 1959, shortly after the announcement of Vatican II and just before that great dream of Church renewal, for which he had worked so hard, became reality.

Even within the Christian Democrats – a variegated and pluralistic organization – a movement formed that did not always follow either the majority party line or the sentiment of the ecclesiastical hierarchy. On the left of the DC, a 'dossettiani' group was organized consisting of Giuseppe Dossetti, Amintore Fanfani, Giuseppe Lazzati and Giorgio La Pira.[78] They supported popular participation in the life of the new Italian nation, born out of the struggle for liberation and resolutely wished for an alliance with the left. Their relationship with the progressive world was based on political and intellectual competition, since they believed that the Church should not merely play the part of an immobile spectator with regard to the changes taking place in society but that it should instead take on a leading role.[79]

In Italy, the labour movement identified itself with the Marxist parties (PCI and PSI) with whom it was necessary to open a dialogue, establishing possible elements of mediation and agreement. Moreover, while it is true that Dossetti and the members of his group always declared a clear theoretical opposition to Marxism, it may also be said that they showed a 'practical sympathy' towards that particular world.[80] It was necessary, in their opinion, to fight the 'sin', but love the 'sinner': denouncing communist heresy did not mean excluding the Communists from the family of civil society, especially given that at the root of their error lay the failure of Christians who, too often, had remained silent in the face of the scandal of poverty. Thus, once the differences between the two worldviews had been defined, collaboration was possible based on a precise series of agreements, since the common objective was the defence of the marginalized. Dossetti proposed 'solidarity between the popular parties' even after the end of the collaboration between the DC and the left in the spring of 1947, because profound social reform was an objective that they all had in common. But it was a goal that proved to be unattainable, given that the majority of the DC now discounted any form of agreement with the Left.

In 1950, Dossetti's ideas became more influential within the party and he was given the role of vice-secretary. One significant factor was the group's openness to the thought of British scholars such as John Maynard Keynes and William Beveridge: Dossetti and his followers studied their economic theories keenly, hoping to find remedies for the enormous problem of unemployment.[81] A link to the theoretical ideas of the British economists was provided above all by Federico Caffè, who contributed to the Dossetti group's journal *Cronache sociale* (1947–1951) and who, in England at the time, was an admirer of Labour politics.[82]

Giorgio La Pira gave a fine demonstration of showing concern towards the poor when, in 1953, as the mayor of Florence, he was one of the leading figures in the difficult struggle – a successful one in the end – against the closure of the chemical and textile company SNIA Viscosa's La Pignone factory: something which meant the dismissal of 1,750 workers. La Pira was convinced that Christianity was a social religion and that its moral principles should be applied not only to individuals but to the whole community: it was, indeed, Christian morality that should lead the faithful to take an interest in social and political issues.[83] Critical of the capitalist West, La Pira believed that the state should intervene on behalf of the poor and he expressed these principles clearly in the article 'L'attesa della povera gente' ('The poor are waiting'), written for *Cronache sociali* in 1950. Here, he upheld the need for unemployment to be fought through decisive public intervention in the economy.[84]

His achievement as mayor was the organization of international conferences in Florence in the fifties, where Palestinian and Israeli, Algerian and French, and Western and Soviet representatives came together in a spirit of dialogue and discussion – something that would be properly valorized in the *Concilio*.[85] La Pira, like Dossetti and Lazzati, was indebted to the ideas of Maritain, who believed that it was not possible to talk about a 'just war' in the atomic age and that it was necessary to work for the creation of a world authority capable of stifling every movement towards military conflict.[86] One significant event was the organization of a conference involving all the mayors of cities that were possible targets for nuclear attack, the result of which was the drafting of a document in favour of peace and detente. On that occasion, the meeting took place between the mayors of Moscow and Florence, and they were photographed shaking hands, an act reported by the whole world's press. It represented the symbolic prefiguring of the audience that Pope John XXIII would grant in the Vatican a few years later to Rada and Aleksei Adjubei, the daughter and son-in-law of Chruščëv.[87] A group of Christians formed around La Pira, including Mario Gozzini, Divo Barsotti, the Piarist Ernesto Balducci and Monsignor Enrico Bartoletti, who worked together with him and invigorated Florentine Catholicism.

It was the *dossettiani* who, in fact, assumed the role of leadership in the DC in the work of the Constituent Assembley, wanting it to ratify the historical confluence of the great ideologies of the twentieth century.[88] The group brought to the drafting of the Charter its ideas concerning the crisis of fascism and the state that it had been developing since the second half of the 1930s. In particular, La Pira transferred the interpretative paradigm of the crisis between religion and the modern world to the level of constitutional structures; he thought that a crisis originated in the Protestant Reformation and then in the philosophical rationalism of the French Revolution, encouraging an individualistic logic and dismembering the organic fabric of society, to effectively pave the way for totalitarian responses. With the collapse of fascism and Nazism, and the emergence of the limits of the Soviet constitutional model, the Dossetti group considered that a constitutional, social and economic 'third way' was possible, and that it was an alternative not only to the models of capitalist democracy but also to the experiences of collectivism.[89]

The historian Paolo Pombeni has pointed out how, unlike the communist Catholics who remained committed to positions of absolute orthodoxy, Dossetti and his followers contemplated 'theological revisionism' and the hypothesis of Church reform.[90] Dossetti, an admirer of the spirituality of Antonio Rosmini,[91] believed in the need for a Church devoted to piousness and poverty, convictions that again emerged during his participation in the *Concilio* as advisor to Cardinal Lercaro.[92]

Relations within the DC were not easy, they were complicated by the variety of political sensibilities and perspectives that made up the party. Thus, in October 1952, Dossetti resigned from his leadership, and then a year later abandoned his parliamentary seat.[93] Lazzati decided to follow Dossetti's example and announced his withdrawal from politics in the spring of 1953.[94]

The experience of the 'Christian avant-garde', while its connotations were those of an elite phenomenon, still had great cultural and political significance: in a period of entrenchment and husbandry, it kept alive the flame of confrontation between the Catholic world and the world of the Left, preparing the way for the new openness in Italian politics that would take place in the following decade.

The new openess to the centre-left

After De Gasperi departed from the scene, following the disappointing results in the 1953 general elections, Italian politics was rocked by great instability. The centrist coalitions – formed by the DC, the Social Democratic Party (PSDI), the Republican Party (PRI) and the Liberal Party (PLI) – could boast of only a small majority in parliament and the government, were always dominated by the Christian Democrats and were unable to survive for a whole legislature. The question then arose of the government's willingness to open up to other parties: the hypothesis on the Left was Pietro Nenni's socialist party; and on the Right the Movimento Sociale Italiano (Italian Social Movement, MSI), a party that had grown out of the fascist experience of the Italian Social Republic and whose secretary was Augusto De Marsanich.[95]

Since the years of the struggle for liberation and until the post-war period, the PSI had links with the PCI, admiring as it did its organizational vigour and ideological fascination; it was thus a party, unlike other European socialist forces, that had the Soviet model as its reference point. The bond with Togliatti was very strong, to the extent that Nenni, during the April 1948 elections, had proposed uniting the two parties under the name of *Fronte popolare* (Popular Front). The disappointing electoral outcome, and especially the voting preferences that went against the PSI, given the organizational strength of the communist association, suggested a certain amount of caution. Greater voice was also given to those in the party who believed that a more autonomous policy was appropriate. During the 31st Party Congress, which took place in Turin between the end of March and the beginning of April 1955, Nenni hypothesized opening up to the Catholics and the DC, and declared his willingness to accept the North Atlantic Treaty, provided its strategy was a defensive one. The turning point, however, occurred in 1956. The 20th Congress of the Communist Party of the Soviet Union (CPSU) followed by the Soviet occupation of Hungary led Nenni to break with Moscow and condemn Soviet violence against the people of Budapest. The Communist Party, faced with the events in Hungary, was dogged by doubts with regard to the legitimacy of Chruščëv's decisions. Criticism of the Soviet military intervention also came from a group of communist intellectuals connected to the journal *Società*. In the end, however, the PCI resolved to support the Soviet leader and accused the Western powers of fomenting the Hungarian uprising. The different positions in relation to Soviet tactics led to a break between the PCI and the PSI, and opened up new perspectives for Italian politics: to many, Nenni seemed to be an ideal figure in terms of engaging in dialogue in order to expand the government majority.

The debate on opening up to the Socialist Party, thanks to the dynamism of Christian Democrat Secretary Fanfani (DC Secretary from 1954 to 1959), was one of the main events of the DC National Council, held in Vallombrosa on 13 and 14 July 1957. Discussion was lively and heated, and there were many members of the party who showed either caution or hostility with regard to Nenni.[96] Equally perplexed were Italy's American allies,[97] the country's industrialists, the influential daily newspaper *Corriere della Sera* and, above all, the Church, quick to once again point out the unreliability of parties who defined themselves as Marxist.[98] Significant attacks in this regard came from the Jesuit Antonio Messineo in *Civiltà Cattolica* in 1957, in particular in the article 'Può il socialista essere democratico?' ('Can a Socialist ever be democratic?').[99]

Despite all this, the Christian Democrat left went on with its policy of opening up to the Left and, on the occasion of the elections of 25 May 1958, the Florentine journal *Politica* – founded by Catholics closely linked to La Pira – played host to a series of articles by figures representing various strands of Italian socialism, including Lelio Basso,[100] Mario Zagari,[101] Matteo Matteotti[102] and Tristano Codignola.[103] The centre-left formula was also supported by the editors of the journal *Il Mulino*, who, sensitive to the new social sciences originating in Anglo-American climes, considered collaboration between the three main Italian political traditions – democratic liberalism, socialist reformism and social Catholicism – as a natural development.[104]

The outcome of the elections, in which the PSI had performed reasonably well, made it possible for Fanfani to establish a new government composed of elements from both the DC and the PSDI, which took office on 1 July 1958, and was welcomed by the Catholic Left but regarded with great suspicion by *La Civiltà Cattolica*.[105] The government clearly intended to open a dialogue with Nenni and his party, but, as early as 26 January 1959, internal and external hostilities forced Fanfani to resign. Without another election, the government was taken on by Antonio Segni, a member of the most conservative part of the DC.

On 7 January 1960, *L'Osservatore Romano* intervened with regard to the possibility of opening up towards the Left, harshly condemning the socialists and any eventual collaboration with a national government. Like the *Civiltà Cattolica*, the Vatican journal held that the PSI, whatever changes the party underwent, was the promulgator of values that were irreconcilable with Catholicism. The journal went on to say that it was illusory to think of 'a definitive detachment of the socialist party from solidarity with communism', given that this was a partnership bound together by a long tradition; above all, it believed that hopes of this kind nourished 'yielding and laxity' in relation to 'ideologies and systems of life' that set themselves in opposition to Catholic doctrine.[106]

While Aldo Moro, the Secretary of the DC from 1959, was working to convince the party of the inevitability of coming to an agreement with the Left, Italian politics was moving in the opposite direction. After the resignation of Antonio Segni, President of the Republic Giovanni Gronchi decided, on 21 March 1960, to appoint Ferdinando Tambroni as prime minister. The latter formed yet another one-party Christian Democrat government, which in parliament obtained the decisive support of twenty-seven deputies from the Italian Social Movement and four former Monarchist deputies.

The establishment of a government supported by these right-wing parties encouraged heated debate within the Catholic world, and the left-wing DC ministers Giulio Pastore, Giorgio Bo and Fiorentino Sullo handed in their resignations. The Jesuits took different positions: while *La Civiltà Cattolica* did not consider the movement to the Right deplorable in itself, an opposing view came from the Milanese Jesuit magazine *Aggiornamenti sociali,* which claimed that 'the gradual acquiescence of the DC in its relations with the MS' could only raise 'apprehension' and create 'immense tension' in the Catholic electorate, 'especially in that part that most felt the need to align political action with the principles that had inspired the DC'.[107]

To reward the MSI for its parliamentary support, Tambroni supported the neo-fascist party's request to hold the national congress in Genoa.[108] The congress should have been chaired by Carlo Emanuele Basile, a leading exponent of the RSI between 1943 and 1945, and responsible for the killing and torture of many members of the Resistance. The Ligurian capital, a fiercely anti-fascist city, saw this as a provocation and left-wing parties organized massive demonstrations which involved clashes with the forces of law and order. Strikes spread throughout the country and the police reacted harshly: never had Republican Italy experienced such difficult days and this led the DC leadership to force Tambroni to resign.[109]

With Tambroni's brief moment of glory at an end, Italian politics once again turned to the possibility of coming to an agreement with the PSI, and on 26 July 1960 Fanfani, with the support of the centrist parties and the abstention of both Socialists and Monarchists, launched his third government, which featured all the leading members of the party.[110] A few months later, another election campaign was held in the country, with the renewal, in early November, of the municipal and provincial councils. Following these administrative elections,[111] Nenni's party opted for a change in its policy, deciding to create local left-wing authorities only where an alternative hypothesis was not possible, and choosing alliance with the DC as its preferred solution. The 34th Socialist Congress was held in Milan from 15 to 20 March 1961, and during the event Nenni repeated his favouring of a gradual approach to the centre-left and supported, in the face of a divided party – his speech obtained only

55 per cent of the votes – the possibility of external support for a government that activated a serious policy of reform.

In the Catholic world, too, discussion continued in relation to the centre-left, and the three Christian Democratic conferences that were held in San Pellegrino in 1961, 1962 and 1963 were treated as important occasions, with the participation of prestigious intellectuals, including Achille Ardigò and Pasquale Saraceno.[112] But it was during the 7th DC congress, held in Naples between the months of January and February in 1962, that the majority of the party, after an extraordinary seven-hour speech from Moro, was persuaded of the inevitability of coming to an agreement with the Left.[113] After the conclusion of the Naples congress, Fanfani, on 21 February, embarked upon his fourth government, with the participation of Social Democrats and Republicans, but, above all – and this was truly a new element – with Socialist abstention. During the parliamentary debate, the exponent of the Christian Democrat Left presented an ambitious project of reforms that included a plan for schools, the nationalization of electricity, changes in public administration, legislation for urban planning and an economic programme. In February 1962, La Pira, who had an excellent personal relationship with Nenni, called 'the fraternal convergence between Catholics and socialists the most important political operation of this century' and added: 'this is a historical operation, a fountainhead and genesis, and, laid out before it, it has a future rich with promise for the good of Italy, of Europe, of the Third World and of all the world's nations!'[114]

It seems evident, therefore, that, from a political point of view, the years between the two decades represented a period of significant thinking and profound change, and that the opening up to the Left, so advocated by some and so opposed by others, was to be considered as the solution for Italy's political instability. This alliance, which many considered a moment of crucial transformation in the country, did not actually live up to expectations: thus, many historians, speaking of the sixties and the experience of centre-left governments, refer to a 'reformist illusion'.[115]

4

Changing Times

Council and post-Council

Kennedy's victory in the American elections, the protest movements for black people's rights, the demonstrations in universities against the war in Vietnam, Pope John XXIII and the Vatican Council II, Che Guevara, Camillo Torres, Mao's China, the Prague revolt: in the 'long sixties' the world was changing and Italian society could no longer remain immobile. The world was heading towards 1968, the year that the great British historian Eric J. Hobsbawn has called the dream-come-true of a simultaneous world uprising, cultivated by revolutionaries since 1917.[1] In the sixties and seventies, a strong movement on behalf of workers' and women's liberation also took root, encouraged by the reflections of new Marxist philosophers.[2]

Historians, and many Catholics, continue to be profoundly divided by the events of the 1960s, and especially by Vatican II. Some conservative Catholics blame the Council for the decline in church-going that took place over the next few decades; others do not blame the Council itself but its misinterpretation by many believers. Some historians – such as Giuseppe Alberigo, professor at the University of Bologna – believe that, in the religious history of the West, the new pontificate of John XXIII and Vatican II marked a positive watershed within Catholic culture.[3] After the long pontificate of Pius XII and its weighty legacy, the community of the faithful started to approach the problems of the contemporary world with the open-minded, sharing spirit embraced by the new pontificate of Pope Angelo Roncalli.[4]

Although this is not the place to start a digression on Vatican II, or refer to the academic literature on the subject,[5] it is nonetheless important to recall that the eschatological tension which has been peculiar to Christianity since its origins finally seemed to have become incorporated into the thinking of that period; so much so that the Council itself has been viewed by some scholars as the 'accomplishment of the prophets' dream'. On this issue Giuseppe Dossetti wrote that 'a certain ecclesiology was brought into the Council, and it was the effect of first-hand experience and of the necessity to keep the Church above worldly matters, and away from, politically and ecclesiologically, debatable political situations'.[6]

Dossetti played an important role during Vatican II, collaborating closely with the cardinals Giacomo Lercaro, Julius August Döpfner, Leon-Joseph Suenens and Kricor Bedros Agagianian. He worked to ensure that a majority would prevail that was favourable to a reformist vision, and in particular because, going back to the thinking of Rosmini, he had arrived at a definition of the Church as 'the people of God'. He was also committed to supporting the decree on ecumenism, which transcended the belief that the religion of Rome had a monopoly on Christian truth, and the declaration *Dignitatis humanae* on religious freedom, which clarified the relationship between authority and freedom.[7] Above all, Dossetti believed that the Council, as the Constitution already stated and as was hoped for in *Pacem in Terris*, should be explicit with regard to the repudiation of conflict. This was something that placed him in opposition to the US episcopate which, directly involved as it was in the Cold War, did not consider it opportune to release a declaration that would undermine support of American foreign policy.[8]

The changes that the Church was undergoing in the 1960s implied transformations in the political sphere as well. As Pietro Scoppola pointed out, there can be no 'real democracy if there is no religious reform first, a way to interpret religious life in accordance with the responsibilities democracy requires'.[9] It is no coincidence, then, that the political dialogue between the Christian Democratic Party (DC) and the Socialist Party (PSI) occurred at that precise time. Pope Roncalli did not intervene in the dispute directly but, in contrast to the prevailing opinions within the Roman Curia, he encouraged Christian Democrat representatives (such as Amintore Fanfani and Aldo Moro), who had turned to him for advice, to pursue their efforts in the direction of an opening up to the PSI.[10]

The research started by the Council encouraged a new ferment in intellectual circles and led to an attempt to recognize the vitality of emerging political energies capable of facing the new challenges arising in Italian society. Those were the necessary conditions for the lively intellectual re-elaborations that were to take place in such journals as *Testimonianze* and *Questitalia*, both founded in 1958. *Testimonianze*, whose editor was Father Ernesto Balducci,[11] addressed those in the Catholic clergy and laity who were disappointed by Italian Catholic Action's

(AC) political activism and, more in general, the rigidity that characterized the pontificate of Pius XII. The intent of those believers was to 'de-clericalise theology and to create a theologically qualified Catholic culture'. The Florentine journal's reference points were represented by the French theologians Henri-Marie de Lubac, Jean Daniélou and Yves Congar, together with Maritain, Mounier, Gabriel Marcel and Georges Bernanos. Their thought and work provided the philosophical background for the ideas promoted by the journal with regard to independence from politics, respect for people, the distinction between spiritual and secular values, and the condemnation of Western civilization.[12]

Questitalia was founded in Venice by Wladimiro Dorigo,[13] who, in 1955, had been admonished by the Church for using language 'suspected of Marxism'. This journal considered itself neither non-Catholic nor written by Catholics – it always denied the legitimacy of such a definition – even though its interests focused on the political organization of Catholics and on the role that they assumed in Italy in the years after Vatican II.[14]

In the wake of the new religious sensibility inaugurated by the papacy of John XXIII, the journal *Relazioni sociali* was launched in Milan in 1960. In its first issues, it revealed a desire to analyse the Italian social and political situation, while regarding the evolution of the PSI with a sympathetic eye, since the latter had now forsaken its extremist positions and abandoned its traditional kowtowing to the Communist Party (PCI).[15] Similarly inspired by the religious currents of the times, in 1965 the journal *Momento* was created in the Milanese dioceses. Describing itself as based on 'testimony and dialogue' and as closely related to the spirituality of Teilhard de Chardin,[16] *Momento* fitted perfectly into the new awareness promoted by the experience of the Council. In its bimonthly issues it displayed three different tendencies: the first deriving from the legacy of Father Primo Mazzolari, the second supporting communitarian personalism and the third promoting dialogue with Marxism in all its various forms.[17]

In May 1964, the Florentine Catholic world published the first issue of *Note di Cultura*. This journal focused mainly on international problems, with an approach towards the Vietnam War and Middle Eastern issues that was close to that of La Pira. That same year, *Il tetto* was founded in Naples, which from the beginning was highly critical of the political choices made by the DC. In June 1967, the weekly magazine *Settegiorni* was also founded: directed by Ruggero Orfei and Piero Pratesi, its aim was to prepare public opinion for a possible separation from the DC.

Certain groups of believers, similar in attitude to the ideas of these journals, also criticized the way in which the guidelines issued by Vatican II had been put into practice and were thus creating a hiatus between the expectations aroused by that event and their realization. For instance, many of those believers thought that the *Instructions* for the application of the liturgical reform, decreeing the use of the vernacular in the Mass and in other rites, did not seem to grant enough freedom and did not satisfy aspirations for a free and creative relationship with the transcendent. Some of the faithful decided to organize celebrations outside the parishes, claiming the right to create new words for prayers and using rhythmic tunes and jazz music instead of traditional Church hymns.[18]

The sixties marked a turning point in the Catholic daily press as well. As a consequence of the dynamic and innovative action of Vatican II, the 'crusading' spirit waned or disappeared in the pages of both *L'Osservatore Romano* and many of the Curia's daily newspapers. Raniero La Valle was appointed director of the Catholic newspaper *L'Avvenire d'Italia* of Bologna, while the Archbishop of Milan, Cardinal Giovanni Battista Montini, entrusted *L'Italia* to Giuseppe Lazzati. This new direction did not last long. In 1966, Lazzati, following the new mood that had arisen against the Vietnam War, took up a position that was anti-imperialist and in favour of peace, but his editorial policy was considered too radical.[19] Using the budget deficit of the periodicals as an excuse, the Conferenza Episcopale Italiana (Italian Episcopal Commettee, CEI) decided to merge the Bolognese and Milanese newspapers. With La Valle's resignation as director, *Avvenire* was established, a newspaper co-owned by the CEI and the Milanese Curia.[20]

In 1967, the evidence that this was a critical moment for political and cultural reflection came with the organization of the congress Impegno e compiti dei cattolici nel tempo nuovo della cristianità (The Duty and Commitment of Catholics in the New Era of Christianity),[21] the goal of which was to encourage the DC to regain its Christian inspiration, which many saw as having dwindled after twenty years of political power. The congress was something that certain intellectuals – Vittore Branca, Sergio Cotta and Gabriele De Rosa – were particularly keen to see realized, and in an open letter they wrote:

> Today, the Catholic world is in ferment: a fruitful ferment, which testifies to its vitality and its ability to sense the new feeling of the times not only in Christianity, but in civil society in general. We believe that the destiny and activity of the Christian Democrats, which is at the centre of the country's public life and represents one of the guarantors of the stability of the democratic state, should involve all Catholics who work in politics and culture, even if they are not of this specific party. It involves us, in particular, who are men of culture and who know well how politics becomes sterile if it does not go to the heart of problems

and does not share the anxieties of the contemporary world; it involves us, as Catholic intellectuals, who demand, from the world of politics, an inspiration that is both profoundly Christian and profoundly human.[22]

Three years later in Fermo, in the Marche region, a new meeting was planned: the aim was to reflect on a troublesome figure in the twentieth-century Catholic world, Romolo Murri, the priest whom the Vatican had consigned to oblivion.[23] In 1972, the publishing house Il Mulino issued the miscellaneous volume *Modernismo, fascismo, comunismo. Aspetti e figure della cultura e della politica dei cattolici nel '90*[24] which focused on exponents of modernism in the first part of the century, a movement that had been condemned by Pius X as dangerous and heretical.

The foundation of numerous research centres also dates back to the sixties. A case in point is the Centro Internazionale di Documentazione e Comunicazione (International Centre of Documentation and Communication, IDOC), which was founded in Rome in 1956 and was devoted to the collection of international and interconfessional documents on human and religious development. In 1972, the centre started publishing its own review, called *Idoc internazionale*. A keen interest in problems relating to development in Third World countries and social and economic transformation was the main feature of the Centro di ricerca per l'emigrazione (Research Centre for Emigration), founded in Rome in 1963 by the Congregation of the Missionaries of St Charles. The Giuseppe Toniolo Centre for Economic and Social Studies was founded in Pisa in 1966, and the following year the Luigi Sturzo Institute organized its first international conference entitled 'Sociologia contemporanea nell'Europa occidentale' ('Contemporary sociology in Western Europe').

Catholic dissent

One of the leading figures of Milanese Catholic dissent – Mario Cuminetti – wrote that internal contestation within the Church 'arose from the effort to put the theological guidelines of Vatican II into practice'.[25] Be that as it may, there is no clear dividing line between radical interpretation of the Council and true dissent, since it was thanks to the Council's reflections that many of the faithful felt legitimized in their search for other ways to express their religiousness. Unable to fulfil their ambition inside the institution, they found themselves experiencing their faith de facto outside of and often in contrast with the strict discipline of the Catholic Church's teachings. However, as historian Guido

Verucci pointed out, the collective movement of 1968 was undoubtedly pivotal to determining a moment 'of great acceleration and a breakthrough for that part of the Italian Catholic world that was engaged in the elaboration of new ways to relate religious faith to the contemporary world'. By the year 1968, then, the phenomena and the features of radical ecclesial contestation had become 'real dissent'.[26] The series of events called *1968* played a role in polarizing the new cultural impulses of the 'long 1960s': it was the time of political radicalization, when everything seemed possible and 'a new age was dawning'. This climate raised intense expectation in the Catholic world, under stress from equally dramatic religious radicalization, involving laymen, priests and nuns.[27]

In Italy, the initial development of the youth protests of the late 1960s was primarily in those universities that were strongly characterized by their religious connotations. In November 1967, protest flared up at the Catholic University of the Sacro Cuore of Milan, which was occupied by students demonstrating vehemently against the considerable rise in tuition fees. The rector, Ezio Franceschini, justified his decision by insisting on the need to balance university accounts,[28] but the students answered with the slogan: 'This is a Catholic university, not a private one.' In their opinion, culture was not 'a commodity that could be bought at production cost' and a democratic country should allow every citizen access to education.[29] Demonstrators argued they were drawing inspiration from the spirit of the Council, which had set the Church free from the political interests of the ruling class and had led believers towards defence of the poor. Student mobilization sparked off a harsh reaction from the academic world and the rector called in the police to have the university shut down. The students continued their protest, organizing demonstrations and then camping out for several days in front of the main entrance of the university. The academic authorities, meanwhile, decided that repression was the best solution: the leaders of the protest were expelled from the university.[30]

Similar protests were organized at the University of Trento, created in the early sixties at the request of the DC's left-wing. Marco Boato, one of the leaders of the protest movement, even went as far as to claim that *Lettera ad una professoressa della scuola di Barbiana* – written by Father Lorenzo Milani,[31] who stigmatized the class-based nature of the Italian school system and fought for equality in the access to knowledge as a condition for human liberation – was a more important point of reference and instrument of research for the struggle of the student movement than *One-Dimensional Man* by Herbert Marcuse.[32]

The Catholic protesters immediately managed to establish a dialogue with the young leftists who at the time were mobilizing in public universities to claim more space for political flexibility and more adequate structures for a student population that had increased exponentially in the sixties. The young people shared an interest in what was going on at an international level, in particular, the war that was taking place in Vietnam and the difficult conditions of Latin America.[33] Many believers looked with interest at those priests and laymen who, on that distant continent, had made a choice of commitment to defend the rights of the dispossessed, not disdaining the revolutionary movements of the Left as comrades in the fields of debate and struggle and accepting Marxism as an instrument with which to analyse and understand the contradictions induced by the capitalist system. Alongside the myths of Che and Fidel, figures shared with the young leftists, these Catholics took Father Camilo Torres as their point of reference: Torres was the revolutionary priest who did not condemn the use of violence, at least as a last resort, and who died in February 1966 fighting together with the guerrillas in Colombia.[34]

There were a number of examples at that time of the new sensitivity to international problems and the taking of positions against the policies of the American superpower. They included the almost one thousand signatures gathered by the young people of the Catholic University of Milan in favour of the Italian government exerting sufficient pressure on the USA in order to suspend the bombardment of Vietnam and the vigil for peace organized on the occasion of Christmas 1967 by Don Enzo Mazzi's Florentine parish of Isolotto. Cardinal Lercaro, meanwhile, on the 'day for peace' that was promoted in all the dioceses on 1 January 1968, expressed himself with great clarity, reading a document, partly written by Dossetti, against the American bombing in Vietnam; and, for this reason, was forced to resign.[35] After Lercaro's removal, Dossetti, dismayed by the harshness of the gesture, moved to Jericho, in the Holy Land, with the aim of promoting dialogue between cultures and religions in one of the most problematic places on the planet.[36]

The young protesters were interested in the Third World Marxist theories of economists Samir Amin and André Gunder Frank, and thus some of the latter's works were published by the Catholic publishing house Jaca Book. In the seventies, the same publisher also produced a theological series, directed by Giuseppe Ruggeri, that investigated the roots of Christian socialism.[37]

The ferment referred to here was a minority phenomenon in the ecclesial panorama: traditional parishes were certainly far more numerous than those in which radical faith flourished, just as the militancy of young people in circles faithful to the Church of Rome was infinitely vaster than that of the 'rebel' groups. But, as Gianenrico Rusconi and Chiara Saraceno point out, 'it is difficult to deny that behind the uncertainties, the confusions and the ambiguities of dissent, a sense of collective awareness was created that was new for church religion'.[38]

Many young people, carried away on the wave of the enthusiasm engendered by the events of 1968, slid towards the New Left and worked with increasing commitment on spreading the word in factories and city neighbourhoods. Linking these two worlds was the need for an all-encompassing approach to an ideal dimension and the myth of a life devoted to the realization of one's own utopia, which could be called 'Christian witness' or 'social justice'. For them, dedicating themselves to political and social commitment represented the authentic realization of the gospel message which requires that a person must, above all, fraternally apply himself to the needs of his fellow man.[39] While it is true that some fell into a political activism and an immanentism that led them to underestimate the dimension of salvation through faith, this did not happen to everyone. Indeed, Don Lorenzo Bedeschi, in an article published in the journal *Religioni oggi* in 1968, criticized those who only looked at 'Catholic dissent' from 'a political angle', because the phenomenon had to be examined in 'doctrinal sources rather than in political phenomenology'.[40]

In 1966, Mario Cuminetti had already recognized the risk that a Christian engaged in the world would slide towards 'a worldisation and politicisation of the Church, to the detriment of the manifestation of its deepest nature'.[41] In the following years, reflecting on the crisis that the Church was experiencing and the community of men that took it as a point of reference, the theologian feared 'the risks of building other idols, of becoming members of other temples and other communities, where the measure, the interest, is not God, but oneself, one's own self-preservation'.[42] *Testimonianze*, for its part, already characterized at the outset by a profound religious sentiment, did not lose its character, even if Maritain's criticism of the West tended over the years to develop into firm opposition to American politics in Vietnam and Latin America. This was not a tendency shared by Balducci, however, who wrote: 'The moral virtues, specific expressions of the human being's orientation towards what is good, are not sufficient to realise and define the Christian life.'[43]

The experience of the 'grassroot groups', too, dates back to this period. Such groups were organized by the journal *Questitalia*, which together with the *Circolo Maritain* from Rimini, *Persona e comunità* from Lucca, *Esprit* from Pescara and the journal *Note e rassegne* from Modena, organized the congress 'Credenti e non credenti per una nuova sinistra' ('Believers and non-believers for a New Left'), held in Bologna on 15 February 1968.[44] The young criticized the political unity of Catholics and the choices made by the DC. They also opposed the capitalist system and positioned themselves politically in the area of the extra-parliamentary Left, judging the PCI not to be sufficiently secular and radical. These grassroots groups, founded in Italy between 1967 and 1969, divided themselves into those who opted for an openly political line and would soon merge with the extra-parliamentary Left, and those more susceptible to religious sentiment, who would first create the Assembly of the Ecclesial Groups and later the Basic Communities. Basic Communities were an international movement, rooted mainly in Latin America, consisting of believers who conceived being Christian as a radical commitment inspired by the gospel: rather than being devoted to the reform of the Church, they aimed to re-found it, drawing legitimacy for their actions from a close relationship with the scriptures, as had happened at the time of the Reformation. In this period, for the first time in Italian contemporary history, there were numerous exchanges between grassroots groups (coming from the Catholic tradition) and the Waldensians.

Both Catholics and non-Catholics joined in the groups, all sharing the same desire to expose 'the ties the Church has with political and economic power', and the same ambition for 'a Church founded on fraternity and the equality of all its members', both lay and religious. Such communities closed ranks against the Concordat between Church and state, the teaching of religion in schools and private confessional schools, while promoting initiatives against compulsory military service.[45]

At that time, many Catholics took a stand against the guidelines of the Church and of the Catholic party. Of great significance was the choice made by Lidia Menapace, a former Catholic partisan and later active member of the DC, who in 1968 decided to resign from the party.[46] In an article in *Settegiorni*, Menapace criticized the DC for its dependence on the ecclesiastic hierarchy.[47] During the meeting of the members of 'Catholic Dissent' held in Reggio Emilia in 1968, she argued that all left-wing activists, whether Catholic or not, should engage in modifying a social situation that appeared anachronistic and in creating a direct, assembly-based democracy.[48]

The crisis the Catholic party went through in these years also surfaced in the decision of Corrado Corghi, regional secretary of the DC in Emilia Romagna from 1956 to 1966, to resign from the party. In an open letter addressed to the party's secretary Mariano Rumor, Corghi stated his aversion to the 'tolerant' positions assumed by the DC towards American policy in Third World countries. In his opinion there was no doubt that 'in order to obtain the liberation of Latin America from neocolonialist slavery it was necessary for western Europe to completely review its policy towards the USA'.[49] In addition, in an interview with the journal *L'Astrolabio* in September 1968, Corghi declared that 'an authentic Christian attitude' implied rebellion against injustice in the world and a struggle for 'radical change'. Such a protest, on a historical and political level, allowed a 'unified struggle and action shared by believers and non-believers, because an authentically human revolutionary ideal was not necessarily in agreement with a religious view or with a lay one'.[50]

In Reggio Emilia, Corghi had gathered a group of young people around him, to whom he spoke of Latin America, Che Guevara, Father Camilo Torres, the Dominican Frei Betto – who had decided to embrace the armed struggle against the Brazilian dictatorship – and of Carlos Marighella, author of the *Mini-Manual do Guerrilheiro Urbano*. Corghi was in close contact with South American events and had travelled there several times in order to try and free Régis Debray, a young French writer, fascinated by the figure of Che, who had been kidnapped in Bolivia. Corghi had thus come into contact with exponents of liberation theology.

One young person listening carefully to Corghi's words was Alberto Franceschini, one of the founders of Brigate Rosse (Red Brigades, BR), who came from a communist family in Reggio Emilia.[51] The Catholic element was also a significant one in the BR; its leaders, Renato Curcio and Mara Cagol,[52] were young AC militants and then students at the faculty of Sociology at the University of Trento.[53] It would be taking things too far to draw a direct line between militancy in Catholic groups and the decision to engage in terrorism, but it was not accidental that one of the first BR documents was drafted during a meeting held in early November 1969 in Chiavari in the Stella Maris hotel, which was the property of the Curia.[54] Don Andrea Gallo, priest of the Carmine parish in Genoa, has underlined how there were many Catholics in those years who felt involved in processes of radical political transformation, sometimes – following the example of Father Torres – resorting to taking up arms.[55] Another BR member was Silvano Girotto, a Franciscan friar who had decided to go to Bolivia as a missionary and who, becoming involved in the armed struggle against the dictator Hugo Banzer, was expelled from the order. Girotto, nicknamed *Frata Mitra* (Friar Machine gun), was certainly an ambiguous character and soon became an informer for General Carlo Alberto Dalla Chiesa: it was Girotto's help that led to the arrest of Curcio in 1974.

Giorgio Bocca argues that, in these terrorist groups, difference in origin was less significant than might be thought, 'given the all-encompassing way, so characteristic of Catholics and communists, in which they confront life and society'; because both the Catholic and the communist have a need 'for total and definitive answers, the rejection of doubt, the replacement of reasoned duty with faith'.[56] The BR members set themselves the goal of 'redeeming Man, indicating the path that led to salvation', practicing, in fact, a secular alternative to religion that had much in common with traditional religion itself.[57]

How thorough Catholic rethinking of the world was at that time is also shown by the experience of the Azione Cattolica which, during the presidency of Vittorio Bachelet (which began in 1964), underwent a profound process of renewal.[58] Opting for the 'religious choice', the association de facto renounced its past of political militancy in support of the DC (as, for example, when it mobilized for the party in the elections of 18 April 1948).[59] Another interesting experience was that of the Associazione Cattolica Lavoratori Italiani (Christian Association of Italian Workers, ACLI). Founded in 1944 to stem the influence of Communists in the world of work, in 1969 it gave its members the freedom to vote.[60] In 1970, the ACLI, in the wake of the workers' united struggle in the factories, supported the 'socialist hypothesis'. Thus, in 1972, Livio Labor, the ACLI president, founded the Movimento Politico dei Lavoratori (Workers' Political Movement, MPL), with the aim of giving life to a second 'left-wing' Catholic party. In his opinion, it was necessary to break the political unity of Catholics and simultaneously contribute to redrafting a new strategy for the Left.

Catholic trade unionism also took a more radical direction: the Confederazione Italiana Sindacati Lavoratori (Italian Confederation of Trade Unions, CISL), in the fifties, under the guidance of Mario Romani, was moderate in nature. Over the following decades, however, with the new sensibility of the Council and the Church paying particular attention to the poor, it became critical in its attitudes in relation to the 'capitalist system'.[61] The FIM-CISL (the metalworkers' union) was involved in a dialogue with the extra-parliamentary left-wing groups. The positions assumed by Sandro Antoniazzi, provincial secretary of the Catholic metalworking workers in Milan, took on a special significance: he upheld the class choice that was also developed by Catholic workers who, on the basis of their experience within the factories, had begun to advance 'theoretical-practical' criticism against Church social doctrine, which was considered insufficient in terms of dealing with contemporary problems.[62]

A crucial turning point occurred at this time: while some believers questioned the collusion of the Catholic world with the political power of the DC and supported, following the Council, a 'religious choice', others placed the religious perspective in the background in order to plunge into extreme political militancy. However, a third option also took shape, namely that of Comunione e Liberazione (Communion and liberation, CL) which, as Father

Turoldo polemically thundered, foreshadowed the return to an updated form of 'Catholic fundamentalism'. Turoldo fiercely opposed this vision of faith and of a rigidly organized Church that avoided any confrontation with those deemed to be 'different',[63] and took the movement's founder, Don Luigi Giussani, harshly to task.[64]

Against the Council and against communism

Inside the world of the Church, however, not everyone interpreted the Council as an encouragement to realign Catholic doctrine with a rapidly transforming society. Monsignor Marcel Lefebvre thought that the Council represented 'the overturning of the pontifical teachings that for more than a century condemned any attempt to bring the Church into line with modernity'.[65] In France he thus founded an anti-Council movement that from 1972 onwards would assume a defiant attitude that led to the breakdown of relations with the Holy See.

The Roman Curia, for its part, was keen to stress its own concern at the spread of radical interpretations of the guidelines arising from Vatican II, expressed by journals such as *Testimonianze*, *Questitalia*, *Il gallo* and *Il Regno*, as well as by the international journal of theology *Concilium*, an Italian edition of which had been issued since 1965 by the Queriniana publishing house in Brescia.

The archbishops of Genoa, Giuseppe Siri,[66] and Palermo, Ernesto Ruffini,[67] were known for their intransigence towards change. Moreover, in 1965, while the Council was still in progress, Mons. Florit, Archbishop of Florence, condemned the position assumed by Father Milani in favour of conscientious objection.[68] In Bologna, in February 1968, Cardinal Giacomo Lercaro – who made an important contribution to the Second Vatican Council – was dismissed for his criticism of the American war in Vietnam, for his collaboration with the Communist administration of Bologna and for having interpreted, in far too radical a way, ideas in favour of the 'Church of the poor'.[69] In addition, the Vatican was determined to reaffirm the traditional principles that were being challenged: in the encyclical *Sacerdotalis coelibatus* (June 1967) the sacred nature of the priesthood was recalled and the promise of celibacy reasserted. In the encyclical *Humanae vitae* of the following July, a stand was taken against contraception, overthrowing the guidelines of the majority on the research commission set up to investigate the matter by Paul VI himself, and rejecting many of the ideas that had already arisen from Council debate.

In Italy, in 1966, the theology journal *Renovatio* was published in order to oppose over-radical interpretations of the *Concilium*, and many groups sprang up which were related to nineteen-century intransigentism, such as the association Silenziosi della Chiesa, or the Mario Fani circles, founded by Luigi Gedda in opposition to the 'religious choice' made by the Catholic Action of Bachelet.

But the most successful organization to take root and gain mass support was Comunione e Liberazione. It was founded in Milan in 1969, following the disintegration of Gioventù Studentesca into a progressive faction, which merged with the Students' Movement, and a more conservative group with links to tradition, led by Father Luigi Giussani. With ideas similar to those of nineteen-century intransigentism, according to which the modern world is the product of the gradual separation from the Church, the CL – supported by the thought of the philosopher Augusto Del Noce[70] – aimed to reaffirm the value of 'Christian civilization'.[71] Besides engaging in a harsh controversy with progressive Catholic groups, Father Giussani clashed with certain sections of the Church and in particular with Giuseppe Lazzati,[72] former president of the Milanese AC, and later rector of the Catholic University of Milan. Lazzati was accused of excessive indulgence towards contemporary innovations: he was guilty in particular, in Giussani's opinion, of being a supporter of the Maritainian thesis of the separation between the supernatural and natural spheres.

Catholics and Marxists: From 'dialogue' to 'common ground'

The Italian Left has always shown an interest in the Catholic world and Gramsci's feelings on this subject have already been highlighted. The Communist Party secretary Palmiro Togliatti followed in the wake of this tradition: Nina Bocenina, Togliatti's secretary during his years of exile in Moscow, recalls in her memoirs that, at Christmas in 1943, Togliatti talked at length about the special characteristics of faith and the organization of the Catholic Church. On that occasion, he stated that: 'Catholicism in Italy is not simply the Church. It is a way of thinking, a complex set of connections between history and politics, culture and philosophy.'[73] This was the starting point for Togliatti's interest in the experience of the Catholic Communists, the group that, under the leadership of Franco Rodano and Adriano Ossicini, originated the idea that it was possible to combine militancy in leftist parties and organizations with faith in the Vatican's religious directives.

In his talk to the Constituent Assembly on 25 March 1947, Togliatti placed emphasis upon the *pace religiosa* (religious peace) that had been adopted during the period of the Resistance, when Catholic workers, military chaplains and priests operated in partisan units alongside communist and socialist militants: the same kind of harmony, he declared, should continue, even though the conflict was over.[74] This was followed by the decision to vote in favour of Article 7 of the Constitution, which implied the acceptance of the Lateran Treaty and comprised part of the project for mutual agreement between the Communist and Catholic masses. Togliatti however, stigmatized every effort to theoretically reconcile Marxism with Christian ideology, and he repeated that the argument should be an exclusively political one. However, the Catholic hierarchy's strong aversion to the Left, exacerbated by the Cold War, prevented the opening of any real form of dialogue and collaboration between the two political cultures for many years.

As we have seen, hope for debate and room for dialogue, albeit limited, remained in some Italian Catholic circles, but most Catholics and Communists continued to regard each other with suspicion, convinced by their own propaganda that the ideological and political opponent was a sworn enemy. This feeling was evident in the articles published in the weekly *Candido* by Giovanni Guareschi, who portrayed these two worlds as being in constant and stubborn opposition. The ecclesiastical authorities, moreover, imposed an absolute political closure to left-wing parties. Togliatti, on the other hand, continued to reaffirm his political interest in the Catholic world even during the Cold War years, and during the 10th PCI Congress, which took place in Rome between 2 and 8 December 1962, stated once again that the relationship with the Catholics was crucial to the party's thought. He also referred to the question in a speech in Bergamo, the birthplace of Pope Roncalli, on 20 March 1963. Although he rejected the attempts to realize an ideological compromise between Catholicism and communism, Togliatti expressed the wish that 'mutual comprehension' could be achieved: 'a mutual acknowledgement of values and therefore an agreement and also a pact to achieve goals which are mutual [...] because they are necessary and indispensable for all humanity'. He lingered over international questions, stressing that the difference between the current period and previous eras was the development of destructive weapons created by men; he then addressed the question of the legality of a war which, if fought with atomic arms, could lead to the end of humanity.[75]

These thoughts arose from the threat posed by the Cuban missile crisis when everyone, believers and atheists alike, was forced to consider the sense of a confrontation which risked compromising the very survival of the planet itself. The Pope's thoughts on the matter are very well known, expressed as they are in the *Pacem in terris* encyclical (April 1963), where he dealt with the problem of war and revealed his concern for the fate of humanity. More importantly, from the point of view of contact between all 'Men of Good Will', he made a distinction between error as such and the person who falls into error. As to Marxist philosophy, the encyclical pointed out that it was necessary to form a clear distinction between doctrines and the historical movements originated by those doctrines.[76] With this conviction, Pope John XXIII showed that he was willing to overcome the scorn and disapproval expressed by Pius XII, as well as to establish the conditions for a debate with others, with those who were different: this attitude had also been part of the 'Christian avant-garde movements' of the forties and fifties. *Gaudium et spes* (December 1965), meanwhile, also warned that all men, whatever their beliefs, 'ought to work for the rightful betterment of this world in which we all live'.[77]

It should also be added that the Second Vatican Council introduced a particularly sensibility into the Catholic world, which led to numerous demands for change, as well as engaging in sharing the rediscovery of the religious dimension which had emerged from the Conciliar assembly and claiming a new leading role in history for the faithful. Many Catholics decided to be more open to the stimuli of the contemporary world, to confront the problems of poverty and underdevelopment, and to interpret the legitimization of the dialogue arising from the Conciliar fathers' reflections as a new opportunity to exchange views with the 'other'.

This new openness in the Marxist world – in France well expressed in the observations of Adam Schaff and Roger Garaudy, who had hypothesized a 'Marxist humanism'[78] – and the new Conciliar sensibility set the scene for the discussion that took place between Marxists and Christians, one of the main figures of which was Mario Gozzini. In 1964, the Florentine Catholic published the book *Dialogo alla prova* ('Dialogue under test') convinced that a relationship between the two cultures was only possible if Communists and Catholics took their respective revisionisms as far as possible; his goal was not to convert Communists but to debate with them. Dialogue was possible, Gozzini argued in his introduction to the book, because 'ecumenical anxiety pushed the Christian beyond the barricades raised in the past' and because Catholics thought it was necessary to open up 'to a charity without which the truth risked remaining sterile'.[79]

In his intellectual research, Gozzini began a dialogue with Lucio Lombardo Radice, an important member of the PCI, who stated that religious ideology was not in fact necessarily reactionary: while religion could, as the communist intellectual explained, be 'the opium of the people', in Marx's description, it could also became a spur towards liberation, as the thought of Teilhard de Chardin revealed.[80] Essays contributed to the book came from Nando Fabro, Luciano Gruppi, Ruggero Orfei, Alberto Cecchi, Giampaolo Meucci, Ignazio Delugu, Danilo Zolo and Salvatore Di Marco.[81] Di Marco's contribution in particular was interesting: referring to the ideas developed in the 1960s amongst Marxist philosophers, he arrived at a re-evaluation of subjectivity and transcendence, and engaged in the search for a link between Marxist philosophy and human problems, in the prospect of 'developing a new philosophy of the human person'.[82] Zolo, for his part, one of the leading figures involved with the journal *Testimonianze*, declared himself a supporter of the comparison between the values present in the personalistic humanism inspired by Christian Revelation, which took Maritain's ideas as a reference point, and Marxist humanism.

A step beyond debate was proposed by the Salesian Giulio Girardi, the author in 1966 of the book *Marxismo e cristianesimo* ('Marxism and Christianity')[83] which foreshadowed the need for an 'encounter' between these two political cultures. Even the journal *Religioni oggi*, as early as 1967, had realized that the time for dialogue was to be considered at an end and sustained the need to 'pass from theory to practice' for the realization of a new society: it was no longer important to distinguish between Christians and Marxists, now was the moment when it was required 'together and equal with one another to confront the great common problems and together solve them'.[84]

The dialogue that developed in Italy was part of a broader international debate: in 1966, in Salzburg, thanks to the commitment of the Paulus-Gesellschaft, a meeting was organized between Catholic theologians and Marxist intellectuals entitled: 'Man and Religion, the future of humanity, the society of tomorrow'. The same association, the following year, organized the conference 'Responsibility for a truly human society' in Mariánské Lázně in Czechoslovakia: the speeches given by Cesare Luperini and Roger Garaudy were then published in *Religioni oggi*,[85] while those by Giulio Girardi, Karl Rahner and Johann Baptist Metz were collected in the volume *Cristiani e marxisti: dialogo per il futuro* ('Christians and Marxists: Dialogue for the future').[86] The journals *Religioni oggi* and *Neuforum Dialog* also promoted a meeting in Vienna in 1968, after which, for a few years, following the Soviet occupation of Prague, the initiatives became less frequent. They resumed with a meeting in October 1975 in Florence – in which, amongst others, Balducci, Gozzini, La Valle and Gruppi took part – on the theme 'The direct evolution of man: A new policy for humanity'. The initiative in this case came from the Paulus-Gesellschaft and the Teilhard de Chardin Association for the Future of Man.[87]

Similar ideas were enlivening the Protestant world in those years, and thus in 1974 the publishing house Jaca Book brought out a book by Friedrich Wilhelm Marquardt on the relationship between theology and socialism in the thought of Karl Barth. The book reconstructed the thought of Barth who, inspired by the religious socialism of Leonhard Ragaz and Hermann Kutter, had based his thinking with regard to God through placing him in strict connection with society and politics. The influence of socialism was evident on Barth's theological ideas, but the interesting thing is that the Protestant intellectual also expressed himself in favour of Marx's thought and employed Marxism to deal with theological arguments.[88]

The dialogue between Marxism and Christianity evolved through journals, and in Italy in particular there were contributions from *Testimonianze, Il tetto* and *Il gallo*, together with the newsletter *Ateismo e cristianesimo* ('Atheism and Christianity') from the Secretariat for Non-Believers. The need for debate between the two cultures also gave rise to periodicals, produced by believers and non-believers, Communists in particular: these included *Religioni oggi*, directed by Alceste Santini, which involved contributions from Lorenzo Bedeschi, Carlo Bo, Corrado Corghi, Giorgio La Pira, Lucio Lombardo Radice, Ambrogio Donini and Giulio Girardi. The journal, which started as a weekly press release in 1964, was transformed into a bimonthly in 1967 and closed in 1969. The journal *Quale società*, also directed by Santini, was published in 1972 and 1973, with the aim of continuing the themes dealt with in *Religioni oggi*, but with more interest in active debate and less in ideological confrontation. The *Rivista internazionale di dialogo*, directed by theologians Karl Rahner and Herbert Vorgrimler, began publication in 1968 as a co-production by the Herder and Morcelliana publishing houses; the Italian edition of the quarterly closed in 1970, the German edition in 1975.[89]

The importance of the development of that period is also testified to by the words of Lombardo Radice who, reflecting on the dialogue between Catholics and Marxists, claimed that it had brought about two main accomplishments: namely that 'Christianity as such does not exclude and does not reject the socialist revolution' and that 'the Marxist science of the proletarian revolution does not entail atheism'. In a letter dated 12 September 1970, sent to Don Carlo Fiore, the director of *Dimensione*, he added: 'I will say at once that Catholic and Christian culture is perhaps further ahead in the study of Marxism than is Marxist culture in the study of Christianity,' and he cited as fundamental the books *Marxismo e cristianesimo* by his esteemed friend Giulio Girardi and *Marxismo e umanesimo* by the director of *Settegiorni*, Ruggero Orfei.[90]

The widespread conviction amongst many believers was therefore that Marxism was not the enemy par excellence but could in fact become a useful instrument of analysis, and that it was necessary to take action in society with determination and, if required, making use of violence. After all, Catholic tradition, contemplating the concept of 'just war', had offered ample food for thought on the legitimacy of the use of force: in the contemporary era in particular, and especially following the analyses of the *Populorum progressio*, a 'just war' was considered to be one that was conducted against the causes of inequality in the world.

Concerned about the debate that was shaking the Catholic world, in May 1971, on the occasion of the 80th anniversary of the *Rerum Novarum*, Pope Paul VI spoke out with regard to the Marxism–Catholicism relationship in the letter *Octogesima adveniens*. His aim was to put a stop to the theoretical and political 'excesses' that had emerged, and he described socialist culture as 'inspired by ideologies incompatible with faith'. The Pope warned against the error of 'accepting elements of Marxist analysis without recognizing its relations with ideology, of entering into the praxes of the class struggle and its Marxist interpretation while neglecting the threat of the type of totalitarian and violent society to which this process leads'.[91] The pontiff's concerns were understandable: the Catholic world was experiencing one of the most radical moments of renewal in its history. However, his exhortations fell on deaf ears, because in the 1970s the need for change was certainly not about to be pacified.

Christians for Socialism

In the post-Council years, following the publication of the documents *Lumen gentium*, *Gaudium et spes* and *Populorum progressio*, Latin American Catholicism was imbued with a new sensibility. The need to work to resolve the problem of social inequality in areas devastated by poverty and underdevelopment had emerged during the second CELAM – the Consejo Episcopal Latinoamericano – conference, held in Medellin, in Colombia, in 1968. It was entitled 'La iglesia en la actual transformación de América Latina a la luz del Vaticano II' ('The Church in the current transformation of Latin America in the light of Vatican II'). It was an event that gave rise to the conviction that the Church could not remain indifferent to the calls for justice, that it should denounce the misery in which many were forced to live. There were three fundamental options for the work of evangelization that came out of that assembly: for the poor, for the *comunità di base* (evangelical Christian communities that did not necessarily follow the dictates of the institutionalized Church) and for integrated liberation – in other words, a liberation both socio-political and spiritual.[92] The final document resulting from the CELAM conference was composed by a group of priests and experts, one of whom in particular stood out in terms of ability and charisma: Father Gustavo Gutiérrez. In that same year, Gutiérrez for the first time used the expression *Teología de la liberación* (Liberation Theology) and called into question the traditional distinction between the profane and sacred spheres, moving towards the conviction of salvation's indivisibility.

It was in this context that the experience of Cristianos por el socialism (Christians for Socialism, CPS) came into being. From 14 to 16 April 1971, eighty priests gathered in Santiago del Chile: they all worked in working-class areas and declared themselves sympathetic to Liberation Theology. On 23 April 1971, twelve professors of theology at Chile Catholic University published a letter expressing their solidarity, and agreement, with the *Declaración de los ochenta*. Three months later, from 16 to 18 July 1971, the first encounter for debate and prayer took place, attended by two-hundred priests: on 1 September the Sacerdotal Secretariat of Christians for Socialism was established.[93] The Chilean CPS set out its programme, which included: a notion of the class struggle as an interpretive element for the Latin American situation and the use of Marxism as an instrument of analysis and social criticism; opposition to the use of Christianity by the dominant classes to justify their social power; and the convergence between the radicality of their faith and the radicality of their political engagement. The first encounter of Latin American Christians for Socialism took place in Santiago from 23 to 30 April 1972. The CPS quickly spread to Europe: in Spain, a group of roughly two-hundred believers, laymen and priests met in Avila and signed a secretly drafted document; a second meeting took place in Burgos in September 1975. Further groups were founded in Portugal (October 1975), France (where they split into several factions), in the USA and in Canada. From 6 to 13 April 1975, Québec City hosted the first CPS international symposium, attended by representatives from Latin America, North America and Europe.[94]

In Italy, in the wake of the long-established 'dialogue' between Christians and Marxists, the CPS experience was particularly relevant for Catholic intellectuals.[95] The foundation of the Christians for Socialism movement took place in Bologna, during a meeting held from 21 to 23 September 1973: it was attended by Christians from the Catholic Left, base communities and evangelical groups as well as by promoters and readers of progressive Catholic journals. Unlike the events in Chile, where the movement had emerged from within the Church itself, in Italy its members were mainly lay people, often members of Catholic associations who were keenly interested in the issues of Vatican II.

During the debate, there appeared to be a general agreement on certain points: the necessity, for Christians, to act within left-wing parties for the 'construction of socialism' without giving up their religious identity; the acceptance of the Marxist analysis of society; the refusal to transform the movement into a religious party, since this would imply the risk of Catholic left-wing integralism; a critical attitude towards the Church, accused of having 'betrayed' the poor and of having therefore become an accomplice and supporter of the 'bourgeois and capitalistic system'.

Giulio Girardi intervened in the debate with a report entitled *I cristiani di oggi di fronte al marxismo* ('Christians today in relation to Marxism'). Already a leading figure during the sixties in the dialogue between Catholics and Marxists, the Salesian priest maintained that the dialogue had, in fact, come to an end: many Christians had made a revolutionary choice, and for them Marxism was no more an alien stance, to be approached with sympathy, but part of their own stance. Girardi further maintained that the 'encounter with Christ' could not solely be limited to the 'spiritual' domain, since it radically transformed the sense of life and history; neither did revolutionary engagement exclusively concern the secular sphere, since it was also a 'globalising project'. Girardi envisaged the possibility of a 'dialectical unity' between Christianity and Marxism, but only if those two systems were able to 'question themselves'.[96]

Rocco Cerrato also addressed the relationship between Christians and Marxists, focusing on the complex structure of Marxism and maintaining that the tradition initiated by Antonio Labriola and Antonio Gramsci – which continued thanks to thinkers such as Lucio Lombardo Radice (who attended the Bologna symposium) – was the highest expression of the movement. Girardi's considerations were in keeping with this line, since he believed that Marxist thought had to revise its notion of religion as a form of alienation and to value its 'subversive virtualities'. Intellectuals such as Ernst Bloch, Leszek Kolakowski, Garaudy and Gramsci who were a point of reference for believers eager to approach Marxist theories, had developed their thought in Engels's wake.[97]

After the Bologna symposium, the CPS movement set roots down in several areas and was involved in the campaign for the referendum on divorce. The national secretariat of Christians for Socialism gathered in Florence on 18 May 1974, a few days after the referendum, and was quick to accuse the movement against divorce for deliberately 'dividing proletarian and popular masses, thus weakening them': the victory of the movement for divorce represented the 'failure of their manoeuvre'.[98]

In Italy, 1977 was characterized by wide-spread social mobilization, which differed from 1968 in terms of the social position of the figures involved. The Settantasettini (the people of '77) supported a radical political project and had a difficult relationship with the PCI, which often led to harsh confrontation. The tense atmosphere eventually also affected the CPS: during the international conference held in Rome from 7 to 9 January 1977, entitled 'Cristiani nella sinistra, militanti nelle lotte di liberazione' ('Christians on the Left, militants in the struggle for liberation'), the dominant positions were the most radical, with their strong aversion for the PCI.

The difference between the Settantasettini and the Christian Left is evident, because while Rodano never wanted to link the liberation process of the oppressed to Church reform, these believers, like the modernists of the early twentieth century, thought that a renewal of society could not be separated from reform that also affected the Church. It is not difficult to understand, therefore, the distrust of the hierarchy towards these Christians and supporters of liberation theology, and the decision to marginalize Girardi. In 1973, the Salesian priest was removed from his teaching position at the Catholic University in Paris and in 1974 from the Istituto Lumen Vitae in Leuven; then, in June 1977, he was expelled from the congregation and could no longer practice as a priest.[99]

The opening up to Marxism and to the world of the Left by many Catholics had already brought about deep unrest and reaction within the Church under the pontificate of Paul VI. However, the real turning point for the Church came with the election of John Paul II and change became evident in January 1979, on the occasion of the Puebla conference. Most liberation theologians, who had emerged as key figures during the Medellín conference, were not allowed to participate. From the very start, Wojtyla voiced his harsh criticism of Marxist thought, mistaken, he believed, in its denial of God. But above all he adopted a persecutory attitude towards liberation movements in Third World countries.[100]

In March 1982, the European movement of Christians for Socialism organized a symposium in Mainz: but by then it had become clear that, with the pontificate of John Paul II and the political disenchantment of the eighties (*riflusso*, 'reflux', as it was called in Italy), it was an experience that was coming to an end. The CPS never formally disbanded: while many of its members returned to a private dimension of faith, others found new ways of voicing their demands for social justice and spiritual renewal (the Noi Siamo Chiesa movement, for example).

5

The Long Seventies

The 'Compromesso storico'

The seventies were characterized by an economic crisis, brought on by international factors, which also had strong repercussions in Italy: after the years of economic boom that had begun after the Second World War, signs of a slowdown began to be visible. From a political point of view, it was a troubled period: after the 1968 crisis involving the government chaired by Aldo Moro, it became clear that it was difficult to return to a centre-left ministerial group. This was the start of a period of political instability and fragile, short-lived governments. Intense social conflict only helped to exacerbate the situation, together with the deployment of what was called the 'strategy of tension'. This began with the Piazza Fontana massacre in December 1969 (orchestrated by members of the extreme right) and continued in 1970 with the attempted coup by former member of the Italian Social Republic Junio Valerio Borghese and the mobilizations organized in Reggio Calabria by members of neo-fascist groups.[1]

Concern about democracy intensified in September 1973 with the coup d'état in Chile.[2] The death of the Chilean president Salvador Allende aroused enormous indignation and anxiety in Italy, where many believed that events in Chile had strong analogies with the Italian situation. In the Latin American country, a left-wing coalition had democratically won an electoral contest in 1970 and was bringing profound change to the country: this led to a coup organized by national right-wing forces and supported by the Americans. What, then, would happen in Italy if, following an election victory, the Communist Party (PCI) and the Socialist Party (PSI) established a government? Would Italy's (extremely active) right-wing circles, and their American allies, permit such a leftward shift in Italian politics, or would they organize a coup d'état?

It was in this context that Enrico Berlinguer, leader of PCI, convinced that the most apocalyptic scenario was also the most likely one, launched a proposal for the 'Compromesso storico' (Historic Compromise). In three articles published in the PCI journal *Rinascita*, Berlinguer drew comparisons between the moderate choice made by Togliatti after the war of liberation, when Italy was a country 'occupied by the armies of the capitalist powers', and the situation in the 1970s: in both cases, a left-wing government was unrealistic because national and international conditions would not allow it.

Berlinguer therefore proposed to abandon the goal of radical transformation and instead put forward the idea of a collaboration with the popular forces inspired by Catholicism, socialism and communism, not unlike that which led to the victory against Nazi fascism.[3]

Only members of the Christian Democrat Left showed a certain interest in the proposal, with Moro the figure who entered into dialogue with Berlinguer the most.[4] In November 1968, Moro had already given a speech to the Democrazia Cristiana (DC) National Council hypothesizing a 'dialectical relationship' with the PCI and a 'challenging debate' with the party that expressed the 'ferment and expectations' of an important part of Italy.[5] After the 1976 general elections, in an article published in the daily newspaper *Il Giorno*, Moro declared that it was necessary to open a dialogue between the large popular parties.[6]

It is clear, however, that while Berlinguer proposed an agreement between the mass parties (DC, PCI and PSI), Moro only thought that it was time for the political legitimation of the PCI.[7] The Christian Democrat statesman was aware that what had taken place in the post-war period in Italy was a warped democracy, paralyzed by ideological contrast, and he thought it was time to assign responsibility to the Communist Party and bestow a legitimacy upon it that would allow it to lead the Italian government.[8]

The debate on divorce and abortion

In 1970, the Italian parliament voted on the law on divorce: it was the final act of a long debate that had been part of the history of the Italian nation since its establishment (1861) and which had gained greater vigour since the end of the fifties.[9] The law was voted in by a parliamentary majority, which did not coincide with the majority that supported the government, composed of secular and left-wing parties, with DC and Italian Social Movement (MSI) deputies voting against. The law was an expression of the new climate that permeated Italian society, pummelled in those years by the challenges of the student movement and the robust participation of factory workers. Everything seemed to be in a state of transformation and even the family itself, that time-honoured bastion of Catholic tradition, was not impregnable to change.

In the months following the parliamentary vote, certain Catholics, spurred on by the pronouncements of Paul VI, mobilized to collect signatures for the repeal of the law on divorce.[10] The most conservative Catholics – in particular the Comunione e Liberazione (CL) movement – declared themselves against the law.[11] The DC, too, invited its members to support the law's repeal.[12] Not all of the Catholic world, however, followed the directions of the Church and the party: the referendum of 1974 represented the litmus test of the changes that had by then established themselves in Catholic spheres, with many believers deciding to uphold the law and take a stand alongside secular and left-wing forces. In February 1974, with the referendum due to take place in May, eighty-eight intellectuals signed an appeal in favour of divorce: these included Don Giovanni Franzoni (the Benedictine abbot of San Lorenzo fuori le Mura in Rome, who, in 1976, would be defrocked for his sympathies with the PCI), the rector of the University of Urbino Carlo Bo, the historian Don Lorenzo Bedeschi, Father David M. Turoldo, Father Camillo De Piaz, Giuseppe Alberigo, Pietro Scoppola and Raniero La Valle. In their appeal, these Catholics made reference to the 'values of civil coexistence and religious freedom, essential in a pluralistic and democratic society'.[13] Scoppola, in a later interview, justified the choice made in 1974: 'the idea of imposing by force of numbers a model of marriage as high as that which derives from Christian tradition seems to me an unacceptable coercion'.[14]

The repeal of the law was opposed by those believers that from Vatican II onwards had adopted a critical stance towards the Church, such as the Cristiani per il socialismo and the Sette novembre group (founded in 1971 with the aim of transforming the Church and taking it back to its original evangelical roots) together with journals such as *Il Regno* of Bologna, *Testimonianze* of Florence, *Idoc* and *Nuovi tempi* of Rome, *Il tetto* of Naples and *Il Foglio* of Turin. The result of the vote (19,138,300 Italians declared themselves in favour of maintaining the law with 13,157,558 against) emphasized that many Christian Democrat voters had not followed their party's instructions and, above all, showed that in Italian society a process was taking place that involved a moving away from the precepts of the Church.[15] The clear majority of Italians in favour of divorce testified to a profound change in mentality and customs, one induced by processes of secularization that had eroded the identity of Catholic culture.[16]

This Italian 'moving away' from the precepts of Catholic morality was even more evident in the case of the debate on abortion. The discussion on this topic began when, at the beginning of the sixties, the effects of a drug – thalidomide – that caused malformations in foetuses emerged, and the hypothesis was raised of the possibility of interrupting pregnancy in such cases.[17] The debate really took off in the seventies as a result of the emergence of the feminist movement and its demand for free choice for women. The PCI did not align itself with the most radical opinions but adopted a position in favour of prevention and decriminalization, avoiding what was considered 'the abortion ideology' of the extremist fringes of the feminist movement.[18] In contrast, the Church took a resolute stand against the law – its reservations made explicit in the document *Aborto e legge di aborto* ('Abortion and the law of abortion') – even though, aside from the official positions, the debate within it was a many-faceted one. The Archbishop of Turin, Cardinal Giovanni Pellegrino, for example, believed that in the face of such an intimate and troubled issue, the Catholic party should leave the matter up to freedom of conscience. The Bishop of Ivrea, Mgr. Luigi Bettazzi, while reaffirming the sacredness of human life wondered what Catholics would do when women were forced to abort in backstreet structures, risking their lives or to go abroad.

The Catholic world was also involved in debating the matter: in January 1973, the Dehonian journal *Il Regno* published an interview by Claudio Zanchettin with the American Dominican father Jacques-Marie Pohier, professor of moral theology and co-director of the 'moral' section of the journal *Concilium*. Father Pohier pointed out that in many civilizations abortion was not considered 'a shameful thing': Aristotle, for example, claimed that the woman who did not accept abortion when the country had reached the maximum number of citizens 'committed a sin against moral justice'. Of course, Pohier did not think that abortion was an 'ideal' solution, but on certain occasions it was a 'less bad and therefore the most moral' choice. Above all, he was convinced that legislation on abortion was necessary and that it should be subordinate to rules on birth control: 'The real solution [...] is limitation of births, not abortion, which should be taken into consideration only when contraceptive methods have proved ineffective or impossible.' Reflecting on therapeutic abortion, Pohier said: 'I do not see what sin there would be against respect for life by eliminating a foetus that, biologically speaking, one knows cannot have a minimum level of human life. On the contrary, it is out of respect for life that it must be eliminated.'[19]

Positions contrary to the Curia's instruction were also taken by Catholics such as La Valle, Balducci and Gozzini: the latter, in particular, was urged to intervene in the matter by his communist friend Lombardo Radice. Thus, in an article that appeared in the Milanese newspaper *Corriere della Sera* on 7 March 1976, he maintained that a law was necessary to regulate the scourge of backstreet abortion; he then pointed out that penal sanctions were not very useful in countering the phenomenon and that most of the abortions in Italy were due to economic and psychological reasons: a good law was therefore necessary, offering the provision of consultants and real support for women who wanted to keep their babies.[20]

The law was passed in the two houses of parliament in 1978, during the very days of the Moro kidnapping, with the votes of the PCI, PSI, Social Democratic Party (PSDI), Republican Party (PRI), Liberal Party (PLI) and the independent Left; it became evident from the final counts that some Christian Democrat parliamentarians had also voted in favour.[21] Approval of the law provoked harsh condemnation from Vatican hierarchies and Catholics who were usually sympathetic towards dialogue with the secular and leftist world, such as Scoppola, also showed their disappointment. Mgr. Bettazzi declared himself in favour of the choice made by parliament and, while reiterating his moral condemnation of abortion, pointed out the useful aspect of the law, which did not leave a woman alone in such a dramatic moment of her existence.[22] Dissenting Catholics and Christian base communities in favour of legislation on the interruption of pregnancy organized a national seminar in Florence on the theme 'Chiesa senza potere e società autogestita' ('A Church without power and a self-managed society') in which they reiterated their solidarity with the women's liberation struggle and condemned Church interference in the public and private sphere.[23]

Events related to the right to terminate pregnancy in Italy had not yet come to an end: the Movimento per la vita (Movement for Life, an association close to Comunione e Liberazione) called for a referendum to limit the right to abortion, which they believed could only be justified if a doctor decided it was necessary in order to save the life of the mother. Radicals, on the other hand, collected signatures for a referendum with the aim of giving greater freedom of choice to women. Gozzini wrote against the referendums in *Testimonianze*, considering it necessary to defend the law and promoting the idea of creating 'Consultori' (public structures arranged for counselling) to spread the practice of contraception throughout the country.[24] Giovanni Franzoni also adopted a position in favour of the law, accusing the Church of having spread the idea of abortion as a kind of plague and of putting pressure on medical and paramedical staff to choose a stance of conscientious objection, something that made the termination of pregnancy difficult in certain parts of Italy.[25] The referendum was held in 1981 with 68 per cent of the votes against repealing the law: further testimony that in Italy customs had changed and few people were willing to renounce the rights that had been acquired.[26]

The years of 'Solidarietà Nazionale'

The era that had seen the DC as the only fulcrum of political equilibrium in Italy came to an end in the mid-seventies: its popular roots, the compactness of the Catholic world and the international panorama had guaranteed it the role of 'obligatory guide' in Italian politics since the post-war period,[27] but the divorce referendum testified that this period had already finished.

The debate on divorce took place at the same time as the growing popularity and upsurge of left-wing parties in the country – something confirmed by the results of the local elections of 15 June 1975, where the PCI was victorious in the country's major cities. The PCI in fact achieved 33.4 per cent of the vote, only two percentage points fewer than the DC. This led the DC to make a change to the leadership of the party: Fanfani was replaced with Benigno Zaccagnini, a figure with a history in the Resistance who enjoyed widespread esteem for his personal integrity and who immediately gave consideration to the appeals coming from Berlinguer's PCI.

The Communist Party's positive results were confirmed in the June 1976 political elections, when Berlinguer's party obtained 7 per cent more of the vote than in 1972, even though it did not succeed in obtaining more votes than the DC. The relevant factor here, however, is that on this occasion certain members of the Catholic intelligentsia – Raniero La Valle, Mario Gozzini, Piero Pratesi, Paolo Brezzi and Angelo Romanò – agreed to run as independent candidates on the PCI list. Gozzini, in a speech delivered at a conference organized by the culture commission of the DC in February 1976, explained his reasons for distancing himself from the party, which he accused of managing power through political patronage and not taking into account the principles expressed by the gospel. The PCI instead had 'exactly what it takes' to be considered a responsible party and capable of taking over the reins of government. It was necessary, therefore, for the collaboration between Christians and Communists that had been interrupted in 1947 to once again become active, as the two political cultures shared 'the rejection of libertarian individualism that distorted the true social dimension of problems'.[28]

The dialogue between Berlinguer and Monsignor Luigi Bettazzi also took place during those months: one of the most radical supporters of Conciliar innovation, Bettazzi had fully accepted the idea of the class struggle which, in his opinion, was a form of 'defence against marginalisation imposed by socially higher categories' and capable of manipulating society.[29] On 6 July 1976, Bettazzi wrote a letter to Berlinguer (published in the diocesan weekly *Il risveglio popolare*) in which, a few days before the elections, he pondered the motivations that had led to the movement of votes towards the Communist Party: 'Many, above all workers, immigrants, the dispossessed, look to you as a hope of renewal, in a society in which they do not find certainty in relation to their work, to their children, to any kind of influence, even the most minimal, with regard to decisions that involve everyone.' And amongst these there were many Christians, many more than in the past, influenced in their choice by 'Christians who were authoritative and publicly committed to remain so' who had decided to stand as independents in the ranks of the PCI.

Berlinguer replied to Bettazzi's letter with an article published in the theoretical journal of the PCI *Rinascita*, in which he laid claim to the party's Marxist patrimony, even though he specified that Marxism was 'understood and used critically as a way of teaching, not accepted and dogmatically read as an immutable text'. Berlinguer considered Marxism a method and a theory for understanding society and recalled Article 2 of the Charter of the PCI which envisaged the possibility for anyone to become a member of the party, regardless of religious faith and philosophical conviction, as long as they accepted its political programme.[30]

The Holy See's daily newspaper *L'Osservatore Romano* also took part in the debate, controversially asking, in a note dated 17 October 1977, for Berlinguer's opinion with regard to Article 5 of the Charter. This spoke of the duty of each party member to 'acquire and deepen [...] their knowledge of Marxism-Leninism', and the paper asked him how this could be reconciled with Article 2 and with the acceptance of religious faith. The Vatican newspaper also reiterated that 'aspects of Marxist theory and practice' appeared 'irreconcilable, or difficult to reconcile, with genuine Christian inspiration', if only for the 'contrast between a practice that privileges a just and responsible freedom as an essential condition of justice and one that has traditionally shown itself ready, in the name of a justice that was often highly partial and questionable, to sacrifice freedom'.[31]

In May 1978, Msgr. Bettazzi, together with Bishop of Livorno Msgr. Alberto Albondi and Auxiliary Bishop of Rome Msgr. Clemente Riva, played an important part in an initiative to try to save the life of Aldo Moro, who had been kidnapped by the Red Brigades (Brigate Rosse, BR): the three prelates intended to offer themselves as hostages in exchange for the politician. This move was, however, blocked by the Vatican Substitute Secretary of State Msgr. Giuseppe Caprio, and Bettazzi's belief was that the Vatican Curia wanted to prevent Moro's release, the Christian Democrat statesman who had dared to enter into dialogue with Berlinguer.[32]

Pope Montini, old and weary though he was – he died just a few months later – was keen to help Moro, his long-standing friend, but came up against a Curia that was hostile to any initiative and determined to support the firm line conveyed by Giulio Andreotti's government. Part of the Catholic world, however, did mobilize and wrote a letter-appeal for negotiation that was published on 18 April 1978, by the extreme Left's daily newspaper *Lotta continua*. In the letter, the Christians appealed to the Brigate Rosse members to respect 'human life' and to the Italian state to agree to a dialogue. Signatories to the appeal included La Valle, Balducci and Turoldo, Giuseppe Alberigo, Domenique Chenu, Jürgen Moltmann, Azione Cattolica president Mario Agnes, Federazione Universitaria Cattolici Italiani president Giuseppe Monni and Domenico Rosati of the Associazione Cattolica Lavoratori Italiani.[33]

The Communist Party, too, expressed themselves to be in favour of the firm line adopted by Andreotti and the Curia, and the former Catholic Communist Antonio Tatò (close to Franco Rodano) clarified the reasons for this position: in his opinion the objective of the BR was to 'block the rise of the PCI in the central organs of the State' because the PCI was 'the only force capable of healing and renewing it'. The PCI had to work to 'move the DC politically, not to prosecute and condemn it' and to apply political pressure so that it would renew itself and make choices consistent with its nature as a party of the people.[34]

Certain foreign chancelleries were not displeased by the murder of Moro at the hands of the BR: there were many in Washington who did not appreciate the hypothesis of a parliamentary majority agreeing to include the Communist Party. Moscow, too, looked on 'Eurocommunism' with hostility, unhappy with the idea that Berlinguer would accept the Western parliamentary and democratic system: the PCI secretary had in fact asserted that the party now had reformist objectives and that he had abandoned those of a revolutionary nature, even while working for the introduction of 'elements of socialism' into national society.[35]

Many mysteries still surround the killing of Moro, and historian Giorgio Galli has pointed out that secret services, the mafia and other shadowy groups have been prominent forces in the history of Republican Italy.[36] One consequence of Moro's assassination was that the PCI, given the democratic emergency, decided to give its support to the Andreotti government. The BR only appeared to emerge victorious from its assault upon the state: their downward spiral began at that very moment and any consensus that they could boast in the country was drastically reduced. However, the organization continued with its terrorist strategy, killing Vittorio Bachelet in 1980, near the Faculty of Political Science in Rome. Bachelet was vice president of the High Council of the Judiciary and an intellectual who was always involved in the modernization of the Azione Cattolica, of which he had been president. On the day of Bachelet's funeral, his son Giovanni read a prayer that, due to its moral and Christian weight, unsettled many members of the BR: 'We also want to pray for those who killed my dad because, without taking anything away from the justice that must be triumphant, there is always forgiveness on our lips and never vendetta, always life and never a plea for the death of others.'[37]

Moro's death triggered a crisis of dialogue between the Catholic and Communist masses. During the XIV Congress of the DC in February 1980, a majority voted for a text that sustained the need to return to the exclusion of the PCI from the sphere of government: something that had to take place not for ideological reasons – Berlinguer had by then led the PCI far from the Soviet orbit – but for political strategy: the PSI was now considered to be a more reliable partner for dialogue. For his part, PSI leader Bettino Craxi agreed to an exclusive relationship with the DC. Thus began a period of competition and conflict between the two left-wing parties, which would only end with the collapse of the so-called 'First Republic' in the early nineties.

The crisis in the politics of collaboration was also fuelled by the intensification of international tension deriving from the Soviet decision to install new missiles in Eastern Europe and the decision of NATO to install Pershing and cruise missiles in Sicily. The mobilization of civil society against the missiles was massive and the demonstration in Rome on 22 October 1981, in addition to the PCI and other left-wing movements, saw the participation of ACLI, Pax Christi, Mani Tese and other Catholic groups. In the following months, peace committees were founded, made up of Catholic and leftist militants, with Fathers Balducci and Turoldo especially involved in the movement.[38]

In the eighties, in Agostino Giovagnoli's view, there began a new phase in the history of the DC, 'characterised by a progressive decline of the party'. One sign of this was in 1981, when the office of prime minister, for the first time in republican history, was given to a non-member of the Christian Democrats, Giovanni Spadolini. It was in this context that, as a moral issue, very different elements such as the Lega democratica (Democratic League, LD) and the Movimento popolare (People's Movement) – founded in 1975 as the political expression of the CL – requested that the party be profoundly transformed and the leadership changed.[39]

The Democratic League

The referendum on divorce clearly revealed the variety of sensibilities that existed within the Catholic world. The political consequences of this were that, in November 1975, a section of the Catholics who had voted for the maintenance of the law on divorce founded the Democratic League in Rome: the main figures in the initiative were a group of intellectuals that included Pietro Scoppola, Achille Ardigò, Luigi Bazoli, Franco Bolgiani, Francesco Traniello, Luigi Pedrazzi and Paolo and Romano Prodi.[40]

The League set itself the goal of establishing a dialogue with Catholics critical of the DC: the intent was not to give rise to a second Catholic party but to operate in the cultural sphere in order to facilitate a process of political change. Some of the members of the League believed that the DC could be reformed as a party and that it was therefore appropriate to operate within it to bring it back to its founding values, which had originated in the experience of the Resistance; others looked beyond the Catholic party and thought that progressive Catholics had to engage in dialogue with the parties of the Left. Ardigò, in particular, proposed that the DC and PCI should carry out common actions in order to correct the most obvious contradictions produced by the 'capitalist system'.[41]

In 1978 the group gave life to the journal *Appunti di cultura e di politica*, directed by Scoppola and focused mainly on political-institutional issues. It took into consideration the political ideas put forward by Moro, even though historians Franco Bolgiani and Paolo Prodi were obliged to indicate the dissent they felt towards what they called too bland a line with regard to the positions of the Christian Democratic Left.

The political and religious perspectives outlined by these believers were not appreciated by the members of Comunione e Liberazione, who accused the members of the League of becoming 'cattocomunisti' (Catholic Communists) and of converting to Marxism. Anchored to traditionalist positions and at a distance from conciliar spirituality, CL members judged that, with totalizing ideologies at an end, space could open up for Christianity to have a new public role, and they refused the idea of a separation between the public sphere and the sphere of faith, between the 'city of man' and the 'city of God'.[42] Members of the League, however, showed themselves to be far from agreement with religious integralism and from the political conservatism of the CL (which was close to Andreotti's way of thinking in the DC).[43]

The clash between the CL and the democratic Catholics was often a harsh one and was mirrored – as had already happened in the sixties – in the opposition between Giuseppe Lazzati, rector of the Catholic University of Milan from 1968 to 1983[44] and 'founding father' of the League, and Don Luigi Giussani, founder of the CL. In 1987, the journalists Antonio Socci and Roberto Fontolan – CL militants – wrote a series of articles in the journal *Il Sabato* in which they attacked the democratic Catholics[45]: they reviled Scoppola and Father Sorge as supporters of Catholic pluralism in the political sphere and for having endorsed the decision of believers who had thought it opportune to present themselves as candidates on the lists of the PCI. But their most vicious attacks were directed against Lazzati, who was even accused of contributing to the Protestant corrosion of Italian Catholicism.[46]

The Democratic League never managed to resolve its ambiguity between political and cultural commitment, splitting up in 1987. But throughout its existence the group helped to form a new Catholic leadership, combining the thought of Sturzo, De Gasperi and Moro with the heritage of Maritain and Dossetti. Above all, while small in numerical terms, the League helped to introduce two intellectuals into Italian politics who would later become prime minister: Romano Prodi and Enrico Letta.

6

The Political System Heads towards Crisis

Volunteers

Between the late seventies and early eighties, the period of collaboration between Catholics and Communists came to a halt, partly due to the arrival in the Vatican, in 1978, of Pope John Paul II.[1] Wojtyla had seen with his own eyes how Catholicism in Poland functioned as the bedrock of national feeling and believed that it should have an analogous role throughout Europe, a continent which, impregnated with the results of Enlightenment thought, had for decades been moving towards the progressive expulsion of God and religion from life and political custom. Unsympathetic to the most innovative tendencies, Wojtyla was a harsh critic of Marxist ideas, which he considered a denial of God, but above all he severely disapproved of the liberation movements in Third World countries. Hence, his condemnation of liberation theology, which believed it was necessary, in order to declare the 'proclamation of Christ', to start from concrete social reality, studied through the instruments offered by Marxist analysis. Opposed to an idea of faith that came from the lowest levels, Wojtyla believed that Catholics were bound to obey the pope, as the successor of Peter, in doctrinal, social and political spheres. This is the context in which to understand the imposition of external management on the Society of Jesus, led from 1965 to 1981 by Father Pedro Arrupe, who was sensitive to the Church's responsibility towards the poor and even willing to engage in dialogue with the world of the Left.

On the other hand, John Paul II showed that in preference to 'political Catholicism' he favoured a new Catholicism committed to social works, one that was active and motivated in terms of reintroducing the values of Catholic tradition and curbing the processes of secularization that were in progress.[2] It was in these years that one of the traditional organizations of the Catholic laity – the Azione Cattolica – found new strength, after the period of crisis of the post-Council era when more radical groups had held sway. In the eighties the Catholic Association of Italian Workers (ACLI) also took on new importance, abandoning the 'intrepid' and left-looking behaviour of the previous decade to assume a more moderate standpoint: and in the 1987 elections Domenico Rosati, who had been president of the association, arrived in the Senate in the ranks of the Democrazia Cristiana (DC).

However, the climate of the times particularly favoured Comunione e Liberazione (CL), which gained important recognition from the new pontiff precisely because it proposed a militant way of understanding faith – putting down roots in the territory and establishing connections with the organs of economic and political power.[3] CL soon threw down the gauntlet against the more progressive fringes of the Catholic world and in particular liberation theology, which was accused of heresy by the theologian Hans Urs von Balthasar in the pages of the CL periodical *Il Sabato*: 'The Church's solidarity with the poor is certainly obvious. To what end do you invent a Christology that, new in terms of detail but false from a general perspective, defines Christ as a political liberator?' Balthasar instead praised the charism of St Francis and declared that it was the duty of the Friars Minor to spread love for the poor; although great care was necessary given that heresy was always lurking, as Gioacchino da Fiore had shown in the Middle Ages when he had attempted to extrapolate 'extreme consequences' from the teachings of St Francis.[4]

This conservative climate has prompted historian Guido Crainz to assert that the eighties, unlike the previous decade, were characterized by the 'denial of collective values', the end of the utopian possibility of transforming the world and a new emphasis in relation to individualism. This was not only true with regard to the Catholic world but, in the wake of what was taking place in other Western countries, to the whole of Italian society: it cannot be forgotten that in 1979 Margaret Thatcher won the elections in Great Britain and the following year Ronald Reagan in the United States. Thus, Crainz points out, in 1980, in the Christian citadel of Assisi, anthropologists, philosophers and theologians discussed the 'new religion of the body', while a few years before the focus had been on 'Christian violence' and liberation theology.[5] Crainz's comments indisputably highlight elements of truth: the eighties were indeed characterized by a reaction to the previous decade's excesses of politicism. Perhaps, however, they do not take into account the complexity of the period: while it is true that the overall climate was conservative and the Polish pope's instructions were very different from the radicality of sentiment in the post-conciliar years, it is equally evident that in the secular and Catholic world a collective ethical tension continued to exist.

Again in 1985, Father Balducci, in the journal *Testimonianze*, wondered what the reason was for the 'clamorous repercussion' of liberation theology on Europe. He identified it in the difficulties of the West, blocked by the 'atomic peril' and the crisis of the two great opposing ideologies, while the only revolutions that could be hypothesized were in Third World countries, and particularly in Latin America. Balducci claimed that the Peace Movement, which had developed in Europe following the installation of Pershing and cruise missiles, represented 'the Western analogue to Liberation theology', because it had the same objectives and combined the struggle for peace with the fight against imperialism: to fight for disarmament meant to fight against capitalism, 'given the natural close connection between the project of seeking security in arms, and capitalism'.[6]

Balducci was referring to the new mobilization for peace that swept through European society in the early 1980s in response to Ronald Reagan's decision to invest heavily in the arms sector. In 1984, during an assembly held in Ariccia, not far from Rome, the Coordinamento nazionale dei comitati per la pace (National Coordination For Peace Committees) was founded, with the aim of organizing the movement and launching the proposal for a popular initiative against nuclear weapons. Catholics played an important role in the struggle for peace, because they succeeded in mobilizing a generation of young people in relation to the subject of non-violence; and it was a struggle that became common ground for a new understanding with the forces of the Left.

Two figures who were particularly active in this battle were Father Eugenio Melandri, a candidate in 1989 for the European Parliament in the ranks of the far-left party Democrazia Proletaria (Proletarian Democracy, DP), and Father Alex Zanotelli, director of the monthly journal of the Comboni Missionaries *Nigrizia* (a post he left in 1987 under pressure from ecclesiastical leaders).[7] The Pax Christi was also committed to the struggle for peace: this was an official Christian movement that had organized protests against conflict in the world since the late 1960s. In the document drawn up on the occasion of the march of 31 March 1987 – which was also signed by Aldo De Matteo of the ACLI, Graziano Zoli of Mani tese and Father Eugenio Melandri of the journal of the Xaverian missionaries *Missione oggi* – Pax Christi affirmed that Jesus was 'the true peace' and that for true peace to be realized in the world Christians had a duty to work for it. In particular, the document challenged the increase in funds for the Ministry of Defence, given that expenditure on armaments contradicted the principles of the Constitution that repudiate war. Pax Christi also called for a law that would ban the arms trade.[8]

In the eighties, with the emphasis on political commitment set aside, the phenomenon of volunteer work took hold.[9] This concentrated on four areas: social marginalization, the Third World, peace and the environment.[10] Non-governmental organizations (NGOs), many of them Catholic, produced the most interesting examples of solidarity: the Federazione Organismi Cristiani Servizio Internazionale Volontario (Federation of Christian International Voluntary Service Organisations, FOCSIV), an association founded in 1970, worked to coordinate Catholics who provided assistance in the Southern Hemisphere. Many of these NGOs were based in the Veneto region, a traditionally Catholic area: the motherhouse of the Comboni Fathers, always keen to address the problems of Africa, was in Verona. The Veneto area also produced the association Beati i costruttori di pace (Blessed are the peace-makers): in November 1985, the group, made up of priests, launched an appeal that gathered broad support throughout the national clergy. This, referring to the words of *Gaudium et Spes*, condemned 'the inhumanity of war' and highlighted the enormous inequalities and injustices that were common around the world, such as the fact that 'a child in a rich country consumed 500 times more in material resources than a Third World child'. To overcome these disparities it was necessary to invest resources not in armaments but in the development of the poorest areas. One of the group's documents read: 'It is time that the problem of peace, connected with that of underdevelopment, becomes a central element in the life of our communities, in catechesis and in the commitment of associations, groups and movements. We are in a state of sin and conversion is therefore essential.'[11] The group also organized important and well-attended meetings at the Verona Arena in October 1986 and May 1987.

In the post-Council years, groups were also formed dedicated to helping the poorest and marginalized in Western societies, such as the Associazione Giovanni XXIII in Rimini, the Comunità di Capodarco in Fermo and the gruppo Abele in Turin, founded by Don Luigi Ciotti.[12] The experience of the Comunità di sant'Egidio provides a good example: created in Rome in 1968 by a group of Catholics around the central figure of Andrea Riccardi in the Sant'Egidio parish of Trastevere, it was recognized as a public association of the Church by the Pontifical Council of the Laity in 1986. The community assisted, and still assists, the poor in the Roman suburbs; it was also, however, involved in trying to find solutions to conflicts in various areas around the world. In October 1992, after more than two years of negotiations, a treaty was finally signed in Rome between the Mozambique government and guerrilla forces: an occasion when Riccardi, together with Msgr. Matteo Zuppi, archbishop of Beira

Gonçalvez, and former Foreign Undersecretary Mario Raffaelli, representing the Italian government, were amongst the mediators. The community has also been involved in ecumenical and interreligious dialogue and has been visited by religious patriarchs such as the Syriac Orthodox Zhakka I Ywas and Ethiopian Orthodox Abune Paulos. In 1992, Riccardi also coordinated the debate with the president of the Muslim World League, Adbullah Omar Nasseef.[13]

The Comunità di San Benedetto in Porto di Genova, meanwhile, founded in the seventies by Don Andrea Gallo, took care of the 'last' in society – the homeless, the prostitutes and the drug addicts. Don Gallo was a Salesian who, while remaining within the Church, often came into conflict with the positions expressed by Church hierarchies on issues such as female priesthood, drug liberalization and abortion. In the field of volunteer work, Caritas played an important role: founded in 1971 as a 'pastoral organism' of the ecclesial community with the task of 'promoting charity', with its roots in the social fabric of the parishes, Caritas has worked to support the movement of conscientious objectors and, in recent years, the reception of refugees and immigrants.

The Gruppo Abele, Caritas, the Comunità di Sant'Egidio and the Comunità di San Benedetto al Porto enjoyed a relationship of fidelity with the Church hierarchy and expressed not only an intensification of religiosity amongst believers but also a transformation of the way of conceiving this religiosity: in fact, they represented a spur to the Vatican so that, following the solicitations that had emerged from the Council, it would stand up more decisively in support of the marginalized.

In the eighties, following the arrest of the majority of those involved in the period of terrorism – known as the *anni di piombo*, the 'years of lead', in Italy – there were many religious figures who decided to visit the prisons and talk about the 'dignity of the people': these figures included Monsignor Antonio Riboldi, Don Salvatore Bussu, chaplain of the special prison in Nuoro, Fathers Turoldo and De Piaz, Don Ciotti and the former priest Mario Cuminetti. At the Badia Fiesolana, an old monastery near Florence, Father Balducci received relatives of imprisoned terrorists and maintained contacts with the militants of the Red Brigades and other terrorist groups. His conviction was that it would not be possible to recover from the anni di piombo if no attempt was made to understand why many young people had been attracted by radical ideas. His opinion with regard to the Italian political class, on the other hand, was a harsh one: 'While we held close around the state under the threat of terrorism, there were those who were representatives of the state who butchered all that was lawful by replacing legality with a mafia-like distribution of power.'[14]

The problem of prison life and of a 'human' response to those who had chosen the path of political violence was very much present in Catholic culture. In September 1983, one group of terrorists, incarcerated in the Le Vallette prison in Turin, contacted the Jesuit Alfonso Bachelet, brother of Vittorio, and asked for a meeting. Father Bachelet accepted the invitation and after the encounter questioned if this form of detention, as organized in Italy, was the only way of dealing with the evil that had been carried out.[15] The Cardinal of Milan, Carlo Maria Martini, also insisted repeatedly on the need to safeguard human dignity and, similarly, Alfredo Carlo Moro, brother of Aldo, sided with a judicial system that took the rights of prisoners into account. Encouraged by these promptings, in 1986 Mario Gozzini drew up a law which bore his name and which set itself the objective of implementing Article 27 of the Constitution. This stated that a sentence should have as its purpose the re-education of the condemned; prisoners were thus granted 'reward' permits, those sentenced to less than three years of imprisonment were placed in rehabilitation programmes through social services, and home detention and other benefits were granted to pregnant women, the seriously ill, the elderly and young people under the age of 21.

This new sensibility that was spreading through society, and which found expression in associationism and voluntary work, was able to transform itself into concrete initiatives thanks to civil service, which presented a possibility to those who, whether lay or Catholic, chose conscientious objection over military service. The question had already been raised in 1962 by the first Catholic objector, the Milanese Giuseppe Gozzini, who, when called upon to do his military service, refused to wear a uniform. Arrested and imprisoned, he was defended by Father Balducci who, for one of his articles that appeared in the journal *La Nazione* in support of the pacifist cause, was sentenced to eight months imprisonment by the Court of Appeal on 15 October 1963, and confirmed the following year in Cassation.[16] In 1966, Don Milani came into conflict with a group of Tuscan military chaplains who had defined conscientious objection as extraneous to the Christian commandment of love and an expression of cowardice. In this case, the episode also had judicial repercussions and Milani was tried for the defence of a criminal act; acquitted at first instance in February 1966, he was then convicted by the Court of Appeal in June 1967, by which time, however, he had died. Following the debate aroused by these sentences and the contemporary social climate in Italy, on 12 December 1972 civil service was introduced into the Italian legal system, proposed by the left-wing DC senator, Giovanni Marcora. The law made it possible for many young people, holding anti-military views – both Catholics and those with leftist ideas – not to carry out the duty of military service and instead to dedicate their commitment to voluntary associations.

The stigmatization of violence *tout court* was not, however, accepted by everyone in the Catholic world: those who worked in Third World areas, where the tragedy of the conditions of society's lowest members was evident, in the wake of Camilo Torres, *Populorum progressio* and the ideas of liberation theology, believed that it was not only possible but indeed necessary to offer forceful opposition to anti-democratic and repressive regimes. These were the years, moreover, when in Nicaragua, after the revolution that had brought the Sandinista National Liberation Front to power in 1979, certain priests and lay people who had taken part in the fight against the dictatorship decided to participate in the Sandinista government (these included Miguel d'Escoto Brockmann and Ernesto Cardenal).[17] John Paul II could hardly look kindly on believers of this kind and, during his visit to Nicaragua in February 1983, he was harshly critical of those members of the Catholic Church who played a part in the Sandinista government.

However, many young people involved in Catholic associations were influenced by the Nicaraguan situation, and certain Italian religious figures were quick to declare their position in relation to the Sandinista experience: the Franciscan Bernardino Formiconi dedicated his book *Nicaragua* 'to the commanders of the revolution on whose shoulders lies the heavy responsibility of being the paladins of a new hope'.[18] Giulio Girardi, who had travelled to the Central American country for the first time in 1980 – and who would return there numerous times and for long periods – was keen to have a full understanding of those revolutionary events, and in 1986 he published the book *Sandinismo, Marxismo, cristianisimo*, published first in Spanish and subsequently translated into Italian.[19] The book, which came out twenty years after *Marxismo e cristianesimo*, expressed not only the ideas of the Council but also those of the theological renewal introduced by liberation theology and in fact represented 'a document of that research'. If *Cristianesimo e marxismo*, explained Girardi, had explored the 'more intellectual than political' relationship of European Christians with revolution, *Sandinismo, Marxismo e cristianesimo* evoked 'the experience of a true revolution, realised with the participation of Christians'.[20]

CL's aversion to pacifist and Third-Worldist movements and to the 'progressive' Catholicism of the 1980s in general was radical, as the polemical words of the philosopher Augusto Del Noce, the movement's ideologist, demonstrate:

> What is asked of Catholics today, if not the reduction of Christianity to a morality, in itself separate from all metaphysics and from all theology, capable in its autonomy and in its self-sufficiency to achieve universality and found a just society? Indeed, this morality would even be capable of putting an end to the centuries-old division between the East and the West, as in fact is being attempted. This universal morality is tolerant: it admits that someone – the Catholic, in fact – can add an otherworldly hope, specifically religious in a transcendent sense; and he feels energised in explicating his practical, human action; this, for humanitarians, is what it means to be Catholic.[21]

The clash between these different faces of Catholicism persisted for many years. Scoppola, having attempted a 'dialogue' by organizing meetings between Catholic exponents of different sensibilities, at the beginning of the new millennium came to the conclusion with regard to the CL:

> I do not trust in the possibilities of a collaboration; I am, rather, convinced that we must let the contradictions already present in their work explode, for example with regard to the use of financial means, which is part of the worst Catholic pragmatism, or, I should say, of the worst clericalism: everything is holy if it serves a holy purpose![22]

It was not only the Catholic world that was smitten with doubt in the eighties, arousing a reconsideration of convictions rooted in the sixties and seventies: the communist culture, too, involved in the crisis of Soviet model and Marxist doctrine, experienced a similar phenomenon. In April 1988, the Marxist economist Claudio Napoleoni, a few months before his death, wrote a letter to Adriano Ossicini in which he raised the question of whether philosophy was sufficient to find a solution to the problems of man, or should it be concluded that salvation could only come from God. Napoleoni's doubts were inspired by the dissolution of all revolutionary projects 'in the sense of the scientific and revolutionary critique of capitalism': the revolutionary role of the working class had come to nothing, as had the certainty that the capitalist system was destined to meet with a general crisis. He observed that the widespread conviction was that Marxism had failed 'as a theory of crisis and as a theory of revolution', while capitalism, opulent and technocratic, seemed to be headed towards a glorious future.[23] Napoleoni argued that it was necessary to go back to the figure of Jesus, in the belief that religion could no longer be conceived, as in a certain secular and liberal tradition, only as a private matter but that it also had a duty with respect to the problems of contemporary society.[24] It is clear that the eighties was a period when the certainties of the past were called into question and the search was launched for new cultural horizons. While all this swept through the world of culture, new challenges also appeared in the sphere of politics.

The Craxi years

After the turning point of the DC's 16th Congress in 1980, the long period of 'pentapartito' (five-party coalition) began in Italy, with governments supported by the DC, the PSI, the Republican Party, the Liberal Party and the Social Democratic Party. The Communist Party was in opposition, even though since 1982 – when Ciriaco De Mita became secretary of the DC – cautious approaches to Berlinguer's party had occurred. In order to curb the ambitions of Craxi's Socialist Party, De Mita decided to entrust the direction of the DC's daily newspaper *Il Popolo* to Giovanni Galloni, from the party's Left. In his editorials, Galloni went back to Moro's line on domestic and international policy and did not shut out the possibility of dialogue with the PCI.[25]

After the June 1983 elections, in which the DC obtained only 32.9 per cent of the vote, the worst result in its history, the party was forced to hand over the helm of government to Bettino Craxi, who went on to become one of the leading political figures of the eighties. Prime minister from 1983 to 1987, Craxi decided to tackle the question of the revision of the Concordat – something that had been under discussion for about ten years – entrusting it to men he had faith in, including Professor Francesco Margiotta Broglio and Gennaro Acquaviva, a member of ACLI who had joined the PSI in 1972.[26] The Costituzione, in force since 1948, had incorporated the Lateran Pacts, which had been signed by Cardinal Gasparri and Mussolini in February 1929 and which recognized the Catholic religion as the religion of the state. But times had changed, society had become secularized and the needs of non-Catholic believers had emerged. This gave rise to Craxi's decision to sign a new Concordat with Cardinal Agostino Casaroli on 18 February 1984 and establish agreements with other religious denominations.[27]

This led to the abolition of the obligation of teaching the Catholic religion in public schools and the direct economic support of priests, who had been paid completely at the expense of the state since 1929. With the revision of the Concordat, a new system of financing religious communities was introduced: each taxpayer could devolve a percentage of his taxes (8 per 1,000) in favour of a religious body recognized by the Italian state (Catholic Church, Waldensian Church, Union of Jewish Communities, Lutheran Church, etc.).

The redefinition of the Concordat prompted discussion within the Socialist Party, where some, in the name of the secular state, believed that no agreement should be signed. Controversy also arose because, as Acquaviva admits, the negotiations were carried out by an elite within the Church and in particular by the group of the Secretariat of State, which excluded the involvement of other figures from the variegated Catholic world.[28] Many believers thus displayed perplexity towards the initiative, with opposition coming especially from those who in the sixties and seventies had declared themselves to be in favour of the abrogation of the agreements between the Italian State and the Holy See. The Florentine journal *Testimonianze*, amongst others, questioned the very idea of the agreement and wondered if it was not enough for the Church 'to have the guarantee of being able to proclaim the Gospel message freely': believers had to share 'their social and political commitment with all people of good will'.[29] A group of Catholics – including Ernesto Balducci, Piero Barbaini, Vittorio Bellavite, Pasquale Colella, Mario Cuminetti, Camillo De Piaz and Enzo Mazzi – issued a document stating that 'an evangelically inspired Church' and a secular state could not allow a 'Constantinian residue' in the legal system, and deprecated the very idea of drawing up the Concordat.[30] At the time of the vote in parliament, the DC, PSI and PCI voted in favour, while the group of the independent Left was divided: while Gozzini voted in favour of the law, La Valle voted against.

On the question of the revision of the Concordat, the PCI and PSI voted in unison. In general, however, relations between the two left-wing parties in this period were not easy; relations were also very cool between Berlinguer and Craxi themselves. Only in 1983, after four years of difficult dealings, did the two leaders officially meet with delegations from the respective parties. The gap between the two left-wing organizations widened in the middle of the decade on the occasion of the 'scala mobile' (escalator) mechanism. Introduced in 1975, the scala mobile provided for the automatic adjustment of wages to the cost of living. Applied in a period of high inflation, the mechanism had however created a spiral that was not a positive one: increase in inflation caused an increase in wages, and then increase in wages provoked inflation.

Prime Minister Craxi, with the support of the DC, decided to intervene and, in February 1984, called a halt to the mechanism. The PCI launched a battle against the socialist leader's decision and on 24 March 1984, together with the communist union CGIL, organized an event in Rome that saw the participation of 700,000 workers. The PCI also decided to support the referendum for the abolition of the law voted by parliament, but the result was a defeat for the Communists, with 54.3 per cent of voters in favour of the law Craxi wanted. In June, Berlinguer, during a meeting to do with the European elections, fell victim to an intracranial hemorrhage and died within a few hours. The response to his death was a hugely emotional one throughout the country, and the images of Berlinguer, despite the stroke, attempting to conclude his speech, aroused great human sympathy for the communist leader. The reaction provoked by this tragedy had repercussions of a political nature, with many people voting for the dead leader's party: thus, for the first time in Italian history, the PCI actually managed to overtake the DC, if only by a handful of votes (33.76 per cent for the PCI against 33.49 per cent for the DC). Alessandro Natta followed Berlinguer as party secretary, chosen in order to provide a sense of continuity with the previous leadership.

The eighties were also characterized by the emergence of the so-called 'moral question', a subject forcefully raised by the PCI which had already, under Berlinguer, stigmatized the high levels of corruption in the Italian political and business system. Embezzlement and waste were present throughout the country but had above all become a dramatic problem in certain southern regions. The infiltration of organized crime in Sicily, Campania and Calabria did, in fact, pose a serious threat to the democratic fabric of the country.

Prominent Christian Democrat figures in Sicily in the post-war era included Salvo Lima, elected mayor of Palermo in 1958 (holding the post until 1966), and Vito Cincimino, the municipality's councillor for public works. During Lima's term of office as mayor, 4,000 building permits were issued, most of them assigned to 'front men' in collusion with the Mafia: this was the so-called 'sacco di Palermo' (sack of Palermo), which radically altered entire neighbourhoods of the city. In 1968, Lima was elected to the Chamber of Deputies, moving closer within the DC to the sphere of Giulio Andreotti, who nominated him several times to the position of government undersecretary.

Then, in October 1970, Ciancimino was elected mayor of Palermo, only to be forced to resign in December because of the inquiries of the Anti-Mafia Commission. In 1976, he entered into a collaborative pact with the Andreotti bloc, giving the latter the support of the Ciancimino group at the DC's national conferences held in 1980 and 1983.

Throughout the post-war period the pressure inflicted by organized crime on Sicilian society was a particularly onerous one, and in the eighties political leverage was joined by a strategy of violent conflict with the state and its representatives.

On 6 January 1980, the Mafia killed Piersanti Mattarella, president of the Sicilian region, for his commitment to the revival of the DC on the island; on 30 April 1982, Pio La Torre, the secretary of the regional PCI, was murdered; on 3 September of the same year, the Prefect of Palermo, Carlo Alberto Dalla Chiesa, was assassinated, together with his wife Emanuela Setti Carraro. The murder of Dalla Chiesa by the Mafia, under the hegemony of Totó Riina,[31] was designed to strike at the very heart of the state and demonstrate the criminal organization's 'influence over the material structure of national power'.[32] On 29 July 1983, a car bomb killed the judge Rocco Chinnici, head of the Palermo Examining Office. As a result of this episode Antonino Caponnetto, a magistrate of Sicilian origins who had lived in Tuscany for years, decided to return to his homeland with the aim of establishing an anti-Mafia pool.[33] Together with Giovanni Falcone, Paolo Borsellino, Giuseppe Di Lello and Leonardo Guarnotta, Caponnetto began a wide-ranging work of sifting and collecting documentation on organized crime, managing to produce cracks in the wall of Mafia *omertà*.[34] This work led in 1984 to the confessions of informers Tommaso Buscetta and Totuccio Contorno,[35] and brought about the sentence of condemnation for the 'Cosa Nostra' at the first maxi-trial, issued on 16 December 1987, by the Palermo Court of Assizes.[36]

Civil society was mobilized to look beyond the traditional parties due to corruption, collusion between the Mafia and political power, and parties unable to transform and revitalize themselves. Many citizens were keen to find new forms of political aggregation, through the rediscovery of the cultural aspect, individual commitment and dedication to voluntary work. In the Sicily of Salvo Lima and Vito Ciancimino, various anti-Mafia initiatives thus came into being: in September 1985, in an assembly of committees against the Mafia, the Centro Studi Peppino Impastato (which took its name from a left-wing activist killed by the Mafia in 1978) launched the idea of establishing a place for community life and social gatherings. The following year the Anti-Mafia Coordination was born, at first it was ancillary to the PCI but progressively it became more and more autonomous.[37] In the same period, in the Catholic sphere, groups arose such as the Centro ricerca (founded by Giuseppe Lumia, a member of Azione Cattolica) and Città per l'uomo (a movement connected to the Jesuits Bartolomeo Sorge and Ennio Pintacuda) with the aim of organizing meetings in Palermo schools in order to raise awareness with regard to the problem of the Mafia.[38] In 1986, Father Bartolomeo Sorge (director of the journal *La Civiltà Cattolica* from 1973 to 1985) founded the Istituto di Formazione politica Pedro Arrupe (Pedro Arrupe Institute of Political Education) in Palermo.[39] Father Sorge specified that his educational project had no wish to have any connections with a particular party:

it was open to anyone who wanted to prepare 'to experience politics in a spirit of service and with true professionalism and, because of this, wanted to understand the Christian vision of life and the social teaching of the Church'.[40] Father Sorge, in his introduction to Ennio Pintacuda's book *Breve corso di politica* ('A short course in politics') – which published the lessons given by the Jesuit writer at the *Istituto Pedro Arrupe* – argued that the problem of Italy was the sickness of its politics and the fact that parties, rather than 'mediate', had invaded society and the state. What was required, in his opinion, was the move from ideological conflict to the idea that for the good of the country the programme should have 'the upper hand over the taking of sides'. Sorge also thought that a renewal was necessary in the world of politics in order to resolve the 'moral question': this, he believed, was possible thanks to the emergence of numerous collective groups, such as the environmental, peace and disarmament movements.[41] It was in this context that the first attempts were made to bring renewal to Sicilian politics: the first 'anomalous council' (partly DC and partly PCI in composition) was realized in Prizzi in 1986. Shortly after this, the mayor of Chiusa Sclafani, Salvatore Pollichino, also decided to establish an administration whose main figures represented the 'healthiest' sectors of the town.[42]

The 'Palermo spring'

In the second half of the eighties, Sicily became an important political laboratory: despite the immobility of the national political panorama, the island was buzzing with a number of projects. The turning point came when, on 15 July 1985, the Christian Democrat Leoluca Orlando became mayor of Palermo, supported by a five-party alliance (DC, PSI, the Republic Party, the Liberal Party and the Social Democratic Party).

Orlando came from an eminent and noble Sicilian family, had had legal training and had worked together with Piersanti Mattarella.[43] The innovative aspect of the new administration stemmed from the fact that Orlando was the first mayor of the Sicilian capital to speak out openly with regard to the Mafia problem. On 3 September 1985, during a torchlight procession in Palermo to mark the third anniversary of the killing of General Dalla Chiesa, he was keen to meet the General's children, Nando and Rita. Then, on 10 February 1986, as the maxi-trial launched by Giovanni Falcone and Paolo Borsellino[44] began, Orlando decided to bring a civil action on behalf of the municipality. Because of this commitment Orlando was forced to live under permanent escort.[45]

However, the national political context was soon to have an influence on politics in Palermo. The latent tensions between the DC and the PSI, brought on by the increasingly central role played by Craxi in Italian political life, in March 1987 led to crisis in the five-party coalition and the call for new parliamentary elections, even though its term had not yet concluded. In the election, held on 14 and 15 June 1987, the DC obtained an increase in consensus with respect to the 1983 general elections (from 32.93 per cent in 1983 to 34.31 per cent in 1987). Craxi's party increased its vote amongst Italian citizens (14.27 per cent), while the PCI saw its results diminish (26.57 per cent). Pondering the electoral outcome, Raniero La Valle was of the opinion that the decline in consensus for the PCI confirmed that the party was no longer able to interpret the need for renewal emanating from Italian society. It was necessary, he believed, for the PCI, representing as it did 'such a great heritage of history, strength and forward movement', to find a new 'driving force' and to specify new goals.[46] Scoppola, for his part, judged the increase in consensus for the DC and PSI as the willingness of the electorate to take a position with regard to one of the two main figures in the debate and added: 'The two-party system has placed itself within the old area of the majority, and it is all within the five-party coalition.'[47]

After the elections, the conflict between the DC and the PSI became more intense. De Mita was insistent in proposing an electoral reform that demanded an explicit declaration of government alliance before the elections; the Christian Democrat secretary clarified that his project was 'that of a government pact, which must be signed before the voting takes place by parties with a common strategy and similar ideas for tackling the problems of the country'.[48] Craxi instead claimed the right to have a 'free hand' in the matter and to choose alliances after the poll result. He also showed concern in relation to the ongoing confrontation between De Mita and the PCI with regard to institutional reforms: he opposed the assignment of the position of prime minister to De Mita, and this, unexpectedly, brought the young Christian Democrat Giovanni Goria to the head of the government.[49]

As a consequence of the intricate national situation, strong disagreements also arose between Christian Democrats and Socialists in the municipality of Palermo, which brought an end to the administration's experience of being run by the five-party coalition. Sergio Mattarella (DC provincial commissioner until July 1988), after noting the impossibility of setting up a council that included the Socialists, endorsed Orlando's idea[50] for following a new path. This involved establishing the 'anomalous council of Palermo' on 15 August 1987, with a majority consisting of the DC, the independent Left, the Green Party, the Social

Democrats and the Catholic Città per l'Uomo civic list. Orlando left the Socialists, Liberals and Republicans in opposition and tried to marginalize the most conservative currents of the DC, linked to the figures of Lima and Ciancimino.[51] In April 1989,[52] Orlando was keen to extend the majority to include the PCI: 'This is not a historical compromise,' he specified, as his political opponents began to hatch plots in order to make life difficult for him.[53] On paper there were fifty-two councillors who were supposed to be on Orlando's side but in the secret vote only forty-one voted in favour of the new Orlando council. Had it not been for the unexpected vote of the member of Democrazia Proletaria, Alberto Mangano, the municipal government would not, thanks to the backstabbers that lurked in its ranks, have had a majority.[54]

During Orlando's mandate, the decision was made to redevelop the most degraded areas of the city (with the help of architects such as Pier Luigi Cervellati, Italo Insolera and Leonardo Benevolo), to ensure transparency in public contracts and tenders, and to curb the deep-rooted system of criminality that impinged upon the life of Palermo's citizens. The council's commitment to combatting the Mafia aroused perplexity in some sectors of the city, with the newspaper *Giornale di Sicilia* accusing Orlando of conveying the idea that Palermo was nothing but Mafia and thus discouraging investment in the city.

The famous Sicilian writer Leonardo Sciascia also took a fierce line in opposition, not only to the mayor but also to the magistrates most involved in the anti-Mafia investigations. On 10 January 1987, he published a long article in the newspaper *Corriere della Sera* in which he accused Orlando of excessive exhibitionism and the magistrate Paolo Borsellino of making use of anti-Mafia activity in order to further his career. Sciascia called them 'anti-mafia professionals', 'people dedicating themselves to a heroism that costs nothing'. His accusations against the mayor were extremely harsh:

> Take, for example, a mayor who, whether by sentiment or calculation, begins to exhibit himself – in interviews on television and in schools, at conventions, in conferences and in processions – as anti-mafia: even if he dedicates all his time to these performances and never finds a moment to deal with the problems of the city he administers, he is sitting pretty. From there within, in the city council or in his party, who would ever dare to propose a vote of no confidence.[55]

Palermo's 'anomalous council' came to an end due to the transformation of the national political balance: between 1989 and 1990, the struggle in the DC involving De Mita in opposition to Andreotti and Forlani, which was essentially based around a dispute over the relationship with Craxi's PSI, reached a conclusion.[56] De Mita, who was relegated to a minority in the party, lost the premiership, the control of RAI TV and the presidency of the Istituto per la Ricostruzione Industriale (Institute for Industrial Reconstruction, IRI), which was taken away from Romano Prodi.[57] In the spring, on the occasion of the elections for the municipal administration of Palermo, Orlando was a candidate and obtained a virtual unanimity of preference, with 71,000 votes: he was, nevertheless, not appointed mayor of the city.[58] Sorge unhesitatingly passed severe judgment on the managerial class that had decided to marginalize Orlando: 'It is impossible to understand why the leaders of this DC should want to break off a flowering branch; why on earth the only Christian Democrat mayor who has been at the helm of a great city has been sacrificed to calculations of power that lack all sense of idealism.'[59] Thus, in November 1990, Orlando decided to abandon the DC and to create another political project, the Rete.

A second Catholic party?

Starting with Vatican II, which introduced religious and ethical pluralism into the Catholic world,[60] the debate regarding Catholic political unity involved an ever-growing number of believers.[61] Two options were identified by 'progressive' Catholics as alternatives to voting for the DC: either diverting votes to parties on the Left or founding a second Catholic party. The first idea was attempted during the political elections of 1968, and provided for the possibility that some believers would present themselves as independents on the PCI lists. The plan was not a successful one but was dusted off and activated on the occasion of the 1976 vote – giving rise to the independent Left group in parliament. The foundation of a left-wing Catholic party was instead realized in 1972 when Livio Labor, president of the ACLI, created the Movimento politico dei lavoratori (Workers' Political Movement, MPL). The MPL were not particularly successful in the political elections held that year and the project quickly faded away.

As we have seen, certain elements within the Democratic League who were critical of the DC also hypothesized new political perspectives: it was an issue that came strongly to the fore in the eighties after the murder of Piersanti Mattarella. Scepticism regarding the possibility of transforming the DC was rife in various Catholic circles, especially because of the blatant collusion between organized crime and the Christian Democratic political system in certain areas of the country. It was in this context in 1980 that the Città per l'Uomo association was founded in Palermo. Inspired by the Jesuit fathers Ennio Pintacuda and

Francesco Paolo Rizzo, it was composed of Christians engaged in civil society, in volunteer work and in trade unions, and was profoundly rooted in the city's various neighbourhoods. The members of the association were critical of the DC, which was viewed as the fulcrum of the region's political-Mafia power, and keen to find new ways to realize their hopes for political transformation.[62]

The need for change did not concern only southern areas. In Milan, in 1985, the Catholic association Città dell'uomo was founded by Giuseppe Lazzati, with the aim of working for the revival and diffusion of a new political culture focused on the individual and democracy.[63] In the very Catholic Trentino, the Rosa Bianca group was created, which took its name, 'White Rose', and inspiration from the Die Weiße Rose group of anti-Nazi students who had stood up to Hitler's regime. The first official meeting of Rosa Bianca occurred in the summer of 1979 at the community of the Comboni Fathers in Limone del Garda, bringing together young people from scouting, the Italian Catholic University Association (FUCI), the AC and volunteer work; many of them gravitating into the orbit of the Democratic League. From 1981, the Rosa Bianca promoted schools of political education to which representatives from the political and religious worlds were invited.[64]

In 1989, in the journal *Il margine*, Michele Nicoletti, one of the leaders of the Rosa Bianca, expressed the 'profound unease' that had developed in the Catholic world in relation to the political world, especially with regard to the Christian Democrats. Nicoletti thought it was necessary to bring to a close the era in which parties had a monopoly on political development and action: it was instead an opportune moment for the social forces that had democratic Catholicism at heart to reappropriate the political initiative and evolve projects dealing with social and economic policies and the fight against corruption and the Mafia.[65] He also stressed the importance of the changes taking place in the West: with the fall of the Berlin Wall the 'ideological smoke screen that had served to justify party occupation of society' had disappeared, and this made misgovernment and corruption even more intolerable.[66]

International upheavals had major repercussions on Italian politics, stimulating a debate on the party system, on the function of parties and on future prospects. In 1990, the review *Micromega* started a discussion on the topic 'How many parties for Catholics?', inviting ideas from the figures most committed to cultural debate in those years. Pietro Scoppola, after noting that there no longer existed any of the conditions that had made Catholic political unity justifiable, urged immediate intervention, including those of an institutional kind, aimed at 'creating the conditions for a physiological shift and a transformation of the leadership'. In his opinion, the invocation of a 'communist threat' no longer made any sense, given the profound change that the PCI had undergone. This awareness had given rise to the Orlando situation in Palermo and the desire, now widespread throughout sizeable sectors of the Catholic world, to sever the preferential relationship with the DC. On the other hand, Scoppola pointed out how it was impossible to consider the coexistence in the same party of both Orlando and those who had worked to plunge his council into crisis.[67]

Father Sorge, for his part, started from the conviction that in Italy 'a presence of Christian inspiration' was still necessary, though it had to 'renew itself and keep pace' with an evolving political panorama. He urged the launching of a 'new initiative in the Catholic world, external to the DC, almost a new constituent of political culture, which would lead to the rediscovery, in a renewed and modern form, of the validity of Sturzo's idea regarding a political presence that, in inspiration, was popular, secular, non-denominational and courageously progressive.' He clearly had in mind Orlando's experience in Palermo, an experience that, in his opinion, corresponded to the need for renewal that was present both in Christians and in Italian society. 'For democratic Catholics', he wrote, 'Palermo was the confirmation that it is possible to translate Sturzo's ideas into an updated and modern form.'[68]

In reality, Orlando, when he left the DC, made it clear that he did not intend to establish a second Catholic party: he began dialogues with members of the political world and of civil society who did not necessarily come from Christian Democratic circles. A group of young people from Turin joined the Rete, led by Diego Novelli – Turin's communist mayor between 1975 and 1985, and someone strongly committed to fighting corruption.[69] The group declared that it appreciated the 'transversality' of Orlando's project, which went beyond 'traditional side-taking'.[70] In the weekly journal *l'Espresso*, it was underlined how Nando Dalla Chiesa's decision to join the Rete was the sign that, as a political venture, it had moved away from a Catholic context to set itself up as a project that was open to a variety of political elements.[71] The son of General Dalla Chiesa, killed in 1982 by the Mafia in Palermo, had founded the group (and then the newspaper) Società civile in Milan, with the aim of highlighting the problem of corruption and the infiltration of organized crime into northern Italy. Dalla Chiesa had never been a member of the PCI, but his sympathies had always been with the world of the Italian Left.

The Rete, therefore, did not start life as a new Catholic party, as Father Sorge had hoped. The Jesuit priest, in an interview with Palermo newspaper *L'Ora*, thus complained that the former mayor had lost his identity as a democratic

Catholic: the coexistence in Orlando's group of different cultures dulled its Christian identity, while Sorge said it was necessary to have 'a presence of clear Christian inspiration in politics'.[72] Father Pintacuda, on the other hand, decided to follow Orlando into the new movement, becoming, in fact, its ideologue. Pintacuda's decision to support Orlando's new political venture created tension with the Society of Jesus, prompting Cardinal Salvatore Pappalardo, archbishop of Palermo,[73] to remove Pintacuda from his teaching post at the city's Centro studi sociali in September 1992.[74]

The end of the 'first republic'

The late eighties and early nineties were a watershed for international and Italian history, as the changes brought about by Michail Gorbačëv started a chain of events that led to the fall of the Berlin Wall and the dissolution of the USSR. The PCI, led from 1988 by Achille Occhetto, who took over from Alessandro Natta, also found itself in profound difficulty. On 12 November 1989, Occhetto, given the crisis that the international communist movement was going through, announced the intention to activate a process of transformation within the party, proposing to 'open a constructive phase to give life to a new political formation of the Italian left'.[75] It was a proposal that initiated a lively confrontation between the leaders and militants of the PCI, which came to the fore during the PCI's 19th Congress, held in Bologna in March 1990. Occhetto's motion obtained 67 per cent of the votes, while the party's left wing – supported by Pietro Ingrao and Alessandro Natta, opposed to changing the party's name and more cautious in severing ties with tradition – received 30 per cent. The motion by Armando Cossutta, seeking to remain in line with the course of Soviet communism, could garner only 3 per cent of the vote. In January 1991, the PCI's 20th Congress opened in Rimini, and the majority of those present voted for the founding of the Partito Democratico della Sinistra (Democratic Party of the Left, PDS). The minority, including Cossutta, Sergio Garavini and Lucio Libertini, instead decided to continue with commitment to the communist line, creating the Partito della Rifondazione Comunista (Communist Refoundation Party, PRC), which also attracted members of Democrazia Proletaria.[76]

Another new element in Italian political life came about in February 1991 with the foundation of the Lega Nord (Northern League) led by Umberto Bossi, which brought together the Liga veneta and the Lega lombarda.[77] The party took root in the areas with a traditional Catholic and Christian Democratic tradition

(Veneto and Lombardy) and represented a further demonstration of the end of Catholic political unity.[78] These changes in the electoral sphere originated in the transformation of the economic fabric: certain areas of the north, once common sites of emigration, had been involved in a tumultuous productive revolution in the seventies and eighties, made possible by family ties that were still cohesive and supportive but also due to a laxity in tax controls guaranteed by the political class.

The creation of this party represented a political revolution: the electoral geography of the north, as it had been delineated by the 1946 elections, was disrupted and the Lega was able to bend to its advantage 'the deep bond between subcultural belonging and localistic orientations'.[79]

In the early 1990s, Mario Segni, a member of the DC and promoter of referendums in 1991 and 1993, founded the Democratic Alliance movement. He was keen to bring a profound renewal to the Italian political system through a reform of the electoral law, transitioning from a proportional to a majority system: his goal was to rescue Italy from the 'swamp' of bargaining that went on between parties and to allow voters to choose between two clear positions.

After a long period of immobility, with the end of international opposition, the Italian electorate began to show more freedom of choice. Catholic political unity, which had represented a barrier to the spread of the Left in Italy and which had guaranteed consensus and votes to the DC, had definitively arrived at a point of crisis. As the political commentator Massimo Franco effectively put it, 'Communism was over, and therefore there was no longer the enemy who held Catholics quarrelsomely united around the DC: the honest and corrupt, the progressive and reactionary, the clerical and Masonic, the northern and southern.'[80]

The parliamentary elections that took place on 5 and 6 April 1992, were a clear sign of the change underway, and voters, for the first time in Republican Italy, chose their own party without worrying about the problem of a possible 'communist danger'. Many Catholics continued to give their consensus to the DC, but others, more progressive in attitude, decided to support the Rete: candidates for the Orlando movement included Raniero La Valle, Paolo Prodi and Paolo Bertezzolo of the Beati i costruttori di Pace group. Father Luigi Ciotti, too, of the Gruppo Abele, declared that he would vote for the Rete, convinced that as a project it was able to 'represent and give voice to civil society, to the people, to their needs and aspirations and also to their dissatisfaction with political degradation'.[81] Other figures in the Catholic world went in different directions: Ermanno Gorrieri[82] and Paola Gaiotti regarded the PDS with interest. In 1992,

Appunti di cultura e di politica dedicated a monographic issue to the PDS programme, highlighting the differences between the PDS and the PCI: 'having abandoned the disasters of real communism and the fog of the ideal version, the PDS programme is characterised by a variety of political cultures, containing ideas deriving from Western socialist experience, from the best examples of liberal thought and from democratic Catholicism'.[83] Scoppola, on the other hand, always with a keen eye on institutional reforms, supported Mario Segni's referendum movement.[84] In an interview he clarified his positions regarding institutional reforms, arguing that a state reform that moved in a presidentialist direction (something Bettino Craxi was very enthusiastic about) would mean 'a break in constitutional continuity' that he thought 'dangerous'. He believed, instead, that a reform of the electoral system was needed to take Italy towards a two-party system. He also considered it necessary 'to adopt measures that would guarantee the stability of the government on the basis of a substantial designation of the executive by the electorate': these objectives would be achieved only by incitement from civil society and making use of the referendum.[85]

As is known, in these elections, despite the Church once again ruling in favour of Catholic political unity, the DC reached its historical minimum: 29.7 per cent of votes for the Camera dei deputati. Marco Follini, a leading party member, reflecting on those years, believed that the 'Christian Democrat winter' began precisely in April 1992, when the party lost 4.6 per cent of its votes compared to the election five years earlier. The DC was still the first party in Italian politics, but behind its apparently solid facade the reasons for its supremacy were crumbling.[86] The communist share, meanwhile, consisting of the PDS and the Rifondazione comunista, fell to 21.7 per cent, losing 2,300,000 votes compared to five years earlier, while the PSI fell below 14 per cent. The Rete could only muster less than 2 per cent of the votes, while Umberto Bossi's Lega managed more than 8 per cent.

In the 1992 elections, given the collapse of both the DC and the traditional left parties, 'a real system breakdown' occurred.[87] Above all, according to left-wing DC member Franco Monaco, what was evident was the intolerance of the electorate 'towards a system of power founded on partitocracy and towards the perverse effects that this provokes'.[88] The electoral results also made it clear that there was a process of secularization taking place in Italian society and a weakening in the rootedness of religious belonging: the DC vote had registered a collapse above all in the 'traditionally Catholic' areas. A great deal of consensus had been awarded to the Lega, to a right-wing party that was 'populist and against solidarity'.[89]

These elections clearly demonstrated the overall defeat of the Catholic world. Many religious lay figures decided to run for various parties, but none of them were elected: the DC put forward characters of great intellectual and moral stature, such as Alberto Monticone, Leopoldo Elia, Nino Andreatta, Domenico Rosati, Tina Anselmi and Guido Bodrato; the PDS presented Paola Gaiotti; the Rete was represented, amongst others, by Raniero La Valle, who was well known and highly esteemed in Christian circles.

The delegitimization of Italian political parties also stemmed from the widespread cases of corruption featured in the press. The *Mani pulite* (Clean Hands) investigation carried out by the Milan Public Prosecutor's Office began when Mario Chiesa, a member of the PSI and president of the Milanese 'Baggina' hospital, was arrested on 17 February 1992, with the money of a freshly accepted bribe in his pocket. It was soon discovered that this was not an isolated case and the whole Italian political system found itself under investigation: the PSI and the DC, who had been running the political and economic power system in Italy for decades, turned out to be the parties most involved. In May 1992, the journalist and historian Giampaolo Pansa wrote sarcastically in *L'Espresso* magazine:

> The Bettino [Craxi] Wall has fallen in Milan; the power system known as the Craxi Holy Family has been toppled in the land of Saint Ambrose. The spread of the scandal that erupted with the hospital of Mario Chiesa brings to an end a historical phase that has lasted twenty years. Of course, the DC has also collected its share of kickbacks. And it is now certain that even the former PCI, today the PDS, has swallowed its slice of that rich and sumptuous cake. But, more than any other, the Milan PSI is the party that has been swept away by a torrent of slime.[90]

The sociologist and Catholic columnist Gianfranco Brunelli felt compelled to point out the responsibilities of the DC: '("Bribesville") does not represent the figure of the DC. But it is the system put in place by the DC, and the political methods adopted and developed to preserve it, that have led to "Tangentopoli"'.[91] Father De Rosa, in *La Civiltà Cattolica*, also described a worrying picture of the situation in the country: 'the worsening of the civil threat of organised crime; the phenomena of corruption and malfeasance brought to light by the magistracy; the crisis of legitimacy for our political parties; the difficult problems of the control and reduction of public spending; the devaluation of the currency and the weakening of Italy's position and image abroad'. All this produced 'an anxiety that pervades each one of us'.[92]

The months that followed the elections were also marked by the re-emergence of a new criminal strategy from the 'Cosa Nostra': on 23 May 1992, the Mafia murdered Giovanni Falcone, his wife Francesca Morvillo and the men who were escorting them. Public opinion was rife with doubt regarding the collusion between organized crime and politics, and Falcone's funeral in the cathedral of Palermo became an opportunity for citizens to externalize, through shouting and protest, their disappointment in the political class. 'But is it only the Mafia?' was how *L'Espresso* headlined their article about the massacre: The magazine interviewed the judge Agostino Cordova, a magistrate engaged in the fight against the 'Cosa Nostra', who aired a number of doubts: 'The first impression is that the Mafia is involved. But we have to see if someone else is involved as well, because the Mafia is not the only criminal organisation in existence in Italy.' And he added: 'It is important to understand why the group that organised the Palermo slaughter has moved with such power and precision at this very moment, such a delicate one as it is'; and he concluded by recalling many times that Italy, throughout its history, had been faced with 'disquieting questions'.[93] The philosopher Norberto Bobbio also commented in the immediate aftermath of Falcone's death: 'The mafia does what it wants, knows how to choose its targets, strikes whenever it wants.' He continued: 'If I think that the people who killed Falcone are Italians, then I am ashamed to be Italian.'[94]

Just a few months later, on 19 July 1992, the judge Paolo Borsellino, Falcone's friend and colleague, was also killed by the Mafia in Palermo, together with the five agents escorting him.[95] The journalist Paolo Gambescia, writing in the newspaper *Il Messaggero*, said: 'This is much, much more than a mafia attack. It is an attack on the state, on Italian democracy.'[96] Similarly Giovanni Pepi in the *Giornale di Sicilia*, spoke of 'open war against the state', adding: 'The mafia thus claims another victory. The state suffers a new defeat.'[97]

Italian instability of those years was increased because the country, governed after the elections by an executive chaired by Giuliano Amato, also had to face the problem of a precarious economic situation, of failing public finances and of limited credibility on the markets: the Italian deficit was over 160 thousand billion lira and the EEC had urged the government to reduce the public debt. There were also disturbing signs coming from the world of production. The distance from the parameters set by the Maastricht treaties (signed on 7 February 1992) seemed unbridgeable without making sacrifices, and this led Amato to present a financial measure of 30,000 billion lira to the Italians, a 7,500 billion lira privatization plan, a property tax on homes and bank deposits, and a pension reform.

It was a very gloomy national political panorama in 1993, in part due to the persistence of the Mafia strategy of terrorism: an attack was organized in Rome in May, then, ten days later, on the night between 26 and 27 May, in Florence, killing five people; in July, another attack was organized in Milan, in Via Palestro, in which five people died. On 15 September, Father Pino Puglisi, the parish priest of Brancaccio, a working-class district of Palermo, was killed, having dared to challenge the territorial hegemony of the Graviano brothers, who had ties to the family of the boss Leoluca Bagarella.[98] Puglisi was not the first priest to fall victim to the Mafia: since the end of the nineteen century, ten priests had been killed in the diocese of Palermo. However, noted Don Cataldo Naro, 'in the previous killings, the exercise of pastoral ministry had never been evident as the motive'. For example, the parish priest of Brancaccio had been killed for reasons connected to his religious activity in a neighbourhood where the Mafia had traditionally held sway.[99] Faced with such a swathe of violence, Giampaolo Pansa wrote apprehensively: 'Italy is at war, we are at war, we live, we will live, in a situation of war.' He added: 'Investigators and magistrates have been winning for a long time. Old political complicities have foundered. Immense patrimonies have been seized. Bosses both old and new are being given tough prison sentences. And they risk remaining inside forever.' To put an end to this situation organized crime had therefore come up with 'a ferocious and desperate assault on the whole anti-mafia hinterland – which means, on the whole of Italy'.[100]

The progressives

In the period following the 1992 elections, the world of the Left, both Catholic and 'secular', began to reflect on the changes taking place in Italian society. Despite the fact that the Left had obtained good results in the administrative elections of June 1993 – the first to take place after the amendment of the electoral law for the mayoral vote, which allowed direct voting – it was widely believed that it was necessary to outline a path and draw up a programme that could be shared by the various forces in the field. Thus, in the first months of 1993, Antonino Caponnetto, one of the magistrates engaged in the fight against the Mafia and a member of the Rete, launched the hypothesis of the establishment of a 'progressive hub'. This would bring together the contributions of the historical Left, popular and democratic Catholicism, the new political movements inspired by environmental protection, and many of the women's and student associations active throughout the country.[101]

Reinforcing this goal of unity, and making it something ineluctable, was Silvio Berlusconi's decision in October 1993 to launch the Forza Italia movement and then, on 26 January 1994, to go into politics. Berlusconi, an entrepreneur first in the field of construction and then in television, wielded great economic and media power, partly thanks to the political and personal dealings he had with Bettino Craxi in the 1980s. His figure aroused a great deal of concern: never before in Italian history had a man with such economic capacity and ability to influence public opinion been part of the political scene. Leoluca Orlando, too, felt compelled to explain his anxieties: 'A normal country is a country where limits are set between politics and information, a country where it cannot be permitted for one person to be involved in politics, and business, and information.'[102]

In *Risotto giallo*, a monthly journal on politics and culture of the Rete,[103] Salvatore Guglielmino, a well-known literary critic, concerned about the fate of democracy, also underlined how Berlusconi combined 'economic power and political power'. He was, he said, opposed to the liberalist view advocated by Forza Italia, which implied 'a kind of social Darwinism' and emphasized how the modern state had been created 'as a constraint and control over the fertility of the appetites of single individuals and groups, with the institution of legality and rights'. Abandoning this perspective would, he suggested, be very dangerous indeed.[104] For his part, ACLI president Giovanni Bianchi, in the journal *Avvenimenti*, published the article 'The Resistible Rise of the Master of the Ether', in which he criticized the close ties between Craxi and Berlusconi, which had led to the concentration of the Italian private television system in the hands of a single person.[105] He also called for the creation of 'a vast democratic cartel', which should encompass 'the best of the great popular traditions'.[106]

What is interesting is that Scoppola, too, revealed that he was convinced 'of the significant and decisive character of the Catholic contribution to the progressive movement'. He believed that Catholics should be leading figures in a project for the 'construction of a new left no longer univocally linked to an ideology, but open to different cultures and to the ethical values of the Christian tradition'.[107] Moreover, Scoppola went on to observe, the political system was moving 'towards a two-party system', and it was therefore natural that Catholics had 'visible preferences for one side or the other'. Commenting on the words of the Pope, who invited believers to be 'united and cohesive', Scoppola called on them to locate this sense of cohesion in values, and not in the sphere of politics.[108]

The elections held on 27 and 28 March 1994 were certainly a watershed, partly because the main figures in the electoral battle had changed. Bloodied and bruised by the *Tangentopoli* scandals and with Craxi involved in judicial investigations, the Socialist Party had decided to break up. Some ex-members decided to throw in their lot with Forza Italia; others instead wanted to support the progressive coalition. During the meeting held in Rome on 28 January 1994, the majority of the party's delegates expressed themselves in favour of the line indicated by the new party secretary Ottaviano Del Turco, which placed the new Socialist Party as 'an integral part of the progressive alignment, but with its own idealistic and political autonomy and with an organisational structure spread throughout the national territory'.[109]

The DC, too, shattered by the investigations of the Milan prosecutors, came to the end of its political journey. Mino Martinazzoli (secretary since October 1992, when he had taken over from Arnaldo Forlani) decided to make a break with the past and imposed strong changes. Above all, he wanted the party to abandon its character as a 'party of power' and return to the original features of the Catholic political tradition, as outlined by Don Sturzo in 1919. To make the new path clear the DC broke up in January 1994, to create the Partito popolare (Italian Popular Party, PPI).

The new Partito Popolare Italiano had the support of the majority of the members of the AC, and Giuseppe Gervasio, in the journal of AC *Orientamenti Sociali*, after noting the change in the 'overall political panorama' and the conclusion of the Christian Democratic project, called for the opening 'of a new credible and effective experience that consistently and transparently intends to keep alive the values of democratic Catholicism in our country'.[110] When asked about possible alliances for the new party, Alberto Monticone (former president of the AC) also placed them in a range that went 'from the democratic left, where possibly, under certain circumstances and with regard to particular objectives, agreement could be found with political exponents of the PDS, up to Segni and exponents of secular and liberal democracy – those, at least, who are not in any way connected with authoritarian, *qualunquiste* (politically apathetic), Leghist or right wing ideas'.[111]

The PPI was therefore defined as a party of the centre, even though it contained elements that were open to dialogue with the Left. It was precisely because of this fear of convergence with the progressives that the party's most conservative members, in particular Clemente Mastella and Pier Ferdinando Casini, decided to break away from the party in order to move towards the centre-right, founding the Centro Cristiano Democratico (Christian Democratic Centre, CCD).

Following extensive discussions the PPI, deeply divided within itself, decided not to make overtures to either Right or Left in the 1994 elections and placed itself at the centre of the political scene, despite the fact that the new electoral mechanism favoured a two-party system logic. Martinazzoli's goal was to end up holding the balance of power between the two political poles, but his strategy turned out to be a losing one: the PPI obtained only 11.1 per cent of the votes and the Patto Segni 4.6 per cent. The person who fully understood the innovative nature of the electoral system was Silvio Berlusconi who, given the incompatibility (more declared than real) between the Northern League and the Alleanza Nazionale (National Alliance, AN; the party that rose from the ashes of the Movimento Sociale Italiano), decided that Forza Italia should ally itself northwards with Bossi's party (Il Polo delle Libertà) and southwards with the heirs of fascism (Il Polo del Buon Governo). The result this produced was amazing, giving them 47.5 per cent of the votes, while L'Alleanza dei Progressisti (the Progressive Alliance) could only reach 32.3 per cent.[112]

The winner of the election battle was clearly Silvio Berlusconi. The sociologist Luca Ricolfi explained that the success of Forza Italia was due to its ability, through the power of television, to move four million votes, acting on 10 per cent of the undecided electorate.[113] Franco Monaco, a member of the Milan AC, noted how the demand for radical change had rewarded the Right and not the Left: the winning coalition was the expression 'of a social bloc' composed of the small and middle bourgeoisie, the productive and technical classes, retailers, artisans and self-employed workers. 'Breaking the ideological shells and attenuating the tension of solidarity connected to them,' he added, 'this social bloc goes in search of a political representation consistent with its own demand to play a leading role.'[114] Above all, observed Monaco, the electorate had perceived the progressive pole as the 'group of continuity and conservation', while the Right had presented itself as an innovator, as 'the new moving forwards'.[115] A disconsolate Claudio Rinaldi, commenting on the electoral outcome in L'Espresso, wrote: 'We can discuss whether a policy based on the TV selling of dreams is the best possible one for Italy in 2000. But it is certain that a whole section of the country was expecting nothing else.'[116]

For the losers, the result of the vote represented the conclusion of a political odyssey: Occhetto resigned and was replaced by Massimo D'Alema. Martinazzoli, too, decided to resign and was succeeded by the provisional leadership of Rosa Russo Jervolino. After the elections, and following such a bitter defeat, the different outlooks that existed within the PPI emerged with more clarity: Rocco Buttiglione and the area of Comunione e Liberazione began to look at Berlusconi's project with interest, while the Left of the PPI declared that they felt more politically inclined towards the progressive group. The internal divisions within the PPI's left wing, between Martinazzoli and De Mita, led to Buttiglione becoming party secretary in July. His obvious sympathy for the centre-right faction meant that his secretariat did not last long; most of the members of the PPI decided to elect Gerardo Bianco as secretary and shift in the direction of the progressive parties, with Romano Prodi nominated as the leader of the new centre-left coalition, which took the name Ulivo. The way was thus open for Prodi's political rise as one of the most prominent proponents of democratic Catholicism, destined for a decade to be a highly significant figure in both national and European political life. The long-cherished project of 'progressive Catholicism' to find a place for itself on the political Left thus came to fruition, sharing ideas for profound social reforms with the progressive forces.[117]

The Church at the crossroads

The end of the Catholic party was much more than the conclusion of the historical parabola of a political organization: it marked 'a profound discontinuity in the forms of the presence of Catholics in Italian political life' and opened a new period in the relationship between the Italian Church and politics.[118] In the nineties, despite the ongoing processes of secularization, the Church became the one single recognized institution in the country and reconfirmed its function as a reference point for Italian society. This came about due to the crisis of the political system and by the weakness that characterized the 'heirs' of the DC, a weakness that forced them to assume positions marked by greater condescension to the hierarchies than had been the case with leaders such as Sturzo, De Gasperi and Moro.

The Church took a stand on the issue of *Tangentopoli* corruption and scandal with a document drawn up by the Ecclesial Justice and Peace Commission on 4 October 1992. This was reported in full in *Avvenire* together with an article by Cardinal Carlo Maria Martini,[119] which made reference to the need to recover the ethics of sociality and solidarity. The observations aroused by the events of *Tangentopoli* were the subject of speeches by bishops and pastoral letters, reaffirming the Church's task of educating people with a sense of state.[120] But above all, faced with the crisis of Catholic political unity, two different strategies emerged in the Church: one, developed by Cardinal Camillo Ruini (president of the Conferenza Episcopale Italiana) and supported by John Paul II, set itself the goal of a direct relationship with civil society in order to reclaim the 'intransigent principles' of Catholicism. Ruini believed that the criterion that should guide believers in their political choices was that of values: the defence of the family, of marriage and of life from its conception; the awareness of the Christian roots of European culture; the fight against relativism; and the recognized role of Catholic schools. Ruini's intention was to lay the foundations, in the heart of Western modernity, of a civilization based on a 'religious identitary reawakening' in the belief that only the Christian faith could assume the role of the unifying principle. It was a vision that involved putting the period of internal dialectic and conciliar renewal behind them: the Church had to be a unified force in the face of a world marked by relativism and atheistic science. This led to a growing uniformity, with the consequent reduction of space for pluralism both in the press and within Catholic institutions. The Vatican assumed an increasingly aggressive profile towards the outside world, assuming the role of political pressure group both nationally and internationally: its goal was no longer to modernize Catholicism but to catholicize modern society.[121] The Church had, after all, already made it clear with the 1995 ecclesial conference in Palermo, in which it announced its intention to develop a new cultural project for Italy, that it wanted to reaffirm its identity and present a precise vision of man and his role in the world.

With the possibility of a single Catholic party abandoned, now unworkable in a two-party system, Ruini's strategy was to insert believers into the two different camps in order to exert an influence on Italian political life.[122] This led to both sides of the Italian political system being swayed by the presence of members following ecclesiastical guidelines: the Church therefore proposed, or boycotted, laws according to its own interests and values.

The other strategy was that of Cardinal Carlo Maria Martini, the archbishop of Milan, who challenged the utilitarian version of liberalism and the spectacularization of politics. He believed the values of Christianity in an increasingly multiethnic society to be solidarity, social justice and hospitality. A scholar of ancient Christianity, and heir to the conciliar experience, Martini put his faith in the religious choice, showing himself to be a stranger to the 'institutional-social option', based on the idea of a Church capable of reshaping the identity of Italian civilization.[123] The cardinal, who retired to Jerusalem after the end of his work in the diocese of Milan, said:

> You can tell a good Christian because they believe in God, they have faith, they know Christ, they learn to know him better as they go along and they listen to him. Knowing him means reading the Bible, talking to him, letting yourself be called by him, becoming like him. A Christian feels their love for Jesus becoming ever stronger. This will increasingly push them to perform social acts, to intercede for others, as Jesus did, who healed the sick, gathered the apostles, criticised the powerful, warned the rich and welcomed foreigners.[124]

Democratic Catholics were moving in the same direction as Martini, and Scoppola declared himself critical of a Church that, he believed, should distance itself from the political options of Left and Right and place itself at 'a higher and more detached level than political contingency'. It should return to its role as the 'ethical inspirer of public consciousness' rather than take on a role in Italian society of a sort of lobby group, capable of exerting great power and influencing the political equilibrium, its preferences oriented towards the centre-right.[125]

The wish to refer back to the radical principles of the gospel was also something at the heart of Noi siamo Chiesa (We are the Church), a European movement founded in 1996 and still highly active today. Its philosophy was based on the most innovative interpretations of Vatican II and it criticized the Church of Wojtila and Ratzinger for having brought back a conception of religion and faith that preceded the conciliar period. These believers perceived the Church as God's people and referred back to the experience of the base communities of the sixties and seventies. They supported the need for a reform of the Catholic Church from a collegial and ecumenical point of view and believed in compatibility between homosexuality and Christianity, in women priests and in the complete separation between religious and 'profane' themes, even going so far as to call into question the utility of the Concordato. Along with other movements such as Pax Christi, the Focolarini and figures such as Comboni missionary Father Alex Zanotelli, Noi siamo Chiesa has always resolutely fought against war and social injustice. Some of these themes would find a sympathetic ear from the new pope, who hailed from one of the poorest continents in the world: following Ratzinger's resignation from the position of Bishop of Rome, Argentine Jorge Mario Bergoglio became pope on 13 March 2013.

7

On the End of the First and Second Millennium

The end of ideologies

The natural question to ask at the end of this book is: what remains of the philosophical developments and ideas of the twentieth century? Are 'progressive' Catholicism and the dialogue between Christians and the Left things of the past or are they still relevant today? It is evident that after the Eastern European crisis and a majority of the left-wing militants revised their ideological convictions, the problem of the relationship between the Catholic and Marxist worlds have been put to one side; but social problems and the need to find solutions to them persist. The end of ideological conflict has certainly made communication easier between different cultures and has led to a search for points of convergence on concrete objectives: the era of 'contamination', marked by the acceptance of reciprocal differences, has thus been launched. It may be easier, now, for a Catholic to share the political perspective of a secular leftist rather than that of a fundamentalist Catholic.

If the seventies are remembered as a decade of violence and ideological clash, and the eighties for the pragmatic and moderate objectives of politics, the nineties were characterized by the emergence of new themes and trends. There was a progressive disaffection with regard to political parties, so much so that – using data from 1992 – only a minority of Italians claimed to have any interest in political issues.[1] This was undoubtedly brought on by the climate of disillusionment that pervaded Western society: after years in which the idea of 'changing the world' was predominant, individualistic attitudes gained the upper hand, aimed only at personal gratification. Those who still showed interest in the problems of society, given the crisis of credibility that parties were going through, preferred to channel their energies into movements and associations, both secular and Catholic. One significant example was that of the Coordinamento antimafia: first an adjunct to the Communist Party (PCI), it became progressively more autonomous and, starting from 1992, after the slaughter of Falcone and Borsellino, was defined as a coordinated assembly of groups and associations.[2] Of these groups, many were composed of Catholics, such as the Centro sociale di San Saverio, founded in 1986 with the aim of working to redeem the most degraded neighbourhoods in the historic centre of Palermo. Another was the Libera association, founded in 1995 and headed by Don Luigi Ciotti, former founder of the Gruppo Abele and director of the journal *Narcomafie*, which was responsible for training in schools and the reuse of assets confiscated from criminal gangs. One of the figures most committed to issues of legality was Don Giuseppe Puglisi, the parish priest in the Brancaccio district of Palermo. With ties to movements such as Azione Cattolica (AC) and Federazione Universitaria Cattolici Italiani (FUCI), he came into conflict with the Graviano brothers, Mafia leaders linked to the family of boss Leoluca Bagarella. The priest was killed in September 1993 in order to prevent him from continuing his work alongside the young people in the Sicilian capital's more difficult neighbourhoods.

The question of what it meant to be a 'left-wing Catholic' after 1989 remains unresolved: up to 1994, they could be considered those who declared themselves critical of the Democrazia Cristiana (DC), sometimes even while staying in the party, with the objective of renewing it from within (the Lega Democratica, for instance). The term could also apply to those who joined left-wing organizations and movements after being members of the DC for most of the time. After the 1990s every definition became more uncertain and problematic, although two basic tendencies could be identified in brief: one made up of the most radical believers, numerically in the minority, the heirs of those who, in the 1960s and 1970s, had interpreted the *Concilio* not only as a 'renewal' of the Church but as an opportunity for its very 'refoundation'. This group had given rise to the experience of the Base Communities, to Cristiani per il Socialismo and, in a more recent period, to Noi siamo Chiesa. These believers took a position, on the occasion of the various international crises (from Kosovo to the Gulf wars to the war in Libya) against any armed conflict, preferring – perhaps in some cases a little naively – dialogue and debate to solutions involving force. They established a dialogue with those parties and left-wing groups (such as the Rifondazione comunista) who shared both this utopian and pacifist vision and an interest in the poorest members of society and in the excluded, who were, in the new millennium, mostly immigrants. It is no coincidence that Nichi Vendola, leader first of Rifondazione Comunista and then of Sinistra ecologia e libertà (the Left for Ecology and Freedom),[3] has always declared himself a believer and a

Catholic, even while disagreeing with many of the positions adopted by the hierarchy, both regarding political choices and civil rights.

Criticism of the ideas of Cardinal Camillo Ruini, president of the Conferenza Episcopale Italiana from 1991 to 2007, seemed in fact to be the defining element of those who still called themselves 'left-wing Catholics'. The substance and form of this criticism was often, however, very different. In fact, while the most radical Catholics bitterly criticized the Church and called for a Third Vatican Council that would finally fulfil the eschatological expectations of the 'people of God', other believers thought it was enough to return to the spirit of the sixties, to realize a community of the faithful along the lines indicated by Pope John. This latter group was keen to emphasize their disagreement with respect to certain Vatican ideas and took part, albeit from minority positions, in the life of the ecclesiastical organism in the hope of restoring to it the sensitivity for dialogue and exploration of the Council years.

One element common to 'left-wing Catholics', both in the 'radical' and 'moderate' versions, was criticism of the nature of 'berlusconismo'. From the eighties, thanks to the diffusion of private television, Italian society had undergone a profound transformation and had bought into the 'myth of consumerism',[4] something alien to the values of that part of the Catholic world that felt it had inherited the conciliar sensibility. Then in the nineties Berlusconi, thanks to his multimedia empire, became a political leader, rising to become the figure of reference for those who – even in the Catholic world – believed it was necessary to curb the left-wing parties.

The opinion on Vatican II was the litmus test to understand where Italian Catholics stood: it is no coincidence that Umberto Bossi's Lega nord had always criticized the religious sensibility that, starting in the sixties, the Church had wished to spread; they were more interested in resurrecting the religious perspective that had been in place before the period of John XXIII. Looking askance at the ideas of Cardinal Carlo Maria Martini (archbishop of Milan from 1979 to 2002) – guilty of supporting the need for dialogue with other religions and welcoming immigrants – members of the Lega nord instead favoured relations with the fundamentalist and anti-council Catholics led by Mgr Marcel François Lefebvre.[5] They were also sympathetic towards prelates such as Alessandro Maggiolini, bishop of Como from 1989 to 2006, and Giacomo Biffi, cardinal and archbishop of Bologna from 1984 to 2003, both with close ties to the Comunione e Liberazione movement. Maggiolini and Biffi were quick to take a stand against the immigration of Muslims into Italy and in favour of the defence of the Italian nation's Catholic specificity.

Conciliar sensibility and dialogue with other cultures and other religions were issues that deeply divided Catholics, bringing forth different religious and political perspectives. Even the problem of *laicità* (secularism), a central issue since the times of the French Revolution, aroused heated debates, given that some Catholics claimed the right not to share the 'non-negotiable values' supported by the Church of Wojtyla and Ratzinger.

From the Ulivo to the Partito Democratico

The experience of the Ulivo, which many Catholics had regarded with interest and hope, was a cause for disappointment: after the electoral victory of 1996, due to internal strife in the centre-left coalition, the Prodi government went into crisis in 1998. Prodi was succeeded as prime minister first by Massimo D'Alema and then, in the final part of the legislature, by Giuliano Amato. Prodi was elected president of the European Commission in 1999, thanks to the influence of D'Alema and Walter Veltroni on European leaders, most of whom had links to the socialist world.[6]

In 1999, there also concluded the seven-year run of Oscar Luigi Scalfaro as president. A fundamentalist Catholic in his youth, during his presidency of the Republic he was a symbol of Catholic 'resistance' to the politics, methods and values of Berlusconi. He was particularly committed to safeguarding the Italian Constitution, an expression of the synthesis between the political cultures that had been involved in the struggle for liberation and which Berlusconi had repeatedly said he wanted to change. In 2002, Scalfaro would take on the role of president of the Istituto Nazionale per la Storia del Movimento di Liberazione in Italia (National Institute for the history of the liberation movement in Italy, INSMLI); meanwhile, in May 1999, his successor as president of the Republic was a man who came from a secular cultural tradition, Carlo Azelio Ciampi.[7]

The year 1999 also saw the election for representatives to the European Parliament, and the Italians found a very different selection of parties on their ballot papers compared to previous years. In 1998, the Partito Democratico della Sinistra (PDS) had broken up and a new party was created: the Democratici di Sinistra (Democrats of the Left, DS), a reformist party linked to the ideals of democratic socialism. In the party logo all reference to the tradition of the PCI had vanished: instead there appeared the term Partito Socialista Europeo (European Socialist Party), of which the new organization was a part. The Democrats saw their consensus reduced in the 1999 elections: in the European elections in 1996 the PDS had obtained 21.1 per cent, while the DS managed only 17.3 per cent.

On the occasion of the 1999 elections, the centre-left fragmented. The most tenacious supporters of the Ulivo presented the list *Democratici per l'Ulivo* which obtained 7.7 per cent, corresponding to seven seats in the European Parliament. Results were disappointing for the Partito Popolare (PPI) at 4.2 per cent. This forced PPI secretary Franco Marini (head of the party since January 1997) to resign, and at the Rimini congress held in September 1999 Pierluigi Castagnetti was elected party secretary. Rifondazione obtained just over 4 per cent of the votes, a result quite similar to that of the Lega nord. Forza Italia, meanwhile, rose from 20.6 per cent in 1996 to 25.2 per cent in 1999.

The 1999 elections showed that division was not appreciated by the centre-left electorate and that the only possible prospect for the progressive forces was to work together in close collaboration, as had happened in 1996 when the Ulivo had been victorious. The claims put forward for the particular specificities of each individual faction, and the conflict that had marked the life of the governments, had not been rewarded by the voters.

Given this blurred image presented by the centre-left, Berlusconi once again grew in strength. An exponent of Milanese democratic Catholicism, Giovanni Colombo, wrote bitterly that Berlusconi was offering 'a neoliberalism sold to the rhythms of commercials', for which life made sense only as a fight in an open battle field: 'it is the epic of continuous challenge, of the never ending frontier, of the head-down struggle to obtain ever greater wealth'.[8]

In May 2001, at the end of the five-year parliamentary term, new elections were called. The Ulivo had been worn out by divisions and Leonardo Benevolo, a democratic Catholic, declared just before the electoral results came out that it was only right that the centre-left coalition should lose its confrontation with Berlusconi: only after a debacle was it possible to find 'unity, respectability, and proactive ability'.[9] Pietro Scoppola, on the other hand, just before the elections, convinced that a Berlusconi victory would represent 'a dangerous step backwards for Italian democracy, a threat to the Constitution', urged people to vote for the Ulivo. However, the vote could not be simply 'against Berlusconi': the Ulivo had to be supported because, despite being compromised by the selfishness of the parties and the leaders running them, it remained a 'great and valid intuition'. With the collapse of communism and the weak performance of Catholic political unity, the conditions for a democracy based on alternation were created: in such a perspective, the Ulivo was the side in opposition to the conservative and moderate right-wing, and it was characterized by the meeting 'of the cultural and political traditions' that had contributed to the birth of the Republic and to the development of democracy. In particular, Scoppola believed that Berlusconi's alliance could not present itself as a bastion of Christian values because it only claimed to protect life and recognize the rights of Catholic schools: its political programme and the cultural positions expressed in it were, in fact, 'radically inconsistent with the vision of solidarity handed down through Christian tradition'.[10]

In the May 2001 elections Berlusconi was at the head of a coalition called the Casa delle libertà (the House of Freedom), which brought together Forza Italia, the Alleanza Nazionale, the Biancofiore (made up of members of the Catholic world) and the Lega nord. The new unity of the centre-right brought the coalition excellent results, with 49.5 per cent of the votes. The centre-left, however, was divided from the start, with the Rifondazione deciding to take an independent path from the Ulivo coalition. This represented the obvious consequence of the arguments and differences that had marked the Rifondazione in relation to the decisions made by Prodi, D'Alema and Amato, and the coalition undoubtedly suffered from this from a consensus point of view: the Ulivo, which proposed Francesco Rutelli as prime minister, obtained 35.47 per cent of the votes and the Rifondazione 5 per cent.

As had already happened in the 1996 elections, in 2001, too, it was clear how Catholic consensus had gone to both sides, with the Ulivo obtaining 43.7 per cent of the Catholic vote and the Casa delle libertà, 45.8 per cent. The 'Catholic question' had, in fact, come to an end in Italy, and believers no longer put their faith in one single political direction, as had happened for years with Christian Democracy: they were now demonstrating their interest in a variety of political possibilities.[11] Filippo Gentiloni, one of the exponents of 'Catholicism of dissent', wrote in *Il Manifesto* that the support for the centre-right had come from the religious 'citadels' and ecclesiastical institutions, while the 'Catholic base' had favoured the centre-left. In the Church, he argued, there were those who, like the faction close to Cardinal Martini, showed confidence in public institutions (the schools and health service) and considered the role of the state was to protect the weakest; the followers of Cardinal Ruini, on the other hand, supported the initiative of private individuals and believed that the state should not intervene.[12]

After the electoral defeat of 2001, the need arose to find a leader for the centre-left and the name of the Catholic Romano Prodi came out because he was the only figure, partly due to the recognition he had obtained in Europe as president of the European Commission, able to face the centre-right. Prodi, on the occasion of the June 2004 European elections, suggested that the centre-left forces (the DS and the Margherita)[13] appear on the list *Uniti nell'Ulivo*. It was an idea that won Scoppola's support: the project, in his opinion, should gather together the legacy of the peace movement, working so that in European consultations the forces of the Left, overcoming their corporate resistance, presented themselves under the same symbol.[14] The *Uniti nell'Ulivo* list obtained 31 per cent in the European elections and the Rifondazione comunista, which took part autonomously, managed 6 per cent. Forza Italia obtained 21 per cent and in general the centre-right forces (going into the vote divided due to the proportional system of the European elections) achieved good results.

When political elections took place in 2006, Prodi proposed that the centre-left should present a united front to the vote in a coalition called Unione. Father Bartolomeo Sorge expressed his support for the idea and, in an article in the journal of the Milan Jesuits *Aggiornamenti sociali*, voiced his fear that, given Berlusconi's entrepreneurial power, both specific and personal interests would take precedence over the common good. Father Sorge instead proposed a government that would put the public accounts in order, thinking not only about the interests of the richest part of the country (as the Northern League did) but also about the development of the south.[15]

In the elections of 9 and 10 April 2006, the centre-left coalition won by a handful of votes in the Chamber of Deputies (49.81 per cent as against 49.74 per cent for the Casa delle Libertà); the Unione had obtained more votes than the sum of the parties, and this was clearly evident in the Senate, where the coalition had not presented a united front.[16] Father Sorge's comments on these results began with a reiteration of his harsh criticism of Berlusconi because of his individualistic and utilitarian conception of politics, something that had led to the loss of civic sense and moral spirit, and to a populism impatient with every rule. He went on to say that the vote signalled a will to call a halt to the direction in which the country was moving, even if he was forced to underline 'the fragility of Prodi's victory'. Sorge proposed the consolidation of the majority and, in order to do so, to proceed to a foundational phase, which would involve the active participation of civil society, in particular of Catholics, and the goal of which would be the constitution of the Partito Democratico.[17]

While it is true that there were many Catholics who supported Prodi's Unione alliance, it is undeniable that the Church played an important role in the election's outcome, guiding electoral preference towards the centre-right. This was evident in polling stations with the highest presence of ecclesiastics and where the consensus in favour of the Berlusconi coalition increased in comparison to previous elections.[18] This shifting of the Catholic electorate was probably motivated by the Unione's decision to ally itself with the Radicals, the party that had been most committed, even as far back as the seventies, to supporting the laws on divorce and abortion, and which insisted strongly on the need for Italian politics to fix strict limits on interference from the Holy See.[19]

The second Prodi government, formed in May 2006, given its narrow margin of advantage in relation to the centre-right coalition, proved to be a very fragile entity indeed, and every parliamentary move proved to be a very difficult one. The Catholic sociologist Gianfranco Brunelli recognized that the executive had worked well in favour of liberalization, in foreign affairs and in terms of wisely managing the public accounts; but he pointed out that one of Prodi's problems was the quarrelling of the parties that supported him. For this reason Prodi needed to put together a single centre-left party, bringing together all like-minded souls into one individual political synthesis; and he hypothesized that it could be called the Partito Democratico.[20] Moreover, even before the 2006 elections, Prodi had promised his supporters that should the list be successful he would push for the foundation of a new political entity, able to unite the tradition of European socialism with liberal-democratic and Catholic reformism.[21]

In April 2007, in an article published in the daily newspaper *La Repubblica*, Prodi declared that the birth of the Democratic Party was imminent: the ideological fences had fallen and political differences between democratic Catholics and the heirs to communist tradition were now, in his opinion, 'very few'. Prodi called for the creation of a pro-European party, one with a 'strong, assertive and just' economic policy, a party that would make Italy more competitive on international markets, would work to make taxes fairer and would pursue a policy in favour of families and young people.[22]

Prodi's proposal pleased the progressive component of the Catholic world: in the journal *Testimonianze*, Jacopo Mazzantini wrote that he agreed with the need to build 'a new political way of thinking, renewing and, in part, abandoning the ideologies of the old centre-left parties, now unsuitable in terms of reading and interpreting a profoundly transformed society'. In his opinion, it was necessary to elaborate a new idea of the state, no longer a 'distributor' but capable of becoming an 'organiser' of wealth. He concluded: 'The Democratic Party represents the last chance for the centre-left.'[23] Alberto Monticone (president of Azione Cattolica from 1980 to 1986), on the other hand, had a more perplexed reaction to the idea of establishing a Democratic Party (PD). He wondered if it was the most appropriate instrument to make the Catholic contribution politically relevant to the growth of democracy: the PD, in his opinion, did not seem to have a conception of humanity that could be shared by those who made 'personalism' the cornerstone of their political project.[24] Rosy Bindi's response to Monticone declared that the cultural plurality of the Democratic Party should be appreciated, calling it 'the natural place where believers and especially Catholics' could best express the autonomy of politics, 'the social function of democratic liberty, the value of cultural mediation on all aspects of reality'.[25]

In the summer of 2007, the Margherita and the Democratici di Sinistra, together with some other minor groups, formed the Partito Democratico, with Walter Veltroni as leader of the new party (a figure who had already had experience in the PCI, the PDS and the DS) flanked by Dario Franceschini, whose background was in Catholic groups, as national deputy secretary.[26] Brunelli immediately pointed out the limits of the new organization: the party, in his opinion, was starting out with an uncertain identity and above all contained a variety of members and interests, and this represented an element of weakness.[27] The disagreements in the centre-left were not, therefore, at an end, and this was made clear when Romano Prodi's government concluded its mandate in January 2008 without a majority in parliament, due to the exit from the majority of a small Catholic party, the UDEUR, led by Clemente Mastella. The parliamentary elections of April 2008 once again handed the majority to the centre-right and Berlusconi was once again installed as Italy's prime minister.

Morals and ethics

In the 'post-ideological' period, following the fall of the Berlin Wall, some themes and methods of protest changed in Western societies, while others persisted. The question of peace continued to be a central one, and in the Balkans a bloody civil war was underway, with slaughter and violence that brought to mind the darkest episodes of the Second World War. The peace movement therefore moved into action once more, and many anti-militarists decided to personally bear witness to the horrors of the conflicts: the ethics of personal responsibility led Catholics and lay people to travel to the war zones, driven by the conviction that solidarity had to be experienced and shared with those involved in the tragedy of war.[28] In 1991 a group of volunteers had made the decision to go to Iraq and remain there, even after the start of the American bombing, putting their own safety at risk. In December 1992, the Beati i costruttori di pace association and the coordinator of Pax Christi, Don Tonino Bello, organized a march towards Sarajevo, with 500 volunteers participating, including priests, nuns, two bishops and some members of parliament. Also taking part was Father Vitaliano della Sala, who had already shown his commitment to peace in 1989 by going to Palestine with the organization Peace Now: on that occasion he had made contact with the Israeli pacifists and participated in the human chain around Jerusalem.

The pacifist movement, strictly opposed to the production and trade of arms and the economic interests that provoked war, was also harshly critical of the capitalist economic structure. It joined together with the 'new global' movement that had made its first appearance in Seattle in November 1999, when over 50,000 people protested against the third World Trade Organisation conference. The 'new global' movement was a global entity involving people from a variety of cultural backgrounds, people who wanted to challenge the 'great of the earth' in the name of a different conception of citizenship and democracy: against the 'globalization of profits', they fought for a 'globalization of rights' and social justice. The movement organized meetings to discuss the problems arising from the new international trade, the most important of which were held in Porto Alegre in 2001 and 2003.[29] The 2003 meeting, which took place during the Iraq war, was entitled 'Resistance to Neoliberalism, War and Militarism: For Peace and Social Justice'.[30]

The movement soon spread to Italy as well, its most significant event taking place on 21 July 2001, organized by the Genoa Social Forum (GSF) against the G8 meeting in the Ligurian capital.[31] The GSF spokesman was Vittorio Agnoletto, who came from a famous Milanese Catholic family and, as a boy, was involved in scouting associations, before becoming a member of Democrazia Proletaria. From 2004, he was a member of the European Parliament for Rifondazione comunista. A significant number of those who participated in the mobilization were, together with leftist group militants, composed of Catholics sensitive to the values of solidarity and critical of globalization. The GSF included the Associazione Agire Politicamente, the Associazione Comunità Giovanni XXIII Liguria, the Chiesa Evangelica Metodista, the Chiesa Evangelica Valdese di Sampierdarena, the Comunità San Benedetto al Porto, the Federazione Chiese Evangeliche Liguria, Mani Tese and the Lilliput Network. Other groups included were the Buon pastore, the Pax Christi movement, Noi Siamo Chiesa, as well as priests such as Don Vitaliano della Sala.[32]

The ACLI, Azione Cattolica, the Comunità of Sant'Egidio, the Consolata and Comboni missionaries, the Movimento giovanile salesiano (Salesian Youth Movement) and the Focolarini also had a keen interest in the issues of just globalization and were present on 7 July 2001 to discuss the contradictions raised by international trade. The questions dealt with largely coincided with those of the Seattle movement and were related to the debt cancellation of poor countries, the abolition of tax havens, the creation of a tax on international transactions and compliance with the Kyoto environmental agreements. Cardinal Dionigi Tettamanzi and Monsignor Antonio Riboldi spoke out in support of the event; and Cardinal Carlo Maria Martini also urged a rethinking in relation to the nature of globalization. As to whether or not to participate in the mobilization of 21 July in Genoa, the meeting left the decision to the freedom of conscience of believers and associations.[33]

The demonstration in Genoa degenerated into conflict and violence, provoked by groups on the margins of the movement but which involved everyone and led to the death of a young man, Carlo Giuliani, killed by the police. Cardinal Silvano Piovanelli, in addition to declaring his own 'sadness' for the young man's death and for the violence of that day, wondered:

> What will the poor think, those who are the very reason for our protest? And the volunteers, starting with the missionaries, the religious and lay priests, who, indeed, fight, and share in, poverty, and walk together with the poorest of the earth? Shame, each for his own part, that we were not able, not even all the Catholic groups, to identify and isolate the violent amongst us.[34]

In the autumn of 2002, the first European Social Forum was held in Florence, which, over three days of seminars, saw the participation of 60,000 people. The meeting was a great success and was held in an atmosphere of discussion and debate and without violence.[35]

The September 11 attack on the Twin Towers in New York in 2001 had major repercussions on the political events of the new Millennium, and was followed by the emergence of an international coalition led by the United States which declared war on Afghanistan and then on Iraq's Saddam Hussein. The pacifist front reacted strongly in Italy, organizing a series of demonstrations and torchlight processions: the first was the Perugia-Assisi march of 14 October 2001 in which 200,000 people took part. The initiative was organized by the association the Tavola della Pace (Table of Peace) which in its appeal wrote: 'We, women and men will march along the road that leads from Perugia to Assisi to promote the globalisation of human rights, democracy and solidarity. […] We are aware that there are no inevitable processes, that "another world is possible" and that to build it, it is necessary to promote globalisation from below.' The appeal was therefore in line with the objectives of the Genoa Social Forum and contained a series of requests aimed at Italian and European institutions and the UN General Assembly.[36] Lay and Catholic groups took part in the 2001 march, alongside some social centre networks and most of the members of the GSF.[37]

The Vatican, too, was keen to comment on the new international tensions: Pope Wojtyla had always reiterated his conviction that the Church held the criteria for living righteously in peace as well as methods for regulating conflict in society.[38] Speaking of Iraq, he chose a different path from the Italian government led by Berlusconi, which was inclined to have faith in the reasons put forward by President George W. Bush, and criticized the war initiative strongly. However, he considered the action of the international community necessary to demand that Iraq be disarmed and its despot removed. The Pope's objective, clearly explained at the Assisi meeting in 2002, was to avoid the so-called 'clash of civilizations' which, according to some, saw Christianity and Islam in opposition to one another; remove religious justifications for the conflict; protect the Christian minorities living in Islamic regions; and bring political debate back to international forums. The Holy See, in fact, emphasized that armed intervention did not have the support of UN deliberations and, above all, rejected the lawfulness of the 'preventive war' supported by the Americans. But neither the appeals of the pontiff nor the diplomatic manoeuvres carried out by the Holy See prevented the outbreak of hostilities against Iraq on 23 March.

The journal *Il Regno* published the official documents of the Holy See dealing with the conflict, which contained a plea for respect of the rules of international law and recognition of the UN Security Council resolutions. The journal then published the joint appeal against armed intervention in Iraq from the Latin Patriarch of Jerusalem, Michel Sabbah, the Archbishop of Sarajevo, Cardinal Vinko Puljic, and the Patriarch of Babylon of the Chaldeans, Raphael Bidawid, exponents of religious communities united by their 'minority' positions in locations with a delicate ethnic, political and religious balance.[39] The Vatican stance aroused the criticism of certain believers. Filippo Gentiloni called it 'ambiguous' and emphasized the rift within the Catholic world: while some argued in the name of defending the values of the West and the legality of the war against Iraq, there were groups, associations, communities and movements within the Church that espoused pacifist opinions that were sometimes more radical than those of the Holy See itself.[40]

The reasons for war and peace were at the centre of debate in the Catholic world: the journal *Testimonianze* maintained that even if 'just wars' existed a 'preventive' war could certainly not be defined as such, both because of the devastating effects it would produce in human and material terms and because it would create the conditions for a post-war period 'bristling with contradictions, overflowing with wounds to heal, fraught with unpredictable scenarios'.[41] Siccardi, more than anyone, revealed his conviction that the war against Iraq was a war dictated by the desire to control the sources of oil and emphasized that President Bush was involved with the American oil lobbies.[42] Father Sorge, too, declared a preventive war to be 'morally unacceptable' given that it was based on 'suspicions' and a 'trial of intentions' that were 'juridically unsustainable', since the United States could not appoint themselves as guarantors of universal peace and claim the right to intervene militarily wherever they wanted in the world. Above all, it was 'politically wrong' given that it would consolidate the Islamic world into a single front and encourage the theorists who believed in a clash between civilizations.[43] The director of the monthly journal *Jesus*, Vincenzo Marras, stated that the 'preventive war' was nothing more than an 'act of aggression', a conflict that the assembly of civilized nations should have condemned without hesitation.[44] An appeal signed by hundreds of well-known figures against hostilities in Iraq, considered 'a threat to the future of civil coexistence on our planet', was also signed by Raniero La Valle, Don Luigi Ciotti, by some members of the AGESCI asociation and by Pietro Pertici of the Tavola della pace.[45] The group Beati i costruttori di pace, meanwhile, given the Berlusconi government's pro-US stance, decided in protest to renounce any help from the Italian state.[46] The missionary Father Alex Zanotelli, together with Don Ciotti, wanted to meet the centre-left leaders Massimo D'Alema, Piero Fassino and Francesco Rutelli in order to encourage them not to give their backing to the war, and Zanotelli, former director of the journal *Nigrizia*, even provocatively suggested a mobilization of Italian civil society involving a simultaneous attack on the website of the Italian Stock Exchange.[47] Certain priests and former priests, including Giovanni Franzoni, Enzo Mazzi, Don Andrea Gallo, Fathers Vitaliano Della Sala and Franco Barbero (of the Pinerolo base community) and Raffaele Garofalo (of the diocese of Sulmona) wrote a letter to Pope Wojtyla in which, in addition to asking to 'open a dialogue' in the Church between all its various members, they declared their adherence to the day of prayer and fasting called by the Pope for Ash Wednesday, reiterated their rejection of preventive war and declared themselves to be 'against the culture of war itself and for global disarmament, for the affirmation of peace as a planetary culture and as a system'.[48]

A large part of the Catholic world was mobilized for peace, and many parishes exhibited the rainbow flag, the symbol of the anti-militarist struggle. Thousands of believers took part in the demonstration on 15 February 2003 organized in over fifty capitals around the world: the communist newspaper *Il Manifesto* noted that for the days of the demonstration the hostels of the nuns in Rome were completely booked out. Hundreds of associations, movements, parishes, the general curias, religious congregations, both male and female, had all decided to be present: 'Franciscans, Salesians and Jesuits will march, together with the Comboni missionary sisters, the young people of the *Azione Cattolica* and the Scouts, the movements that are traditionally in the front line for peace, such as *Pax Christi* and *Beati i costruttori di pace*, and the many young people from the parishes who have amassed a host of rainbow flags.'[49] Three million people took part in the Rome demonstration,[50] and the Turin daily newspaper *La Stampa* pointed out how 'nuns and communists' marched together, united by the goal of peace.'[51]

The enormous demonstrations significantly shifted the orientation of public opinion[52] and, wrote Saccardi in *Testimonianze*, reinforced the political ideas of the Ulivo: once again there was the possibility 'to give life to an alliance', which saw the forces of the Left and the world of associationism brought together.[53] Guido Formigoni was more cautious in judgment, noting that these mobilizations for peace were 'problematic and immature' in character, incapable of translating such imposing events into 'farsighted and responsible political positions'. 'To build political synthesis', he went on, 'much greater effort is required at an intellectual level': it was necessary, in terms of objectives, to build a 'credible perspective'.[54]

Not all believers, however, shared this pacifist and anti-militarist point of view: the attack on the West by Islamic extremists brought to the fore the question of not only the military but also the cultural defence of Europe. Certain Christians (but also laymen), the so-called *theocons*, first in the United States and then in Europe, saw in Christianity the perfect bulwark to the spread of a multiethnic, multiracial and multireligious society.[55] The writer Oriana Fallaci – a champion in her youth of battles for the secular state – now called herself an 'atheo-Christian' and declared that she had no love for a Catholic Church that welcomed immigrants, that provided them with asylum and support, and that was silent when the crucifix was offended, humiliated and removed from classrooms. Islam had declared war on Western civilization, a war that was above all cultural, which wanted to 'strike at our soul', our way and philosophy of life, our way of thinking, acting and loving, and, more than anything, our freedom. The Catholic religion, in Fallaci's opinion, as an identitary element in the European community should thus rise to provide protection against the new 'barbarians'.[56] In 2004, Marcello Pera, president of the Italian Senate, and Cardinal Joseph Ratzinger, Prefect of the Congregation for the Doctrine of the Faith, published a book they had composed together with the significant title *Radici* (Roots). Here, they reflected in two autonomous essays on the crisis of a Europe, incapable, according to Pera, of defending its cultural and religious roots, the supporter of relativistic ideas that denied universal values and called into question its own principles, principles that had civilized the world. Thus, in the face of the 'holy war' that Islamic fanaticism had launched against the West, the old continent had responded with manifestations of peace and the constant use of 'politically correct' language. Pera also said that he was critical of a Church that had shown itself too inclined to ask forgiveness for mistakes made in the past, for the violence that had accompanied the campaigns of evangelization; and that he had no time for a West that lived in a state of 'guilt' in relation to imperialism, fascism, Nazism, communism and anti-Semitism. This was a mindset that could not grasp the fact that 'war had been declared on the West' and, faced with this challenge, European Christianity appeared 'stunned, bewildered, resigned, too often either silent or shouting down what should be the banners of its culture'.[57]

Ratzinger, for his part, analysing the founding values of Western civilization, identified them in human dignity and rights, not created by a legislator, convention or political decision but which were derived directly from God. Thus, the value of the family, and of monogamous marriage, were derived in this way, as cells of the formation of a community. In the contemporary age, however, these basic assumptions were challenged by the progress of medicine (which had created cloning and genetic manipulation), as well as the spread of erroneous customs, which had led to cohabitation, divorce and homosexual unions. The conclusion reached by the cardinal was that the West, which intended to be 'laudably open with full understanding to external values', showed, however, that it no longer loved itself, 'now seeing in its history only what is deplorable and destructive and no longer able to perceive what is great and pure'. The acceptance of multiculturalism meant denying the identity of Europe and its roots in Christianity: it was necessary, instead, to reaffirm the common foundations of the West and the 'respect for that which is sacred'.[58]

These were ideas shared by many lay and Catholic intellectuals, keen to recognize a social and political role for the Christian religion: for their argumentative verve, it is worth mentioning the former member of Partito Radicale Gaetano Quagliariello, the former communists Giuliano Ferrara and Ferdinando Adornato, and the former feminists Nicoletta Tiliacos, Anna Bravo and Lucietta Scaraffia.[59] In an ecclesiastical context, such opinions found supporters in Monsignor Maggiolini and Cardinal Biffi, worried about the 'passive colonisation' produced by the uncontrolled influx of Muslim immigrants and advocates of the need to defend a European identity that, in their opinion, coincided with that of the Catholic Church.[60] Perplexity towards this approach, on the other hand, was expressed by Massimo Teodori, a secular liberal who stigmatized the new neo-traditionalist crusade led by 'holy atheists', repentant laymen and bigoted liberals, figures who, in accordance with Vatican directives, insisted on imposing the idea that the Church constituted the only source of public morality, effectively imposing a new obscurantism.[61] Criticism also came from the philosopher Roberto Escobar, alarmed by the politics of fear and hatred that, instilled by newspapers and television, had convinced many Italians that 'the weakest of the weak and the poorest of the poor' were the 'poisoners of our identity, the subtle invaders that creep into our home'.[62] Even a liberal Catholic like Dario Antiseri, who said of himself that he was 'Christian because he was relativist' and 'relativist because Christian', distanced himself from the theocons, in the belief that, in the Christian faith, 'only God is absolute' and consequently all that is human is historical, perfectible, contestable.[63]

The temptation to propose an 'identitary Christianity' in defence of Europe was thus something a large part of the Church could identify with. In recent years, given the crisis of the great historical and historicist ideologies and the fact that religion has once again come to the fore, the Catholic Church, as historian Francesco Traniello pointed out, has not limited itself to proclaiming *erga omnes* that 'its truths about humanity are irrevocable'; the Church has also wanted to argue that to lack respect for them would bring about destructive consequences of every kind. Religion was thus understood as a factor of collective identity and social cohesion, assuming the role, in fact, of 'civil religion'.[64]

This was not, obviously, a perspective shared by everyone, and Franco Monaco, a disciple of Lazzati and one of Cardinal Martini's closest collaborators, stated his perplexity with Pera in the journal *Jesus*. Pera, he said, was a 'laicist', sympathetic towards the philosophy of Karl Popper, who confused his own idea of 'absolute' with that of the Church: while for Pera the absolute was 'the dogma of Occidentalism', for the Christian the appreciation of Western civilization did not authorize triumphalism and its hierarchy of values was not considered indisputable. Moreover, Monaco explained, Christianity by its very nature and mission had a universalistic value, and therefore had to live with a plurality of models of civilization.[65] Scoppola, too, hit out at those who made instrumental use of Christianity,[66] and Vito Mancuso, professor of theology at the Università Vita e Salute San Raffaele, pointed out that the term 'catholic' in its most radical sense means 'universal' and that a thought was authentically Catholic not if it 'supinely obeyed the dictates of Church teaching, but if it had at heart the good and the life of everyone'.[67]

In *Aggiornamenti sociali*, Giannino Piana denounced the policy that deployed the Christian religion to defend the identity of the West from the incursion of other cultural and religious traditions, and the kind of Christianity that exploited the support of politics to influence the processes that determined the collective life. The attempt of some 'to take possession of the Christian religion for purely utilitarian ends' was absolutely deplorable: the task of faith was, according to conciliar teachings, 'to provide human activity with a horizon of transcendent meaning': only in this way could religion recover its impact on social and political reality.[68] Enzo Bianchi, the prior of the monastic community of Bose, also spoke out against the Christian-Western equation and the reduction of the Church to an ethico-social lobby, criticizing those 'authoritative ecclesiastics' who wanted a 'powerful, massively visible Church, present in the spaces left empty by ideologies'. This was not an approach that could be accepted by 'witnesses of Jesus Christ, made a man like us, who died and rose in order to restore the full communion of humanity and of the entire cosmos with God'.[69] The risk was, he added, that faced with the affirmation of fundamentalism in some sectors of the Islamic world the Church would respond with a similar simplification, because 'this form of intolerance has long lived within Churches, not excluding the Catholic Church'.[70] Above all, warned Umberto Brancia in the journal *Confronti*, if fundamentalist visions and proclamations in defence of indisputable principles moved out of television discussion programmes and settled in community life, then their fanaticism and hatred could produce 'infernal consequences'.[71] Rosy Bindi, too, arguing against the theocons, urged Catholics not to 'lend themselves to the risk of reducing Christianity to a "civil religion" and an improper use of faith': in her opinion, the Catholic-democratic culture had to recognize the 'religious foundation to the freedom of man' but not to surrender 'to the search for political consensus or the exercise of power'.[72]

Recent years

John Paul II died in April 2005. He was a pope who had determinedly demanded firm doctrinal steadfastness from every member of the Church, and this was an approach that had provoked a crisis in the conciliar spirit, in episcopal collegiality and in the freedom of theological research. There was, in other words, a preponderance of disciplinary measures during the Woytla pontificate, its targets notable theologians such as Küng, Schillebeeckx, Curran, Boff, Balasuriya and Dupuis. Censorship had also affected religious communities such as the Jesuits, the Carmelites and the Paulines, and there were also moments of tension between the Roman Curia and the Dutch, American, German, Brazilian, Indian, Austrian, English and Australian episcopal conferences. John Paul II was particularly hard in his attitude towards Oscar Romero, the Salvadoran bishop who had dedicated himself to human rights and social justice in relation to the people of his homeland and who, isolated from the Church and given no support in his fight against government violence, was killed at the altar in 1980.[73]

During his long pontificate, John Paul II was able to nominate 118 cardinals, 117 of whom would then go on to elect his successor, thus effectively controlling the direction of the Church in the period after his death.[74] Cardinal Ratzinger's ascent to the papal throne was therefore carried out in a spirit of continuity, and Filippo Gentiloni argued that the choice had taken place under the banner of 'the most rigid Catholic orthodoxy'. Ratzinger had always talked about the modern world and its culture in negative terms and had referred to a 'dictatorship of relativism' that the Catholic Church must oppose. It was no coincidence, then, that the appointment pleased 'reactionaries all around the world', the American president Bush, all fundamentalists and, in Italy, leading theocon exponent Marcello Pera. Behind this appointment, accused *Il Manifesto*'s Vatican expert, there was no Vatican II, 'with its openness to dialogue and modern culture, but rather Vatican Council I, that of a Church entrenched within the alleged infallibility of Rome'.[75] David Gabrielli, meanwhile, in the pages of *Confronti*, declared that he had no wish to lose hope that Benedict XVI would find the courage to create a 'discontinuity' with his own past as a 'conservative' cardinal and predicted that if Ratzinger went on his way as a 'severe chastiser' of Catholic exponents of the conciliar tradition, the Church could find itself experiencing 'a dramatic polarisation, almost a latent schism', which would deeply lacerate people's consciences.[76]

In the Italian Church, as we have already seen, opinions varied, and this was evident during the fourth Ecclesial Convention held in Verona from 16 to 20 October 2006: while Cardinal Ruini reiterated the possibility of 'a renewal in continuity' on the basis of the 'hermeneutics of the reform' indicated by Benedict XVI, Cardinal Dionigi Tettamanzi (archbishop of Milan from 2002 to 2011) focused his speech on the theme of conciliar reception in the Italian Church.[77] Ruini denounced secularism and ethical relativism, and called for a greater commitment from Christians in the public arena, promoting the 'religion of values' capable of finding consensus amongst the laity who shared with the Church the defence of tradition and national culture.[78] Against this alliance between Christians and 'holy atheists',[79] Cardinal Tettamanzi instead reiterated the need to return to the spirit of the Council.[80] There was great applause from those present at the Verona meeting when Tettamanzi stated 'it is better to be Christian without saying so rather than proclaiming it without being so', since this was interpreted as the Archbishop of Milan distancing himself from the positions of those within the Church who dialogued with the 'holy atheists'.[81]

Alberto Melloni (director of Bologna's Istituto di Scienze religiose Giovanni XXIII), reflecting on the Verona conference, denounced the weakness of the Italian Church, the evident tiredness, conformity, frustration, and surrender towards those who wanted to exploit faith. According to Melloni, in recent years Italian politics had not only been one of the areas of interest at the Italian Episcopal Conference but had been 'the privileged object', and so dialectic within Catholicism had been extinguished and a lack of interest in 'Christian experience' and in faith itself had emerged.[82] The Italian Church had chosen to open a dialogue with right-wing parties especially, and the latter had made themselves available to legislate in defence of the family, against stem cell research and assisted procreation. The centre-right had then granted funding to Catholic private schools, consented to fixed positions for religious teachers and allowed tax breaks to ecclesiastical properties.

The choices of the Conferenza Episcopale Italiana (CEI) were in step with the more general 'conservative' climate of Benedict XVI's pontificate. There was perplexity in the Muslim sphere, amongst the laity and in some sectors of the Catholic world, at Ratzinger's *lectio magistralis* in Regensburg on 12 September 2006, in which he quoted the Byzantine emperor Manuel II Palaeologus regarding the relationship between faith and reason: the Pope stated that while Christianity rejected conversion through violence, in the Muslim religion the nature of God was not linked to the human category of reasonableness. The reactions to the pontiff's words were very critical: he was accused of an 'occidentalist' vision of Christianity as well as a lack of respect for the religion of Muhammad.

Gentiloni, commenting on the speech, underlined the condemnation of Darwin's theories, 'because the pope does not seem to want to consider the possibility of an evolutionism that excludes God' and of relativism, considered 'the greatest evil of the century'. A journalist of *Il Manifesto* noted that ideas of this kind distanced Ratzinger from 'a good part of modern culture and also from Catholic theology', and was instead a move in the direction of the theocon: 'the various forms of fundamentalism are getting closer, while modern thought, with its uncertainties and openness to others and to history, moves away'.[83]

The concern of a part of the Catholic world was also manifested in the face of the Pope's willingness to pay heed to the followers of Monsignor Lefebvre, in order to induce them to return to the Church, and of the concession granted to them to celebrate Mass according to the old rite of Pius V. The Vatican decision provoked the reaction of the French Church and, in particular, the president of the episcopal conference, Cardinal Jean-Pierre Ricard, while the ecclesiastical provinces of Besançon and Rouen were keen to give voice to the anxiety of the faithful in relation to this concession. The growing suspicion in priests and laity in the various Western countries was that a strategy was underway to downsize the changes introduced by Vatican II.[84]

The political scientist Gian Enrico Rusconi noted that theological argument was now absent or irrelevant in Church debate, so much so that there was no mention of the great traditional theological dogmas, original sin, redemption, salvation, revelation or the Trinitarian doctrine. The (repentant) laity who sided with the Church claimed to do so in order 'to fight the lax, relativist and Jacobin drift of contemporary society' and to put a stop to the 'moral threat of scientism, (Darwinist) evolutionary naturalism and the abusive nature of biotechnology'.

The effects of all this, on a political level, were evident when the subject of 'public ethics' came up: instead of finding a point of compromise between citizens who had different ideas, the 'non-negotiability' of the Church's ideas prevailed. Confusion was thus created between 'their legitimate convictions and the moral obligation for all citizens to share them'; there was a lack of good sense, a vital element for building a society of 'mature citizens', of believers, non-believers and those with different beliefs.[85]

Certain believers sympathetic towards the ideas of Vatican II also indicated their discomfort and declared that they felt marginalized and humiliated 'by the sometimes overbearing and biased imposition' of a conservative and politically slanted religion.[86] The Vatican expert Giancarlo Zizola pointed out the 'fundamentalist fever' that distinguished the Catholic Church; critical of the conformist tendencies induced by the excessive power of the papal magisterium he expressed his hope for a recovery of the conciliar spirit and the development of 'new criteria for consultation and participation at all levels of the ecclesiastical system'.[87] And Don Michele Do, the priest of a small mountain town, from his retreat in the parish of St Jacques of Champoluc, invoked the Council that had called the certainties of Christians into question, thus helping them to be reborn: 'Being let loose and free is a great challenge, everything we know and are must be overthrown, we cannot stop but renew ourselves, wash our eyes clear once again.'[88]

Within the Catholic world, no one denied European culture's profound basis in the Christian tradition but, as Maurizio Abbà said in *Testimonianze*, this should not serve as an excuse to justify the exclusion of non-Christians;

indeed, Christianity had in itself the characteristics of acceptance and debate, and could be the inspiration for a richer and more plural Europe.[89] Franco Toscani also wrote on the subject, again in *Testimonianze*, arguing that the values of coexistence, acceptance, dialogue and solidarity had to inspire the new European citizenship: it was necessary, in his opinion, to start from the premise of the recognition of the positive legacy of all religions.[90]

The concern spreading throughout Italy was above all related to the considerable influx of migrants from Eastern Europe, South America, Africa and Asia. This was due to a number of factors within the various countries but essentially responded to the Italian production system's need for workers to perform tasks that the native population were no longer willing to do. Nonetheless, the sociologist Maurizio Ambrosini (a collaborator with Don Virginio Colmegna's Casa della Carità) noted that in recent electoral strategies, and victories of the centre-right, the issue of immigration was central, because it tapped into the fears and insecurities inherent in society with regard to 'foreigners'.[91] Guido Formigoni, too, addressing the issue of immigration, has shown how the media and certain political forces created the psychosis in Italy of an 'invasion' of non-EU citizens. In particular, he stressed that the only freedom that right-wing politicians did not contemplate, given the force with which they advocated liberalism in the economic sphere, was to allow the 'movement of human beings, to migrate in search of sources of livelihood and emancipation from misery and decay'. The centre-left, on the other hand, tried to anticipate and deal with the phenomenon by giving it a sense of order, setting up public programmes aimed at social inclusion, orientation and introduction into the world of work.[92] Rosario Iaccarino, meanwhile, noted how a feeling of social selfishness induced by uncertainty with regard to the future grew in Italian society, and he stigmatized political messages that related immigration to crime and public order.[93]

Romano Prodi also spoke out about the issue, saying that the goal was to 'export our stability and our prosperity'. It was therefore necessary to work to overcome conflict and delays in development in the countries at the borders of Europe, in the Balkans, Russia and the Mediterranean. In addition, it was vital to support the peace process in the Middle East and to strengthen political relations with the Maghreb countries. Europe had to re-propose its role as a supportive partner with developing countries, in order to stand alongside them in the fight against poverty. Hope lay in 'the worldwide projection of our fundamental values' and the goal of sustainable development had to 'translate into powerful solidarity'.[94]

In *Testimonianze*, Maurizio Bassetti wrote in favour of a multi-ethnic society based on mutual respect and free from intolerant attitudes, calling for the creation of a new culture of security and rights for all. His conviction was that in a globalized world it was impossible to prevent the birth of multicultural societies.[95] Andrea Bigalli, involved in the Caritas charity association, said it was crucial to deal with the problems of poverty, alienation and marginality, convinced that knowledge, courage and dialogue were the conditions for coexistence. If acceptance was conceived as a 'guarantee of rights with the definition of corresponding duties', the migratory influx could be handled well and to everyone's benefit.[96]

Father Enzo Bianchi, for his part, urged Christians to 'look for ways in which the equality of the rights and dignity of persons, economic equality, the equality of all citizens', regardless of their faith or principles, could find 'realisation', because this was the measure of their fidelity to the gospel.[97] He recalled, in fact, that in the Old Testament the category of foreigner, or stranger, was the one that best represented 'the various aspects of the needy' but above all that the evangelist Matthew had given Jesus the words: 'I was a stranger, and you took me in.'[98] Regarding the reception of immigrants, Father Andrea Gallo said: 'Jesus was a traveller, Abraham was a foreigner, the children of Israel were foreigners in Egypt, Aeneas escaped from war and founded Rome, Ulysses left his homeland, thirsty for knowledge.' And concluded, therefore, that making illegal immigration a crime was itself 'a crime against humanity'. It was 'a violation of a universal law'.[99]

Ratzinger's Church showed more attention to moral issues than to social problems, supported in this by the conservative climate that existed in society and in Italian politics, and by the compliance demonstrated by a good part of the political class towards the 'ethical suggestions' that emanated from within the Vatican walls. The centre-right coalition in particular revealed a sensitivity to such indications: in February 2004, the Berlusconi government promulgated a law on 'assisted procreation' (law 40/2004) that was aimed at regulating and restricting this medical practice. The law was immediately the subject of heated debate and in June 2005 was the focus of an abrogative referendum, first proposed by the Radicals and then supported by the Democratici di Sinistra. The CEI intervened at this point, proposing to make the referendum ineffective through mass abstention. The centre-left Catholics (and in particular the Margherita group) decided to leave voting to individual freedom of conscience. Romano Prodi took a different tack: he affirmed the importance of the vote as an act of civil responsibility, showing that he was not frightened to go up against the Vatican. In the end, only 25.6 per cent of Italians went to the polls, the law was not abolished (though later Constitutional Court pronouncements strongly undermined it) and Cardinal Ruini considered the result a victory.

The direct intervention of the Church in the political debate aroused a certain bewilderment. Pietro Scoppola pointed out how the centre-right, from 1994 onwards, had secured the support of Catholic hierarchies through a policy of compliance with the wishes of the CEI, allowing the 'Church to act as a powerful lobby in the field of politics'.[100] In the pages of *Testimonianze*, Vittoria Franco argued that the law on assisted fertilization was one of the 'most cruel and anachronistic' texts 'that could be imagined, the result of an intolerable submissiveness to the imperatives of the ecclesiastical hierarchies'.[101] Filippo Gentiloni also took a position on the matter, placing the crisis of the secular state at the centre of his observations, together with the arrogance of the ecclesiastical hierarchy that dictated the political agenda and openly influenced the citizens' vote.[102]

Secularism became a central theme in debates of that period, as evidenced by the publication of Giovanni Boniolo's book *Laicità*, which contrasted intellectuals of different cultural sensibilities.[103] In June 2006, at the Rome head office of the publisher Laterza, a debate was organized between the jurist Gustavo Zagrebelsky (former president of the Constitutional Court) and Pietro Scoppola on the issues of ethics, freedom and dogma.[104] On that occasion Scoppola replied to the layman Zagrebelsky, who said that faith was incompatible with democracy if it was other-directed by a dogmatic power, by recalling the phrase of Cardinal John Henry Newman: 'I shall drink to the Pope, if you please, still, to Conscience first, and to the Pope afterwards.' Scoppola argued that democracy required ethical resources and thus also required the Church, and that, on the other hand, the Church should open itself to democracy to immunize itself from fundamentalism and integrism, and to escape from the 'merchants of the temple'.[105]

A lively discussion took place in the coalition that brought Prodi to the premiership in 2006 regarding something that had already come to the surface during the period of the drafting of the programme, the issue of civil rights and in particular the recognition of cohabiting unmarried couples and same-sex unions. Francesco Rutelli and Giuseppe Fioroni were both against such matters, as opposed to the Radicals of Emma Bonino, supported by many members of the Left. In February 2007, the Prodi government passed a bill drafted by two ministers, Rosy Bindi (Family) and Barbara Pollastrini (Equal Opportunities). The intention, said Bindi, was not to introduce a surreptitious basis for marriage between homosexuals but 'to regulate the rights and duties of cohabiting people without discriminating against sexual orientation'.[106] The legal adviser to Bindi was Renato Balduzzi, president of the Movimento ecclesiale di impegno culturale (Ecclesial Movement of Cultural Commitment), while the head of Pollastrini's legislative office was Professor Stefano Ceccanti, former president of FUCI.[107]

The debate on rights was a difficult moment for the fragile Prodi government, with some Members of Parliament, obviously perplexed about the law, forcing it to be withdrawn. In addition, the theodem Paola Binetti (a member of the Margherita) was quick to clarify that, with regard to ethical issues, 'the logic of side-taking' was not valid, hypothesizing parliamentary majorities different from those expected by the executive.[108] Mons. Giuseppe Betori, secretary general of the CEI, spoke out trenchantly:

> Those who intend to live together, thus forming heterosexual or homosexual couples, are free to do so and in this they suffer no impediment or any kind of discrimination; but this choice does not produce any form of para-family unit and cannot therefore justify the assignment of rights that are identical or similar to those deriving from the conjugal union founded on marriage.[109]

Fulvio De Giorgi, former member of the Lega democratica, while placing emphasis on the value of the family for Christians, admitted that in Europe there was now a 'plurality of matrimonial situations and forms of cohabitation, recognised both legally and *de facto*', and this should not be seen as frightening.[110] Rosy Bindi went even further, declaring her appreciation for the 'desire for stability and mutual solidarity', the commitment to a common life and the desire to build a 'family', also on the part of homosexual couples.[111]

Another occasion for the discussion of ethical issues arose in 2006 with the debate centring around the case of Piergiorgio Welby, a radical activist who was seriously ill with muscular dystrophy and who fought for the recognition of the right to refuse undesired medical treatment in favour of euthanasia. It was a question that divided the country, and while Welby finally succeeded in having his suffering brought to an end, the reaction from Cardinal Ruini was a harsh one, forbidding the deceased a religious funeral. The theologian Vito Mancuso called this decision a scandal 'for which those responsible will be accountable to God'.[112] Gentiloni, meanwhile, pointed out polemically that, in the very days when Welby had been denied a church funeral, the Chilean Church had raised no objection to a religious ceremony for the recently deceased dictator Augusto Pinochet.[113]

The former priest Giovanni Franzoni, for his part, was keen to reiterate his conviction that it was up to the patient to decide, either directly, if they were able, or through a living will, while doctors had to put themselves in the 'humble role of therapist both of the living and of the dying'.[114] And Don Andrea Gallo wondered: 'Is not the protection of individual rights one of the cornerstones of the Gospel message?' And he continued: 'Where is love? Where is respect for the primacy of personal conscience? Where is mercy? There is a void of love in this Catholic crusade and an oppressive fundamentalism is on the march.'[115] The base communities also took part in the debate. In an open letter to Welby, they declared that they recognized his right to freedom of conscience, adding: 'we believe it is right and humane that you can conclude your existence of life in peace, without being forced to endure a treatment that is not respectful of your dignity'.[116] The theme of euthanasia divided the world of believers, with a poll conducted by the newspaper *La Repubblica* showing that 50 per cent of practicing Catholics and 71 per cent of non-practitioners were said to favour the interruption of treatment in Welby's case.[117]

The clash of opinions broke out again with the case of Eluana Englaro, a young girl who had remained in a vegetative state for 17 years, following a traffic accident. Her father, after a long battle, managed to obtain the interruption of artificial nutrition, and Eluana died in February 2009. On this occasion, too, the Catholic world was divided: while *Famiglia cristiana* published an article entitled 'Eluana Englaro: Everything is Ready for Her Execution. Death at Christmas' (the subtitle was: 'While we are tucking into our *panettone*, the girl could be allowed to die of hunger and thirst. By judicial order.'),[118] the theologian Vito Mancuso praised a policy which had 'the ability to mediate between various personal convictions in search of the common good'.[119]

Today

During Ratzinger's pontificate, there was no lack of controversy with regard to his work in Italy and abroad: the rigid and conservative character of his magisterium seemed to many to have little to do with the needs of a society undergoing profound and rapid transformation. This, together with a progressive loss of physical strength and the difficulties he encountered in relations with the Roman Curia, led him to resign. He was succeeded in March 2013 by the cardinal Jorge Mario Bergoglio, the first pontiff in the history of the Church to be a member of the Society of Jesus: the new pope chose the name of Francis, in memory of the friar of Assisi, famous for his devotion to the poor and his own life of poverty.

It is not easy for a historian to analyse recent times, lacking the necessary gap in order to reconstruct and interpret events. Pope Bergoglio's succession to Ratzinger has certainly, however, meant a profound change in the Church. Unlike Wojtyla, from Eastern Europe, and Ratzinger, a learned theologian, Bergoglio has experienced the life of the Argentine *favelas* and has a clear idea concerning the privations and hardships resulting from poverty and underdevelopment. The son of Italian immigrants, he knows about the problems of hospitality and integration, and so it was no coincidence that for his first trip outside Rome he chose the island of Lampedusa, the arrival point for migrants coming from North Africa to Italy. He has been called a 'pope of the left'. Certainly, anyway, a pope with whom the world of the Left can engage in dialogue and debate.

Conclusion

Italian Catholicism emerges from this research as multifaceted, with a variety of ideas and opinions in relation to social issues; and it is clear that even those believers who engaged with the world of the Left did so from different perspectives. The progressive front, on the other hand, was marked by division: first the Socialist Party, then after 1921 the Communist Party and then in the seventies groups belonging to the radical Left, believing in the importance of religion in Italian society, engaged the Catholic world in dialogue but for their own specific reasons and in a number of ways.

Five different sensibilities and modes of relationship with regard to progressive culture and parties can be identified in the Catholic world:

1. Foremost in the research are those Catholic figures who felt they had to engage with the Left due to their belief that in both cultures there was a strong focus on the poor and that common elements could be found in both traditional Christian eschatology and Marxist utopia. They looked back to the myth of early Christianity, powerfully egalitarian and communist in nature, and believed that the Church should return to those principles, abandoning its hierarchical and oligarchical character. The conviction that action for social justice could not be separated from wide-ranging Church reform was shared by many of the modernist thinkers of the early twentieth century: Ernesto Buonaiuti in particular highlighted the discrepancies between a 'People of God' Church and the largely political-administrative role that the ecclesiastical institution had assumed over the centuries.

After the Second World War, the idea of a Church that was both close to the poor and poor itself was shared by believers such as Don Primo Mazzolari, the Servants of Mary David Maria Turoldo and Camillo De Piaz, the Piarist Ernesto Balducci, Giuseppe Dossetti, Giorgio La Pira and Giuseppe Lazzati. Many of whom were leading figures in the Council and post-Council years, when the conviction strongly re-emerged that it was necessary to work for a change in the role of believers in the religious community and for the abandonment of any compromise with power.

2. Other believers developed the idea that it was possible to clearly divide the religious from the political sphere and therefore to be Catholics in conformity with the directives of the Church and at the same time supporters of a political leftist culture. They believed that it was not appropriate to question the ecclesiastical structure, given that the Church was a metahistorical entity and as such not subject to adaptation to change over the centuries. This conception, which originated in the thinking of Benedetto Croce, was supported above all by Franco Rodano, advocate of the secular principle of the division between religious and temporal spheres.

The proposal of the 'Historical Compromise' elaborated by Enrico Berlinguer in the seventies was also an expression of this vision: the secretary of the PCI preferred to engage in dialogue with those moderate Catholic sectors that still saw themselves as linked to the DC rather than believers who had for years criticized Catholic political unity. Rodano's ideas clearly lay behind Berlinguer's political decisions, the former being Togliatti's advisor on issues related to the Catholic world, mediated through the presence of Antonio Tatò, former member of the Sinistra cristiana and Berlinguer's secretary in the 1970s.

3. The third category is formed by those moderate Catholics who, under particular conditions (for example, when faced with fascist violence in the early twenties), hypothesized political collaboration with the Left. Amongst these were the members of the Partito Popolare who, in the name of preserving democracy, tried to establish coalitions that included Reformist Socialists; these Catholics were thus disowned by the Holy See, and resolved to come to an agreement with Mussolini. It was a policy that the centre-left governments of the sixties would also find themselves in line with, representing as they did the programmatic meeting between Socialists and Christian Democrats, two political forces in dialogue with one another, each of them with their own identity and specificity, on the basis of having a political programme to realize.

4. Also significant was the choice of those believers who worked to ensure that Catholic associations abandoned their militant and often political aspect, to opt for a 'religious choice' and a commitment to the poor and oppressed. This was a minority sensibility – at least in Italy – until the end of the fifties, only to spread widely during the Council and post-Council period.

5. In the post-war period, members of the Christian Democrat Left, who often also belonged to Catholic associations, were leading figures in the party and, through the Dossetti group, in grassroots groups as well as the Lega

democratica, they were powerfully engaged with the question of confrontation with the socialist and communist world. Composed mostly of young intellectuals, the left-wing groups developed their political line in journals and became leading figures in the Ulivo period of the 1990s, the coalition made up of former Christian Democrats and former Communists picked Romano Prodi, an exponent of democratic Catholicism, as their leader.

One detail that emerges from the analysis carried out here is the close connection between politics and religion in Italy and the great influence that the Church has always wielded in the nation's events. It is also evident, however, that the process of modernization cannot be separated from the affirmation of the secular nature of politics and institutions. Awareness of this was something that had a profound impact on part of the Catholic world, in particular on those who were most determined to challenge the desire of the Italian Church to impose Catholic political unity. The belief that religious principles could find expression in a political party had already been a source of conflict between the Vatican and Don Romolo Murri, convinced as he was that one should join a party on the basis of a political programme and not for reasons of faith. The priest's ideas were important for all Catholics involved in politics, and their validity was especially proven by the tumultuous events that shook the Partito Popolare, sundered and paralyzed by the variety of political orientations within it. After the Second World War, the Vatican's choice to channel votes towards the Christian Democrats at first seemed a way to stem the right-wing direction that the so-called 'partito romano' – the 'Roman party', in other words the most conservative part of the Catholic Church – had taken. Very soon, however, the DC began to appear too 'limiting' to those Catholics who, especially after the Council, wanted to express their political (and religious) militancy in a manner more respectful of evangelical precepts, claiming the primacy of conscience that liberal Catholics had upheld in the nineteenth century. The end of Catholic political unity – foreshadowed in the 1976 elections by the presentation of certain Catholics as independents on the PCI lists – actually took place with the conclusion of the First Republic and the dissolution of the DC.

During the course of the twentieth century, the question of the theoretical confrontation between Marxism and Christianity emerged on various occasions. Encouraged by the ideas of Benedetto Croce, first echoed by Murri and then by exponents of the Sinistra cristiana in the 1940s, many Catholics supported the need to separate historical materialism from dialectical materialism. They believed that Marxism should be used as a tool for understanding contemporary society: the interpretation of historical reality therefore involved the assumption of modern methods of analysis, unrelated to Catholic culture. In the sixties and seventies many believers were of the opinion that, going beyond the matter of 'dialogue', it was possible to identify points of convergence between the two philosophies and that Marxism and Christianity both shared an interest in humanity and its happiness, a happiness that was also terrestrial.

In the international debate, Christians engaged in dialogue with those Marxist thinkers – such as Adam Schaff and Roger Garaudy – who had mostly attempted to follow independent paths of research, in the direction of a 'Marxist humanism'; in Italy, the debate's leading figures were the Catholics Giulio Girardi, Mario Gozzini, Nando Fabro and Ruggero Orfei and the Communists Lucio Lombardo Radice, Luciano Gruppi and Concetto Marchesi.

In the new millennium, the twentieth century's cultural and ideological pillars have begun to crumble, the old parties have broken up and new and different faces are to be found gracing the political arena. None of the current parties in the Italian parliament officially claim inspiration from either religious principles or Marxist ideology. Even the distinction between Right and Left seems increasingly labile: a new direction has opened in the world of Italian politics – and not only there – and problems and prospects have now taken on a different appearance. In the digital age, newspapers and journals that forged public opinion and political conviction saw their sales halved compared to just a few years before, with information increasingly conveyed via the internet. Societies based on 'direct democracy' are emerging, reluctant to employ the mediation of intermediate bodies such as parties and trade unions, and the most common terms in politics nowadays are 'populism' and 'postmodernity'.

Notes

Introduction

1 Rosario Forlenza and Bjørn Thomassen, *Italian Modernities. Competing Narratives of Nationhood* (New York: Palgrave Macmillan, 2016), 1–2.
2 Ibid., 58.
3 Jose Pedro Zúquete, 'Populism and Religion', in *The Oxford Handbook of Populism*, eds, Cristóbal Rovira Kaltwasser, Paul Taggart, Paulina Ochoa Espejo and Pierre Ostiguy (Oxford: Oxford University Press, 2017); Daniel Nilsson DeHaunas and Marat Shterin, 'Religion and the Rise of Populism', *Religion, State & Society* 46, no. 3 (2018): 177–185.
4 Letter from Giuseppe Rensi to Romolo Murri, Bellinzona, 12 November 1905, Archivio Romolo Murri, Fondazione Romolo Murri di Urbino, box 8.
5 Benedetto Croce, *Materialismo storico ed economia marxistica* (Palermo: Sandron, 1900).
6 Franco Rodano, *Questione democristiana e compromesso storico* (Rome: Editori Riuniti, 1977).

Chapter 1

1 Jacques Oliver Boudon, *Napoléon et les cultes. Les religions en Europe à l'aube du XIX siècle (1800–1815)* (Paris: Fayard, 2002); Alyssa Goldstein Sepinwall, *The abbé Grégoire and the French Revolution. The Making of Modern Universalism* (Berkeley: University of California Press, 2005); Bernard Plongeron, *Des résistences religieus à Napoleon* (Paris: Letouzey, 2006); Marina Caffiero, 'Lo scontro con la Rivoluzione francese. Strategie di una riconquista', in *Le religioni e il mondo moderno*, vol. 1, *Cristianesimo*, ed. Daniele Menozzi (Turin: Einaudi, 2008), 203–229.
2 Vernon L. Lidtke, 'August Bebel and German Social Democracy's Relation to the Christian Churches', *Journal of the History of Ideas* 27, no. 2 (1966): 245–264; Roger Aubert, ed., *Histoire de l'Église depuis les origines jusqu'à nos jours*, vol. 12, *Le Pontificat de Pie IX (1846–1878)* (Paris: Blound & Gay, 1964); Bernard Plongeron, 'Le Christianisme comme messianisme social', in *Histoire du Christianisme*, vol. 10, *Les défis de la modernité (1750–1840)*, eds Jean-Marie Mayeur, Charles and Luce Pietri, André Vauchez and Marc Venard (Paris: Desclée, 1997), 866–886. Sebastian

Prüfer, *Sozialismus statt Religion. Die deutsche Sozialdemokratie vor der religiösen Frage 1863–1890* (Göttingen: Vanderhoeck & Ruprecht, 2002); Patrick Pasture, 'Between Cross and Class. Christian Labor in Europe', in *Between Cross and Class. Comparative Histories of Christian Labor in Europe (1840–2000)*, eds Lex Heerma Van Voss, Patrick Pasture and Jan De Maeyer (Bern: Peter Lang, 2005), 9–48; Yvon Tranvouez, *Catholicisme et société dans la France du XX siècle* (Paris: Karthala, 2011); Lisa Dittrich, *Antiklerikalismus in Europa. Öffentlichkeit und Säkularisierung in Frankreich, Spanien und Deutschland (1848–1914)* (Göttingen: Vandenhoeck & Ruprecht, 2014); Daniela Saresella, 'Christianity and Socialism in Italy in the Early Twentieth Century', *Church History* 84, no. 3 (September 2015): 585–607.

3   On this, see Paolo Pombeni, *Socialismo e cristianesimo (1815–1975)* (Brescia: Queriniana, 1977); Daniele Menozzi, *Chiesa, poveri, società nell'età moderna e contemporanea* (Brescia: Queriniana, 1980), 59–68; René Epp, 'L'Église et les Révolutions', in *Le droit et les institutions de l'Église catholique latine de la fin du XVIII siècle a 1978*, eds René Epp, Charles Lefebvre and René Metz (Paris: Editions Cujas, 1981), 79–84; Daniele Menozzi, 'La Chiesa cattolica', in *Storia del cristianesimo. L'età contemporanea*, eds Giovanni Filoramo and Daniele Menozzi (Roma-Bari: Laterza, 1997), 166–171; Joe Holland, *Modern Catholic Social Teaching: The Popes Confront The Industrial Age (1740–1958)* (Mahwah, NJ: Paulist Press, 2003).

4   Claude Langlois, *Le catholicisme au féminin: les congrégations françaises à supérieure générale au 19 siècle* (Paris: Cerf, 1984); Giancarlo Rocca, *Donne religiose. Contributo ad una storia della condizione femminile nei secoli XIX–XX* (Rome: Edizioni Paoline, 1992).

5   André Biéler, *Chrétiens et socialistes avant Marx* (Geneva: Labor et fides, 1981), 81–97.

6   Karl Kautsky, *Die Sozialdemokratie und die katholische Kirche* (Berlin: Vorwärts, 1902), 15–16.

7   Philippe Levillain and Jean-Marc Ticchi, eds, *Le Pontificat de Léon XIII: Renaissance du Saint-Siège?* (Rome: École Française de Rome, 2006), 225–244.

8   Camillo Brezzi, *Laici, cattolici. Chiesa e Stato dall'Unità d'Italia alla Grande guerra* (Bologna: Il Mulino, 2011), 122–135.

9   See Silvia Dominici, *La lotta senz'odio: il socialismo evangelico del «Seme» (1901–1915)* (Milan: Angeli, 1995).

10 Carlo Maria Curci, *Di un socialismo cristiano nella questione operaia* (Rome: Fratelli Bencini Editori, 1885), V–VII.

11 Paolo Pombeni, 'Movimento cattolico e movimento socialista', in *Dizionario storico del movimento cattolico in Italia (1860–1980)*, vol. 1, *I fatti e le idee*, eds Francesco Traniello and Giorgio Campanini (Turin: Marietti, 1981), 17–19.

12 Giorgio Spini, *Italia liberale e protestanti* (Turin: Claudiana, 2002).

13 Valdo Vinay, *Storia dei Valdesi*, vol. 3 (Turin: Claudiana, 1980), 291–293.

14 Alfredo Luciani, *Cristianesimo e socialismo in Europa (1700–1989)* (Rome: ASCE, 1989), 748–749.
15 Giorgio Vecchio, 'I cattolici milanesi e la locale Camera del lavoro (1889–1896)', *Bollettino dell'archivio per la storia del movimento sociale cattolico in Italia* 12, no. 1 (1977): 151–179.
16 Francesca Anzi, 'Le origini delle Camere del lavoro', *Critica sociale* 39, no. 15 (1947): 297–298.
17 Luisa Osnaghi Dodi, *L'azione sociale dei cattolici nel milanese (1878–1904)* (Milan: Sugarco, 1974), 149–161.
18 Letter from F. S. Cabrini to 'mia figlia carissima', Milan, 9 May 1998, in the Archivio Generale Congregazione del Sacro Cuore; see Daniela Saresella, *Cattolicesimo italiano e sfida americana* (Brescia: Morcelliana, 2001), 165–166. Cabrini (1850–1917) was an Italian missionary, founder of the Congregation of the Missionaries of the Sacred Heart of Jesus.
19 Albertario (1846–1902) was an Italian priest and journalist, editor of the *Osservatore Cattolico* newspaper, which brought together intransigent positions concerning faith with open positions on social issues.
20 Murri (1870–1944), a priest since 1893, promoted the Democratic Catholic movement in Italy in the early twentieth century. A critic of the conservatism of the ecclesiastical hierarchy, he tried to reconcile socialism and social doctrine.
21 Turati (1857–1932) was an Italian politician and journalist. In 1892, he was one of the founders of the Italian Socialist Party.
22 Pietro Scoppola, *Coscienza religiosa e democrazia nell'Italia contemporanea* (Bologna: Il Mulino, 1966), 61.
23 Romolo Murri, 'La crisi del liberalismo in Italia', *Cultura Sociale* 1, no. 12 (1898): 178.
24 Romolo Murri, 'Il momento e i cattolici', *Cultura Sociale* 1, no. 10 (1898): 146.
25 Scoppola, *Coscienza religiosa e democrazia*, 112.
26 Labriola (1843–1904) was an Italian philosopher, with particular interest in the field of Marxism. He was one of the founders of the Italian Socialist Party.
27 See Daniela Saresella, *Romolo Murri e il movimento socialista (1891–1907)* (Urbino: Quattro Venti, 1994), 21–35. On Murri, see Ilaria Biagioli, Alfonso Botti and Rocco Cerrato, eds, *Romolo Murri e i murrismi in Italia e in Europa cent'anni dopo* (Urbino: Quattro Venti, 2004); Daniela Saresella, ed., 'Romolo Murri dalla democrazia cristiana al fascismo', special issue, *Modernism* 1, no. 1 (2015), 11–220.
28 The Italian Socialist Party, reflecting the ongoing debate in the Second International, was divided between two factions: a reformist one, led by Filippo Turati, and a revolutionary one, led by Arturo Labriola. Murri showed interest in Turati's ideas.
29 Pius X (Giuseppe Melchiorre Sarto, 1835–1914) was Pope from 1903 to 1914. He supported the alliance between Catholics and liberals, against the socialists.

30 Benedetto Croce (1866–1952) was an Italian philosopher, historian, politician, literary critic and writer. He was the ideologist of twentieth-century Italian liberalism.
31 Romolo Murri, 'Partiti ed accordi', *Cultura sociale* 8, no. 187 (1905): 305–306.
32 Letter from Giuseppe Rensi to Romolo Murri, Bellinzona 12 November 1905, Archivio Romolo Murri, Fondazione Romolo Murri di Urbino, box 8.
33 Romolo Murri, 'La guerra santa', *Cultura Sociale* 9, no. 192 (1906): 2.
34 In Belgium abbé Adolphe Daens founded the Christene Volkspatij in 1893. On several occasions the latter came to local agreements with the Socialist Party (for example for the local elections in Alost in 1899).
35 See Claudio Giovannini, 'Lega democratica nazionale', in *Dizionario storico del movimento cattolico in Italia 1860–1980*, vol. 1, *I fatti e le idee*, eds Francesco Traniello and Giorgio Campanini (Turin, Italy: Marietti, 1981), 304–309.
36 Giuseppe Rossini, 'Introduzione', in Giuseppe Donati, *Scritti politici* (Rome: Cinque Lune, 1956), X.
37 Scoppola, *Coscienza religiosa e democrazia*, 123.
38 Ernesto Vercesi, *Democrazia cristiana in Italia* (Milan: Tipografia e Libreria dell'Unione, 1910), 33–34.
39 Gallerati Scotti (1878–1966) was a member of Italian Catholic modernism. An aristocrat and a writer, in 1907 he founded the journal *Rinnovamento*, with Alessandro Casati and Stefano Jacini. See Nicola Raponi, *Tommaso Gallarati Scotti tra politica e cultura* (Milan: Vita e Pensiero, 1971); and Fulvio De Giorgi and Nicola Raponi, eds, *Rinnovamento religioso e impegno civile in Tommaso Gallarati Scotti* (Milan: Vita e Pensiero, 1994); Luciano Pazzaglia and Claudia Crevenna, eds, *Tommaso Gallarati Scotti tra totalitarismo fascista e ripresa democratica* (Milan: Cisalpino, 2013).
40 'A proposito delle Lettere di un prete modernista', *Nova et vetera* 1, nos 11–12 (1908): 379–382. See Alfonso Botti, 'Rinnovamento religioso e riforma della Chiesa: "Nova et vetera"', in *La riforma della Chiesa nelle riviste religiose di inizio Novecento*, eds Marina Benedetti and Daniela Saresella (Milan: Edizioni Biblioteca Francescana, 2010), 77–91.
41 There is a considerable bibliography dealing with modernism. As regards France, the following are still essential reading: Émile Poulat, *Histoire, dogme et critique dans la crise moderniste* (Paris: Casterman, 1962); Pierre Colin, *L'audace et le soupçon. La crise moderniste dan le catholicisme française* (Paris: Desclée De Brouwer, 1997); Émile Goichot, *Alfred Loisy e ses amis* (Paris: Les editions du cerf, 2002). Regarding England: Alexander Roper Vidler, *A Variety of Catholic Modernism* (London: Cambridge University Press, 1970). The following are more recent works: David G. Schultenover, *A View from Rome. On the Eve of the Modernist Crisis* (New York: Fordham University Press, 1993); Darrell Jodock, ed., *Catholicism Contending with Modernity: Roman Catholic Modernism and Anti-*

Modernism in Historical Contexts (Cambridge: Cambridge University Press, 2000); Hubert Wolf and Judith Schepers, eds, *In wilder zügelloser Jagd nach Neuem. 100 Jahre Modernismus und Antimodernismus in der katholischen Kirche* (Paderborn: Ferdinand Schöningh, 2009); Guido Verucci, *L'eresia del Novecento. La Chiesa e la repressione del modernismo in Italia* (Turin: Einaudi, 2010); Claus Arnold and Giovanni Vian, eds, *La condanna del modernismo. Documenti interpretazioni, conseguenze* (Rome: Viella, 2010); Luciano Vaccaro and Marco Vergottini, eds, *Modernismo. Un secolo dopo* (Brescia: Morcelliana, 2010); Daniela Saresella, 'O modernismo italiano entre história e historiografia', *OPSIS* 17, no. 2 (2017): 194–215; Ilaria Biagioli, Matteo Caponi and Maria Paiano, eds, 'Modernismo e antimodernismo cattolico nella Grande Guerra', special issue, *Modernism*, no. 3 (2017): 11–243.

42 The Radical Party was founded in the late nineteenth century by Felice Cavallotti and Agostino Bertani, heirs to the culture of the Risorgimento and advocates of a secular and liberal spirit, which aimed to promote suffrage and the secular school system on a wider scale. See Alfonso Botti, *Romolo Murri e l'anticlericalismo negli anni de 'La Voce'* (Urbino: Quattro Venti, 1996), 34–35; and Lucio D'Angelo, *Il radicalismo sociale di Romolo Murri (1912–1920)* (Milan: Angeli, 2007).

43 Many of the journals and newspapers quoted in the essay were basically typewritten sheets, very cheap and irregularly printed; publication was frequently suspended for economic reasons. They might – as in the case of the journal *Rinnovamento* – be subsidized by their rich directors.

44 The veteran work by Emilio Sereni, *Il capitalismo nelle campagne* (Turin: Einaudi, 1947) is essential reading on this subject.

45 'Cristianizzare i socialisti e socializzare i cristiani', *La Plebe*, 1 November 1905: 2.

46 Franco Boiardi, '"La Plebe" (1904–1907) e i radicali cristiani di Reggio Emilia', *Rinnovamento* 32, no. 4 (1960): 61.

47 'Chi siamo', *La Plebe*, 30 April 1905: 2.

48 Camillo Prampolini (1859–1930) was an Italian socialist politician. Born in Reggio Emilia, he was the most important exponent of Evangelical Socialism. See Arnaldo Nesti, *Gesù socialista* (Turin: Claudiana, 1974): 38–44. See also Dominici, *La lotta senz'odio*; Patrizia Audenino, *L'avvenire del passato. Utopia e moralità nella sinistra italiana alle soglie del XX secolo* (Milan: Angeli, 2002).

49 Il prete della plebe, 'Fra la gens emiliana', *Cultura Sociale* 8, no. 181 (1905): 221. The letter was also published in *La Plebe* on 9 July 1905.

50 Murri's reply appears at the bottom of the letter 'Il prete della plebe' and was subsequently republished in *La Plebe* on 6 August 1905.

51 See Enrico Decleva, 'Anticlericalismo e religiosità nel socialismo italiano', in *Prampolini e il socialismo riformista* (Rome: Mondo operaio-Edizioni Avanti!, 1979), 258–260.

52 'Gli eccessi del materialismo. Socialismo e sindacalismo', *La Plebe*, 9 July 1905: 3. See Saresella, *Romolo Murri e il movimento socialista*, 118–121.

53 Lorenzo Bedeschi, 'Le correnti cattoliche novatrici nell'Umbria all'inizio del secolo', *Studi economici e sociali* 15, no. 3 (1966): 125–136.

54 Lorenzo Bedeschi, *Cattolici e comunisti: dal socialismo cristiano ai cristiani marxisti* (Milan: Feltrinelli, 1974), 20–22.

55 Avolio (1848–1928), a friend of Murri's, was the organizer in Naples of Christian Democrat groups. See Ulderico Parente, *Riformismo religioso e sociale a Napoli tra Ottocento e Novecento: la figura e l'opera di Gennaro Avolio* (Urbino: Quattro Venti, 1995).

56 Luciani, *Cristianesimo e socialismo in Europa*, 741–742.

57 *Fonti e documenti*, no. 1 (1972) is devoted to the Roman radical group. See also Lorenzo Bedeschi, 'Il processo del Sant'Uffizio contro i modernisti romani', *Fonti e documenti* 6, no. 8 (1978): 7–24.

58 Buonaiuti (1881–1946), a historian and priest, was one of the leaders of Italian modernism. See Fausto Parente, *Ernesto Buonaiuti* (Rome: Istituto dell'Enciclopedia Italiana, 1971); Annibale Zambarbieri, *Il cattolicesimo tra crisi e rinnovamento, Ernesto Buonaiuti ed Enrico Rosa nella prima fase della polemica modernista* (Brescia: Morcelliana, 1979); Giordano Bruno Guerri, *Eretico e profeta. Ernesto Buonaiuti, un prete contro al Chiesa* (Milan: Mondadori, 2001); Rocco Cerrato, 'E. Buonaiuti e l'essenza del cristianesimo', *Filosofia e teologia*, no. 1 (1991): 58–68; Rocco Cerrato, 'Filosofia e teologia nella crisi modernista', in *Il modernismo in Italia e in Germania nel contesto europeo*, eds Michele Nicoletti and Otto Weiss (Bologna: Il Mulino, 2010), 99–135; Fabrizio Chiappetti, *La formazione di un prete modernista. Ernesto Buonaiuti e 'Il Rinnovamento'* (Urbino: Quattro Venti, 2012); Rocco Cerrato and Alfonso Botti, eds, 'Buonaiuti nella cultura europea del Novecento', special issue, *Modernism* 2 (2016): 21–236.

59 See Ernesto Buonaiuti, *Lo gnosticismo. Storia di antiche lotte religiose* (Rome: Ferrari, 1907).

60 See Annibale Zambarbieri, 'La ricerca e la disciplina. Ernesto Buonaiuti e la condanna della Rivista storico critica delle scienze teologiche', in *Fede e libertà. Scritti in onore di p. Giacomo Martina*, eds Maurilio Guasco, Alberto Monticone and Pietro Stella (Brescia: Morcelliana, 1998), 423–481; Rocco Cerrato, 'La Rivista storico critica delle scienze teologiche e il progresso della ricerca contemporanea', in *La riforma della Chiesa nelle riviste religiose di inizio Novecento*, eds Marina Benedetti and Daniela Saresella (Milan: Edizioni Biblioteca Francescana, 2010), 45–76.

61 *Perché siamo socialisti e cristiani* (Rome: Libreria Editrice Romana, 1908), 28.

62 Rossi (1885–1971) was an Italian philosopher and scholar of English. Turchi (1882–1958) was a priest and historian of religions. See Rocco Cerrato, 'Nova et vetera, una rivista modernista a Roma', *Annali di storia dell'educazione e delle istituzioni scolastiche* 16, no. 16 (2009): 311–334.

63 Nesti, *Gesù socialista*, 50–51.
64 Pombeni, 'Movimento cattolico e movimento socialista', 23.
65 See Pietro Scoppola, *Crisi modernista e rinnovamento cattolico in Italia* (Bologna: Il Mulino, 1963), 261–262; Zambarbieri, 'Prime censure a Buonaiuti: tra cultura e appartenenza religiosa', in *La condanna del modernismo*, 13–44.
66 Felice Perroni and, Guglielmo Quadrotta, 'Possono i socialisti cristiani iscriversi nel nostro partito? Lettera di Perroni e Quadrotta', *Avanti!*, 17 July 1908: 1.
67 Filippo Turati, 'Possono i socialisti cristiani iscriversi nel nostro partito?', *Critica sociale* 18, no. 8 (1 August 1908): 227–228.
68 On the debate over the letter from Perroni and Quadrotta, see *Socialismo e religione* (Rome: Libreria Editrice Romana, 1911). For a historical reconstruction of the facts, see Alberto De Sanctis, *Un dibattito politico su religione e socialismo (1908–1910)* (Florence: Centro Editoriale Toscano, 2010).
69 Paolo Vinci [Ernesto Buonaiuti], 'Polemiche. Socialismo cristiano', *Nova et vetera* 1, no. 11 (1908): 88–89.
70 Bonomi (1873–1951) joined the Socialist Party in 1993, and became one of the most prominent members of the organization. A Member of Parliament, he was expelled from the party in 1912 for his support for the Italian war in Libya.
71 Ivanoe Bonomi, 'Possono i socialisti cristiani iscriversi nel nostro partito?', *Avanti!*, 17 July 1908: 1.
72 Giuseppe Rensi, 'Socialismo e cristianesimo', *Critica sociale* 18, nos 23–24 (1908): 52–53.
73 Domenico Spadoni, 'Dal cristianesimo al socialismo', *Critica sociale* 18, nos 23–24 (1908): 365–367.
74 Daniela Saresella, 'Angelo Crespi collaboratore di Coenobium e la crisi religiosa di inizio Novecento', in *Spiritualità e utopia: la rivista Coenobium*, eds Fabrizio Panzera and Daniela Saresella (Milan: Cisalpino, 2007), 297–320.
75 Angelo Crespi, *Le vie della fede* (Rome: Libreria Editrice Romana, 1908), 20. See De Sanctis, 'Introduzione' to *Un dibattito politico su religione e socialismo (1908–1910)*, 47–49.
76 Born in the Ukraine, and a student of Antonio Labriola's, at the beginning of the 1900s, Angelica Balabanoff lived between Lugano (Switzerland) and Italy.
77 Angelica Balabanoff, 'Religione e socialismo', *Avanti!*, 13 August 1908: 1.
78 Alberto Malatesta, 'Possono i socialisti cristiani iscriversi al nostro partito?', *Avanti!*, 11 August 1908: 1.
79 In winter 1900, Adolf Harnack (1851–1930), Professor of Church History at Berlin University, gave a series of lectures on the original substance of the Christian message. The lectures were brought together in the book *Das Wesen des Christentums* (Leipzig: J. C. Hinrichs'sche Buchhandlung, 1902). Harnack was sceptical about subordinating the means of salvation to the church authorities, believing that the spirit was sufficient to attain the salvation of human beings. In

reply, Loisy wrote *L'Évangile et de l'Église* (Paris: Alphonse Picard et fils, 1902) in which he challenged the conclusions of the German Lutheran theologian, using the same scientific research criteria. See Harvey Hill, *The Politics of Modernism: Alfred Loisy and the Scientific Study of Religion* (Washington, DC: Catholic University of America Press, 2002).

80 Guglielmo Quadrotta, 'Polemiche coi cristiani', *Avanti!*, 14 August 1908: 1.
81 Redazione Avanti!, 'Polemiche coi cristiani. Il Vangelo vero e quello falsificato', *Avanti!*, 14 August 1908: 1.
82 Bignami (1873–1951), a member of the Italian Socialist Party, moved to Lugano in 1898 and tried to spread the ideals of pacifism through the review *Coenobium*, published from 1906 to 1919.
83 Ghisleri (1855–1938), close to the political thought of Giuseppe Mazzini, was, in 1895, one of the founders of the Partito Repubblicano.
84 Laura Demofonti, *La riforma nell'Italia del primo Novecento. Gruppi e riviste di ispirazione evangelica* (Rome: Edizioni di Storia e Letteratura, 2003), 54–65.
85 Alberto Cavaglion, 'La cultura italiana del '900 attraverso le riviste. La linea cenobitica', in *Coenobium (1906-1919), Un'antologia* (Comano: Edizioni Alice, 1992), 37.

Chapter 2

1 Giorgio Vecchio, *Luigi Sturzo. Il prete che portò i cattolici alla politica* (Milan: Centro Ambrosiano, 1997), 43–45; see also Gabriele De Rosa, *L'utopia politica di Luigi Sturzo* (Brescia: Morcelliana, 1975).
2 See Gabriele De Rosa, *Il Partito Popolare Italiano* (Bari: Laterza, 1966).
3 Edith Pratt Howard, *Il Partito Popolare Italiano* (Florence: La nuova Italia, 1957), 131.
4 Francesco Malgeri, 'Guido Miglioli nella dialettica politica dall'età giolittiana al fascismo', in *La figura e l'opera di Guido Miglioli (1879-1979)*, ed. Franco Leonori (Rome: Quaderni del CDCD, 1982), 96.
5 Giorgio Vecchio, *Alla ricerca del partito. Cultura politica ed esperienze dei cattolici italiani nel primo Novecento* (Brescia: Morcelliana, 1987), 67–69. See also John Foot, '"White Bolsheviks"? The Catholic Left and the Socialism in Italy 1919–1920', *Historical Journal* 40, no. 2 (June 1997): 415–433; Claudia Baldoli, 'With Rome and with Moscow: Italian Catholic Communism and the Anti-Fascist Exile', *Contemporary European History* 25, no. 4 (November 2016): 619–643.
6 'In margine alla lotta agraria', *L'Azione*, 1 January 1921: 1.
7 Guido Miglioli, *Con Roma e con Mosca* (Milan: Garzanti, 1945), 41.
8 'I lavoratori delle organizzazioni bianche sono anch'essi per l'unità sindacale. Una nostra intervista con l'on. Miglioli', *L'Unità*, 11 December 1924.

9   Guido Miglioli, *La collectivisation des campagnes soviétiques* (Paris: 1935).
10 Guido Miglioli, *Études historiques. Humanisme et réalisme dans la question agraire soviétique* (Brussels: 1938).
11 Carlo Felice Casula, *Fronte democratico popolare e Costituente della terra* (Rome: Edizioni Lavoro, 1981), 8.
12 Giorgio Vecchio, *I cattolici milanesi e la* politica (Milan: Vita e Pensiero, 1982), 144–150.
13 Giorgio Campanini, *Cultura e ideologia del popolarismo. Micheli, Ferrari, Donati* (Bescia: Morcelliana, 1982), 10.
14 Mario G. Rossi, *Francesco Luigi Ferrari. Dalle leghe bianche al Partito popolare* (Modena: Riccardo Franco Levi Editore, 1977), 73–83.
15 Paolo Trionfini, *Francesco Luigi Ferrari. Accompagnò i cattolici al senso dello Stato* (Milan: Centro ambrosiano, 1997), 41.
16 See Francesco Luigi Ferrari, '*Il Domani d'Italia' e altri scritti del Primo dopoguerra (1919–1926)*, ed. Mario G. Rossi (Rome: Edizioni di Storia e Letteratura, 1983).
17 'Interview with Filippo Turati', *Il Domani d'Italia*, 24 December 1922: 1.
18 Mario G. Rossi, 'Introduzione', in Ferrari,'*Il Domani d'Italia' e altri scritti del Primo dopoguerra (1919–1926)*, XVII.
19 Giuseppe Ignesti, 'Introduzione', in Francesco Luigi Ferrari, *Il regime fascista italiano*, ed. Giuseppe Ignesti (Rome: Edizioni di Storia e Letteratura, 1983), XI–CX.
20 Francesco Luigi Ferrari, *Lettera a Salvemini*, in *Antifascisti cattolici* (Vicenza: La Locusta, 1968), 43–62. See Maria Cristina Giuntella, 'Introduzione', in Francesco Luigi Ferrari, *Scritti dall'esilio. 'Azione cattolica e il Regime' e altri saggi editi e inediti sui rapporti Chiesa-Stato* (Rome: Edizioni di Storia e Letteratura; Modena: Edizioni S.I.A.S., 1991), X–XXIV.
21 Lorenzo Bedeschi, 'Esperienza di fede e coscienza storica in F.L. Ferrari: gli anni modenesi', in *Francesco Luigi Ferrari a cinquant'anni dalla morte*, ed. Giorgio Campanini (Rome: Edizioni di Storia e Letteratura, 1983), 61–62.
22 Letter from Salvemini to Sturzo of 16 May 1933, in Luigi Sturzo and Gaetano Salvemini, *Carteggio (1925–1957)*, ed. Giuseppe Grasso (Soveria Mannelli: Rubbettino, 2009), 22–23.
23 Lorenzo Bedeschi, *Giuseppe Donati* (Rome: Cinque Lune, 1959), 36–37.
24 Gianandrea De Antonellis, *Un coscienza pulita. Giuseppe Donati tra impegno politico e religioso* (Milan: Ned, 1981), 12–14; Claudio Giovannini, 'La collaborazione a *La Voce* e a *L'Unità* di Salvemini', in *Giuseppe Donati tra impegno politico e problema religioso*, eds Roberto Ruffilli and Pietro Scoppola (Milan: Vita e Pensiero, 1983), 51–56.
25 Giuseppe Rossini, 'Introduzione', in Giuseppe Donati, *Scritti politici* (Rome: Cinque Lune, 1956), LXXVI.
26 Ibid., CXVII–CXVIII.

27 Giovanni Antonazzi, 'Introduzione' in Luigi Sturzo and Alcide De Gasperi, *Carteggio (1920–1953)* (Brescia: Morcelliana, 1999), 24–25.
28 Gabriele De Rosa, *Luigi Sturzo* (Turin: Unione tipografico-Editrice torinese, 1977), 212–213.
29 De Rosa, *L'utopia politica di Luigi Sturzo*, 129.
30 Vecchio, *Luigi Sturzo*, 55.
31 Giuseppe Ignesti, 'Momenti del popolarismo in esilio', in *I cattolici tra fascismo e democrazia*, eds Pietro Scoppola and Francesco Traniello (Bologna: Il Mulino, 1975), 78–79.
32 Giorgio Vecchio, 'Alcide De Gasperi (1918–1942). Le sconfitte di un politico di professione', in Alcide De Gasperi, *Scritti e discorsi politici*, vol. 2, *Alcide De Gasperi dal Partito Popolare italiano all'esilio interno 1919–1942*, scientific coordination by Paolo Pombeni (Bologna: Il Mulino, 2007), 9–186.
33 Alberto Melloni, 'Alcide De Gasperi alla biblioteca vaticana', in *Alcide De Gasperi: un percorso europeo*, eds Gustavo Corni and Paolo Pombeni (Bologna: Il Mulino, 2005), 142–143.
34 Stefano Trinchese, 'Giordani Igino', in *Dizionario biografico degli italiani*, vol. 55 (Rome: Istituto dell'Enciclopedia Italiana, 2000), 207–212.
35 Piero Craveri, *De Gasperi* (Bologna: Il Mulino, 2006), 101–122.
36 Antonio Scornajenghi, *L'alleanza difficile. Liberali e popolari tra massimalismo socialista e reazione fascista (1919–1921)* (Rome: Studium, 2006), 56–60.
37 Mario Casella, *Cultura, politica e socialità negli scritti e nella corrispondenza di Igino Giordani* (Naples: Edizioni Scientifiche Italiane, 1992), 23–28.
38 Igino Giordani, *Rivolta Cattolica* (Turin: Gobetti, 1925).
39 Saresella, *Cattolicesimo italiano e sfida americana*, 212–214; see also Igino Giordani, *Memorie d'un cristiano ingenuo* (Rome: Città Nuova editrice, 1981), 80.
40 The letter is reproduced in: Ignesti, 'Momenti del popolarismo in esilio', 80–81.
41 Pombeni, 'Movimento cattolico e movimento socialista', 25.
42 Giovanni Sale, *La Chiesa di Mussolini. I rapporti tra fascismo e religione* (Milan: Rizzoli, 2011), 41–57.
43 Nicola Palumbi, *Don Giovanni Minzoni. Educatore e martire* (Cinisello Balsamo: San Paolo, 2003), 21–22.
44 Lorenzo Bedeschi, ed., *Il diario di don Minzoni* (Brescia: Morcelliana, 1965), 98–99.
45 Lorenzo Bedeschi, 'Introduzione', in ibid., 9–54.
46 Bartolo Gariglio, *Cattolici democratici e clerico-fascisti. Il mondo cattolico torinese alla prova del fascismo (1922–1927)* (Bologna: Il Mulino, 1976), 129–131.
47 Ibid., 145–169.
48 Daniela Saresella, 'Introduction' in Primo Mazzolari, *La pieve sull'argine* (Bologna: Dehoniane, 2008).

49 Primo Mazzolari, 'I cattolici italiani e il comunismo. Una visione obiettiva e un programma di lavoro', *La vita cattolica*, 5 March 1937: 1. See Matteo Truffelli, 'Introduzione', in Primo Mazzolari, *Scritti Politici* (Bologna: Dehoniane, 2010), 32–40.
50 Primo Mazzolari, *Il compagno Cristo: Vangelo del reduce* (Milan: Martini e Chiodi, 1945).
51 Address by His Holiness Pius XI to the professors and students of the Catholic University of the Sacred Heart in Milan, 13 February 1929, available online:https://w2.vatican.va/content/pius-xi/it/speeches/documents/hf_p-xi_spe_19290213_vogliamo-anzitutto.html (accessed 11 May 2019). See Christopher Duggan, *Fascist Voices. An Intimate History of Mussolini's Italy* (London: The Bodley Head, 2012), 95–112; Emilio Gentile, *Contro Cesare. Cristianesimo e totalitarismo nell'epoca dei fascismi* (Milan: Feltrinelli, 2016).
52 Ridolfi's words are mentioned in: Francesco Ridolfi, 'Un caso di coscienza', in *Antifascisti Cattolici* (Vicenza: La Locusta, 1968), 80–81.
53 Giorgio Vecchio, *Lombardia 1940-1945. Vescovi, preti e società alla prova della guerra* (Brescia: Morcelliana, 2005), 29, 110.
54 Gioacchino Malavasi, *L'antifascismo cattolico. Il Movimento guelfo d'azione (1928-1948)* (Rome: Edizioni Lavoro, 1982), 12. See Paolo Trionfini, *'L'antifascismo cattolico' di Gioacchino Malavasi* (Rome: Edizioni Lavoro, 2004), 9–134.
55 Vincenzo Schirripa, *Giovani sulla frontiera. Guide e scout cattolici nell'Italia repubblicana* (Rome: Studium, 2006), 34–35.
56 Renato Moro, *La formazione della classe dirigente cattolica (1929-1937)* (Bologna: Il Mulino, 1979), 84. See Maria Cristina Giuntella, *La Fuci tra modernismo, Partito popolare e fascismo* (Rome: Studium, 2000). See also Jorge Dagnino, 'The Intellectuals of Italian Catholic Action and the Sacralisation of Politics in 1930s Europe', *Contemporary European History* 21, no. 2 (May 2012): 215–233. See also Richard J. Wolff, *Between Pope and Duce: Catholic Students in Fascist Italy* (New York: Peter Lang, 1990).
57 Ibid., 208–211.
58 Ibid., 10–11.
59 'Note a margine', *L'Ossevatore Romano*, 24 May 1931: 1.
60 Silvana Antonioli and Gianna Cameroni, *Cattolici Clandestini. Federico Sorbaro e il Movimento guelfo d'azione* (Milan: NED, 1985), 15–17.
61 Guido Verucci, *La Chiesa nella società contemporanea* (Rome: Laterza, 1988), 37.
62 Antonio Acerbi, *La Chiesa e la democrazia. Da Leone XIII al Vaticano II* (Milan: Vita e Pensiero, 1991), 112–113.
63 Giovanni Miccoli, 'La Chiesa e il fascismo', in *Fascismo e società italiana*, ed. Guido Quazza (Turin: Einaudi, 1973), 203.
64 Moro, *La formazione della classe dirigente cattolica*, 42.
65 Daniele Menozzi, *Sacro Cuore. Un culto tra devozione interiore e restaurazione cristiana della società* (Rome: Viella, 2001).

66 See Maria Bocci, *Agostino Gemelli, rettore e francescano. Chiesa, regime, democrazia* (Brescia: Morcelliana, 2003).
67 See Verucci, *L'eresia del Novecento*, 66–70.
68 Carlo Fantappiè, *Arturo Carlo Jemolo. Riforma religiosa e laicità dello Stato* (Brescia: Morcelliana, 2011), 21–22. See also Annibale Zambarbieri, 'La Koinonìa di Ernesto Buonaiuti', *Humanitas* 61, no. 56 (2001): 213–230; Ottavia Niccoli, ed., *Una rete di amicizie. Carteggi dalla Koinonia di Ernesto Buonaiuti* (Rome: Viella, 2014); Francesco Torchiani, *L'oltretevere da oltreoceano* (Rome: Donzelli, 2015), 67–73.
69 Guerri, *Eretico e profeta*, 4.
70 Luigi Salvatorelli and Giovanni Mira, *Storia d'Italia nel periodo fascista* (Turin: Einaudi, 1962), 497.
71 Ernesto Buonaiuti, *La Chiesa romana* (Milan: Gilardi e Noto, 1932).
72 Lorenzo Bedeschi, 'Introduction', in ibid., 24–25.
73 Guerri, *Eretico e profeta*, 244.
74 P. Olivi [Ernesto Buonaiuti], 'Chiesa e comunismo', *L'Ambrosiano*, 23 January 1937, 1.
75 Ernesto Buonaiuti, *La Chiesa e il comunismo* (Rome: Bompiani, 1945), 5–8, 36–37.
76 Regarding the whole affair, see Francesco Margiotta Broglio, *Italia e Santa Sede dalla Grande guerra alla Conciliazione* (Bari: Laterza, 1966).
77 On 24 January 1945, he wrote to Remo Missir: 'I have not yet been reinstated to my university chair. I would like to think and hope that it will not take much longer for justice to be done for me.' (Ernesto Buonaiuti, *La vita allo sbaraglio. Lettere a Missir (1926–1946)*, ed. Ambrogio Donini (Florence: La nuova Italia editrice, 1980), 543.
78 Francesco Margiotta Broglio, 'Ernesto Buonaiuti', in *Modernismo, fascismo, comunismo. Aspetti e figure della cultura e della politica del cattolici nel '900*, ed. Giuseppe Rossini (Bologna: Il Mulino, 1972), 79–99.
79 'Modernism', Giorgio La Piana Papers, bMS 104, Andover-Harvard Theological Library, Harvard Divinity School, Cambridge, MA. On this, see Daniela Saresella, 'Giorgio La Piana and the Religious Crisis in Italy at the Beginning of the 20th Century', *Harvard Theological Review* 110, no. 1 (2017): 75–99.
80 Giorgio Levi Della Vida, *Fantasmi ritrovati* (Vicenza: Neri Pozza, 1966), 153.
81 Ernesto Buonaiuti, *Pellegrino di Roma* (Rome: Darsena, 1945), 214, 344.
82 Ambrogio Donini, *Sessant'anni di militanza comunista* (Milan: Teti, 1988), 109–110.
83 Ibid., 30, 178.
84 Buonaiuti, *Pellegrino di Roma*, 345–346.
85 Ambrogio Donini, *Stato laico e libertà di coscienza*, conference held at Milan's Teatro Lirico on 15 December 1946, mimeograph.
86 Leonardo Rapone, *Cinque anni che paiono secoli. Antonio Gramsci dal socialismo al comunismo* (Rome: Carocci, 2011).

87 Paolo Spriano, *Storia del Partito comunista*, vol. 1, *Da Bordiga a Gramsci* (Turin: Einaudi, 1976); Albertina Vittoria, *Storia del Pci (1921-1991)* (Rome: Carocci, 2006).
88 A useful text on the relationship between Labriola and Gramsci is Guido Liguori's *Sentieri gramsciani* (Rome: Carocci, 2006), 113-123.
89 'Il Partito comunista', *L'Ordine nuovo*, 4 September 1920: 1; now in Antonio Gramsci, *L'Ordine nuovo 1919-1920* (Turin: Einaudi, 1954), 154. Gramsci, on 11 October 1919, also wrote the article *Giorgio Sorel* in *Ordine nuovo* (now in Antonio Gramsci, *Masse e partito. Antologia 1910-1926*, ed. Guido Liguori [Rome: Editori Riuniti, 2016], 198-200).
90 Hugues Portelli, *Gramsci e la questione religiosa* (Milan: Mazzotta, 1976), 9. See also Antonio Gramsci, *Il Vaticano e l'Italia* (Rome: Editori Riuniti, 1967). See Forlenza and Thomassen, *Italian Modernities*, 91-118.
91 *Socialisti e cristiani*, 26 August 1920, quoted in Antonio Gramsci, *Sotto la mole (1916-1920)* (Turin: Einaudi, 1960), 495.
92 Gabriele De Rosa, 'Gramsci e la questione cattolica', in *Atti del convegno internazionale di studi gramsciani*, Florence, 9-11 December 1977, ed. Franco Ferri (Rome: Editori Riuniti-Istituto Gramsci, 1977), 262-263.
93 'Il Partito comunista', 154.
94 Ibid., 155.
95 The *Quaderni del carcere* (Prison Notebooks) are the collection of comments, texts and notes that Antonio Gramsci began writing from 8 February 1929, during his incarceration in fascist prisons. See Giuseppe Cospito, *Il ritmo del pensiero. Per una lettura diacronica dei 'Quaderni del carcere' di Gramsci* (Naples: Bibliopolis, 2011); Angelo D'Orsi, *Gramsci. Una nuova biografia* (Milan: Feltrinelli, 2017), 261-279.
96 *Le Tesi di Lione* (the Lyon Theses) are the political documents elaborated by Gramsci and presented at the Third Congress of the Italian Communist Party, held clandestinely in Lyon in January 1926. See Gramsci, *Masse e partito*, 333-388.
97 Filippo Mazzonis, 'Gramsci e la questione cattolica', *Trimestre* 14, nos 2-3 (1980): 173. See especially Fabio Frosini, *La religione dell'uomo moderno. Politica e verità nei* Quaderni del carcere *di Antonio Gramsci* (Rome: Carocci, 2010), 40-42. Cosimo Zene, 'I subalterni nel mondo: tipologie e nesso con le differenti forme dell'esperienza religiosa', *International Gramsci Journal* 1, no. 4 (June 2015): 66-82. Fabio Frosini, 'Subalterns, Religion, and the Philosophy of Praxis in Gramsci's Prison Notebooks', *Rethinking Marxism* 28, nos 3-4 (December 2016): 523-539.
98 Antonio Gramsci, *Quaderni dal carcere*, vol. 2, *Il materialismo storico e la filosofia di Benedetto Croce*, ed. Valentina Gerratana (Turin: Einaudi, 2012), 1383-1384.
99 Gramsci also communicated his personal aversion to the Society of Jesus in a letter to Tania of 7 April 1930, in which he expressed a negative judgment with regard to Fr. Alberto Bresciani (Antonio Gramsci and Tatiana Schucht, *Lettere 1926-1935*, eds Aldo Natoli and Chiara Daniele [Turin: Einaudi, 1997], 494-497).

100 Ernesto Vercesi *I papi del secolo XIX*, vol. I, *Pio VII* (Milan: Società Editrice internazionale, 1932). Gramsci had also read Ernesto Vercesi's *Storia del movimento cattolico in Italia (1870–1922)* (Florence: Edizioni de La Voce, 1923) (Letter from Gramsci to Tania of 25 March 1929, in Gramsci and Schucht, *Lettere 1926–1935*, 331–335).
101 Gramsci, *Quaderni dal carcere*, vol. 2, 1383–1384.
102 A. G., untitled article, *Avanti!*, Piemontese edition, 22 December 1918; cited from Antonio Gramsci, *Scritti giovanili (1914–1918)* (Turin: Einaudi, 1958), 349.
103 'I popolari', *L'Ordine nuovo*, 1 November 1919; cited from Antonio Gramsci, *L'Ordine nuovo*, 284.
104 Ibid., 285–286.
105 Ibid., 286.
106 Bartolo Gariglio, *Con animo liberale. Piero Gobetti e i popolari 1918–1926)* (Milan: Angeli, 1997), 17–48. See also Paolo Spriano, *Gramsci e Gobetti. Introduzione alla vita e alle opere* (Turin: Einaudi, 1977).
107 Claudio Treves, 'La Chiesa e il nuovo assetto europeo', *Critica sociale* 31, no. 23 (1–15 December 1919): 336.
108 Claudio Treves, 'I popolari e la proprietà', *Critica sociale* 32, no. 8 (16–30 April 1920): 113.
109 Untitled article, *L'Ordine nuovo*, 20 March 1920; now in Gramsci, *L'Ordine nuovo*, 476.
110 *Socialisti e cristiani*, 26 August 1920; now in Gramsci, *Sotto la Mole 1916–1920*, 495.
111 Untitled article, *L'Unità*, 24 February 1926; cited in Antonio Gramsci, *La costruzione del Partito comunista 1923–1926* (Turin: Einaudi, 1978), 107–108.
112 'La sostanza della crisi', *L'Ordine nuovo*, 5 February 1922; cited in Antonio Gramsci, *Socialismo e fascismo* (Rome: Editori Riuniti, 1972), 454.
113 'La situazione', *L'Ordine nuovo*, 21 February 1922; cited in Antonio Gramsci, *Per la verità. Scritti 1913–1926*, ed. Renzo Martinelli (Rome: Editori Riuniti, 1974), 253.
114 'Che fare?', *Voce della gioventù*, 1 November 1923; cited in Gramsci, *Per la verità*, 268. In relation to this, see Renzo Martinelli, 'Il "che fare" di Gramsci nel 1923', *Studi storici* 13, no. 4 (1972): 790–802.
115 Unsigned article in *L'Unità*, 24 February 1926; cited in Gramsci, *La costruzione del Partito comunista*, 106.
116 'Il Partito comunista II'; now in Gramsci, *L'Ordine nuovo*, 159.
117 'Il Partito popolare', *L'Unità*, 22 February 1924; now in Gramsci, *La costruzione del Partito comunista*, 11.
118 'La sostanza della crisi', *L'Ordine nuovo*, 5 February 1922; now in Gramsci, *Socialismo e fascismo*, 454.
119 'Il processo della crisi', *L'Ordine nuovo*, 13 February 1922; now in Gramsci, *Socialismo e fascismo*, 459.

120 'Il Partito comunista', 159.
121 Ibid.
122 The bill, officially against Freemasonry, in fact proposed to restrict the areas of action of anti-fascist parties. For Gramsci's intervention, see 'Campagna Nazionale contro l'Art. 270 e tutti I Reati Associativi'. Available online: https://www.inventati.org/reati_associativi/testi%20raccolti/011.html (accessed 11 May 2019).
123 *Origini e scopi della legge sulle associazioni segrete*, in *L'Unità*, 23 May 1925; now in Gramsci, *La costruzione del Partito comunista*, 84.
124 'Il Partito popolare', 10.
125 Ibid., 10–11.
126 Ibid., 12.
127 'Un dibattito su Gramsci e la storia d'Italia', *Studi storici* 8, no. 3 (July–September 1967): 637–649.
128 'La Ceka', *L'Unità*, 7 December 1924; cited in Gramsci, *La costituzione del Partito comunista*, 372.
129 *La Correspondance internationale* was the bulletin of information of the Komintern, published in French, English and German.
130 'Il Vaticano', *Correspondance internationale*, 12 March 1924; cited in Gramsci, *La costruzione del Partito comunista*, 523.
131 *Un esame della situazione italiana*, a text that Gramsci submitted to the Communist Party's Executive Committee on 2–3 August 1926; cited in Gramsci, *La costruzione del Partito comunista*, 116.
132 'Il Vaticano', 524.
133 Emile Vandervelde, 'Conclusions. Le résultats de l'enquête', *Mouvement socialiste*, 15 April 1903, 667. From December 1902 to April 1903, the *Mouvement socialiste* had launched an investigation into anticlericalism and socialism in which the leading exponents of the Second International had participated.
134 George Sorel, *Lettere a Benedetto Croce*, ed. Salvatore Onufrio (Bari: De Donato, 1980). Modernism and figures linked to the movement are discussed on several occasions in the letters.
135 *Quaderni dal carcere,* vol. 2, 1384.
136 Antonio Gramsci, *Quaderni dal carcere*, vol. 3, *Letteratura e vita nazionale* (Rome: Editori Internazionali Riuniti, 2013), 1711.
137 Ibid., 2013.
138 George Sorel, 'Le illusioni del progresso', in George Sorel, *Scritti politici*, ed. Roberto Vivarelli (Turin: Unione Tipografica Torinese, 1963), 678. With regard to this, see Giuseppe La Ferla, *Ritratto di Georges Sorel* (Milan: La Cultura, 1933), 55–58; Marco Gervanoni, *Georges Sorel. Una biografia intellettuale. Socialismo e liberalismo nella Francia della Belle époque* (Milan: Unicopli, 2006).
139 George Sorel, 'Le modernisme et le nouveau Syllabus', *Pages libres*, 7 September 1907, 247.

140 Benedetto Croce, 'Il risveglio filosofico e la cultura italiana (1908)', in *Cultura e vita morale* (Bari: Laterza, 1914), 14.
141 Luigi M. Bottazzi, 'Il Sillabo di Pio X', *Critica sociale*, 1 August 1907, 230. In relation to the judgement of European Socialists on Modernism, see Daniela Saresella, 'Il movimento socialista, il modernismo e la questione religiosa (1898-1907)', in *Il modernismo tra cristianità e secolarizzazione*, eds Alfonso Botti and Rocco Cerrato (Urbino: Quattro Venti, 2000), 145-159.
142 *Quaderni dal carcere*, vol. 2, 1265-1266.
143 Félix Sartiaux, *Joseph Turmel: prêtre historien des dogmes* (Paris: Les Éditions Rieder, 1931).
144 *Quaderni dal carcere*, vol. 3, 1713. Alfred Loisy, *Mémoires pour servir à l'histoire religieuse de notre temps* (Paris: Nourry, 1930-1931).
145 Lorenzo Bedeschi, *Interpretazioni e sviluppo del modernismo cattolico* (Milan: Bompiani, 1975).
146 Antonio Gramsci, *Quaderni dal carcere*, vol. 1, *Gli intellettuali e l'organizzazione della cultura* (Rome: Editori Internazionali Riuniti, 2012), 69.
147 *Quaderni dal carcere*, vol. 3, 1712.
148 *Quaderni dal carcere*, vol. 2, 1304.
149 Ibid., 1213.
150 Ibid., 1304.
151 Gentile was – together with Benedetto Croce – one of the greatest exponents of the Italian Philosophical neo-idealism.
152 Prezzolini was a journalist, writer, editor, professor at the University, and Italian writer.
153 *Quaderni dal carcere*, vol. 2, 1304-1305. Regarding the relationship between Gramsci and Gentile, see Giuseppe Vacca, *Modernità alternative. Il Novecento di Antonio Gramsci* (Turin: Einaudi, 2017), 47-48.
154 Missiroli was an Italian writer and journalist.
155 *Quaderni dal carcere*, vol. 2, 1304-1305.
156 Ibid. There is an interesting handwritten note, found by Giuseppe Vacca in the papers of Tania Schucht at the Gramsci Institute in Rome, which reflects on the repression of the Modernist movement (Giuseppe Vacca, *Vita e pensieri di Antonio Gramsci (1926-1937)* [Turin: Einaudi, 2012], 260-261, n. 36).
157 *Quaderni dal carcere*, vol. 3, 2089-2091.
158 Bedeschi, *Cattolici e comunisti*, 32.
159 Elisa Giunipero, 'Le inchieste sul comunismo in Cina?', in *Pius XI*, eds Alberto Guasco and Raffaella Perin (Münster: LIT, 2010), 393-445.
160 Verucci, *La Chiesa nella società contemporanea*, 98-99. Giulia Albanese, *Dittature mediterranee. Fascismo e colpo di Stato in Italia, Spagna e Portogallo* (Rome: Laterza, 2016).
161 Philippe Chenaux, *L'Église catholique et le communisme en Europe (1917-1989). De Lénine à Jean-Paul II* (Paris: Cerf, 2009), 85-118.

162 Piero Treves, *Scritti novecenteschi*, eds Alberto Cavaglion and Sandro Gerbi (Bologna: Il Mulino, 2006), 110–111.
163 See Roberto Pertici, *Chiesa e Stato in Italia. Dalla Grande Guerra al nuovo concordato (1914–1984)* (Bologna: Il Mulino, 2009), 262–264.
164 Emma Fattorini, *Hitler, Mussolini and the Vatican: Pope Pius XI and the Speech That Was Never Made* (Cambridge: Polity Press, 2011).
165 Agostino Giovagnoli, *La cultura democristiana* (Rome: Laterza, 1991), 210.
166 See Francesco Malgeri, 'La formazione della DC tra scelte locali e urgenze nazionali', in *Cattolici, Chiesa, Resistenza*, ed. Gabriele De Rosa (Bologna: Il Mulino, 1997), 533–563.
167 *A colloquio con Dossetti e Lazzati*, interview by Leopoldo Elia and Pietro Scoppola (Bologna: Il Mulino, 2003), 30.
168 See Francesco Malgeri, *La Chiesa italiana e la guerra* (Rome: Studium, 1980), 130.
169 Andrea Riccardi, *L'inverno più lungo (1943–1944): Pio XII, gli ebrei e i nazisti a Roma* (Rome: Laterza, 2008), V–XVIII.
170 Giacomo De Antonellis, 'I cattolici lombardi a difesa della libertà', *Civiltà ambrosiana* II, no. 2 (1985), 136; see also Giacomo De Antonellis, *Cattolici ambrosiani per la libertà* (Milan: Ned, 1995).
171 After the fall of fascism, which took place on 25 July 1943, and following the armistice of 8 September (signed by King Vittorio Emanuele and Prime Minister Badoglio), the north of Italy was invaded by German troops and there began the political experience of the Italian Social Republic, headed by Mussolini. The liberation of Italy took place on 25 April 1945.
172 There is a useful bibliography regarding Catholics, war and resistance edited by Paolo Trionfini, 'I cattolici italiani, la seconda guerra mondiale, la resistenza: una bibliografia', *Bollettino dell'Archivio per la storia del movimento sociale cattolico in Italia* 31, no. 1 (1996), 35–184.
173 Piero Malvestiti, 'La confusione delle lingue e la lingua delle confusioni', *L'Italia*, 7 September 1943; republished in Piero Malvestiti, *La lotta politica in Italia dal 25 luglio 1943 alla Costituente* (Milan: Bernabò, 1948), 22–23.
174 *Idee e programmi della DC nella Resistenza*, introduction by Giovanni Battista Varnier (Rome: Civitas, 1984), 51–54. See Alberto Caracciolo, *Teresio Olivelli* (Brescia: La Scuola, 1975), 144–151; Nazareno Fabbretti, *Teresio Olivelli* (Milan: Edizioni Paoline, 1992).
175 See Enrico Galavotti, *Il giovane Dossetti: gli anni della formazione, 1913–1939* (Bologna: Il Mulino, 2006); Enrico Galavotti, *Il professorino: Giuseppe Dossetti tra crisi del fascismo e costruzione della democrazia 1940–1948* (Bologna: Il Mulino, 2013); Paolo Pombeni, *Giuseppe Dossetti: l'avventura politica di un riformatore cristiano* (Bologna: Il Mulino, 2013); Alberto Melloni, *Dossetti l'indicibile. Il quaderno scomparso di Cronache sociali: i cattolici per un nuovo partito a sinistra della Dc* (Rome: Donzelli, 2013).

176 *Idee e programmi della Dc nella Resistenza*, 105-111. See also Giorgio Campanini, 'I programmi del partito democratico cristiano (1942-1947)', in *Cristiani in politica. I programmi politici dei movimenti cattolici democratici*, ed. Bartolo Gariglio (Milan: Angeli, 1987), 196-208.

177 Giacomo De Antonellis, *Il caso Puecher. Morire a vent'anni partigiano e cristiano* (Milan: Rizzoli, 1984).

178 Ezio Franceschini, *Attività clandestina dell'Associazione professori e assistenti universitari APAU e del Comitato di Liberazione Nazionale dei professori e assistenti universitari* (Milan: Comitato direttivo provvisorio dell'Associazione professori e assistenti universitari, 1945).

179 Marilena Dorini, *Giuseppe Lazzati: gli anni del lager (1943-1945)* (Rome: Ave, 1989).

180 Giuseppe Lazzati, 'La Resistenza continua', in *Per amore ribelli*, eds Gianfranco Bianche and Bruno De Marchi (Milan: Vita e Pensiero, 1976), 13-17.

181 See Truffelli, 'Introduzione', 21-32.

182 Vecchio, *Lombardia 1940-1945*, 325-387.

183 See Alfonso Botti, Rocco Cerrato and Stefano Pivato, 'L'itinerario storiografico di Lorenzo Bedeschi', *Fonti e documenti* 13, no. 13 (1984): 13-43.

184 Lorenzo Bedeschi, *Uno che ha attraversato la linea* (Ravenna: Istituto Storico della Resistenza di Ravenna, 1966), 47.

185 See Pietro Scoppola, *25 aprile. Liberazione* (Turin: Einaudi, 1995).

Chapter 3

1 Hubert Wolf, *Papst und Teufel. Die Archive des Vatikan und das Dritte Reich* (Munich: Verlag, 2008); Fattorini, *Hitler, Mussolini and the Vatican*. See also George Passelecq and Bernard Suchecky, *L'Encyclique Cache ´e de Pie XI: Une occasion manque ´ de l'E ´glise face a l'antisemitisme* (Paris: Le Découverte, 1995); Raffaella Perin, ed., *Pio XI e la crisi europea* (Venice: Edizioni Cà Foscari, 2016); Giovanni Coco, 'Un inviato molto special. Spionaggio fascista e diplomazia italiana nel Conclave del 1939', *Revue d'Histoire Ecclésistique* 113, nos 1-2 (1918): 273-318.

2 Lucia Ceci, *L'interesse superiore. Il Vaticano e l'Italia di Mussolini* (Rome: Laterza, 2013), 212-260.

3 Marisa Rodano, *Diario minimo del mutare dei tempi. L'età dell'inconsapevolezza, il tempo della speranza (1921-1948)*, vol. 1 (Rome: Memori, 2008), 149-150.

4 Giovanni Pioli, a contributor to a number of journals (*Coenobium, Nova et vetera* and *Bilychnis*), was a frequent visitor to the modernist circles in Rome that centred on the figure of Buonaiuti. Considered as belonging to the group of radical Modernists, he decided to renounce priesthood, in the belief that the Roman

Church was not consistent with the true values of Christianity, oppressed as it was by rigidity of doctrine (See Demofonti, *La riforma nell'Italia del primo Novecento*, 112). In the aftermath of the Second World War Pioli collaborated with radical pacifist movements; he died in 1969.

5 Bedeschi, *Cattolici e comunisti*, 51.
6 Daniela Saresella, *Cattolici a sinistra. Dal modernismo ai giorni nostri* (Rome: Laterza, 2011), 35–41.
7 Adriano Ossicini, *Un'isola sul Tevere. Il fascismo al di là del ponte* (Rome: Editori Riuniti, 1999), 42.
8 Bedeschi, *Cattolici e comunisti*, 52–53.
9 The document is included in F. Leonori, 'Una Sinistra cristiana d'altri tempi', *Astrolabio* 12, no. 65 (28 February 1973): 62.
10 Ibid., 62.
11 Francesco Malgeri, *La Sinistra cristiana (1937–1945)* (Brescia: Morcelliana, 1982), 21–22. See also Adriano Ossicini, *Cristiani non democristiani* (Rome: Editori Riuniti, 1980), 51–65.
12 Ossicini, *Un'isola sul Tevere*, 132.
13 Renato Zangrandi, *Il lungo viaggio attraverso il fascismo. Contributo alla storia di una generazione* (Milan: Feltrinelli, 1962), 542–544.
14 Franceso Malgeri, 'Cultura e politica in Felice Balbo: l'esperienza della sinistra cristiana', in *Felice Balbo tra filosofia e società*, ed. Giorgio Campanini (Milan: Angeli, 1985), 17–18.
15 Augusto Del Noce, *Il cattolico comunista* (Milan: Rusconi, 1981), 197–198.
16 Malgeri, *La sinistra cristiana*, 23–24.
17 Lucio Lombardo Radice, 'La Sinistra Cristiana e la collocazione politica dei cattolici rivoluzionari', *Rinascita* XXIV, no. 11 (1967): 19–20; collected in Lucio Lombardo Radice, *Socialismo e libertà* (Rome: Editori Riuniti, 1968), 119–127.
18 Adriano Ossicini, 'Cattolici a pugno chiuso', *Rinascita* 30, no. 45 (1973): 21–22.
19 The document is preserved in the Archivio Centrale dello Stato (Central State Archives in Rome), Ministero degli Interni, 1903–1941, cat. F1, folder 16, sheet 198.
20 *Documento del MCC* [MCC Document], s.d. (but 1943), in the Archivio Storico dell'Istituto Luigi Sturzo, Fondo Partito Sinistra Cristiana, box 9, folder C51, sheet 6.
21 Letter by Adriano Ossicini, in Archivio Storico dell'Istituto Luigi Sturzo, Fondo Partito Sinistra Cristiana, box 9, folder C51, sheet 5.
22 See Donald Sassoon, *Togliatti e il partito di massa. Il Pci dal 1944 al 1964* (Rome: Castelvecchi, 2014).
23 Letter from Rodano to Balbo, in the Archivio Storico dell'Istituto Luigi Sturzo, Fondo Partito Sinistra Cristiana, box 9, folder C51, sheet 7.

24 *Il comunismo e i cattolici* (Rome: Ed. Voce Operaia, 1944), 36–44.
25 'Nel blocco attorno al Comitato di Liberazione Nazionale sta la sicura vittoria delle masse popolari', *Voce operaia*, 4 December 1943: 1.
26 Francesco Malgeri, 'Introduzione', in *Voce operaia. Dai cattolici comunisti alla Sinistra cristiana* (Rome: Studium, Rome 1992), 35–36.
27 Ossicini, *Cattolici a pugno chiuso*, 21–22.
28 *A colloquio con Dossetti e Lazzati*, interview by Elia and Scoppola, 47.
29 Mariano Cordovani, 'Cattolici comunisti', *L'Osservatore Romano*, 23 July 1944: 1.
30 'Un passo avanti', *Voce operaia*, 4 September 1944: 1.
31 *Ordine del giorno del Partito della Sinistra Cristiana* ('Agenda of the Party of the Christian Left'), 4 September 1944, in the Archivio Storico dell'Istituto Luigi Sturzo, Fondo Partito Sinistra Cristiana, box 2, folder B6, sheet 7.
32 *Statuto del partito della Sinistra Cristiana* ('Statute of the Party of the Christian Left'), in the Archivio Storico dell'Istituto Luigi Sturzo, Fondo Partito Sinistra Cristiana, box 1, folder B3, sheet 3.
33 Francesco Malgeri, *La sinistra cristinana*, 113–115.
34 'Nota', *L'Osservatore Romano*, 2 January 1945: 1.
35 *Direzione Centrale del Partito* ('Party Executive Committee'), 5 January 1945, in the Archivio Storico dell'Istituto Luigi Sturzo, Fondo Partito Sinistra Cristiana, box 2, folder B6, sheets 6 and 8.
36 [Palmiro Togliatti], 'Il caso della "Sinistra cristiana"', *Rinascita* 2, no. 1 (January 1945): 16–17.
37 *Direzione central* ('Executive Committee'), 4 August 1945, in the Archivio Storico dell'Istituto Luigi Sturzo, Fondo Partito Sinistra Cristiana, box 2, folder B6, sheet 16. See also Mario Cocchi and Pio Montesi, eds, *Per una storia della Sinistra cristiana. Documenti 1937–1945* (Rome: Coines, 1975), 214–271.
38 See Jean-François Durand, *L'Église catholique dans le crise de l'Italie* (Rome: École française de Rome, 1991), 621–628.
39 See Carlo Felica Casula, *Cattolici-comunisti e sinistra cristiana (1938–1945)* (Bologna: Il Mulino, 1976), 178–179; Antonio Parisella, 'Christian Movements and Parties of Left in Italy (1938–1958)', in *Left Catholicism (1943–1945). Catholicism and Society in Western Europe at the Point of Liberation*, eds Emmanuel Gerard and Gerd-Rainer Horn (Leuven: Leuven University Press, 2001), 142–173.
40 Balbo's intervention is in Cocchi and Montesi, *Per una storia della Sinistra cristiana*, 238–241.
41 Adriano Ossicini, *Contro la sconfitta della politica* (Rome: Editori Riuniti, 2002), 10.
42 Malgeri, 'Cultura e politica in Felice Balbo', 26.
43 Bedeschi, *Cattolici e comunisti*, 87–120.
44 Palmiro Togliatti, *Comunisti e cattolici* (Rome: Editori Riuniti, 1966), 14–15.
45 *A colloquio con Dossetti e Lazzati*, interview by Elia and Scoppola, 68.

46 After the excommunication of 1949, Balbo and his group decided not to renew their PCI membership as an act of allegiance to the Church; three years later (5 February 1952) they would publish a declaration of allegiance to pontifical directions in the *Osservatore Romano*.
47 Adriana Zavoli, 'Gerardo Bruni e i cristiano-sociali', *Discorsi e immagini* 2, no. 9 (1981): 8–21.
48 Luciani, *Cristianesimo e socialismo in Europa*, 763–765, 780–781. Olivetti (Ivrea 1901–Aigle 1960), engineer, entrepreneur and Italian politician, was distinguished for his innovative industrial projects. He thougth that the company's profit would be reinvested for the benefit of the community.
49 Gerardo Bruni, 'In tema di ideologia socialista', *Quaderni del socialismo* 1, no. 1 (1953): 5.
50 Antonio Parisella, 'Gerardo Bruni', in *Dizionario storico del movimento cattolico in Italia*, vol. 1, *Protagonisti*, eds Francesco Traniello and Giorgio Campanini (Casale Monferrato: Marietti, 1982), 56–58. See also Antonio Parisella, ed., *Gerardo Bruni e i cristiano-sociali* (Rome: Edizioni Lavoro, 1984).
51 Vittorini, writer and translator, from 1945 (until 1947) headed the journal *Il Politecnico*, close to the PCI. See Irene Piazzoni, 'Per una nuova cultura politica', in *1945. La transizione del dopoguerra*, eds Guido Formigoni and Daniela Saresella (Rome: Viella, 2017), 209–228.
52 See Giorgio Campanini, *Cristianesimo e democrazia: studi sul pensiero politico cattolico del Novecento* (Brescia: Morcelliana, 1980, 139–152.
53 Lorenzo Bedeschi, 'L'opposizione cattolica nel decennio 1949–1959', in *I cristiani nella sinistra dalla Resistenza a oggi* (Rome: Coines, 1976), 111–112.
54 See Craveri, *De Gasperi*; Guido Formigoni, 'Alcide De Gasperi 1943–1948. Il politico vincente alla guida della transizione', in Alcide De Gasperi, *Scritti e discorsi politici*, vol. 3, *Alcide De Gasperi e la fondazione della Democrazia cristiana (1943–1948)*, eds Vera Capperucci and Sara Lorenzini (Bologna: Il Mulino, 2008), 119–147. On this period, see also Christopher Duggan and Christopher Wagstaff, eds, *Italy in the Cold War. Politics, Culture and Society (1948–1958)* (Oxford: Berg, 1995).
55 On this, see Marta Margotti, *Lavoro manuale e spiritualità. L'itinerario dei preti operai* (Rome: Studium, 2001). See also Robert Wattebled, *Stratégies catholiques en monde ouvrier dans la France d'après-guerre* (Paris: Ed. Ouvrières, 1990); Emmanuel Gerard E. Paul Wynants, ed., *Histoire du mouvement ouvrier chrétien en Belgique* (Leuven: Leuven University Press, 1994); Bruno Duriez and Étienne Fouilloux, eds, *Chrétiens et ouvriers en France (1937–1970)* (Paris: Éditions de l'Atelier, 2001); Marta Margotti, *La fabbrica dei cattolici. Chiesa, industria e organizzazioni operaie a Torino (1948–1965)* (Turin: Angolo Manzoni, 2012).
56 Giuseppe Carlo Marino, *Autobiografia del Pci staliniano 1946–1953* (Rome: Editori Riuniti, 1991), 47–57. See Vittoria, *Storia del PCI*.

57 Patrizia Gabrielli, *Vivere da protagoniste: donne tra politica, cultura e controllo sociale* (Rome: Carocci, 2001).

58 Daniela Saresella and Giorgio Vecchio, eds, *Mazzolari e il cattolicesimo italiano prima del Concilio Vaticano II* (Brescia: Morcelliana, 2012); Paolo Zanini, *La rivista Il gallo: dalla tradizione al dialogo (1946–1965)* (Milan: Biblioteca Francescana, 2012).

59 Lorenzo Bedeschi, 'La presenza politica dei cristiani nella sinistra italiana. Appunti per una interpretazione', in *I cristiani nella sinistra dalla Resistenza ad oggi* (Rome: Coines, 1976), 34.

60 Remo Rinaldi, *Don Zeno, Turoldo, Nomadelfia. Era semplicemente Vangelo* (Bologna: Dehoniane, 1998), 129.

61 Michele Ranchetti, *Gli ultimi preti. Figure del cattolicesimo contemporaneo* (Fiesole: ECP, 1997), 11. With regard to this, see Maurilio Guasco and Paolo Trionfini, eds, *Don Zeno e Nomadelfia. Tra società civile e società religiosa* (Brescia: Morcelliana, 2001).

62 'Note', *L'Italia*, 26 May 1952: 1.

63 David Maria Turoldo, 'Meditazione sul voto del 18 aprile', *Cronache sociali* 2, no. 8 (1948): 1–2.

64 See Daniela Saresella, *David Maria Turoldo, Camillo De Piaz e la Corsia dei Servi di Milano* (Brescia: Morcelliana, 2008); Paolo Zanini, *David Maria Turoldo: nella storia religiosa e politica del Novecento* (Milan: Paoline, 2013).

65 See Agostino Giovagnoli, 'L'Azione cattolica italiana dal 1948 al 1958', in *Chiesa e progetto educativo nell'Italia del secondo dopoguerra* (Brescia: La scuola, 1988), 117–154.

66 Mario Rossi, *La terra dei vivi* (Rome: Ave, 1954), 13, 19.

67 'Faziose speculazioni', *L'Osservatore Romano*, 23 April 1954: 1.

68 The letter is given at the end of the book by Mario Rossi, *I giorni dell'onnipotenza* (Rome: Coines, 1975), 200.

69 Miglioli, *Con Roma e con Mosca*, 9.

70 Casula, *Fronte democratico popolare e Costituente della terra*, 10–11.

71 See Giorgio Campanini, *La rivoluzione cristiana. Il pensiero politico di Emmanuel Mounier* (Brescia: Morcelliana, 1968), 20–39. See also Yvonne Tranvouez, *Catholiques et communistes. La crise du progressisme chrétien 1950–1955* (Paris: Cerf, 2000).

72 Campanini, *Cristianesimo e democrazia*, 118–119.

73 See Primo Mazzolari, *Cattolici e comunisti* (Vicenza: La Locusta, 1966), 85–91.

74 Primo Mazzolari, 'Impegni cristiani istanze comuniste', in ibid., 5–35.

75 Giorgio Vecchio, *Pacifisti e obiettori nell'Italia di De Gasperi (1948–1953)* (Rome: Studium, 1993), 40–43.

76 'Non dite', *L'Osservatore Romano*, 15 January 1950: 1.

77 Primo Mazzolari, 'Editoriale', *Adesso* 1, no. 1 (1949): 1, 8.

78 See Vera Capperucci, *Il partito dei cattolici. Dall'Italia degasperiana alle correnti democristiane* (Soveria Mannelli: Rubbettino, 2010).

79 Alberto Melloni, 'Cronache sociali. La produzione di cultura politica come filo della utopia di Giuseppe Dossetti', in *Cronache sociali 1947–1951*, ed. Alberto Melloni (Bologna: Istituto per le Scienze Religiose, 2007), XXI–XXII.
80 Giorgio Campanini, *Dossetti Politico* (Bologna: Dehoniane, 2004), 27–29.
81 Luigi Guerzoni, 'Le riflessioni di Dossetti sullo Stato: spunti di ricerca', in *Giuseppe Dossetti: la fede e la storia. Studi nel decennale della morte*, ed. Alberto Melloni (Bologna: Il Mulino, 2007), 299–309.
82 Paolo Pombeni, *Il gruppo dossettiano e la fondazione della democrazia italiana (1938–1948)* (Bologna: Il Mulino, 1979), 375–380.
83 Giorgio Galli and Paolo Facchi, *La sinistra democristiana. Storia e ideologie* (Milan: Feltrinelli, 1962), 296–298.
84 Giorgio La Pira, 'L'attesa della povera gente', *Cronache sociali* 4, no. 1 (1950): 1–6.
85 See Massimo De Giuseppe, *Giorgio La Pira. Un sindaco e le vie della pace* (Milan: Centro Ambrosiano, 2001).
86 Jacques Maritain, *L'uomo e lo Stato* (Milan: Vita e Pensiero, 1982) (the first edition was published in Chicago in 1951).
87 Agostino Giovagnoli, *Il partito italiano. La Democrazia cristiana dal 1942 al 1994* (Rome: Laterza, 1996), 92–94. See also Agostino Giovagnoli and Luciano Tosi, eds, *Amintore Fanfani e la politica estera italiana* (Venice: Marsilio, 2010).
88 Paolo Pombeni, *La costituente. Un problema storico-politico* (Bologna: Il Mulino, 1995), 92–93.
89 Nicola Antonetti, 'Dottrine politiche e dottrine giuridiche. I cattolici democratici e i problemi costituzionali (1943–1946)', in *I cattolici democratici e la Costituzione*, eds Nicola Antonetti, Ugo De Siervo and Francesco Malgeri (Bologna: Il Mulino, 1998), 157–159.
90 Pombeni, *Il gruppo dossettiano*, 108–109.
91 See Galavotti, *Il giovane Dossetti*.
92 See Giuseppe Trotta, *Giuseppe Dossetti. La rivoluzione nello Stato* (Florence: Camunia, 1996), 435–437.
93 Giuseppe Chiarante, *Tra De Gasperi e Togliatti. Memorie degli anni Cinquanta* (Rome: Carocci, 2006), 46.
94 Marcello Malpensa and Alessandro Parola, *Lazzati. Una sentinella nella notte (1909–1986)* (Bologna: Il Mulino, 2005), 567–572.
95 Giorgio Vecchio, Daniela Saresella and Paolo Trionfini, *Storia dell'Italia contemporanea* (Bologna: Monduzzi, 2002), 292–294.
96 Francesco Malgeri, 'Gli anni di transizione: da Fanfani a Moro (1954–1962)', in *Storia della Democrazia cristiana*, vol. 3, ed. Francesco Malgeri (Rome: Cinque Lune, 1988), 103.
97 See Umberto Gentiloni Silveri, *L'Italia e la nuova frontiera. Stati Uniti e centro-sinistra 1958–1965* (Bologna: Il Mulino, 1998).

98   See Yannis Voulgaris, *L'Italia del centro-sinistra (1960–1968)* (Rome: Carocci, 1998), 116–128; Simona Colarizi, *Storia del Novecento italiano. Cent'anni di entusiasmo, di paure, di speranza* (Milan: BUR, 2000), 360–363. Above all, see Augusto D'Angelo, *Moro, i vescovi e l'apertura a sinistra* (Rome: Studium, 2005); Eliana Versace, *Montini e l'apertura a sinistra. Il falso mito del 'vescovo progressista'* (Milan: Guerini e associati, 2007).

99   Antonio Messineo, 'Può il socialista essere democratico?' *La Civiltà Cattolica* 108, no. 15 (1957): 337–349.

100 Lelio Basso, 'Insieme alla sinistra laica?' *Politica* 4, no. 1 (1958): 3.

101 Mario Zagari, 'Domani è troppo tardi', *Politica* 4, no. 2 (1958): 3.

102 Matteo Matteotti, 'Prima l'unificazione dei socialisti', *Politica* 4, no. 3 (1958): 3.

103 Tristano Codignola, 'L'accordo non giova ai socialisti', *Politica* 4, no. 3 (1958): 3.

104 Marzia Maccaferri, 'Intellettuali italiani tra società opulenta e democrazia del benessere: il caso de Il Mulino', *Mondo contemporaneo* 5, no. 1 (2009): 45–77.

105 Daniela Saresella, *Dal Concilio alla contestazione. Riviste cattoliche negli anni del cambiamento* (Brescia: Morcelliana, 2005), 187–191.

106 'Cattolici e socialisti', *L'Osservatore Romano*, 7 January 1960: 1.

107 'Cattolici e neofascismo', *Aggiornamenti sociali* 11, no. 6 (1960): 321–326. See also Pietro Scoppola, *La repubblica dei partiti. evoluzione e crisi di un sistema politico (1945–1996)* (Bologna: Il Mulino, 1991), 339–351.

108 See Enzo Santarelli, *Storia critica della Repubblica. L'Italia dal 1945 al 1994* (Milan: Feltrinelli, 1996), 115–118.

109 Vecchio, Saresella and Trionfini, *Storia dell'Italia contemporanea*, 303.

110 Nicola Tranfaglia, 'La modernità squilibrata. Dalla crisi del centrismo al compromesso storico', in *Storia dell'Italia repubblicana, II La trasformazione dell'Italia: sviluppo e squilibri*, vol. 2, *Istituzioni, movimenti, culture*, ed. Francesco Barbagallo (Turin: Einaudi, 1995), 45.

111 In the administrative vote, the DC held steady (40.3 per cent), the PSI fell (14.4 per cent) and the PCI made gains (24.5 per cent).

112 Pietro Scoppola's observations are interesting in this regard, in '*La nuova cristianità' perduta* (Rome: Studium, 1985), 97.

113 On Moro's speech, see Vecchio, Saresella and Trionfini, *Storia dell'Italia contemporanea*, 308–309. See also Aldo Moro, *L'intelligenza e gli avvenimenti. Testi 1959–1978* (Milan: Garzanti, 1979), 64–65; Guido Formigoni, *Aldo Moro. Lo statista e il suo dramma* (Bologna: Il Mulino, 2016).

114 Letter from La Pira to Nenni, s. l. 18 February 1962, in Archivio la Pira (Florence), file 21, folder 9, doc. 5. Nenni replied with a note: 'Let's hope that Fanfani, too, brings to the thing the fervour that it deserves' (Note from Nenni to La Pira, Rome, 7 March 1962, in Archivio la Pira (Florence), file 21, folder 9, doc. 11).

115 A chapter of the book by Silvio Lanaro, *Storia dell'Italia repubblicana: l'economia, la politica, la cultura, la società dal dopoguerra agli anni '90* (Venice: Marsilio, 2001), 307–342 is entitled 'L'illusione riformista'.

Chapter 4

1. Eric J. Hobsbawn, *The Age of Extremes: The Short Twentieth Century (1914–1991)* (London: Abacus, 1995), 351.
2. See Angelo Ventrone, *Vogliamo tutto. Perché due generazioni hanno creduto nella rivoluzione 1960–1988* (Rome: Laterza, 2012).
3. Giuseppe Alberigo, *Transizione epocale. Studi sul Vaticano II* (Bologna: Il Mulino, 2009), 765–849. See also Giuseppe Ruggieri, 'Ricezione e interpretazioni del Vaticano II. Le ragioni di un dibattito', in *Chi ha paura del Vaticano II?*, eds Alberto Melloni and Giuseppe Ruggieri (Rome: Carocci, 2009), 17–44.
4. See Marco Roncalli, *Giovanni XXIII. Angelo Giuseppe Roncalli, una vita nella storia* (Milan: Lindau, 2006); Alberto Melloni, *Papa Giovanni. Un cristiano al Concilio* (Turin: Einaudi, 2009). Also Daniela Saresella, 'Ecclesial Dissent in Italy in the Sixties', *Catholic Historical Review* 102, no. 1 (Winter 2016): 46–68.
5. See Jared Wicks, 'More Light on Vatican II', *Catholic Historical Review* 94, no. 1 (2008): 75–101; Massimo Faggioli, 'Council Vatican II: Bibliographical Overview 2007–2010', *Cristianesimo nella storia* 32 (2011): 755–791; Daniela Saresella, 'La Chiesa contemporanea tra modernità e tradizione', *Passato e presente* 94, no. 1 (2012): 139–153.
6. *A colloquio con Dossetti e Lazzati,* interview by Elia and Scoppola, 106. Dossetti (Genova 1913–Oliveto di Monteveglio 1996) was an exponent of the left-wing of the DC who abandoned politics in 1951. After becoming a monk, he founded the Piccola famiglia dell'Annunziata. He died in 1996. See Galavotti, *Il giovane Dossetti*; Galavotti, *Il professorino*; Pombeni, *Giuseppe Dossetti*; and Melloni, *Dossetti l'indicibile. Il quaderno scomparso di 'Cronache sociali'*.
7. Trotta, *Giuseppe Dossetti*, 435–437.
8. Guido Formigoni, *Alla prova della democrazia. Chiesa, cattolici e modernità nell'Italia del '900* (Trento: Il Margine, 2008), 130–153.
9. Pietro Scoppola, *Un cattolico a modo suo* (Brescia: Morcelliana, 2008), 63. Scoppola (Rome 1926–Rome 2007) was an exponent of democratic Catholicism and an important historian of the twentieth-century Italian Catholic world. See Agostino Giovagnoli, *Chiesa e democrazia. La lezione di Pietro Scoppola* (Bologna: Il Mulino, 2011); Giordano Frosini, *Pietro Scoppola. Un cristiano del nostro tempo* (Bologna: Il Mulino, 2012).
10. Giovagnoli, *Il partito italiano*, 100–107. See also D'Angelo, *Moro, i Vescovi e l'apertura a sinistra*; Formigoni, *Aldo Moro*.
11. Balducci (Santa Fiona 1922–Cesena 1992) was one of the most prominent names in Italian Catholic culture at the time of the Second Vatican Council and in the post-Council period.
12. Maria Cristina Giuntella, '*Testimonianze* e l'ambiente cattolico fiorentino', in *Intellettuali cattolici tra riformismo e dissenso*, ed. Sergio Ristuccia (Milan: Edizioni

di Comunità, 1975), 230–245. See also Bruna Bocchini Camaiani, *Ernesto Balducci: la Chiesa e la modernità* (Rome: Laterza, 2002), 155–169; Saresella, *Dal Concilio alla contestazione,* 117–144.

13   Dorigo (Venice 1927–Venice 2006), was a partisan from 1943 to 1945, and then, after the war, joined the DC. He left the party in 1958, when he founded the review *Questitalia,* which was published until 1970.

14   Wladimiro Dorigo, 'Lettera aperta', *Questitalia* 1, no. 1 (1958): 1.

15   'Il Partito socialista sta uscendo dalla prigione del suo massimalismo?' *Relazioni sociali* 2, no. 2 (1962): 1.

16   Marcello Gentili, 'La realtà terrestre in Teilhard de Chardin e nel nuovo cattolicesimo', *Momento* 1, no. 1 (1965): 3–15.

17   Angelo Monasta, 'Il dissenso cattolico nell'esperienza di quattro riviste: "Momento, Note di Cultura, Note e Rassegne, Il tetto"', in Ristuccia, *Intellettuali cattolici tra riformismo e dissenso,* 320–321.

18   See Michael Hornsby-Smith, *The Changing Parish: A Study of Parishes, Priests and Parishioners after Vatican II* (London: Routledge, 1989), 36–42.

19   On Montini's politics regarding the problem of peace, see Daniele Menozzi, *Chiesa, pace e guerra nel Novecento. Verso una delegittimazione religiosa dei conflitti* (Bologna: Il Mulino, 2008), 271–287. See also Frank J. Coppa, 'The Contemporary Papacy from Paul VI to Benedict XVI: A Bibliographical Essay', *Catholic Historical Review* 92, no. 4 (April 2006): 597–608.

20   Paolo Murialdi and Nicola Tranfaglia, *La stampa italiana del neocapitalismo* (Rome: Laterza, 1976), 23–24.

21   Giuseppe Rossini, ed., *L'impegno e i compiti dei cattolici nel tempo nuovo della cristianità* (Rome: Ave, 1967).

22   Giuseppe Rossini, 'Ai cattolici che operano nella politica e nella cultura', in *L'impegno e i compiti dei cattolici nel tempo nuovo della cristianità. Atti del convegno di studio della Democrazia Cristiana,* ed. Giuseppe Rossini, Lucca, 28–30 April 1967 (Rome: Cinque Lune, 1967), VII.

23   Giuseppe Rossini, ed., *Romolo Murri nella storia politica e religiosa del suo tempo* (Rome: Cinque lune, 1972).

24   See Giuseppe Rossini, ed., *Modernismo fascismo, comunismo. Aspetti e figure della cultura e della politica dei cattolici nel '900* (Bologna: Il Mulino, 1972).

25   Mario Cuminetti, *Il dissenso cattolico in Italia (1965–1980)* (Milan: Rizzoli 1983), 23.

26   Verucci, 'La Chiesa postconciliare', in *Storia dell'Italia repubblicana,* ed. Francesco Barbagallo (Turin: Einaudi, 1995), 328–330. For an international overview, see Denis Pelletier, *La crise catholique: Religion, societé et politique en France (1965–1978)* (Paris: Payot, 2002); Andrew Greeley, *The Catholic Revolution: New Wine, Old Wineskins and Second Vatican Council* (Berkeley: University of California Press, 2004); Agostino Giovagnoli, ed., *1968 tra utopia e Vangelo. Contestazione e mondo cattolico* (Rome: Ave, 2000).

27 Hugh McLeod, *The Religious Crisis of the 1960s* (Oxford: Oxford University Press, 2010), 141–160; see also Julian Bourg, *From Revolution to Ethics: May 1968 and Contemporary French Thought* (Montreal: McGill-Queen's University Press, 2007), 257–275; Jay Corrin, *Catholic Progressives in England after Vatican II* (Notre Dame, IN: University of Notre Dame Press, 2013); Gerd-Rainer Horn, *The Spirit of Vatican II. Western European Progressive Catholicism in the Long Sixties* (Oxford: Oxford University Press, 2015); Saresella, 'Ecclesial dissent in Italy in the Sixties', 46–68.
28 Pietro Zerbi, 'Per una biografia di Ezio Franceschini (1906–1983). Letture, ricordi, documenti', *Aevum* 61, no. 3 (1987): 521–564.
29 The students' document was published in *L'Unità* on 2 January 1968. A detailed account of the events can be found in Giancarlo Lizzeri and Pippo Ranci, eds, *Università Cattolica. Storia di 3 occupazioni, repressioni, serrate* (Milan: Edizioni Relazioni Sociali, 1968). Reconstructions of the events are to be found in many books on the protests of 1968; see Roberto Beretta, *Il lungo autunno. Controstoria del sessantotto cattolico* (Milan: Rizzoli, 1998), 22–34.
30 'Sempre occupata la Cattolica', *La Stampa*, 29 May 1968: 1.
31 Father Milani was a priest, teacher and educator. In Barbiana, near Florence, he founded a school for the working classes. Opposed by ecclesiastical authorities for his commitment against compulsory military service, he died of illness at the age of 44 in 1967. See Richard Drake, 'Catholics and Italian Revolutionary Left of the 1960s', *Catholic Historical Review* 94, no. 3 (2008): 450–475.
32 Marco Boato, *Il '68 è morto: viva il '68* (Verona: Bertani, 1979), 7.
33 Daniela Saresella, 'The Vietnam War, the Church, the Christian Democratic Party and the Italian Left Catholics', *Social Sciences* 7, no. 55 (3 April 2018): 1–12.
34 See Massimo De Giuseppe, *L'altra America: i cattolici italiani e l'America latina. Da Medellín a Francesco* (Brescia: Morcelliana, 2017).
35 See Lorenzo Bedeschi, *Il cardinale destituito: documenti sul caso Lercaro* (Turin: Gribaudi, 1968); Giuseppe Battelli, 'I vescovi italiani e la dialettica pace-guerra. Giacomo Lercaro (1947–1968)', *Studi storici* 45, no. 2 (2004): 367–417.
36 Roberto Villa, *A un anno dalla scomparsa di Dossetti. La testimonianza profetica nella Chiesa del Concilio Vaticano* (Portogruaro: Nuova dimensione, 1997), 14–25. With regard to Montini's policies in relation to the problem of peace, see Menozzi, *Chiesa, pace e guerra nel Novecento*, 271–287.
37 Of the publications in the series, see Friedrich-Wilhelm Marquardt, *Teologia e socialismo. L'esempio di K. Barth* (Milan: Jaca Book, 1974); Wolfgang Deresch, ed., *La fede dei socialisti religiosi* (Milan: Jaca Book, 1974).
38 Gian Enrico and Chiara Saraceno, *Ideologia religiosa e conflitto sociale* (Bari: De Donato, 1970), 217.
39 Carlo Falconi, *La contestazione nella Chiesa. Storia e documenti del movimento cattolico antiautoritario in Italia e nel mondo* (Milan: Feltrinelli, 1969), 91–120.

40 Lorenzo Bedeschi, 'Riflessioni sul dissenso cattolico', *Religioni oggi* 2, no. 2 (1968): 1–12.
41 Mario Cuminetti, 'Un ruolo da precisare', *Relazioni Sociali* 6, no. 10 (1966): 64.
42 Mario Cuminetti, unpublished, undated manuscript notes (presumably from the very early seventies), Istituto nazionale Storia del Movimento di Liberazione, Milan, Fondo Cuminetti, b. 10, F. 68, 71.
43 Ernesto Balducci, *In fede*, unreferenced document, in Fondazione Balducci (Fiesole), public archive, section 1, file 1/2.
44 See Alessandro Santagata, *La contestazione cattolica. Movimenti, cultura e politica dal Vaticano II al '68* (Florence: Viella, 2016).
45 Verucci, 'La Chiesa postconciliare', 332–333. See also Silvia Inaudi and Marta Margotti, eds, *La Rivoluzione del Concilio. La contestazione cattolica negli anni Sessanta e Settanta* (Rome: Studium, 2017).
46 'Le dimissioni della Menapace: verso la fine della mistificazione della sinistra DC', *Questitalia* 11 (1968): 39–44.
47 Lidia Menapace, 'Sinistra vecchia e nuova', *Settegiorni* 41 (1968): 18.
48 Francesco Coïsson, 'Dissenso cattolico. Il confronto di Reggio Emilia', *L'Astrolabio* 6, no. 39 (1968): 6–7. See Saresella, *Cattolici a sinistra,* 285–301.
49 Complete letter published in *L'unità*, 3 March 1968: 3.
50 'Una nuova strategia. Intervista con Corrado Corghi', *L'Astrolabio* 6, no. 39 (1968): 12–14. Corghi, on this occasion, received a letter expressing friendship and esteem from Lucio Lombardo Radice (See Carte di L. L. Radice, in Archivio Istituto Gramsci di Rome, scatola Dialogo [2]).
51 Annachiara Valle, *Parole opere e omissioni. La Chiesa nell'Italia degli anni di piombo* (Milan: Rizzoli, 2008), 127–130.
52 See Stefania Podda, *Nome di battaglia Mara. Vita e morte di Mara Cagol, il primo capo delle Br* (Milan: Sperling & Kupfer, 2007).
53 Jean-Dominique Durand, 'Catholiques et violence terroriste en Italie durant les années de plomb', in *L 'Italie des années de plomb. Le terrorisme entre histoire et mémoire*, eds Marc Lazar and Marie-Anne Matard-Bonucci (Paris: Éditions Autrement, 2010), 81–97.
54 Giorgio Galli, *Il partito armato. Gli «anni di piombo» in Italia 1968–1986* (Milan: Kaos Edizioni, 1993), 16. See also Guido Panvini, *Cattolici e violenza politica* (Venice: Marsilio, 2014).
55 Valle, *Parole opere e omissioni*, 153.
56 Giorgio Bocca, *Il terrorismo italiano. 1970–1978* (Milan: Rizzoli, Milan 1979), 7–8.
57 Alessandro Orsini, *Anatomia delle Brigate Rosse. Le radici ideologiche del terrorismo rivoluzionario* (Soveria Mannelli: Rubbettino, 2009), 53–57. See also Gianfranco Pasquino, ed., *La prova delle armi* (Bologna: Il Mulino, 1984); Donatella Della Porta, *Il terrorismo di sinistra* (Bologna: Il Mulino, 1990); Raimondo Catanzaro, ed., *Ideologie, movimenti, terrorismo* (Bologna: Il Mulino, 1990); and Raimondo Catanzaro, ed., *Storie di lotta armata* (Bologna: Il Mulino, 1995).

58 Angelo Bertani and Luca Diliberto, *Vittorio Bachelet. Un uomo uscì a seminare* (Rome: Ave, 1994), 41–63; Mario Casella, 'Introduzione' in Vittorio Bachelet, *Il servizio è la gioia. Scritti associativi ed ecclesiali (1959-1973)* (Rome: Ave, 1992), 11–18.
59 Vittorio De Marco, *Le barricate invisibili. La Chiesa in Italia tra politica e società (1945-1978)* (Galatina: Congedo, 1994), 208–216.
60 Ibid., 195–208.
61 Paolo Trionfini, *La laicità della CISL. Autonomia e unità sindacale negli anni Sessanta* (Brescia: Morcelliana, 2014).
62 Sandro Antoniazzi, 'Cattolici e scelta di classe in Italia', in *Cristiani e internazionalismo* (Rome: Coines, 1974), 67–74.
63 David Maria Turoldo, 'Presentazione', in *Gli estremisti di centro. Il neo-integralismo cattolico degli anni '70: Comunione e Liberazione* (Rimini: Guaraldi, 1975).
64 Alberto Melloni, 'Turoldo e Cl, primavera 1975', in *Laicità e profezia. La vicenda di David Maria Turoldo* (Palazzago: Servitium, 2003), 281–328.
65 See Bernard Tissier de Mallerais, *Marcel Lefebvre: une vie* (Paris: Clovis, 2002); Philippe Levillain, *Rome n'est plus dans Rome. Mgr Lefebvre et son église* (Paris: Clovis, 2010); Giovanni Miccoli, *La Chiesa dell'anticoncilio. I tradizionalisti alla conquista di Roma* (Rome: Laterza, 2011).
66 See Nicla Buonasorte, *Siri. Tradizione e Novecento* (Bologna: Il Mulino, 2006).
67 Giuseppe Petralia, *Il cardinal Giuseppe Ruffini arcivescovo di Palermo* (Città del Vaticano: Libreria editrice vaticana, 1989).
68 See Maria Grazia Fida, *Educare alla pace. La via di don Milani* (Milan: Edizioni Paoline, 2012), 23–28.
69 See Bedeschi, *Il cardinale destituito*.
70 Del Noce (Pistoia 1910–Rome 1989), an Italian philosopher, focused on the crisis of contemporary civilization and upheld the values of Christian tradition. See Massimo Borghesi, *Augusto Del Noce. La legittimazione critica del moderno* (Genoa: Marietti, 2011).
71 See Salvatore Abruzzese, *Comunione e Liberazione* (Bologna: Il Mulino, 2001); Massimo Camisasca, *Comunione e Liberazione: le origini (1954-1968)* (Milan: San Paolo, 2001); Maria Bocci, 'Il Concilio indiviso. Da Gioventù Studentesca a Comunione e Liberazione', in *Da Montini a Martini: il Vaticano II a Milano*, vol. 1, *Le figure*, eds Gilles Routhier, Luca Bressan and Luciano Vaccaro (Brescia: Morcelliana, 2012), 473–531.
72 See Malpensa and Parola, *Lazzati*. See also 'L'associazionismo cattolico, i cattolici democratici e il progetto di don Giussani', in *Cattolicesimo e laicità. Politica, Cultura e fede nel secondo Novecento*, eds Alfredo Canavero and Daniela Saresella (Brescia: Morcelliana, 2015), 227–241.
73 Nina Bocenina, *La segretaria di Togliatti: memorie di Nina Bocenina* (Florence: Ponte alle Grazie, 1993), 41–42.

74 Togliatti, *Comunisti e cattolici*, 14–15.
75 Palmiro Togliatti, *Opere*, vol. 6, *1956–1964*, ed. Luciano Gruppi (Rome: Editori Riuniti, 1984), 697–699.
76 John XXIII, 'Encyclicals: PACEM IN TERRIS', The Holy See, 11 April 1963. Available online: http://www.vatican.va/holy_father/john_xxiii/encyclicals/documents/hf_j-xxiii_enc_11041963_pacem_en.html (accessed 17 May 2019).
77 Pope Paul VI, 'GAUDIUM ET SPES', The Holy See, 7 December 1965. Available online: http://www.vatican.va/archive/hist_councils/ii_vatican_council/documents/vat-ii_cons_19651207_gaudium-et-spes_en.html (accessed 17 May 2019).
78 Donald Sassoon, *One Hundred Years of Socialism. The West European Left in the Twentieth Century* (New York: Tauris, 2010), 241–273.
79 Mario Gozzini, ed., *Il dialogo alla prova* (Florence: Vallecchi, 1964), 7–9. See Daniela Saresella, 'The Dialogue between Catholics and Communists in 1960s Italy', *Journal of History of Ideas* 75, no. 3 (2014): 493–512.
80 Lucio Lombardo Radice, 'Un marxista di fronte a fatti nuovi nel pensiero e nella coscienza religiosa', in Gozzini, *Il dialogo alla prova*, 81–112.
81 See Saresella, *Dal Concilio alla contestazione*, 301–322.
82 Salvatore Di Marco, 'La filosofia marxista e i problemi dell'uomo', in Gozzini, *Il dialogo alla prova*, 389–426.
83 Giulio Girardi, *Marxismo e cristianesimo*, preface by Franziskus Koenig (Assisi: Cittadella, 1966).
84 Editorial proposal for issue no. 1 di *Quale società*, in Carte di L. L. Radice, in Archivio Istituto Gramsci, box Dialogo 2.
85 Cesare Luperini, 'Le nuove prospettive del marxismo', *Religioni oggi* 1, no. 1 (1967): 1.
86 Luigi Fabbri, ed., *Cristiani e marxisti: dialogo per il futuro* (Rome: Ave, 1967).
87 On the international context of the debate, see Chenaux, *L'Église catholique et le communisme en Europe (1917–1989)*, 298–308.
88 Marquardt, *Teologia e socialismo*.
89 Luigi Accattoli, 'L'età del dialogo (1963–1968)', in Bedeschi, *I cristiani nella sinistra*, 137–138.
90 Letter from Lombardo Radice to Fiore, in Carte di L. L. Radice, in Archivio Istituto Gramsci, box Dialogo 1 and 2. See Ruggero Orfei, *Marxismo e umanesimo* (Rome: Coines, 1970).
91 Paolo VI, 'Octogesima adveniens', in *Enchiridion delle Encicliche*, vol. 7 (Bologna: Dehoniane, 1994), 1021–1037.
92 'Povertà della chiesa', in *Medellin. Documenti* (Bologna: Dehoniane, 1969), 123–127.

93 *Cristianos por el socialismo consecuencia cristiana o aleinación política?* (Santiago de Chile: Editorial del Pacífico, 1972); Pablo Richard, *Origen y desarrollo del movimiento Cristianos per el Socialismo: Chile 1970-1973* (Paris: Centre Lebret Foi et développement, 1975); Teresa Donoso Loero, *Los Cristianos por el socialismo en Chile* (Santiago de Chile: Editorial Vaitea, 1975). See also Daniela Saresella, 'I Cristiani per il Socialismo in Italia', *Studi Storici* 59, no. 2 (2018): 525-549.

94 José Ramos-Regidor, 'Storia, tendenze, problematica e prospettive del movimento Cristiani per il socialismo', in *Cristiani per il socialismo*, eds José Ramos-Rigidor and Aldo Gecchelin (Milan: Arnoldo Mondadori, 1977), 20-21. See Bartolomeo Sorge, 'Il movimento dei "Cristiani per il Socialismo"', *La Civiltà cattolica* 124, vol. 2 (20 April 1974), quad. 2972: 111-130; *Origen y desarrollo del movimiento 'Cristianos por el socialismo'*; Brian H. Smith, *The Church and Politics in Chile: Challenges to Modern Catholicism* (Princeton, NJ: Princeton University Press, 2014), 248-250.

95 Gozzini, *Il dialogo alla prova*; see also Filippo Gentiloni, *Oltre il dialogo. Cattolici e Pci: le possibili intese tra passato e presente* (Rome: Editori Riuniti, 1989).

96 Giulio Girardi, typescript, *Fondo Giulio Girardi*, ed. Fondazione Basso (Rome), busta 29.

97 Rocco Cerrato, 'Scelta di classe ed esperienza di fede', *Idoc internazionale* 3, no. 20 (30 November 1973): 40-44.

98 'Cristiani per il socialismo e la vittoria del NO', *Testimonianze* 17, no. 163 (March 1974): 204-205.

99 'Caso Girardi', *Com-Nuovi Tempi* 4, no. 22 (1977): 3.

100 Giovanni Miccoli, *In difesa della fede. La Chiesa di Giovanni Paolo II e Benedetto XVI* (Milan: Rizzoli, 2007), 41-44.

Chapter 5

1 Mirco Dondi, *L'eco del boato. Storia della strategia della tensione 1965-1974* (Rome: Laterza, 2015).

2 See Jonathan Haslam, *The Nixon Administration and the Death of Allende's Chile* (London: Verso, 2005).

3 Enrico Berlinguer, 'Riflessione sull'Italia dopo i fatti del Cile', *Rinascita* 30, no. 38 (1973): 3-4; Enrico Berlinguer, 'Riflessione sull'Italia dopo i fatti del Cile', *Rinascita* 30, no. 39 (1973): 3-4; Enrico Berlinguer, 'Riflessione sull'Italia dopo i fatti del Cile', *Rinascita* 30, no. 40 (1973): 3-4; then published in Enrico Berlinguer, *La 'questione comunista' (1969-1975)*, ed. Antonio Tatò (Rome: Editori Riuniti, 1975), 609-639. See Francesco Barbagallo, *Enrico Berlinguer* (Rome: Carocci, 2006), 186-188; Silvio Pons, *Berlinguer e la fine del comunismo* (Turin: Einaudi, 2006), 43-45.

4   Piero Craveri, *La Repubblica dal 1958 al 1992* (Turin: Utet, 1995), 611–612.
5   Formigoni, *Aldo Moro*.
6   Aldo Moro, 'La terza fase', *Il Giorno*, 10 December 1976.
7   Pietro Scoppola, *La coscienza e il potere* (Rome: Laterza, 2007), XII–XIII.
8   Pietro Scoppola, 'Il detonatore Craxi', *Appunti di cultura e di politica* 1, no. 6 (1978): 8–11.
9   Daniela Saresella, 'The Battle for Divorce in Italy and Opposition from the Catholic World (1861–1974)', *Journal of Family History* 42, no. 4 (2017): 401–418.
10 Carlo Falconi, *La crociata di Paolo VI. La svolta reazionaria di papa Montini* (Milan: Kaos edizioni, 1968), 110–118.
11 See Giovanni Tassani, 'Nuovi movimenti e politica in area cattolica', in Traniello and Campanini, *Dizionario storico del Movimento cattolico*, 176–178.
12 Diana De Vigili, *La battaglia sul divorzio. Dalla Costituente al Referendum* (Milan: Angeli, 2000), 163–164.
13 See Gianbattista Scirè, *Il divorzio in Italia: partiti, Chiesa, società civile dalla legge al referendum (1965–1974)* (Milan: Bruno Mondardori, 2007).
14 Scoppola, *Un cattolico a modo suo*, 46.
15 See Arturo Parisi, *Questione cattolica e referendum. L'inizio di una fine* (Bologna: Il Mulino, 1974).
16 Pietro Scoppola, 'La fine del partito cristiano', in Traniello and Campanini, *Dizionario storico del movimento cattolico*, 155.
17 This was a drug prescribed during pregnancy that was found to be responsible for the birth of children with phocomelia.
18 Lorenza Perini, *Il corpo della cittadina. Nilde Iotti e il dibattito sull'aborto in Italia negli anni Settanta*, in *Nilde Iotti. Dalla Cattolica a Montecitorio* (Milan: Biblion, 2010), 155–210.
19 Carlo Zanchettin, 'La Chiesa e l'aborto. Intervista a Jaques-Marie Pohier', *Il Regno* 18, no. 258 (1973): 15–18.
20 Mario Gozzini, 'Referendum sull'aborto: tre scelte per il cattolico', *Il Corriere della Sera*, 7 March 1976: 1.
21 See Gennaro Acquaviva and Luigi Covatta, eds, *Moro-Craxi. Fermezza e trattativa trent'anni dopo* (Venice: Marsilio, 2009).
22 Bettazzi's declarations are cited in Giambattista Sciré, *L'aborto in Italia. Storia di una legge* (Milan: Bruno Mondadori, 2008), 177.
23 'Le Comunità cristiane di base sull'aborto', *Adista*, 29–30 June 1978, 5–6.
24 Mario Gozzini, 'Aborto: la posta in gioco', *Testimonianze* 23, no. 229 (1980): 41–50.
25 See Sciré, *L'aborto in Italia*, 215–216.
26 Franco Garelli, *La Chiesa in Italia* (Bologna: Il Mulino, 2007), 14.
27 Marco Follini, *L'arcipelago democristiano* (Bari: Laterza, 1990), 78–79.
28 Mario Gozzini, *Oltre gli steccati* (Milan: Sperling & Kupfer, 1994), 227–241.
29 Mario Pancera, *Conversazioni con Bettazzi* (Vicenza: La Locusta, 1978), 40–41.

30 Enrico Berlinguer, 'Comunisti e cattolici: chiarezza di principi e basi di un'intesa', *Rinascita* 34, no. 34 (1977): 3–5. The same issue also contained the letter from the Bishop of Ivrea.
31 'Partito comunista e cattolici in Italia', *L'Osservatore Romano*, 17 October 1977: 1.
32 See Valle, *Parole opere e omissioni*, 29–35.
33 Agostino Giovagnoli, *Il caso Moro. Una tragedia repubblicana* (Bologna: Il Mulino, 2005), 176–177.
34 *Caro Berlinguer. Note e appunti riservati di Antonio Tatò a Enrico Berlinguer* (Turin: Einaudi, 2003), 65–73.
35 Enrico Berlinguer, *Il Pci e la crisi italiana* (Rome: Editori Riuniti, 1976), 50–51.
36 Giorgio Galli, *Mezzo secolo di Dc (1943–1993): da De Gasperi a Mario Segni* (Milan: Rizzoli, 1993), 317. With regard to this, see *Relazioni della commissione parlamentare d'inchiesta sulla strage di via Fani, sul sequestro e assassinio di Aldo Moro e sul terrorismo in Italia*, 2 vols (Rome: Camera dei Deputati, 1993); Sergio Flamigni, *Il mio sangue ricadrà su di loro'. Gli scritti di Aldo Moro prigioniero delle Br* (Milan: Kaos, 1997).
37 Valle, *Parole opere e omissioni*, 194–195.
38 See Giovanni Maria Ceci, 'Il mondo cattolico italiano e la crisi degli euromissili', in *Guerra e pace nell'Italia del Novecento. Politica estera, cultura politica e correnti dell'opinione pubblica*, eds Luigi Goglia, Renato Moro and Leopoldo Nuti (Bologna: Il Mulino, 2006), 437–460. See also. Angela Santese, *La pace atomica. Ronald Reagan e il movimento antinucleare (1979–1987)* (Florence: Le Monnier, 2016).
39 Agostino Giovagnoli, 'La Democrazia cristiana dal 1980 al 1994', in Traniello and Campanini, *Dizionario storico del Movimento cattolico*, 124–133.
40 Fulvio De Giorgi, 'L'esperienza della Lega democratica e la storia di Appunti', *Appunti di cultura e di politica* 25, no. 4 (2008): 23–29. See also Lorenzo Biondi, *La Lega democratica. Dalla Democrazia cristiana all'Ulivo* (Rome: Viella, 2013); Daniela Saresella, 'I cattolici democratici e la fine dell'unità politica dei cattolici', in *L'Italia contemporanea dagli anni Ottanta ad oggi*, vol. 3, *Istituzioni e politica*, eds Simona Colarizi, Agostino Giovagnoli and Paolo Pombeni (Rome: Carocci, 2014), 205–225.
41 The essay is in *Atti del convegno nazionale*, Rome, 16–17 November 1976, published by the national secretary of the Lega democratica (Rome: 1976), 23–44.
42 Gaetano Quagliariello, *Cattolici, pacifisti, teocon. Chiesa e politica in Italia dopo la caduta del muro* (Milan: Mondadori, 2006), 35–36.
43 Paola Gaiotti De Biase, 'Riaggregazione cattolica', *Appunti di cultura e di politica* 2, no. 3 (1979): 34–36.
44 Armando Oberti, 'Lazzati e l'Università Cattolica: da una testimonianza per la causa di beatificazione?' in *Giuseppe Lazzati (1909–1986). Contributi per una biografia*, ed. Giuseppe Alberigo (Bologna: Il Mulino, 2000), 213–228.

45 The articles were republished in Antonio Socci and Roberto Fontolan, *Tredici anni della nostra storia* (Milan: Editoriale italiana, 1988).
46 See Daniela Menozzi, *La Chiesa italiana e la secolarizzazione* (Turin: Einaudi, 1993), 232–263.

Chapter 6

1 Giovanni Miccoli, *In difesa della fede*.
2 Andrea Riccardi, *Governo carismatico. Venticinque anni di pontificato* (Brescia: Morcelliana, 2003); and Daniele Menozzi, *Giovanni Paolo II. Una transizione incompiuta? Per una storicizzazione del pontificato* (Brescia: Morcelliana, 2006).
3 Massimo Faggioli, *Breve storia dei movimenti cattolici* (Rome: Carocci, 2008), 79–81. See also Abruzzese, *Comunione e liberazione. Identità religiosa e disincanto laico*; Marco Gervasoni, *Storia d'Italia degli anni Ottanta* (Venice: Marsilio, 2010), 155–167.
4 Hans Urs von Balthasar, 'Madre Teresa, san Francesco e frate Boff', *Il Sabato* 9, no. 10 (1986): 11.
5 Guido Crainz, *Autobiografia di una repubblica. Le radici dell'Italia attuale* (Rome: Donzelli, 2009), 73, 132.
6 Ernesto Balducci, 'Teologia della Liberazione e movimento per la pace', *Testimonianze* 28, no. 6–7 (1985): 7–17.
7 Candido Cannavò, *Pretacci. Storia di uomini che portano il Vangelo sul marciapiedi* (Milan: Rizzoli, 2008), 141–143.
8 See Alberto Melloni, 'Pacifismo cattolico e ruolo internazionale della Chiesa', *Il Mulino* 52, no. 2 (2003): 390–398.
9 With regard to the data about associationism and volunteer work in this period, cf. Vecchio, Saresella and Trionfini, *Storia dell'Italia contemporanea*, 640–641.
10 See Mario Diani, *Le isole nell'arcipelago. Il movimento ecologista in Italia* (Bologna: Il Mulino, 1988); Roberto Biorcio, ed., *La sfida verde. Il movimento ecologista in Italia* (Padua: Liviana Editrice, 1988); Roberto Della Seta, *La difesa dell'ambiente in Italia. Storia e culture del movimento ecologista* (Milan: Franco Angeli, 2000); Donatella Della Porta and Mario Diani, *Movimenti senza protesta? L'ambientalismo in Italia* (Bologna: Il Mulino 2004).
11 See *Beati i costruttori di pace. Appello, testimonianza, schede di lavoro* (Padua: Messaggero, 1986).
12 Cannavò, *Pretacci*, 224–227. See also Annachiara Valle, 'Dieci anni di Libera? Annuncio e denuncia', *Jesus* 26, no. 6 (2004): 10–12.
13 Andrea Riccardi, 'Tra diplomazia, storia e religioni', in *Chiesa in Italia 1993*, annals of *Il Regno* (Bologna: Dehoniane, 1994), 165–166. See also Massimo Faggioli, 'The

New Elites of Italian Catholicism: 1968 and the New Catholic Movements', *Catholic Historical Review* 98, no. 1 (January 2012): 18–40.

14 Ernesto Balducci, 'Dal carcere una nuova cultura?' *Testimonianze* 27, no. 267 (1984): 7–20.

15 Valle, *Parole opere e omissioni*, 214.

16 Amoreno Martellini, *Fiori nei cannoni. Non violenza e antimilitarismo nell'Italia del Novecento* (Rome: Donzelli, 2006), 144–153.

17 John W. Murphy and Manuel J. Caro, *Uriel Molina and the Sandinist Popular Movement in Nicaragua* (Jafferson, NC: McFarland & Company Publisher, 2006).

18 Bernardino Formiconi, *Nicaragua la nuova speranza. Una testimonianza sul Nicaragua, la sua problematica e il nuovo cammino* (Assisi: Cittadella, 1980).

19 Giulio Girardi, *Sandinismo, marxismo, cristanismo en la nueva Nicaragua: la Confluencia* (Managua: Centro Ecuménico Antonio Valdivieso, 1986); in the same year the book was published in Italy by Borla. See. De Giuseppe, *L'altra America*, 186–189.

20 Giulio Girardi, *Sandinismo, marxismo, cristianesimo* (Rome: Borla, 1986), 10–11. See also Giulio Girardi, ed., *'Le rose non sono borghesi'. Popolo e cultura nel nuovo Nicaragua* (Rome: Borla, 1986).

21 Augusto Del Noce, 'E' tutto vero', *Il Sabato* 11, no. 1 (1988): 4.

22 *A colloquio con Dossetti*, interview by Elia and Scoppola, 102.

23 Riccardo Bellofiore, 'Le origini di un dissenso', *Bozze 89* 11, no. 2 (1989): 45–46.

24 Claudio Napoleoni, *Cercate ancora. Lettera sulla laicità e ultimi scritti*, ed. Raniero La Valle (Rome: Editori Riuniti, 1990), 119–121.

25 See Simona Colarizi and Marco Gervasoni, *La cruna dell'ago. Craxi, il Partito socialista e la crisi della Repubblica* (Rome: Laterza, 2005), 221–223.

26 Maurizio Punzo, 'Il dibattito sulla revisione del Concordato. I socialisti', *Civitas*, series four, 3, no. 1 (2006): 45–64.

27 Pertici, *Chiesa e Stato in Italia*, 460.

28 Gennaro Acquaviva and Giuseppe Re Rita, *La Chiesa galassia e l'ultimo Concordato* (Milan: Rusconi, 1987), 14.

29 'Concordato: revisione profonda?', *Testimonianze* 27, no. 263 (1984): 3–7.

30 *Documento dei cattolici anticoncordatari in occasione della ratifica parlamentare del nuovo Concordato*, March 1985, in Pertici, *Chiesa e Stato in Italia dalla Grande Guerra al Concordato*, 464.

31 Totò Riina was an Italian mobster tied to 'Cosa nostra'. He was considered the head of the organization from 1982 until his arrest on 15 January 1993.

32 Nando Dalla Chiesa, *Delitto imperfetto. Il generale, la mafia, la società italiana* (Rome: Editori Riuniti, 2003), 7–8. See also Guido Crainz, *Il Paese reale. Dall'assassinio di Moro all'Italia di oggi* (Rome: Donzelli, 2012), 121–124.

33 See Antonino Caponnetto, *I miei giorni a Palermo. Storie di mafia e di giustizia raccontate a Saverio Lodato* (Milan: Garzanti, 1992), 23–24. See also Raffaello Canteri, *Rete Italia* (Trento: Publiprint, 1993), 35–36.

34 Giuseppe Carlo Marino, *Storia della mafia* (Rome: Newton Compton, 2012), 295–296.
35 See Simona Colarizi and Marco Gervasoni, *La tela di Penelope. Storia della seconda repubblica* (Rome: Laterza, 2012), 7–8.
36 John Dickie, *Cosa nostra. Storia della mafia siciliana* (Rome: Laterza, 2005), 419–426.
37 Marino, *Storia della mafia*, 297–298.
38 See Paul Ginsborg, *L'Italia del tempo presente. Famiglia, società civile, Stato (1980–1996)* (Turin: Einaudi, 1998), 392–394; Ennio Pintacuda, *Il guado. Il travaglio delle democrazia in vent'anni di storia italiana* (Molfetta: Edizioni La meridiana, 1995), 108–113.
39 Father Sorge had arrived in Palermo in 1985, after having worked for twenty-five years at *La Civiltà cattolica*. See Pierluigi Diaco and Andrea Scrosati, eds, *Padre Ennio Pintacuda. Un prete e la politica* (Acireale: Bonanno Editore, 1992), 8–9.
40 Bartolomeo Sorge, *Uscire da tempio. Intervista autobiografica* (Genoa: Marietti, 1989), 150–151.
41 Bartolomeo Sorge, 'Prefazione. Riscoprire la politica', in *Breve corso di Politica*, ed. Ennio Pintacuda (Milan: Rizzoli, 1988), VII–XXII.
42 See Canteri, *Rete Italia*, 24–25.
43 See Paolo Giuntella, 'Introduzione', in Leoluca Orlando, *Fede e politica. Paolo Giuntella intervista Leoluca Orlando* (Casale Monferrato: Marietti, 1992), 3–5.
44 The judges Falcone and Borsellino were killed in a Mafia bombing in 1993.
45 Ginsborg, *L'Italia del tempo presente*, 393.
46 Raniero La Valle, 'Il problema dell'identità', *Rinascita* 94, no. 27 (11 July 1987): 6–7.
47 Pietro Scoppola, 'La fine del bipolarismo', *Appunti di cultura e di politica* 10, no. 5 (June 1987): 15–17.
48 Consiglio Nazionale, 12–13 September 1984, in Archivio Storico dell'Istituto Sturzo, Fondo Democrazia cristiana, Serie Consiglio nazionale, box 69, file 170,
49 Francesco Barbagallo, *L'Italia repubblicana. Dallo sviluppo alle riforme mancate (1945–2008)* (Rome: Carocci, 2009), 193.
50 'Orlando sindaco con Verdi e sinistra', *Repubblica*, 11 August 1987: 16–17.
51 'La svolta al comune. Tutto sta nel programma', *L'Ora*, 11–12 August 1987.
52 'Palermo. I pericoli di Orlando', *La Stampa*, 17 April 1989.
53 'Orlando: non è un compromesso storico', *La Stampa*, 11 April 1989.
54 Canteri, *Rete Italia*, 40–41.
55 Leonardo Sciascia, 'I professionisti dell'antimafia', *Corriere della Sera*, 10 January 1987: 1. See Salvatore Lupo, *Che cos'è la mafia. Sciascia, Andreotti, l'antimafia e la politica* (Rome: Donzelli, 2007), 3–36. Emanuele Macaluso, *Sciascia e i comunisti* (Milan: Feltrinelli, 2010).
56 See Colarizi and Gervasoni, *La cruna dell'ago*; Gervasoni, *Storia dell'Italia degli anni Ottanta: quando eravamo moderni* (Venice: Marsilio, 2010), 165–167.

57 Colarizi and Gervasoni, *La tela di Penelope,* 13–14.
58 Pietro Scoppola, 'La Democrazia cristiana', in *La politica italiana. Dizionario critico 1945-1995*, ed. Gianfranco Pasquino (Rome: Laterza, 1995), 228–229.
59 Sorge's words are cited in: Orlando, *Fede e politica. Paolo Giuntella intervista Leoluca Orlando,* 64–65.
60 Enzo Pace, *L'unità dei cattolici in Italia. Origini e decadenza di un mito collettivo* (Milan: Guerini e Associati, 1995), 9–10.
61 Scoppola, 'La fine del partito cristiano', 155.
62 Fabrizio Lentini, *La primavera breve. Quando Palermo sognava una Città per l'Uomo* (Cinisello Balsamo: Paoline, 2011), 37–43. See Ennio Pintacuda, *La scelta* (Casale Monferrato: Piemme, 1993), 49–61.
63 Luigi Filippo Pizzolato, 'Alle origini di Città dell'uomo', in Guido Formigoni and Luigi Filippo Pizzolato, *Giuseppe Lazzati e il progetto di 'Città dell'uomo'* (Milan: In Dialogo, 2002), 21–46.
64 Vincenzo Passerini, 'La Rete e la Lega', in *Storia del Trentino. Fatti, personaggi, istituzioni di un paese di confine,* vol. 2, ed. Sergio Benvenuti (Trento: Edizioni Panorama, 1995), 297–300.
65 Michele Nicoletti, 'Un secondo partito cattolico?' *Il margine* 11, no. 6 (1989): 3–9.
66 Donatella Della Porta, *Movimenti collettivi e sistema politico in Italia (1960-1995)* (Rome: Laterza, 1996), 155–156.
67 Pietro Scoppola, 'Quanti partiti per i cattolici?', *Micromega*, no. 2 (1990): 7–15.
68 Bartolomeo Sorge, 'Manifesto per la costituente cattolica', *Micromega* 24, no. 2 (1990): 16–23.
69 Sante Cruciani, 'Diego Novelli, sindaco di Torino. Il compagno giornalista', in *Storie di sindaci per la storia d'Italia (1889-2000)*, eds Oscar Gaspari, Rosario Forlenza and Sante Cruciani (Rome: Donzelli, 2009), 203–207.
70 Diego Novelli, 'Partiti e potere', *Avvenimenti* 14, no. 1 (2 January 1991): 10.
71 Renzo Di Rienzo, 'Laici in Rete', *L'Espresso* 55, no. 50 (16 December 1990): 25.
72 Interview with Father Sorge by Marina Pino, *L'Ora*, 13 July 1991: 1; see Davide Camarrone, *La rete: un movimento per la democrazia* (Rome: Edizioni Associate, 1992), 60–62. See also 'I gesuiti criticano la neonata Rete. Per padre Sorge è un aborto politico', *Corriere della Sera*, 25 November 1991.
73 Orlando, *Fede e politica. Paolo Giuntella intervista Leoluca Orlando*, 54–55.
74 Canteri, *Rete Italia*, 30.
75 Achille Occhetto, 'Una costituente per aprire una nuova prospettiva della sinistra', in *Documenti per il congresso straordinario del Pci*, vol. 1, *Comitato centrale della svolta* (Rome: l'Unità, 1990), 16.
76 Piero Ignazi, *Dal PCI al PDS. Vero un nuovo modello di partito?* (Bologna: Il Mulino, 1997); Paolo Bellucci, Marco Maraffi and Paolo Segatti, *PCI, PDS, DS. La trasformazione dell'identità politica della sinistra di governo* (Rome: Donzelli, 2000). See also Giorgio Napolitano, *Dal PCI al socialismo europeo. Un'autobiografia*

politica (Roma: Laterza, 2008), 243–259; Iginio Ariemma, *La casa brucia. I Democratici di Sinistra dal PCI ai nostri giorni* (Venice: Marsilio, 2000); Alessandro De Angelis, *I comunisti e il partito. Dal 'partito nuovo' alla svolta dell'"89* (Rome: Carocci, 2002); Andrea Possieri, *Il peso della storia. Memoria, identità, rimozioni dal PCI al PDS (1970-1991)* (Bologna: Il Mulino, 2007); Sandro Guerrieri, 'Il PCI di Occhetto e le riforme istituzionali. Dalla critica al consociativismo alla via referendaria', in *L'Italia contemporanea dagli anni Ottanta a oggi*, vol. 3, *Istituzioni e politica*, eds Simona Colarizi, Agostino Giovagnoli and Paolo Pombeni (Rome: Carocci, 2014), 253–268.

77 See Daniele Vimercati, *I lombardi alla nuova crociata. Il 'fenomeno Lega' dall'esordio al trionfo* (Milan: Mursia, 1990); Giovanni De Luna *Figli di un benessere minore. La Lega 1979-1993* (Firenze: La Nuova Italia, 1994); Ilvo Diamanti, *La Lega Nord. Geografia, storia e sociologia di un soggetto politico* (Rome: Donzelli, 1995); Roberto Biorcio, *La rivincita del Nord. La Lega dalla contestazione al governo* (Rome: Laterza, 2010); Guido Passalacqua, *Il vento della Padania. Storia della Lega Nord 1984-2009* (Milan: Mondadori, 2010); Renzo Guolo, *Chi impugna la croce. Lega e Chiesa* (Rome: Laterza, 2011); Gianluca Passarelli and Dario Tuorto, *La Lega di Salvini. Estrema destra di governo* (Bologna: Il Mulino, 2018).

78 Ilvo Diamanti, *La Lega: geografia, storia e sociologia di un nuovo soggetto politico* (Rome: Donzelli, 1993).

79 Paolo Segatti, 'L'offerta politica e i candidati della Lega alle elezioni amministrative del 1990', *Polis* 56, no. 6 (1992): 257.

80 Massimo Franco, *Tutti a casa. Il crepuscolo di mamma Dc* (Milan: Mondadori, 1993), 24.

81 Typescript document, 9 March 1992, in *Fondo Diego Novelli, attività politica e parlamentare* 1981–2001, until 2001, sc. 13, f. 22, 'Rete documenti vari', until 2001, at the Fondazione istituto piemontese Antonio Gramsci.

82 Mirco Carrattieri, *Una democrazia in crisi di trasformazione. Tra ricerca sociale e nuovi percorsi politici (1981-2004)*, in *Ermanno Gorrieri (1920-2004). Un cattolico sociale nelle trasformazioni del Novecento*, eds Mirco Carrattieri, Michele Marchi and Paolo Trionfini (Bologna: Il Mulino, 2009), 507–828.

83 'Un programma meditato. Ma quanto definisce questo PSD?', *Appunti di cultura e di politica* 15, no. 1 (January 1992): 1–2.

84 Pietro Scoppola, 'Un Patto per la riforma', *Appunti di cultura e di politica* 15, no. 2 (February 1992): 1–3.

85 Pietro Scoppola, 'Intervista. Costituzione e riforme istituzionali', *Orientamenti Sociali* 54, no. 1 (March 1992): 79–82. See also Pietro Scoppola, 'Qualche storica ragione per respingere il presidenzialismo', *Il Mulino* 40, no. 335 (May–June 1991): 442–455.

86 Marco Follini, *C'era una volta la DC* (Bologna: Il Mulino, 1994), 7.

87 Paolo Pombeni, 'Il sistema dei partiti dalla Prima alla Seconda Repubblica', in Colarizi, Giovagnoli and Pombeni, *L'Italia contemporanea dagli anni Ottanta a oggi*, 311–312.
88 Franco Monaco, 'I cattolici italiani nell'attuale congiuntura politica', *Aggiornamenti sociali* 44, no. 2 (1993): 101–120.
89 Gianfranco Brunelli, 'Scadenze 1992', *Regno attualità* 36, no. 670 (15 May 1992): 309–315.
90 Gianpaolo Pansa, 'Cade il Muro di Bettino', *L'Espresso*, 10 May 1992, 10–14. See Jonathan Dunnage, *Twenties Century Italy. A Social History* (London: Pearson, 2002), 213–220; John Foot, *Modern Italy* (New York: Palgrave, 2003), 192–193.
91 Gianfranco Brunelli, 'La mutazione democristiana', *Regno attualità* 38, no. 675 (15 August 1993): 470–473.
92 Giuseppe De Rosa, 'Un'Italia inquieta e disorientata', *La Civiltà Cattolica* 54, no. 144 (2 January 1993), quad. 3421: 73–78.
93 'Ma è solo Mafia?', *L'Espresso*, 31 May 1992: 6–9.
94 'Bobbio: mi vergogno di essere italiano', *Il Messaggero*, 26 May 1992: 1.
95 Giuseppe Lo Bianco and Sandra Rizza, *L'agenda rossa di Paolo Borsellino* (Milan: Chiarelettere, 2007).
96 Paolo Gambescia, 'Stage a Palermo, assalto allo Stato', *Il Messaggero*, 20 July 1992: 1.
97 Giovanni Pepi, 'Altra strage. Ucciso giudice Borsellino. E' guerra aperta contro lo Stato', *Giornale di Sicilia*, 20 July 1992: 1.
98 See Francesco Deliziosi, *Pino Puglisi il prete che fece tremare la mafia con un sorriso* (Milan: Rizzoli, 2013).
99 Cataldo Naro, 'Il martirio di don Puglisi e la pastorale "moderna" delle Chiese in Sicilia', *La voce di Campofranco* 33, nos 9–10 (November–December 1993): 8.
100 Gianpaolo Pansa, 'Una bomba dal passato', *L'Espresso*, 6 June 1993, 40–45. See Salvatore Lupo, *La mafia non ha vinto* (Rome: Laterza, 2014).
101 Antonino Caponnetto, 'Coponnetto: un polo progressista per una società più giusta e solidale', *La Stampa*, 17 September 1993: 1.
102 Leoluca Orlando, *Relazione introduttiva. Così l'Italia libera l'Italia*, from 14 January 1994, in Archivio privato di Guido Formigoni.
103 The journal *Risotto giallo* began in December 1993, with an editorial board that included, amongst others, Sergio Chillé and Guido Formigoni.
104 Salvatore Guglielmino, 'In cabina elettorale pensando: Rete!', *Risotto giallo* 1, no. 2 (February 1994): 2–3.
105 Giovanni Bianchi, 'La resistibile ascesa del padrone dell'etere', *Avvenimenti* 1, no. 8 (2 March 1994): 14–15.
106 Giovanni Bianchi, 'Per un cartello democratico', *Aggiornamenti sociali* 44, no. 12 (1993): 847–852.
107 Pietro Scoppola, 'Ipotesi per la presenza politica dei cattolici', *Aggiornamenti sociali* 45, no. 1 (1994): 53–62.

108 'Uniti nei valori, divisi nel voto. Colloquio con Pietro Scoppola', *L'Espresso*, 21 January 1994, 42.
109 'Manifesto di adesione agli Stati generali per la Costituente socialista', Rome, 29 January 1994, mimeographed document, in the *Archivio privato di Giuliana Nuvoli*.
110 Giovanni Gervasio, 'Cattolici e politici nella transizione', *Orientamenti Sociali* 55, no. 4 (October–December 1993): 3–7.
111 Alberto Monticone, 'Intervista. Facciamo il punto sul nuovo Partito Popolare', *Orientamenti Sociali* 55, no. 4 (October–December 1993): 83–92.
112 Agostino Giovagnoli, *La Democrazia cristiana dal 1980 al 1994*, 152. Forza Italia was first with 21 per cent of the votes, followed by the PDS with 20.3 per cent, AN with 13.5 per cent and the Lega with 8.4 per cent.
113 Luca Ricolfi, 'Elezioni e mass-media. Quanti voti ha spostato la Tv', *Il Mulino* 98, no. 6 (1994): 1031–1046.
114 Franco Monaco, 'L'Italia vira a destra', *Aggiornamenti sociali* 45, no. 5 (1994): 325–332.
115 Sonia Stefanizzi, Guido Martinotti, 'Basic instinct, qui sotto c'è un'onda lunga', *Reset* II, no. 5 (April 1994): 4–6.
116 Claudio Rinaldi, 'Altro che miracolo', *L'Espresso*, 8 April 1994, 40–43.
117 Gianni Baget Bozzo, *L'intreccio. Cattolici e comunisti 1945-2004* (Milan: Mondadori, 2004), 11–12.
118 Scoppola, *La fine del partito cristiano*, 153.
119 Carlo Maria Martini, 'Per restaurare la legalità violata', *Avvenire*, 10 October 1992: 1.
120 Gianfranco Brunelli, 'Chiesa, società e politica: i cattolici e le prospettive del paese', *Regno attualità* 38, no. 687 (15 May 1994): 92–93.
121 Riccardo Chiaberge, *Lo scisma. Cattolici senza papa* (Milan: Longanesi, 2009), 11–12. See Massimiliano Livi, 'The Ruini system and Berlusconismo: synergy and transformation between the Catholic Church and Italian politics in the Second Republic', *Journal of Modern Italian Studies* 21, no. 3 (2016): 399–418.
122 See Sandro Magister, *Chiesa extraparlamentare* (Naples: L'ancora del Mediterraneo, 2001).
123 Formigoni, *Alla prova della democrazia*, 253–254. See also Giovanni Bianchi, *Martini 'politico' e la laicità dei cristiani* (Cinisello Balsamo: San Paolo, 2007).
124 Carlo Maria Martini, *Conversazioni notturne a Gerusalemme. Sul rischio della fede* (Milan: Mondadori, 2008), 19.
125 Scoppola, *La coscienza e il potere*, XVII–XIX.

Chapter 7

1 Roberto Biorcio, 'Cittadini e politica negli anni Novanta', in *L'Italia che cambia*, ed. Marino Livolsi (Florence: Nuova Italia, 1993), 123–149.

2   Della Porta, *Movimenti collettivi e sistema politico in Italia (1960-1995)*, 129-142.
3   *Sinistra ecologia e libertà* was a small left-wing party founded in December 2009; it broke up in 2016.
4   See Irene Piazzoni, *Storia delle televisioni in Italia* (Rome: Carocci, 2014).
5   Guolo, *Chi impugna la croce*, 21-42.
6   See Giuseppe Tognon, ed., *La tela di Prodi. Una costituzione per un'Europa più democratica* (Milan: Baldini & Castoldi, 2003).
7   See Rosario Forlenza, *La Repubblica del Presidente. Gli anni di Carlo Azelio Ciampi (1999-2006)* (Reggio Emilia: Diabasis, 2011).
8   Giovanni Colombo, 'Autunno italiano', *Appunti di cultura e di politica* 23, no. 6 (2000): 1-8.
9   Luciano Benevolo, 'Il centrosinistra deve perdere', *Appunti di cultura e di politica* 23, no. 8 (2000): 12-15.
10 Pietro Scoppola, 'Votare per l'Ulivo e non solo contro Berlusconi', *Appunti di cultura e di politica* 24, no. 2 (2001): 8-11.
11 Gianfranco Brunelli, 'Chiesa e politica: quel che resta della questione cattolica', *Annale de Il Regno* 96, no. 711 (2002): 149-160.
12 Filippo Gentiloni, 'Cosa passa tra Martini e Ruini', *Il Manifesto*, 11 February 2001: 1.
13 The La Margherita party was officially formed in March 2002 and nominated Francesco Rutelli as its leader. It gathered together a number of figures from the Partito Popolari, including Marini, Castagnetti, Bindi, Dario Franceschini and Enrico Letta; a liberal democratic section, composed of Rutelli and Paolo Gentiloni; and an Ulivo faction with ties to Romano Prodi, its prominent figures including Arturo Parisi and Enzo Bianco.
14 Pietro Scoppola, 'L'Ulivo non può attendere', *Appunti di cultura e politica* 26, no. 4 (2003): 5-8.
15 Bartolomeo Sorge, 'Valutare con sapienza i programmi', *Aggiornamenti sociali* 57, no. 3 (2006): 193-198.
16 Ettore Scappini and Dario Tuorto, 'I risultati difformi del voto alla Camera e al Senato', *Il Mulino* 55, no. 3 (2006): 461-464.
17 Bartolomeo Sorge, 'Ripartire dalla Costituzione', *Aggiornamenti sociali* 57, no. 6 (2006): 461-466.
18 Ilvo Diamanti, 'Se la Chiesa sta all'opposizione', *la Repubblica*, 11 June 2006: 1.
19 Paolo Segatti, 'Cattolici e voto', in *L'Italia a metà. Dietro il voto del paese divisoi*, eds Renato Mannheimer and Paolo Natale (Milan: Cairo Editore, 2006), 84-96.
20 Gianfranco Brunelli, 'I nodi al pettine', *Il Regno attualità* 51, no. 18 (2006): 591.
21 See Aldo Cristadoro, 'Ds e Margherita verso il Partito democratico?', in Mannheimer and Natale, *L'Italia a metà*, 97-104.
22 Romano Prodi, 'Una maratona di 12 anni e ora l'ultimo chilometro', *la Repubblica*, 22 April 2007: 1.

23 Jacopo Mazzantini, 'Un'identità democratica, oltre il socialismo', *Testimonianze* 50, no. 455 (2007): 14–18.
24 Alberto Monticone, 'Partito democratico: un partito di sinistra che guarda al centro', *Aggiornamenti sociali* 58, nos 7–8 (2007): 495–499.
25 Rosy Bindi, *Quel che è di Cesare* (Rome: Laterza, 2009), 7.
26 See Gianfranco Pasquino, ed., *Il Partito democratico: elezione del segretario, organizzazione e potere* (Bologna: Bonomia University Press, 2009).
27 Gianfranco Brunelli, 'La democrazia come rappresentazione', *Nuova umanità* 23, no. 138 (2007): 597–599.
28 Simone Tosi and Tommaso Vitale, *Individual Responsibility: A Grammar's Journey. The Legacy of the Italian Catholic Movement for Peace*, paper presented at the 3rd ECPR Conference – Budapest, 8–10 September 2005, New Developments in Political Sociology, Panel 'Sociology of Collective Action', Panel Chair M. Oliver Fillieule.
29 Mario Pianta, *Globalizzazione dal basso. Economia mondiale e movimenti sociali* (Rome: Manifestolibri, 2001), 81–109.
30 Massimiliano Andretta, 'Il framing del movimento contro la globalizzazione neoliberista', *Rassegna italiana di sociologia* 46, no. 2 (2005): 249–274.
31 See Massimiliano Andretta and Donatella Della Porta, eds, *Global, neoglobal, new global. La protesta contro il G8 a Genova* (Rome: Laterza, 2002).
32 The Rete Lilliput, established in 1999, was composed of various groups, including: Nigrizia, Mani Tese, Pax Christi and Beati i costruttori di Pace. The Lilliput Network was inspired by Father Alex Zanotelli.
33 Roberto Zuccolini, 'G8, sfilano i cattolici anti-globalizzazione', *Corriere della Sera*, 7 July 2001: 1.
34 Silvano Piovanelli, 'Io provo vergogna anche per noi cattolici', *Corriere della Sera*, 27 July 2001: 1.
35 Donatella Della Porta, *I new global. Chi sono e cosa vogliono i critici della globalizzazione* (Bologna: Il Mulino, 2003), 7–13.
36 'Assisi, marcia della pace e della discordia', *La Stampa*, 14 October 2001: 4.
37 Donatella Della Porta, Massimiliano Andretta and Lorenzo Mosca, 'Movimenti sociali e sfide globali: politica, antipolitica e nuova politica dopo l'11 settembre', *Rassegna italiana di sociologia* 44, no. 1 (2003): 43–76.
38 Daniele Menozzi, *Chiesa, pace e guerra. Verso una legittimazione religiosa dei conflitti* (Bologna: Il Mulino, 2008), 305–308.
39 'Di fronte alla crisi irachena', *Il Regno documenti* 92, no. 5 (2003): 129–133.
40 Filippo Gentiloni, 'Il Vaticano, pacifista ma non troppo', *Confronti* 30, no. 2 (2003): 4.
41 Sergio Siccardi, 'Cuori di pace e venti di guerra', *Testimonianze* 46, no. 427 (2003): 5–10.
42 Sergio Saccardi, 'Dopo l'Iraq', *Testimonianze* 46, no. 428 (2003): 5–7.

43 Bartolomeo Sorge, 'Guerra preventiva all'Iraq?' *Popoli. Mensile internazionale di cultura e informazione missionaria della Compagnia di Gesù* 14, no. 1 (2003): 1.
44 Vincenzo Marras, 'La guerra preventiva', *Jesus* 25, no. 2 (2003): 3.
45 'Una guerra contro il diritto', *Il Manifesto*, 6 February 2003: 1.
46 Angelo Mastrandrea, 'Le ong: rifiuteremo i soldi del governo', *Il Manifesto*, 12 February 2003: 1.
47 Goffredo Parise, 'A piedi nudi contro i cannoni', *la Repubblica*, 7 January 2003: 1.
48 Gian Mario Gillio, 'Otto preti al Papa: pace nel mondo ma anche nella Chiesa', *Confronti* 30, no. 4 (2003): 8.
49 Mimmo De Cillis, '15 febbraio, tutto esaurito tra i cattolici di base', *Il Manifesto*, 13 February 2003: 1. See also 'Preti e suore in movimento. Tanti religiosi in manifestazione', *Il Manifesto*, 16 February 2003: 1.
50 Fabrizio Roncone, 'I pacifisti sfilano a Roma: siamo tre milioni', *Corriere della Sera*, 16 February 2003: 1.
51 Filippo Ceccarelli, 'La piazza. Giovani e vecchi, suore e comunisti. Siamo tre milioni e vogliamo la pace', *La stampa*, 16 February 2003: 1.
52 Renato Mannheimer, 'Effetto blix e manifestazioni, salgono al 70% i contrari alla guerra in ogni caso', *Corriere della Sera*, 17 February 2003.
53 Saccardi, 'Cuori di pace e venti di guerra', 5–10.
54 Guido Formigoni, 'La crisi internazionale: angosce, speranze, impegni', *Appunti di cultura e politica* 26, no. 1 (2003): 1–5.
55 See Enzo Pace, 'Politics of Paradise. Conflitti di religione e conflitti d' identità prima e dopo l'11 settembre', *Rassegna italiana di sociologia*, 44, no. 1 (2003): 25–42; Flavio Felice, *Neocon e teocon. Il ruolo della religione nella vita pubblica statunitense* (Soveria Mannelli: Rubbettino, 2006); Quagliariello, *Cattolici, pacifisti, teocon*.
56 Oriana Fallaci, *La forza della ragione* (Milan: Rizzoli, 2004).
57 Marcello Pera, 'Il relativismo, il cristianesimo e l'Occidente', in Marcello Pera and Joseph Ratzinger, *Radici* (Milan: Mondadori, 2004), 42–45.
58 Joseph Ratzinger, 'Europa. I suoi fondamenti spirituali ieri, oggi, domani', in Pera and Ratzinger, *Radici*, 67–70.
59 Dario Fertilio, 'Devoti contro relativisti, i liberali alla guerra', *Corriere della Sera*, 30 April 2006: 1.
60 Guolo, *Chi impugna la croce*, 52–60.
61 Massimo Teodori, *Laici. L'imbroglio italiano* (Venice: Marsilio, 2006).
62 Roberto Escobar, *La paura del laico* (Bologna: Il Mulino, 2010), 9–10.
63 Dario Antiseri, *Cristiano perché relativista, relativista perché cristiano. Per un relativismo della contingenza* (Soveria Mannelli: Rubbettino, 2003), VII–VIII.
64 Francesco Traniello, 'Verso un nuovo profilo dei rapporti tra Stato e Chiesa in Italia', in Francesco Traniello, Franco Bolgiani and Francesco Margiotta Broglio, *Stato e Chiesa in Italia. Le radici di una svolta* (Bologna: Il Mulino, 2009), 13–52.

65 Franco Monaco, 'La "religione civile" secondo Pera, supporto ideologico dell'occidentalismo', *Jesus* 26, no. 6 (2004): 13.

66 See Giovagnoli, *Chiesa e democrazia*, 257–259.

67 Vito Mancuso, *Per amore. Rifondazione della fede* (Milan: Mondadori, 2005), 15.

68 Giannino Piana, 'Cristianesimo come "religione civile?"' *Aggiornamenti sociali* 57, no. 3 (2006): 223–234.

69 Enzo Bianchi, 'Che ne sarà del cristianesimo?', in *Lettera agli amici dell'Avvento 2003*. Available online: www.monasterodibose.it (accessed 12 May 2019).

70 Enzo Bianchi and Gilles Kepel, *Dentro il fondamentalismo* (Turin: Bollati Boringhieri, 2008).

71 Umberto Brancia, 'Neocons all'italiana e illuministi old style', *Confronti* 31, no. 12 (2004): 5–6.

72 Bindi, *Quel che è di Cesare*, 5–6.

73 See Massimo De Giuseppe, *Oscar Romero. Storia, memoria, attualità* (Bologna: Sermis, 2006).

74 Gianfranco Brunelli, 'Giovanni Paolo II: un pontificato carismatico', *Annale del Il Regno* 95, no. 731 (2006): 153–169. See Menozzi, *Giovanni Paolo II*, 118–126.

75 Filippo Gentiloni, 'Papa in nero', *Il Manifesto*, 20 April 2005: 1. There are similar opinions in Paolo Flores d'Arcais, *La sfida oscurantista di Joseph Ratzinger* (Milan: Ponte alle Grazie, 2010).

76 David Gabrielli, 'E se Benedetto XVI fosse diverso da Ratzinger?' *Confronti* 32, no. 5 (2005): 3.

77 'Il futuro del cattolicesimo italiano', *Il Regno attualità* 51, no. 18 (2006): 589–590.

78 See Ilvo Diamanti, 'Se la Chiesa sta all'opposizione', *La Repubblica*, 11 June 2006: 1.

79 The term 'holy atheist' was coined by Beniamino Andreatta. See Gianni Valente, 'Dall'Action française agli atei devoti', in *Le Chiese e gli altri. Culture, religioni, ideologie e Chiese cristiane nel Novecento*, ed. Andrea Riccardi (Milan: Guerini e associati, 2008), 411–428.

80 Franco Garelli, 'I movimenti, visibili e invisibili', *Il Mulino* 55, no. 6 (2006): 1075–1085.

81 Marco Politi, 'Tettamanzi richiama la Chiesa: Cristiani non solo a parole', *la Repubblica*, 17 October 2006: 1.

82 Alberto Melloni, 'Tre fasi nel rapporto fra Chiesa, episcopato e politica', *Il Mulino* 55, no. 6 (2006): 1056–1065.

83 Filippo Gentiloni, 'L'islam violento interpretato da papa Ratzinger', *Il Manifesto*, 13 September 2006: 1.

84 Luigi Prezzi, 'Latino o Concilio?' *Il Regno attualità* 51, no. 20 (2006): 672.

85 Gian Enrico Rusconi, 'Discorso pubblico e discorso teologico', *Il Mulino* 56, no. 5 (2007): 771–780. See also Franco Garelli, *L'Italia cattolica nell'epoca del pluralismo* (Bologna: Il Mulino, 2006), 18–19.

86 Fulvio De Giorgi, *Il brutto anatroccolo. Il laicato cattolico italiano* (Milan: San Paolo, 2008), 24–26.
87 Giancarlo Zizola, 'La democrazia nella Chiesa', *Il Mulino* 57, no. 4 (2008): 674–687.
88 Michele Do, *Amare la Chiesa*, preface by E. Bianchi (Magnano: Edizioni Qiqajon, 2008), 16–17.
89 Maurizio Abbà, 'Radici e frutti dell'albero Europa', *Testimonianze* 46, no. 427 (2003): 22–32.
90 Franco Toscani, 'Come pensare l'Europa', *Testimonianze* 46, no. 427 (2003): 33–45.
91 Maurizio Ambrosini, *Richiesti e respinti. L'immigrazione in Italia. Come e perché* (Milan: Il Saggiatore, 2010).
92 Guido Formigoni, 'Gli immigrati, frontiere discriminante della politica italiana', *Appunti di cultura e di politica* 24, no. 3 (2003): 6–9.
93 Rosario Iaccarino, 'Italia: sos razzismo', *Appunti di cultura e di politica* 26, no. 3 (2004): 6–10.
94 Romano Prodi, 'Stabilizzare l'Europa e rafforzare la sua presenza a livello mondiale', *Appunti di cultura e di politica* 26, no. 5 (2004): 1–3.
95 Maurizio Bassetti, 'Contro la sindrome del riccio', *Testimonianze* 46, no. 432 (2003): 20–25.
96 Andrea Bigalli, 'Immigrazione sulla pelle', *Testimonianze* 46, no. 432 (2003): 38–45.
97 Enzo Bianchi, 'Cristiani nella società. Il valore dell'uguaglianza', *Il Mulino* 56, no. 4 (2007): 585–592.
98 Enzo Bianchi, *L'altro siamo noi* (Turin: Einaudi, 2010).
99 Andrea Gallo, *Così in cielo come in terra* (Milan: Mondadori, 2010), 19.
100 Pietro Scoppola, 'Il dialogo tra la Chiesa e la sinistra', *Repubblica*, 27 September 2005: 1; now in Scoppola, *La coscienza e il potere*, 221–226.
101 Vittoria Franco, 'Se viene messa sotto assedio la laicità', *Testimonianze* 47, no. 440 (2005): 96–101.
102 Filippo Gentiloni, 'Interloquire alla pari', *Testimonianze* 47, no. 440 (2005): 75–76.
103 Giovanni Boniolo, ed., *Laicità. Una geografia delle nostre radici* (Turin: Einaudi, 2006), 25–46.
104 Marco Politi, 'Ratzinger, i cattolici e la democrazia', *la Repubblica*, 8 June 2006: 1.
105 Pietro Scoppola, 'Ma la Chiesa è in movimento', *la Repubblica*, 8 June 2006: 1.
106 Bindi, *Quel che è di Cesare*, 37–40.
107 Alberto Bobbio, 'Dopo la legge sui Dico, parla il ministro Bindi. E adesso la famiglia', *Famiglia cristiana* 77, no. 7 (2007): 24–26.
108 Giacomo Galeazzi, 'Dico, parte la corsa ai ritocchi', *La Stampa*, 12 February 2007: 1.
109 Giuseppe Betori, 'La famiglia, fonte di vita della società civile', *Famiglia cristiana* 77, no. 6 (2007): 3.

110 De Giorgi, *Il brutto anatroccolo,* 132–134.
111 Bindi, *Quel che è di Cesare*, 38.
112 Corrado Augias and Vito Mancuso, *Disputa su Dio e dintorni* (Milan: Mondadori, 2009), 45–46.
113 Filippo Gentiloni, 'Welby: il discutibile legalismo della Chiesa', *Il Manifesto*, 29 December 2006: 1.
114 Giovanni Franzoni, 'La cura del morire', *Confronti* 33, no. 11 (2006): 4.
115 Andrea Gallo, 'La crociata di una Chiesa materialista', *Micromega* 31, no. 1 (2007): 77–79.
116 'Lettera a aperta a Piergiorgio Welby dalla Comunità di base', *Micromega* 41, no. 1 (2007): 89–90.
117 Caterina Pasolini, 'Eutanasia, il no del medico di Welby', *la Repubblica*, 29 November 2006: 1.
118 'La morte a Natale', *Famiglia cristiana*, 78, no. 12 (2008): 3–4.
119 Augias and Mancuso, *Disputa su Dio e dintorni*, 88.

Bibliography

A colloquio con Dossetti e Lazzati, interview by L. Elia and P. Scoppola (Bologna: Il Mulino, 2003).

Abbà, M., 'Radici e frutti dell'albero Europa', *Testimonianze* 46, no. 427 (2003), pp. 22–32.

Abruzzese, S., *Comunione e liberazione. Identità religiosa e disincanto laico* (Rome: Laterza, 2001).

Acerbi, A., *La Chiesa e la democrazia. Da Leone XIII al Vaticano II* (Milan: Vita e Pensiero, 1991).

Acquaviva, G. and L. Covatta, eds, *Moro-Craxi. Fermezza e trattativa trent'anni dopo* (Venice: Marsilio, 2009).

Acquaviva, G. and G. De Rita, *La Chiesa galassia e l'ultimo Concordato*, ed. L. Accattoli (Milan: Rusconi, 1987).

Albanese, G., *Dittature mediterranee. Fascismo e colpo di Stato in Italia, Spagna e Portogallo* (Rome: Laterza, 2016).

Alberigo, G., *Transizione epocale. Studi sul Vaticano II* (Bologna: Il Mulino, 2009).

Ambrosini, M., *Richiesti e respinti. L'immigrazione in Italia. Come e perché* (Milan: Il Saggiatore, 2010).

Andretta, M., 'Il framing del movimento contro la globalizzazione neoliberista', *Rassegna italiana di sociologia* 46, no. 2 (2005), pp. 249–274.

Andretta, M. and D. Della Porta, eds, *Global, neoglobal, new global. La protesta contro il G8 a Genova* (Rome: Laterza, 2002).

Anon., 'A proposito delle Lettere di un prete modernista', *Nova et vetera* 1, nos 11–12 (1908), pp. 379–382.

Antiseri, D., *Cristiano perché relativista, relativista perché cristiano. Per un relativismo della contingenza* (Soveria Mannelli: Rubbettino, 2003).

Antonetti, N., U. De Siervo and F. Malgeri, eds, *I cattolici democratici e la Costituzione* (Bologna: Il Mulino, 1998).

Antoniazzi, S., 'Cattolici e scelta di classe in Italia', in *Cristiani e internazionalismo* (Rome: Coines, 1974).

Antonioli, S. and G. Cameroni, *Cattolici Clandestini. Federico Sorbaro e il Movimento guelfo d'azione* (Milan: Ned, 1985).

Ridolfi, F., 'Un caso di coscienza', in *Antifascisti cattolici* (Vicenza: La Locusta, 1968), pp. 80–81.

Anzi, F., 'Le origini delle Camere del lavoro', *Critica sociale* 39, no. 15 (1947), pp. 291–299.

Ariemma, I., *La casa brucia. I democratici di sinistra dal PCI ai nostri giorni* (Venice: Marsillo, 2000).

Arnold, C. and G. Vian, eds, *La condanna del modernismo. Documenti interpretazioni, conseguenze* (Rome: Viella, 2010).

Aubert, R., ed., *Histoire de l'Église depuis les origines jusqu'à nos jours*, vol. 12, *Le Pontificat de Pie IX (1846–1878)* (Paris: Blound & Gay, 1964).

Audenino, P., *L'avvenire del passato. Utopia e moralità nella sinistra italiana alle soglie del XX secolo* (Milan: Angeli, 2002).

Augias, C. and V. Mancuso, *Disputa su Dio e dintorni* (Milan: Mondadori, 2009).

Bachelet, V., *Il servizio è la gioia. Scritti associativi ed ecclesiali (1959–1973)* (Rome: Ave, 1992).

Baget Bozzo, G., *L'intreccio. Cattolici e comunisti 1945–2004* (Milan: Mondadori, 2004).

Baldoli, C., 'With Rome and with Moscow: Italian Catholic Communism and the Anti-Fascist Exile', *Contemporary European History* 25, no. 4 (November 2016), pp. 619–643.

Balducci, E., 'Dal carcere una nuova cultura?' *Testimonianze* 27, no. 267 (1984), pp. 7–20.

Balducci, E., 'Teologia della Liberazione e movimento per la pace', *Testimonianze* 28, no. 6–7 (1985), pp. 7–17.

Barbagallo, F., *Enrico Berlinguer* (Rome: Carocci, 2006).

Barbagallo, F., *L'Italia repubblicana. Dallo sviluppo alle riforme mancate (1945–2008)* (Rome: Carocci, 2009).

Barbagallo, F., ed., *Storia dell'Italia repubblicana, II La trasformazione dell'Italia: sviluppo e squilibri*, vol. 2, *Istituzioni, movimenti, culture* (Turin: Einaudi, 1995).

Bassetti, M., 'Contro la sindrome del riccio', *Testimonianze* 46, no. 432 (2003), pp. 20–25.

Basso, L., 'Insieme alla sinistra laica?' *Politica* 4, no. 1 (1958), p. 3.

Battelli, G., 'I vescovi italiani e la dialettica pace-guerra. Giacomo Lercaro (1947–1968)', *Studi storici* 45, no. 2 (2004), pp. 367–417.

Beati i costruttori di pace. Appello, testimonianza, schede di lavoro (Padua: Messaggero, 1986).

Bedeschi, L., ed., *Il diario di don Minzoni* (Brescia: Morcelliana, 1965).

Bedeschi, L., *Cattolici e comunisti: dal socialismo cristiano ai cristiani marxisti* (Milan: Feltrinelli, 1974).

Bedeschi, L., 'Esperienza di fede e coscienza storica in F.L. Ferrari: gli anni modenesi', in *Francesco Luigi Ferrari a cinquant'anni dalla morte*, 61–62.

Bedeschi, L., *Giuseppe Donati* (Rome: Cinque Lune, 1959).

Bedeschi L., *I cristiani nella sinistra dalla Resistenza ad oggi* (Rome: Coines, 1976).

Bedeschi, L., *Il cardinale destituito: documenti sul caso Lercaro* (Turin: Gribaudi, 1968).

Bedeschi, L., 'Il processo del Sant'Uffizio contro i modernisti romani', *Fonti e documenti* 6, no. 8 (1978): 7–24.

Bedeschi, L., *Interpretazioni e sviluppo del modernismo cattolico* (Milan: Bompiani, 1975).

Bedeschi, L., *La sinistra cristiana e il dialogo con i comunisti* (Parma, 1966).
Bedeschi, L., 'Riflessioni sul dissenso cattolico', *Religioni oggi* 2, no. 2 (1968), pp. 1–12.
Bedeschi, L., *Uno che ha attraversato la linea* (Ravenna: Istituto Storico della Resistenza di Ravenna, 1966).
Bellofiore, R., 'Le origini di un dissenso', *Bozze 89* 11, no. 2 (1989), pp. 45–46.
Bellucci, P., M. Maraffi and P. Segatti, *PCI, PDS, DS. La trasformazione dell'identità politica della sinistra di governo* (Rome: Donzelli, 2000).
Benevolo, L., 'Il centrosinistra deve perdere', *Appunti di cultura e di politica* 23, no. 8 (2000), pp. 12–15.
Beretta, R., *Il lungo autunno. Controstoria del sessantotto cattolico* (Milan: Rizzoli, 1998).
Berlinguer, E., *Il Pci e la crisi italiana* (Rome: Editori Riuniti, 1976).
Berlinguer, E., *La 'questione comunista' (1969–1975)*, ed. A. Tatò (Rome: Editori Riuniti, 1975).
Bertani, A. and L. Diliberto, *Vittorio Bachelet. Un uomo uscì a seminare* (Rome: Ave, 1994).
Betori, G., 'La famiglia, fonte di vita della società civile', *Famiglia cristiana* 77, no. 6 (2007), p. 3.
Heerma Van Voss, L., P. Pasture and J. De Maeyer, eds, *Between Cross and Class. Comparative Histories of Christian Labor in Europe (1840–2000)* (Bern: Peter Lang, 2005).
Biagioli, I., A. Botti and R. Cerrato, eds, *Romolo Murri e i murrismi in Italia e in Europa cent'anni dopo* (Urbino: Quattro Venti, 2004).
Biagioli, I., M. Caponi and M. Paiano, eds, 'Modernismo e antimodernismo cattolico nella Grande Guerra', special issue, *Modernism*, no. 3 (2017).
Bianchi, E., 'Cristiani nella società. Il valore dell'uguaglianza', *Il Mulino* 56, no. 4 (2007), pp. 585–592.
Bianchi, E., *L'altro siamo noi* (Turin: Einaudi, 2010).
Bianchi, E. and G. Kepel, *Dentro il fondamentalismo* (Turin: Bollati Boringhieri, 2008).
Bianchi, 'G., La resistibile ascesa del padrone dell'etere', *Avvenimenti* 1, no. 8 (2 March 1994), pp. 14–15.
Bianchi, G., *Martini 'politico' e la laicità dei cristiani* (Cinisello Balsamo: San Paolo, 2007).
Bianchi, G., 'Per un cartello democratico', *Aggiornamenti sociali* 44, no. 12 (1993), pp. 847–852.
Biéler, A., *Chrétiens et socialistes avant Marx* (Geneva: Labor et fides, 1981).
Bigalli, A., 'Immigrazione sulla pelle', *Testimonianze* 46, no. 432 (2003), pp. 38–45.
Bindi, R., *Quel che è di Cesare* (Rome: Laterza, 2009).
Biondi, L., *La Lega democratica. Dalla Democrazia cristiana all'Ulivo* (Rome: Viella, 2013).
Biorcio, R., 'Cittadini e politica negli anni Novanta', in M. Livolsi, ed., *L'Italia che cambia* (Florence: Nuova Italia, 1993), pp. 123–149.
Biorcio, R., *La rivincita del Nord. La Lega dalla contestazione al governo* (Rome: Laterza, 2010).

Boato, M., *Il '68 è morto: viva il '68* (Verona: Bertani, 1979).
Bobbio, A., 'Dopo la legge sui Dico, parla il ministro Bindi. E adesso la famiglia', *Famiglia cristiana* 77, no. 7 (2007), pp. 24–26
Bocca, G., *Il terrorismo italiano. 1970–1978* (Milan: Rizzoli, 1979).
Bocchini Camaiani, B., *Ernesto Balducci: la Chiesa e la modernità* (Rome: Laterza, 2002).
Bocci, M., *Agostino Gemelli, rettore e francescano. Chiesa, regime, democrazia* (Brescia: Morcelliana, 2003).
Bocci, M., 'Il Concilio indiviso. Da Gioventù Studentesca a Comunione e Liberazione', in G. Routhier, L. Bressan and L. Vaccaro, eds, *Da Montini a Martini: il Vaticano II a Milano*, vol. 1, *Le figure* (Brescia: Morcelliana, 2012), pp. 473–531.
Bocenina, N., *La segretaria di Togliatti: memorie di Nina Bocenina* (Florence: Ponte alle Grazie, 1993).
Boiardi, F., '"La Plebe" (1904–1907) e i radicali cristiani di Reggio Emilia', *Rinnovamento* no. 4 (1960), p. 61.
Borghesi, M., *Augusto Del Noce. La legittimazione critica del moderno* (Genoa: Marietti, 2011).
Botti, A., 'Rinnovamento religioso e riforma della Chiesa: "Nova et vetera"', in M. Benedetti and D. Saresella, eds, *La riforma della Chiesa nelle riviste religiose di inizio Novecento* (Milan: Edizioni Biblioteca Francescana, 2010), pp. 77–91.
Botti, A., *Romolo Murri e l'anticlericalismo negli anni de 'La Voce'* (Urbino: Quattro Venti, 1996).
Botti, A., R. Cerrato and S. Pivato, 'L'itinerario storiografico di Lorenzo Bedeschi', *Fonti e documenti* 13, no. 13 (1984), pp. 13–43.
Boudon, J. O., *Napoléon et les cultes. Les religions en Europe à l'aube du XIX siècle (1800–1815)* (Paris: Fayard, 2002).
Bourg, J., *From Revolution to Ethics: May 1968 and Contemporary French Thought* (Montreal: McGill-Queen's University Press, 2007).
Brancia, U., 'Neocons all'italiana e illuministi old style', *Confronti* 31, no. 12 (2004), pp. 5–6.
Brezzi, C., *Laici, cattolici. Chiesa e Stato dall'Unità d'Italia alla Grande guerra* (Bologna: Il Mulino, 2011).
Brunelli, G., 'Chiesa e politica: quel che resta della questione cattolica', *Annale de Il Regno* (2002), pp. 149–160.
Brunelli, G., 'I nodi al pettine', *Il Regno attualità* 51, no. 18 (2006), p. 591.
Brunelli, G., 'La democrazia come rappresentazione', *Nuova umanità* 23, no. 138 (2007), pp. 597–599.
Brunelli, G., 'La mutazione democristiana', *Regno attualità* 38, no. 675 (15 August 1993), pp. 470–473.
Brunelli, G., 'Scadenze 1992', *Regno attualità* 36, no. 670 (15 May 1992), pp. 309–315.
Bruni, G., 'In tema di ideologia socialista', *Quaderni del socialismo* 1, no. 1 (1953), p. 5.
Buonaiuti, E., *La Chiesa e il comunismo* (Rome: Bompiani, 1945).

Buonaiuti, E., *La Chiesa romana* (Milan: Gilardi e Noto, 1932).
Buonaiuti, E., *La vita allo sbaraglio. Lettere a Missir (1926-1946)*, ed. A. Donini (Florence: La nuova Italia editrice, 1980).
Buonaiuti, E., *Lo gnosticismo. Storia di antiche lotte religiose* (Rome: Ferrari, 1907).
Buonaiuti, E., *Pellegrino di Roma* (Rome: Darsena, 1945).
Buonasorte, N., *Siri. Tradizione e Novecento* (Bologna: Il Mulino, 2006).
Caffiero, M., 'Lo scontro con la Rivoluzione francese. Strategie di una riconquista', in D. Menozzi, ed., *Le religioni e il mondo moderno*, vol. 1, *Cristianesimo* (Turin: Einaudi, 2008), pp. 203-229.
Camisasca, M., *Comunione e Liberazione: le origini (1954-1968)* (Milan: San Paolo, 2001).
Campanini, G., *Cristianesimo e democrazia: studi sul pensiero politico cattolico del Novecento* (Brescia: Morcelliana, 1980).
Campanini, G., *Cultura e ideologia del popolarismo. Micheli, Ferrari, Donati* (Bescia: Morcelliana, 1982).
Campanini, G., *Dossetti Politico* (Bologna: Dehoniane, 2004).
Campanini, G., 'I programmi del partito democratico cristiano (1942-1947)', in B. Gariglio, ed., *Cristiani in politica. I programmi politici dei movimenti cattolici democratici* (Milan: Angeli, 1987), pp. 196-208.
Campanini, G., *La rivoluzione cristiana. Il pensiero politico di Emmanuel Mounier* (Brescia: Morcelliana, 1968).
Canavero, A. and D. Saresella, eds, *Cattolicesimo e laicità. Politica, Cultura e fede nel secondo Novecento* (Brescia: Morcelliana, 2015).
Cannavò, C., *Pretacci. Storia di uomini che portano il Vangelo sui marciapiedi* (Milan: Rizzoli, 2008).
Canteri, R., *Rete Italia* (Trento: Publiprint, 1993).
Caponnetto, A., *I miei giorni a Palermo. Storie di mafia e di giustizia raccontate a Saverio Lodato* (Milan: Garzanti, 1992).
Capperucci, V., *Il partito dei cattolici. Dall'Italia degasperiana alle correnti democristiane* (Soveria Mannelli: Rubbettino, 2010).
Caracciolo, A., *Teresio Olivelli* (Brescia: La Scuola, 1975).
Caro Berlinguer. Note e appunti riservati di Antonio Tatò a Enrico Berlinguer (Turin: Einaudi, 2003).
Carrattieri, M., M. Marchi and P. Trionfini, eds, *Ermanno Gorrieri (1920-2004). Un cattolico sociale nelle trasformazioni del Novecento* (Bologna: Il Mulino, 2009).
Casella, M., *Cultura, politica e socialità negli scritti e nella corrispondenza di Igino Giordani* (Naples: Edizioni Scientifiche Italiane, 1992).
Casula, C. F., *Cattolici-comunisti e sinistra cristiana (1938-1945)* (Bologna: Il Mulino, 1976).
Casula, C. F., *Fronte democratico popolare e Costituente della terra* (Rome: Edizioni Lavoro, 1981).
Catanzaro, R., ed., *Storie di lotta armata* (Bologna: Il Mulino, 1995).
Catanzaro, A., ed., *Ideologie, movimenti, terrorismo* (Bologna: Il Mulino, 1990).

Cavaglion, A., ed., *Coenobium (1906-1919), Un'antologia* (Comano: Edizioni Alice, 1992).
Ceci, G. M., 'Il mondo cattolico italiano e la crisi degli euromissili', in L. Goglia, R. Moro and L. Nuti, eds, *Guerra e pace nell'Italia del Novecento. Politica estera, cultura politica e correnti dell'opinione pubblica* (Bologna: Il Mulino, 2006), pp. 437–460
Ceci, L., *L'interesse superiore. Il Vaticano e l'Italia di Mussolini* (Rome: Laterza, 2013).
Cellini, J., *Universalism and Liberation. Italian Catholic Culture and the Idea of International Community* (Leuven, 2017).
Cerrato, R., 'E. Buonaiuti e l'essenza del cristianesimo', *Filosofia e teologia*, no. 1 (1991), pp. 58–68.
Cerrato, R., 'Filosofia e teologia nella crisi modernista', in M. Nicoletti and O. Weiss, eds, *Il modernismo in Italia e in Germania nel contesto europeo* (Bologna: Il Mulino, 2010), pp. 99–135.
Cerrato, R., 'La Rivista storico critica delle scienze teologiche e il progresso della ricerca contemporanea', in M. Benedetti and D. Saresella, eds, *La riforma della Chiesa nelle riviste religiose di inizio Novecento* (Milan: Edizioni Biblioteca Francescana, 2010), pp. 45–76.
Cerrato, R., 'Nova et vetera, una rivista modernista a Roma', *Annali di storia dell'educazione e delle istituzioni scolastiche* 16, no. 16 (2009), pp. 311–334.
Cerrato, R., 'Scelta di classe ed esperienza di fede', *Idoc internazionale*, no. 20 (30 November 1973), pp. 40–44.
Cerrato, R. and A. Botti, eds, 'Buonaiuti nella cultura europea del Novecento', special issue, *Modernism*, no. 2 (2016).
Chenaux, P., *L'Église catholique et le communisme en Europe (1917-1989). De Lénine à Jean-Paul II* (Paris: Cerf, 2009).
Chiaberge, R., *Lo scisma. Cattolici senza papa* (Milan: Longanesi, 2009).
Chiarante, G., *Tra De Gasperi e Togliatti. Memorie degli anni Cinquanta* (Rome: Carocci, 2006).
Chiappetti, F., *La formazione di un prete modernista. Ernesto Buonaiuti e 'Il Rinnovamento'* (Urbino: Quattro Venti, 2012).
Cocchi, M. and P. Montesi, eds, *Per una storia della Sinistra cristiana. Documenti 1937-1945* (Rome: Coines, 1975).
Coco, G., 'Un inviato molto special. Spionaggio fascista e diplomazia italiana nel Conclave del 1939', *Revue d'Histoire Ecclésistique* 113, nos 1–2 (1918), pp. 273–318.
Codignola, T., 'L'accordo non giova ai socialisti', *Politica* 4, no. 3 (1958), p. 3.
Coïsson, F., 'Dissenso cattolico. Il confronto di Reggio Emilia', *L'Astrolabio* 6, no. 39 (1968), pp. 6–7.
Colarizi, S., *Storia del Novecento italiano. Cent'anni di entusiasmo, di paure, di speranza* (Milan: BUR, 2000).
Colarizi, S. and M. Gervasoni, *La cruna dell'ago. Craxi, il Partito socialista e la crisi della Repubblica* (Rome: Laterza, 2005).

Colarizi, S. and M. Gervasoni, *La tela di Penelope. Storia della seconda repubblica* (Rome: Laterza, 2012).

Colin, P., *L'audace et le soupçon. La crise moderniste dan le catholicisme française* (Paris: Desclée De Brouwer, 1997).

Colombo, G., 'Autunno italiano', *Appunti di cultura e di politica* 23, no. 6 (2000), pp. 1–8.

Coppa, F. J., 'The Contemporary Papacy from Paul VI to Benedict XVI: A Bibliographical Essay', *Catholic Historical Review* 92, no. 4 (April 2006), pp. 597–608.

Corni, G. and P. Pombeni, eds, *Alcide De Gasperi: un percorso europeo* (Bologna: Il Mulino, 2005).

Corrin, J., *Catholic Progressives in England after Vatican II* (Notre Dame, IN: University of Notre Dame Press, 2013).

Cospito, G., *Il ritmo del pensiero. Per una lettura diacronica dei 'Quaderni del carcere' di Gramsci* (Naples: Bibliopolis, 2011).

Crainz, G., *Autobiografia di una repubblica. Le radici dell'Italia attuale* (Rome: Donzelli, 2009).

Crainz, G., *Il Paese reale. Dall'assassinio di Moro all'Italia di oggi* (Rome: Donzelli, 2012).

Craveri, P., *De Gasperi* (Bologna: Il Mulino, 2006).

Craveri, P., *La Repubblica dal 1958 al 1992* (Turin: Utet, 1995).

Crespi, A., *Le vie della fede* (Rome: Libreria Editrice Romana, 1908).

Croce, B., 'Il risveglio filosofico e la cultura italiana (1908)', in *Cultura e vita morale* (Bari: Laterza, 1914), p. 14.

Croce, B., *Materialismo storico ed economia marxistica* (Palermo: Sandron, 1900).

Cruciani, S., 'Diego Novelli, sindaco di Torino. Il compagno giornalista', in O. Gaspari, R. Forlenza and S. Cruciani, eds, *Storie di sindaci per la storia d'Italia (1889–2000)* (Rome: Donzelli, 2009), 203–207.

Cuminetti, M., *Il dissenso cattolico in Italia (1965–1980)* (Milan: Rizzoli, 1983).

Cuminetti, M., 'Un ruolo da precisare', *Relazioni Sociali* 6, no. 10 (1966), p. 64.

Curci, C. M., *Di un socialismo cristiano nella questione operaia* (Rome: Fratelli Bencini Editori, 1885).

D'Angelo, A., *Moro, i vescovi e l'apertura a sinistra* (Rome: Studium, 2005).

D'Angelo, L., *Il radicalismo sociale di Romolo Murri (1912–1920)* (Milan: Angeli, 2007).

D'Orsi, A., *Gramsci. Una nuova biografia* (Milan: Feltrinelli, 2017).

Dagnino, J., 'The Intellectuals of Italian Catholic Action and the Sacralisation of Politics in 1930s Europe', *Contemporary European History* 21, no. 2 (May 2012), pp. 215–233.

Dalla Chiesa, N., *Delitto imperfetto. Il generale, la mafia, la società italiana* (Rome: Editori Riuniti, 2003).

De Angelis, A., *I comunisti e il partito. Dal 'partito nuovo' alla svolta dell'*89 (Rome: Carocci).

De Antonellis, G., *Cattolici ambrosiani per la libertà* (Milan: Ned, 1995).

De Antonellis, G., 'I cattolici lombardi a difesa della libertà', *Civiltà ambrosiana* 2, no. 2 (1985), p. 136.

De Antonellis, G., *Il caso Puecher.Morire a vent'anni partigiano e cristiano* (Milan: Rizzoli, 1984).

De Antonellis, G., *Una coscienza pulita. Giuseppe Donati tra impegno politico e religioso* (Milan: Ned, 1981).
De Biase, P. G., 'Riaggregazione cattolica', *Appunti di cultura e di politica* 2, no. 3 (1979), pp. 34–36.
De Gasperi, A., *Scritti e discorsi politici*, vol. 2, *Alcide De Gasperi dal Partito popolare all'esilio interno (1919–1942)*, scientific coordination by P. Pombeni (Bologna: Il Mulino, 2007).
De Gasperi, A., *Scritti e discorsi politici*, vol. 3, *Alcide De Gasperi e la fondazione della democrazia italiana (1943–1948)*, eds V. Capperucci and S. Lorenzini (Bologna: Il Mulino, 2008).
De Gasperi, A., *Scritti e discorsi politici*, vol. 4, *Alcide De Gasperi e la stabilizzazione della Repubblica (1948–1954)* (Bologna: Il Mulino, 2009).
De Gasperi, A., *Scritti e discorsi politici*, vol. 1, *Alcide De Gasperi nel Trentino asburgico* (Bologna: Il Mulino, 2006).
De Giorgi, F., *Il brutto anatroccolo. Il laicato cattolico italiano* (Milan: San Paolo, 2008).
De Giorgi, F., 'L'esperienza della Lega democratica e la storia di Appunti', *Appunti di cultura e di politica*, no. 4 (2008), pp. 23–29.
De Giorgi, F. and N. Raponi, eds, *Rinnovamento religioso e impegno civile in Tommaso Gallarati Scotti* (Milan: Vita e Pensiero, 1994).
De Giuseppe, M., *Giorgio La Pira. Un sindaco e le vie della pace* (Milan: Centro Ambrosiano, 2001).
De Giuseppe, M., *L'altra America: i cattolici italiani e l'America latina. Da Medellín a Francesco* (Brescia: Morcelliana, 2017).
De Giuseppe, M., *Oscar Romero. Storia, memoria, attualità* (Bologna: Sermis, 2006).
De Luna, G., *Figli di un benessere minore. La Lega 1979–1993* (Firenze: La Nuova Italia, 1994).
De Marco, V., *Le barricate invisibili. La Chiesa in Italia tra politica e società (1945–1978)* (Galatina: Congedo, 1994).
De Marco, V., *Storia dell'Azione Cattolica Italiana negli anni Settanta* (Rome, 2007).
De Rosa, G., 'Gramsci e la questione cattolica', in F. Ferri, ed., *Atti del convegno internazionale di studi gramsciani*, Florence, 9–11 December 1977 (Rome: Editori Riuniti-Istituto Gramsci, 1977), 262–263.
De Rosa, G., *Il Partito popolare italiano* (Bari: Laterza, 1966).
De Rosa, G., *L'utopia politica di Luigi Sturzo* (Brescia: Morcelliana, 1975).
De Rosa, G., 'Un'Italia inquieta e disorientata', *La Civiltà Cattolica*, no. 144 (2 January 1993), quad. 3421, pp. 73–78.
De Rosa, G., *Luigi Sturzo* (Turin: Unione tipografico-Editrice torinese, 1977).
De Sanctis, A., ed., *Un dibattito politico su religione e socialismo (1908–1910)* (Florence: Centro Editoriale Toscano, 2010).
De Vigili, D., *La battaglia sul divorzio. Dalla Costituente al Referendum* (Milan: Angeli, 2000).
Del Noce, A., 'E' tutto vero', *Il Sabato* 11, no. 1 (1988), p. 4.

Del Noce, A., *Il cattolico comunista* (Milan: Rusconi, 1981).
Della Porta, D., *I new global. Chi sono e cosa vogliono i critici della globalizzazione* (Bologna: Il Mulino, 2003).
Della Porta, D., *Il terrorismo di sinistra* (Bologna: Il Mulino, 1990).
Della Porta, D., *Movimenti collettivi e sistema politico in Italia (1960-1995)* (Rome: Laterza, 1996).
Della Porta, D. and M. Diani, *Movimenti senza protesta? L'ambientalismo in Italia* (Bologna: Il Mulino, 2004).
Della Porta, D., M. Andretta and L. Mosca, 'Movimenti sociali e sfide globali: politica, antipolitica e nuova politica dopo l'11 settembre', *Rassegna italiana di sociologia* 44, no. 1 (2003), pp. 43-76.
Della Seta, R., *La difesa dell'ambiente in Italia. Storia e culture del movimento ecologista* (Milan: Franco Angeli, 2000).
Della Vida, G. L., *Fantasmi ritrovati* (Vicenza: Neri Pozza, 1966).
Decleva, E., 'Anticlericalismo e religiosità nel socialismo italiano', in *Prampolini e il socialismo riformista* (Rome: Mondo operaio-Edizioni Avanti!, 1979), pp. 258-260.
Deliziosi, F., *Pino Puglisi il prete che fece tremare la mafia con un sorriso* (Milan: Rizzoli, 2013).
Demofonti, L., *La riforma nell'Italia del primo Novecento. Gruppi e riviste di ispirazione evangelica* (Rome: Edizioni di Storia e Letteratura, 2003).
Deresch, W., ed., *La fede dei socialisti religiosi* (Milan: Jaca Book, 1974).
Di Nucci, L. *La democrazia distributiva* (Bologna, 2016).
Di Rienzo, R., 'Laici in Rete', *L'Espresso*, no. 50 (16 December 1990), p. 25.
Diaco, P. and A. Scrosati, eds, *Padre Ennio Pintacuda. Un prete e la politica* (Acireale: Bonanno Editore, 1992).
Diamanti, I., *La Lega Nord. Geografia, storia e sociologia di un soggetto politico* (Rome: Donzelli, 1995).
Diani, M., *Le isole nell'arcipelago. Il movimento ecologista in Italia* (Bologna: Il Mulino, 1988).
Dickie, J., *Cosa nostra. Storia della mafia siciliana* (Rome: Laterza, 2005).
Dittrich, L., *Antiklerikalismus in Europa. Öffentlichkeit und Säkularisierung in Frankreich*, Spanien *und Deutschland (1848-1914)* (Göttingen: Vandenhoeck & Ruprecht, 2014).
Do, M., *Amare la Chiesa*, preface by E. Bianchi (Magnano: Edizioni Qiqajon, 2008).
Dominici, S., *La lotta senz'odio: il socialismo evangelico del «Seme» (1901-1915)* (Milan: Angeli, 1995).
Donati, G., *Scritti politici* (Rome: Cinque Lune, 1956).
Dondi, M., *L'eco del boato. Storia della strategia della tensione 1965-1974* (Rome: Laterza, 2015).
Donini, A., *Sessant'anni di militanza comunista* (Milan: Teti, 1988).
Donoso Loero, T., *Los Cristianos por el socialismo en Chile* (Santiago de Chile: Editorial Vaitea, 1975).

Dorigo, W., 'Lettera aperta', *Questitalia* 1, no. 1 (1958), p. 1.

Dorini, M., *Giuseppe Lazzati: gli anni del lager (1943–1945)* (Rome: Ave, 1989).

Galli Della Loggia, E. and L. Di Nucci, eds, *Due nazioni, Legittimazione e delegittimazione nella storia dell'Italia contemporanea* (Bologna, 2003).

Drake, R., 'Catholics and Italian Revolutionary Left of the 1960s', *Catholic Historical Review* 94, no. 3 (2008), pp. 450–475.

Duggan, C. and C. Wagstaff, eds, *Italy in the Cold War. Politics, Culture and Society (1948–1958)* (Oxford: Berg, 1995).

Duggan, C., *Fascist Voices. An Intimate History of Mussolini's Italy* (London: Bodley Head, 2012).

Dunnage, J., *Twenties Century Italy. A Social History* (London: Pearson, 2002).

Durand, J.-F., *L'Église catholique dans le crise de l'Italie* (Rome: École française de Rome, 1991).

Duriez, B. and É. Fouilloux, eds, *Chrétiens et ouvriers en France (1937–1970)* (Paris: Éditions de l'Atelier, 2001).

Enrico, G. and C. Saraceno, *Ideologia religiosa e conflitto sociale* (Bari: De Donato, 1970).

Epp, R., 'L'Église et les Révolutions', in R. Epp, C. Lefebvre and R. Metz, eds, *Le droit et les institutions de l'Église catholique latine de la fin du XVIII siècle a 1978* (Paris: Editions Cujas, 1981), pp. 79–84.

Escobar, R., *La paura del laico* (Bologna: Il Mulino, 2010).

Fabbretti, N., *Teresio Olivelli* (Milan: Edizioni Paoline, 1992).

Fabbri, L., ed., *Cristiani e marxisti: dialogo per il futuro* (Rome: Ave, 1967).

Faggioli, M., *Breve storia dei movimenti cattolici* (Rome: Carocci, 2008).

Faggioli, M., 'Council Vatican II: Bibliographical Overview 2007–2010', *Cristianesimo nella storia* 32 (2011), pp. 755–791.

Faggioli, M., 'The New Elites of Italian Catholicism: 1968 and the New Catholic Movements', *Catholic Historical Review*, 98, no. 1 (January 2012), pp. 18–40.

Falconi, C., *La contestazione nella Chiesa. Storia e documenti del movimento cattolico antiautoritario in Italia e nel mondo* (Milan: Feltrinelli, 1969).

Falconi, C., *La crociata di Paolo VI. La svolta reazionaria di papa Montini* (Milan: Kaos edizioni, 1968).

Fallaci, O., *La forza della ragione* (Milan: Rizzoli, 2004).

Fantappiè, C., *Arturo Carlo Jemolo. Riforma religiosa e laicità dello Stato* (Brescia: Morcelliana, 2011).

Fattorini, E., *Hitler, Mussolini and the Vatican: Pope Pius XI and the Speech that was Never Made* (Cambridge: Polity Press, 2011).

Favretto, I., 'The Italian Left in Search of Ideas: The Re-discovery of the Political Ideas of the Action Party', *Journal of Modern Italian Studies* 7, no. 3 (2002), pp. 392–415.

Favretto, I., 'Rough Music and Factory Protest in Post-1945 Italy', *Past and Present* 228, no. 1 (2015), pp. 207–247.

Felice, F., *Neocon e teocon. Il ruolo della religione nella vita pubblica statunitense* (Soveria Mannelli: Rubbettino, 2006).

Ferrari, F. L., *'Il Domani d'Italia' e altri scritti del Primo dopoguerra (1919-1926)*, ed. M. G. Rossi (Rome: Edizioni di Storia e Letteratura, 1983).

Ferrari, F. L., *Il regime fascista italiano*, ed. G. Ignesti (Rome: Edizioni di Storia e Letteratura, 1983).

Ferrari, F. L., *Scritti dall'esilio. 'Azione cattolica e il Regime' e altri saggi editi e inediti sui rapporti Chiesa-Stato* (Rome: Edizioni di Storia e Letteratura; Modena: Edizioni S.I.A.S., 1991).

Flamigni, S., *Il mio sangue ricadrà su di loro. Gli scritti di Aldo Moro prigioniero delle Br* (Milan: Kaos, 1997).

Flores d'Arcais, P., *La sfida oscurantista di Joseph Ratzinger* (Milan: Ponte alle Grazie, 2010).

Follini, M., *C'era una volta la DC* (Bologna: Il Mulino, 1994).

Follini, M., *L'arcipelago democristiano* (Bari: Laterza, 1990).

Foot, J., *Modern Italy* (New York: Palgrave, 2003).

Foot, J., '"White Bolsheviks"? The Catholic Left and the Socialism in Italy 1919-1920', *Historical Journal* 40, no. 2 (June 1997), pp. 415-433.

Forlenza, R., *La Repubblica del Presidente. Gli anni di Carlo Azelio Ciampi (1999-2006)* (Reggio Emilia: Diabasis, 2011).

Forlenza, R., *On the Edge of Democracy. Italy 1943-1945* (Oxford, 2019).

Forlenza, R., 'The Enemy within: Catholic Anti-Communism in Cold War Italy', *Past & Present*, 235, no. 1 (May 2017), pp. 207-242.

Forlenza, R. and B. Thomassen, 'Catholic Modernity and the Italian Constitution', *History Workshop Journal*, 81, no. 1 (1 April 2016), pp. 231-251.

Forlenza, R. and B. Thomassen, *Italian Modernities. Competing Narratives of Nationhood* (New York: Palgrave Macmillan, 2016).

Formiconi, B., *Nicaragua la nuova speranza. Una testimonianza sul Nicaragua, la sua problematica e il nuovo cammino* (Assisi: Cittadella, 1980).

Formigoni, G., *Aldo Moro. Lo statista e il suo dramma* (Bologna: Il Mulino, 2016).

Formigoni, G., *Alla prova della democrazia. Chiesa, cattolici e modernità nell'Italia del '900* (Trento: Il Margine, 2008).

Formigoni, G., 'Gli immigrati, frontiere discriminante della politica italiana', *Appunti di cultura e di politica* 24, no. 3 (2003), pp. 6-9.

Formigoni, G., 'La crisi internazionale: angosce, speranze, impegni', *Appunti di cultura e politica* 26, no. 1 (2003), pp. 1-5.

Formigoni, G., *Storia d'Italia nelle Guerra fredda (1943-1978)* (Bologna, 2016).

Franceschini, E., *Attività clandestina dell'Associazione professori e assistenti universitari APAU e del Comitato di Liberazione Nazionale dei professori e assistenti universitari* (Milan: Comitato direttivo provvisorio dell'Associazione professori e assistenti universitari, 1945).

Franco, M., *Tutti a casa. Il crepuscolo di mamma Dc* (Milan: Mondadori, 1993).

Franco, V., 'Se viene messa sotto assedio la laicità', *Testimonianze* 47, no. 440 (2005), pp. 96-101.

Franzoni, G., 'La cura del morire', *Confronti* 33, no. 11 (2006), p. 4.
Frosini, F., *La religione dell'uomo moderno. Politica e verità nei* Quaderni del carcere *di Antonio Gramsci* (Rome: Carocci, 2010).
Frosini, F., 'Subalterns, Religion and the Philosophy of Praxis in Gramsci Prisona Notebooks', *Rethinking Marxism* 28, nos 3–4 (December 2016), pp. 523–539.
Gabrielli, D., 'E se Benedetto XVI fosse diverso da Ratzinger?' *Confronti* 32, no. 5 (2005), p. 3.
Gabrielli, P., *Vivere da protagoniste: donne tra politica, cultura e controllo sociale* (Rome: Carocci, 2001).
Galavotti, E., *Il giovane Dossetti: gli anni della formazione, 1913–1939* (Bologna: Il Mulino, 2006).
Galavotti, E., *Il professorino: Giuseppe Dossetti tra crisi del fascismo e costruzione della democrazia 1940–1948* (Bologna; Il Mulino, 2013).
Galli, G., *Il partito armato. Gli «anni di piombo» in Italia 1968–1986* (Milan: Kaos Edizioni, 1993).
Galli, G., *Mezzo secolo di Dc (1943–1993): da De Gasperi a Mario Segni* (Milan: Rizzoli, 1993).
Galli G. and P. Facchi, *La sinistra democristiana. Storia e ideologie* (Milan: Feltrinelli, 1962).
Gallo, A., *Così in cielo come in terra* (Milan: Mondadori, 2010).
Gallo, A., 'La crociata di una Chiesa materialista', *Micromega*, no. 1 (2007), pp. 77–79.
Garelli, F., 'I movimenti, visibili e invisibili', *Il Mulino* 55, no. 6 (2006), pp. 1075–1085.
Garelli, F., *L'Italia cattolica nell'epoca del pluralismo* (Bologna: Il Mulino, 2006).
Garelli, F. *La Chiesa in Italia* (Bologna: Il Mulino, 2007).
Gariglio, B. *Cattolici democratici e clerico-fascisti. Il mondo cattolico torinese alla prova del fascismo (1922–1927)* (Bologna: Il Mulino, 1976).
Gariglio, B., *Con animo liberale. Piero Gobetti e i popolari 1918–1926)* (Milan: Angeli, 1997).
Gentile, E., *Contro Cesare. Cristianesimo e totalitarismo nell'epoca dei fascismi* (Milan: Feltrinelli, 2016).
Gentili, M., 'La realtà terrestre in Teilhard de Chardin e nel nuovo cattolicesimo', *Momento* 1, no. 1 (1965), pp. 3–15.
Gentiloni, F., 'Il Vaticano, pacifista ma non troppo', *Confronti* 30, no. 2 (2003), p. 4.
Gentiloni, F., 'Interloquire alla pari', *Testimonianze* 47, no. 440 (2005), pp. 75–76.
Gentiloni, F. *Oltre il dialogo. Cattolici e Pci: le possibili intese tra passato e presente* (Rome: Editori Riuniti, 1989).
Gentiloni Silveri, U., *L'Italia e la nuova frontiera. Stati Uniti e centro-sinistra 1958–1965* (Bologna: Il Mulino, 1998).
Gerard, E. and G.-R. Horn, eds, *Left Catholicism 1943–1955. Catholics and Society in Western Europe at the Point of Liberation* (Leuven: Leuven University Press, 2001).
Gervanoni, M., *Georges Sorel. Una biografia intellettuale. Socialismo e liberalismo nella Francia della Belle époque* (Milan: Unicopli, 2006).

Gervasio, G., 'Cattolici e politici nella transizione', *Orientamenti Sociali*, no. 4 (October–December 1993), pp. 3–7.
Gervasoni, M., *Storia dell'Italia degli anni Ottanta. Quando eravamo moderni* (Venice: Marsilio, 2010).
Gillio, G. M., 'Otto preti al Papa: pace nel mondo ma anche nella Chiesa', *Confronti* 30, no. 4 (2003), p. 8.
Ginsborg, P., *L'Italia del tempo presente: famiglia, società civile, Stato (1980–1996)* (Turin: Einaudi, 1998).
Girardi, G., ed., *'Le rose non sono borghesi'. Popolo e cultura nel nuovo Nicaragua* (Rome: Borla, 1986).
Giordani, I., *Memorie d'un cristiano ingenuo* (Rome: Città Nuova editrice, 1981).
Giordani, I., *Rivolta cattolica* (Turin: Gobetti, 1925).
Giovagnoli A. and L. Tosi, eds, *Amintore Fanfani e la politica estera italiana* (Venice: Marsilio, 2010).
Giovagnoli, A., *Chiesa e progetto educativo nell'Italia del secondo dopoguerra* (Brescia: La scuola, 1988).
Giovagnoli, A., *Il caso Moro. Una tragedia repubblicana* (Bologna: Il Mulino, 2005).
Giovagnoli, A., *Il partito italiano. La Democrazia cristiana dal 1942 al 1994* (Rome: Laterza, 1996).
Giovagnoli, A., *La cultura democristiana* (Rome: Laterza, 1991).
Giovagnoli, A., 'La Democrazia cristiana dal 1980 al 1994', in F. Traniello and G. Campanini, eds, *Dizionario storico del Movimento cattolico. Aggiornamento 1980–1995* (Genoa: Marietti, 1997), 124–133.
Giovagnoli, A., *La repubblica degli italiani (1946–2016)* (Rome, 2016)
Giovagnoli, A., *Sessantotto. La festa della contestazione* (Cinisello Balsamo, 2018).
Giovagnoli, A., ed., *1968 tra utopia e Vangelo. Contestazione e mondo cattolico* (Rome: Ave, 2000).
Giovannini, C., 'Lega democratica nazionale', in F. Traniello and G. Campani, eds, *Dizionario storico del movimento cattolico in Italia 1860–1980*, vol. 1, *I fatti e le idee* (Turin: Marietti, 1981), pp. 304–309.
Girardi, G., *Marxismo e cristianesimo*, preface by F. Koenig (Assisi: Cittadella, 1966).
Girardi, G., *Sandinismo, marxismo, cristianesimo* (Managua: Centro Ecuménico Antonio Valdivieso; Rome: Borla, 1986).
Giunipero, E., 'Le inchieste sul comunismo in Cina?', in A. Guasco and R. Perin, eds, *Pius XI* (Münster: LIT, 2010), pp. 393–445.
Giuntella, M. C., *La Fuci tra modernismo, Partito popolare e fascismo* (Rome: Studium, 2000).
Goichot, É., *Alfred Loisy e ses amis* (Paris: Les editions du cerf, 2002).
Goldstein Sepinwall, A., *The abbé Grégoire and the French Revolution. The Making of Modern Universalism* (Berkeley: University of California Press, 2005).
Gozzini, M., *Oltre gli steccati* (Milan: Sperling & Kupfer, 1994).
Gozzini, M., ed., *Il dialogo alla prova* (Florence: Vallecchi, 1964).

Gramsci, A., *Il Vaticano e l'Italia* (Rome: Editori Riuniti, 1967).
Gramsci, A., *La costruzione del Partito comunista 1923–1926* (Turin: Einaudi, 1978).
Gramsci, A., *L'Ordine nuovo 1919–1920* (Turin: Einaudi, 1954).
Gramsci, A., *Masse e partito. Antologia 1910–1926*, ed. G. Liguori (Rome: Editori Riuniti, 2016).
Gramsci, A., *Per la verità. Scritti 1913–1926*, ed. Renzo Martinelli (Rome: Editori Riuniti, 1974).
Gramsci, A., *Quaderni dal carcere*, vol. 1, *Gli intellettuali e l'organizzazione della cultura* (Rome: Editori Riuniti, 2012).
Gramsci, A., *Quaderni dal carcere*, vol. 2, *Il materialismo storico e la filosofia di Benedetto Croce*, ed. V. Gerratana (Turin: Editori Riuniti, 2012).
Gramsci, A., *Quaderni dal carcere*, vol. 3, *Letteratura e vita nazionale* (Rome: Editori Riuniti, 2013).
Gramsci, A., *Scritti giovanili (1914–1918)* (Turin: Einaudi, 1958).
Gramsci, A., *Socialismo e fascismo* (Rome: Editori Riuniti, 1972).
Gramsci, A., *Sotto la mole (1916–1920)* (Turin: Einaudi, 1960).
Gramsci, A. and T. Schucht, *Lettere 1926–1935*, eds A. Natoli and C. Daniele (Turin: Einaudi, 1997).
Grazia Fida, M., *Educare alla pace. La via di don Milani* (Milan: Edizioni Paoline, 2012).
Greeley, A., *The Catholic Revolution: New Wine, Old Wineskins and Second Vatican Council* (Berkeley: University of California Press, 2004).
Guasco, A., *Cattolici e fascisti. La Santa Sede e la politica italiana all'alba del regime (1919–1925)* (Bologna, 2013).
Guasco, A., *Le due Italie. Azionismo e qualunquismo (1943–1948)* (Milan, 2018).
Guasco, M., *Carità e giusticia. Don Luigi Di Liegro (1928–1997)* (Bologna, 2012).
Guasco, M., *Modernismo. I fatti e gli idee* (Milan, 1995).
Guasco, M. and P. Trionfini, eds, *Don Zeno e Nomadelfia. Tra società civile e società religiosa* (Brescia: Morcelliana, 2001).
Guerri, G. B., *Eretico e profeta. Ernesto Buonaiuti, un prete contro la Chiesa* (Milan: Mondadori, 2001).
Guerrieri, S., 'Il PCI di Occhetto e le riforme istituzionali. Dalla critica al consociativismo alla via referendaria', in S. Colarizi, A. Giovagnoli and P. Pombeni, eds, *L'Italia contemporanea dagli anni Ottanta a oggi*, vol. 3, *Istituzioni e politica* (Rome: Carocci, 2014), pp. 253–268.
Guglielmino, S., 'In cabina elettorale pensando: Rete!', *Risotto giallo* 1, no. 2 (February 1994), pp. 2–3.
Guolo, R., *Chi impugna la croce. Lega e Chiesa* (Rome: Laterza, 2011).
Harnack, A., *Das Wesen des Christentums* (Leipzig: J. C. Hinrichs'sche Buchhandlung, 1902).
Haslam, J., *The Nixon Administration and the Death of Allende's Chile* (London: Verso, 2005).
Hill, H., *The Politics of Modernism: Alfred Loisy and the Scientific Study of Religion* (Washington, DC: Catholic University of America Press, 2002).

Hobsbawn, E. J., *The Age of Extremes: The Short Twentieth Century (1914–1991)* (London: Abacus, 1995).
Holland, J., *Modern Catholic Social Teaching: The Popes Confront The Industrial Age (1740–1958)* (Mahwah, NJ: Paulist Press, 2003).
Horn, G.-R., *The Spirit of Vatican II. Western European Progressive Catholicism in the Long Sixties* (Oxford: Oxford University Press, 2015).
Horn, G.-R., *Western European Liberation Theology (1924–1959)* (Oxford, 2008).
Horn, G.-R. and E. Gerard, eds, *Catholicism and Society in Western Europe at the Point of Liberation* (Leuven, 2001).
Hornsby-Smith, M., *The Changing Parish: A Study of Parishes, Priests and Parishioners after Vatican II* (London: Routledge, 1989).
Iaccarino, R., 'Italia: sos razzismo', *Appunti di cultura e di politica* 26, no. 3 (2004), pp. 6–10.
Idee e programmi della DC nella Resistenza, introduction by G. Battista Varnier (Rome: Civitas, 1984).
Ignazi, P., *Dal PCI al PDS. Vero un nuovo modello di partito?* (Bologna: Il Mulino, 1997).
Il comunismo e i cattolici (Rome: Ed. Voce Operaia, 1944).
Il prete della plebe, 'Fra la gens emiliana', *Cultura Sociale* 8, no. 181 (1905), p. 221.
Jodock, D. ed., *Catholicism Contending with Modernity: Roman Catholic Modernism and Anti-Modernism in Historical Contexts* (Cambridge: Cambridge University Press, 2000).
Kautsky. K., *Die Sozialdemokratie und die katholische Kirche* (Berlin: Vorwärts, 1902).
La Ferla, G., *Ritratto di Georges Sorel* (Milan: La Cultura, 1933).
La Pira, G., 'L'attesa della povera gente', *Cronache sociali* 4, no. 1 (1950), pp. 1–6.
La Valle, R., 'Il problema dell'identità', *Rinascita* 94, no. 27 (11 July 1987), pp. 6–7.
Lanaro, S., *Storia dell'Italia repubblicana: l'economia, la politica, la cultura, la società dal dopoguerra agli anni '90* (Venice: Marsilio, 2001).
Langlois, C., *Le catholicisme au féminin: les congrégations françaises à supérieure génerale au 19 siècle* (Paris: Cerf, 1984).
Lazar, M. and M.-A. Matard-Bonucci, eds, *L'Italie des années de plomb. Le terrorisme entre histoire et mémoire* (Paris: Éditions Autrement, 2010).
Inaudi, S. and M. Margotti, eds, *La rivoluzione del Concilio. La contestazione cattolica negli anni Sessanta e Settanta* (Rome: Studium, 2017).
Biorcio, R., ed., *La sfida verde. Il movimento ecologista in Italia* (Padua: Liviana Editrice, 1988).
Tognon, G., ed., *La tela di Prodi. Una costituzione per un'Europa più democratica* (Milan: Baldini & Castoldi, 2003).
Boniolo, G., ed., *Laicità. Una geografia delle nostre radici* (Turin: Einaudi, 2006).
Lazzati, G., 'La Resistenza continua', in G. Bianche and B. De Marchi, eds, *Per amore ribelli* (Milan: Vita e Pensiero, 1976), pp. 13–17.
Lentini, F., *La primavera breve. Quando Palermo sognava una Città per l'Uomo* (Cinisello Balsamo: Paoline, 2011).

Levillain, P., *Rome n'est plus dans Rome. Mgr Lefebvre et son église* (Paris: Clovis, 2010).
Levillain, P. and J.-M. Ticchi, eds, *Le Pontificat de Léon XIII: Renaissance du Saint-Siège?* (Rome: École Française de Rome, 2006).
Lidtke, V. L., 'August Bebel and German Social Democracy's Relation to the Christian Churches', *Journal of the History of Ideas* 27, no. 2 (1966), pp. 245–264.
Liguori, G., *Sentieri gramsciani* (Rome: Carocci, 2006).
Livi, M., 'The Ruini System and Berlusconismo: Synergy and Transformation between the Catholic Church and Italian Politics in the Second Republic', *Journal of Modern Italian Studies* 21, no. 3 (2016), pp. 399–418.
Lizzeri, G. and P. Ranci, eds, *Università Cattolica. Storia di 3 occupazioni, repressioni e serrate* (Milan: Edizioni Relazioni Sociali, 1968).
Lo Bianco, G. and S. Rizza, *L'agenda rossa di Paolo Borsellino* (Milan: Chiarelettere, 2007).
Loisy, A., *L'Évangile et de l'Église* (Paris: Alphonse Picard et fils, 1902).
Loisy, A., *Mémoires pour servir à l'histoire religieuse de notre temps* (Paris: Nourry, 1930–1931).
Lombardo Radice, L., *Socialismo e libertà* (Rome: Editori Riuniti, 1968).
Luciani, A., *Cristianesimo e socialismo in Europa (1700–1989)* (Rome: ASCE, 1989).
Lupo, S., *Che cos'è la mafia. Sciascia, Andreotti, l'antimafia e la politica* (Rome: Donzelli, 2007).
Lupo, S., *La mafia non ha vinto* (Rome: Laterza, 2014).
Macaluso, E., *Sciascia e i comunisti* (Milan: Feltrinelli, 2010).
Maccaferri, M., 'Intellettuali italiani tra società opulenta e democrazia del benessere: il caso de Il Mulino', *Mondo contemporaneo* 5, no. 1 (2009), pp. 45–77.
Magister, S., *Chiesa extraparlamentare* (Naples: L'ancora del Mediterraneo, 2001).
Malavasi, G., *L'antifascismo cattolico. Il Movimento guelfo d'azione (1928–1948)* (Rome: Edizioni Lavoro, 1982).
Malgeri, F., 'Cultura e politica in Felice Balbo: l'esperienza della sinistra cristiana', in G. Campanini, ed., *Felice Balbo tra filosofia e società* (Milan: Angeli, 1985), pp. 17–18.
Malgeri, F., 'Guido Miglioli nella dialettica politica dall'età giolittiana al fascismo', in F. Leonori, ed., *La figura e l'opera di Guido Miglioli (1879–1979)* (Rome: Quaderni del CDCD, 1982).
Malgeri, F., 'Introduzione', in *Voce operaia. Dai cattolici comunisti alla Sinistra cristiana* (Rome: Studium, 1992), pp. 35–36.
Malgeri, F., *La Chiesa italiana e la guerra* (Rome: Studium, 1980).
Malgeri, F., 'La formazione della DC tra scelte locali e urgenze nazionali', in G. De Rosa, ed., *Cattolici, Chiesa, Resistenza* (Bologna: Il Mulino, 1997), pp. 533–563.
Malgeri, F., *La Sinistra cristiana (1937–1945)* (Brescia: Morcelliana, 1982).
Malgeri, F., ed., *Storia della Democrazia cristiana*, vol. 3 (Rome: Cinque Lune, 1988).
Malpensa, M. and A. Parola, *Lazzati. Una sentinella nella notte (1909–1986)* (Bologna: Il Mulino, 2005).
Malvestiti, P., *La lotta politica in Italia dal 25 luglio 1943 alla Costituente* (Milan: Bernabò, 1948).

Mancuso, V., *Per amore. Rifondazione della fede* (Milan: Mondadori, 2005).
Margiotta Broglio, F., 'Ernesto Buonaiuti', in G. Rossini, ed., *Modernismo, fascismo, comunismo. Aspetti e figure della cultura e della politica dei cattolici nel '900* (Bologna: Il Mulino, 1972).
Margiotta Broglio, F., *Italia e Santa Sede dalla Grande guerra alla Conciliazione* (Bari: Laterza, 1966).
Margotti, M., *La fabbrica dei cattolici. Chiesa, industria e organizzazioni operaie a Torino (1948-1965)* (Turin: Angolo Manzoni, 2012).
Margotti, M., *Lavoro manuale e spiritualità. L'itinerario dei preti operai* (Rome: Studium, 2001).
Marino, G. C., *Autobiografia del Pci staliniano 1946-1953* (Rome: Editori Riuniti, 1991).
Marino, G. C., *Storia della mafia* (Rome: Newton Compton, 2012).
Maritain, J., *L'uomo e lo Stato* (Milan: Vita e Pensiero, 1982) (first published in Chicago in 1951).
Mariuzzo, A., *Communism and Anti-Communism in Early Cold War Italy. Language, Symbols and Myths* (Manchaster, 2018).
Marquardt, F.-W., *Teologia e socialismo. L'esempio di K. Barth* (Milan: Jaca Book, 1974).
Marras, V., 'La guerra preventiva', *Jesus* 25, no. 2 (2003), p. 3.
Martellini, A., *Fiori nei cannoni. Non violenza e antimilitarismo nell'Italia del Novecento* (Rome: Donzelli, 2006).
Martinelli, R., 'Il "che fare" di Gramsci nel 1923', *Studi storici* 13, no. 4 (1972), pp. 790-802.
Martini, C. M., *Conversazioni notturne a Gerusalemme. Sul rischio della fede* (Milan: Mondadori, 2008).
Matteotti, M., 'Prima l'unificazione dei socialisti', *Politica* 4, no. 3 (1958), p. 3.
Mazzantini, J., 'Un'identità democratica, oltre il socialismo', *Testimonianze* 50, no. 455 (2007), pp. 14-18.
Mazzonis, F., 'Gramsci e la questione cattolica', *Trimestre*, nos 2-3 (1980), p. 173.
Mazzolari, P., *Cattolici e comunisti* (Vicenza: La Locusta, 1966).
Mazzolari, P., *Il compagno Cristo: Vangelo del reduce* (Milan: Martini e Chiodi, 1945).
Mazzolari, P., *La pieve sull'argine*, ed. D. Saresella (Bologna: Dehoniane, 2008).
Mazzolari, P., *Scritti politici*, ed. M. Truffelli (Bologna: Dehoniane, 2010).
McLeod, H., *The Religious Crisis of the 1960s* (Oxford: Oxford University Press, 2010).
Melloni, A., *Dossetti l'indicibile. Il quaderno scomparso di Cronache sociali: i cattolici per un nuovo partito a sinistra della Dc* (Rome: Donzelli, 2013).
Melloni, A., 'Pacifismo cattolico e ruolo internazionale della Chiesa', *Il Mulino* 52, no. 2 (2003), pp. 390-398.
Melloni, A., *Papa Giovanni. Un cristiano al Concilio* (Turin: Einaudi, 2009).
Melloni, A., 'Tre fasi nel rapporto fra Chiesa, episcopato e politica', *Il Mulino* 55, no. 6 (2006), pp. 1056-1065.
Melloni, A., 'Turoldo e Cl, primavera 1975', in *Laicità e profezia. La vicenda di David Maria Turoldo* (Palazzago: Servitium, 2003), pp. 281-328.

Melloni, A., ed., *Cronache sociali 1947–1951* (Bologna: Istituto per le Scienze Religiose, 2007).

Melloni, A., ed., *Giuseppe Dossetti: la fede e la storia. Studi nel decennale della morte* (Bologna: Il Mulino, 2007).

Melloni, A. and G. Ruggieri, eds, *Chi ha paura del Vaticano II?* (Rome: Carocci, 2009).

Menapace, L., 'Sinistra vecchia e nuova', *Settegiorni* 41 (1968), p. 18.

Menozzi, D., *Chiesa, pace e guerra nel Novecento. Verso una delegittimazione religiosa dei conflitti* (Bologna: Il Mulino, 2008).

Menozzi, D., *Chiesa, pace e guerra. Verso una legittimazione religiosa dei conflitti* (Bologna: Il Mulino, 2008).

Menozzi, D., *Chiesa, poveri, società nell'età moderna e contemporanea* (Brescia: Queriniana, 1980).

Menozzi, D., *Giovanni Paolo II. Una transizione incompiuta? Per una storicizzazione del pontificato* (Brescia: Morcelliana, 2006).

Menozzi, D., 'La Chiesa cattolica', in G. Filoramo and D. Menozzi eds, *Storia del cristianesimo. L'età contemporanea* (Roma-Bari: Laterza, 1997), pp. 166–171.

Menozzi, D., *La Chiesa italiana e la secolarizzazione* (Turin: Einaudi, 1993).

Menozzi, D., *Sacro Cuore. Un culto tra devozione interiore e restaurazione cristiana della società* (Rome: Viella, 2001).

Messineo, A., 'Può il socialista essere democratico?' *La Civiltà Cattolica* 108, no. 15 (1957), pp. 337–349.

Miccoli, G., *In difesa della fede. La Chiesa di Giovanni Paolo II e Benedetto XVI* (Milan: Rizzoli, 2007).

Miccoli, G., *La Chiesa dell'anticoncilio. I tradizionalisti alla conquista di Roma* (Rome: Laterza, 2011).

Miccoli, G., 'La Chiesa e il fascismo', in G. Quazza, ed., *Fascismo e società italiana* (Turin: Einaudi, 1973), p. 203.

Miglioli, G., *Con Roma e con Mosca* (Milan: Garzanti, 1945).

Miglioli, G., *Études historiques. Humanisme et réalisme dans la question agraire soviétique* (Brussels, 1938).

Miglioli, G., *La collectivisation des campagnes soviétiques* (Paris: Les Éditions Rieder, 1935).

Monaco, F., 'I cattolici italiani nell'attuale congiuntura politica', *Aggiornamenti sociali* 44, no. 2 (1993), pp. 101–120.

Monaco, F., 'L'Italia vira a destra', *Aggiornamenti sociali* 45, no. 5 (1994), pp. 325–332.

Monaco, F., 'La "religione civile" secondo Pera, supporto ideologico dell'occidentalismo', *Jesus* 26, no. 6 (2004), p. 13.

Monticone, A., 'Intervista. Facciamo il punto sul nuovo Partito Popolare', *Orientamenti Sociali*, no. 4 (October–December 1993), pp. 83–92.

Monticone, A., 'Partito democratico: un partito di sinistra che guarda al centro', *Aggiornamenti sociali* 58, nos 7–8 (2007), pp. 495–499.

Moro, A., *L'intelligenza e gli avvenimenti. Testi 1959–1978* (Milan: Garzanti, 1979).

Moro, R., *La formazione della classe dirigente cattolica (1929–1937)* (Bologna: Il Mulino, 1979).

Murialdi, P. and N. Tranfaglia, *La stampa italiana del neocapitalismo* (Rome: Laterza, 1976).

Murphy, J. W. and M. J. Caro, *Uriel Molina and the Sandinist Popular Movement in Nicaragua* (Jafferson, NC: McFarland & Company Publisher, 2006).

Murri, R., 'Il momento e i cattolici', *Cultura Sociale* 1, no. 10 (1898), p. 146.

Murri, R., 'La crisi del liberalismo in Italia', *Cultura Sociale* 1, no. 12 (1898), p. 178.

Murri, R., 'La guerra santa', *Cultura Sociale* 9, no. 192 (1906), p. 2

Murri, R., 'Partiti ed accordi', *Cultura sociale* 8, no. 187 (1905), pp. 305–306.

Napoleoni, C., *Cercate ancora. Lettera sulla laicità e ultimi scritti*, ed. R. La Valle (Rome: Editori Riuniti, 1990).

Napolitano, G., *Dal PCI al socialismo europeo. Un'autobiografia politica* (Roma: Laterza, 2008).

Naro, C., 'Il martirio di don Puglisi e la pastorale "moderna" delle Chiese in Sicilia', *La voce di Campofranco* 33, nos 9–10 (November–December 1993), p. 8.

Nesti, A., *Gesù socialista* (Turin: Claudiana, 1974).

Niccoli, O., ed., *Una rete di amicizie. Carteggi dalla Koinonia di Ernesto Buonaiuti* (Rome: Viella, 2014).

Nicoletti, M., 'Un secondo partito cattolico?' *Il margine*, no. 6 (1989), pp. 3–9.

Nilsson DeHaunas, D. and M. Shterin, 'Religion and the Rise of Populism', *Religion, State & Society* 46, no. 3 (2018), pp. 177–185.

Novelli, D., 'Partiti e potere', *Avvenimenti*, no. 1 (2 January 1991), p. 10.

Oberti, A., 'Lazzati e l'Università Cattolica: da una testimonianza per la causa di beatificazione?' in G. Alberigo, ed., *Giuseppe Lazzati (1909–1986). Contributi per una biografia* (Bologna: Il Mulino, 2000), pp. 213–228.

Occhetto, A., 'Una costituente per aprire una nuova prospettiva della sinistra', in *Documenti per il congresso straoridnario del Pci*, vol. 1, Comitato centrale della svolta (Rome: l'Unità, 1990), p. 16.

Orlando, L., *Fede e politica. Paolo Giuntella intervista Leoluca Orlando* (Casale Monferrato: Marietti, 1992).

Orfei, R., *Marxismo e umanesimo* (Rome: Coines, 1970).

Orsini, A., *Anatomia delle Brigate rosse. Le radici ideologiche del terrorismo rivoluzionario* (Soveria Mannelli: Rubbettino, 2009).

Osnaghi Dodi, L., *L'azione sociale dei cattolici nel milanese (1878–1904)* (Milan: Sugarco, 1974).

Ossicini, A., 'Cattolici a pugno chiuso', *Rinascita* 30, no. 45 (1973), pp. 21–22.

Ossicini, A., *Contro la sconfitta della politica* (Rome: Editori Riuniti, 2002).

Ossicini, A., *Cristiani non democristiani* (Rome: Editori Riuniti, 1980).

Ossicini, A., *Un'isola sul Tevere. Il fascismo al di là del ponte* (Rome: Editori Riuniti, 1999).

Pace, E., *L'unità dei cattolici in Italia. Origini e decadenza di un mito collettivo* (Milan: Guerini e Associati, 1995).

Pace, E., 'Politics of Paradise. Conflitti di religione e conflitti d' identità prima e dopo l'11 settembre', *Rassegna italiana di sociologia* 44, no. 1 (2003), pp. 25–42.

Palumbi, N., *Don Giovanni Minzoni. Educatore e martire* (Cinisello Balsamo: San Paolo, 2003).

Pancera, M., *Conversazioni con Bettazzi* (Vicenza: La Locusta, 1978).

Panzera, F. and D. Saresella, eds, *Spiritualità e utopia: la rivista Coenobium* (Milan, 2007).

Panvini, G., *Cattolici e violenza politica* (Venice: Marsillo, 2014).

Parisella, A., ed., *Gerardo Bruni e i cristiano-sociali* (Rome: Edizioni Lavoro, 1984).

Parente, F., *Ernesto Buonaiuti* (Rome: Istituto dell'Enciclopedia Italiana, 1971).

Parente, U., *Riformismo religioso e sociale a Napoli tra Ottocento e Novecento: la figura e l'opera di Gennaro Avolio* (Urbino: Quattro Venti, 1995).

Parisella, A., 'Gerardo Bruni', in F. Traniello and G. Campanini, eds, *Dizionario storico del movimento cattolico in Italia*, vol. 1, *Protagonisti* (Casale Monferrato: Marietti, 1982), pp. 56–58.

Parisi, A., *Questione cattolica e referendum. L'inizio di una fine* (Bologna: Il Mulino, 1974).

Pasquino, G., ed., *La prova delle armi* (Bologna: Il Mulino, 1984).

Pasquino, G., ed., *Il Partito democratico: elezione del segretario, organizzazione e potere* (Bologna: Bonomia University Press, 2009).

Passalacqua, G., *Il vento della Padania. Storia della Lega Nord 1984–2009* (Milan: Mondadori, 2010).

Passarelli, G. and D. Tuorto, *La Lega di Salvini. Estrema destra di governo* (Bologna: Il Mulino, 2018).

Passelecq, G. and B. Suchecky, *L'Encyclique cachée de Pie XI. Une occasion manquée de l'Eglise face à l'antisémitisme* (Paris: Le Découverte, 1995).

Passerini, V., 'La Rete e la Lega', in S. Benvenuti, ed., *Storia del Trentino. Fatti, personaggi, istituzioni di un paese di confine*, vol. 2 (Trento: Edizioni Panorama, 1995), 297–300.

Pazzaglia, L. and C. Crevenna, eds, *Tommaso Gallarati Scotti tra totalitarismo fascista e ripresa democratica* (Milan: Cisalpino, 2013).

Pelletier, D., *La crise catholique: Religion, societé et politique en France (1965–1978)* (Paris: Payot, 2002).

Pera, M. and J. Ratzinger, *Radici* (Milan: Mondadori, 2004).

Perché siamo socialisti e cristiani (Rome: Libreria Editrice Romana, 1908).

Perin, R., ed., *Pio XI e la crisi europea* (Venice: Edizioni Cà Foscari, 2016).

Perini, L., *Il corpo della cittadina. Nilde Iotti e il dibattito sull'aborto in Italia negli anni Settanta*, in *Nilde Iotti. Dalla Cattolica a Montecitorio* (Milan: Biblion, 2010).

Pertici, R., *Chiesa e Stato in Italia. Dalla Grande Guerra al nuovo concordato (1914–1984)* (Bologna: Il Mulino, 2009).

Pertici, R., 'Il vario anticomunismo italiano (1936–1960): lineamenti di una storia', in E. Galli Della Loggia and L. Di Nucci, eds, *Due nazioni, Legittimazione e delegittimazione nella storia dell'Italia contemporanea* (Bologna, 2003), pp. 330–345.

Petralia, G., *Il cardinal Giuseppe Ruffini arcivescovo di Palermo* (Città del Vaticano: Libreria editrice vaticana, 1989).

Piana, G., 'Cristianesimo come "religione civile?"' *Aggiornamenti sociali* 57, no. 3 (2006), pp. 223–234.

Pianta, M., *Globalizzazione dal basso. Economia mondiale e movimenti sociali* (Rome: Manifestolibri, 2001).

Piazzoni, I., 'Per una nuova cultura politica', in G. Formigoni and D. Saresella, eds, *1945. La transizione del dopoguerra* (Rome: Viella, 2017), pp. 209–228.

Piazzoni, I., *Storia delle televisioni in Italia* (Rome: Carocci, 2014).

Pintacuda, E., *Breve corso di Politica* (Milan: Rizzoli, 1988).

Pintacuda, E., *Il guado. Il travaglio della democrazia in vent'anni di storia italiana* (Molfetta: Edizioni La meridiana, 1995).

Pizzolato, L. F., 'Alle origini di Città dell'uomo', in G. Formigoni and L. F. Pizzolato, *Giuseppe Lazzati e il progetto di 'Città dell'uomo'* (Milan: In Dialogo, 2002), pp. 21–46.

Plongeron, B., *Des résistences religieus à Napoleon* (Paris: Letouzey, 2006).

Plongeron, B., 'Le Christianisme comme messianisme social', in *Histoire du Christianisme*, vol. 10, *Les défis de la modernité (1750–1840)*, under the direction of J.-M. Mayeur, C. and L. Pietri, A. Vauchez and M. Venard (Paris: Desclée, 1997), pp. 866–886.

Podda, S., *Nome di battaglia Mara. Vita e morte di Mara Cagol, il primo capo delle Br* (Milan: Sperling & Kupfer, 2007).

Pombeni, P., *Giuseppe Dossetti: l'avventura politica di un riformatore cristiano* (Bologna: Il Mulino, 2013).

Pombeni, P., *Il gruppo dossettiano e la fondazione della democrazia italiana (1938–1948)* (Bologna: Il Mulino, 1979).

Pombeni, P., 'Il sistema dei partiti dalla Prima alla Seconda Repubblica', in S. Colarizi, A. Giovagnoli and P. Pombeni, eds, *L'Italia contemporanea dagli anni Ottanta a oggi*, vol. 3, *Istituzioni e politica* (Rome: Carocci, 2014), 311–312.

Pombeni, P., *La costituente. Un problema storico-politico* (Bologna: Il Mulino, 1995).

Pombeni, P., 'Movimento cattolico e movimento socialista', in F. Traniello and G. Campanini, eds, *Dizionario storico del movimento cattolico in Italia (1860–1980)*, vol. 1, *I fatti e le idee* (Turin: Marietti, 1981), pp. 17–19.

Pombeni, P., *Socialismo e cristianesimo (1815–1975)* (Brescia: Queriniana, 1977).

Pons, S., *Berlinguer e la fine del comunismo* (Turin: Einaudi, 2006).

Portelli, H., *Gramsci e la questione religiosa* (Milan: Mazzotta, 1976).

Possieri, A., *Il peso della storia. Memoria, identità, rimozioni dal PCI al PDS (1970–1991)* (Bologna: Il Mulino, 2007).

Poulat, É., *Histoire, dogme et critique dans la crise moderniste* (Paris: Casterman, 1962).

Pratt Howard, E., *Il Partito Popolare Italiano* (Florence: La nuova Italia, 1957).

Prezzi, L., 'Latino o Concilio?' *Il Regno attualità* 51, no. 20 (2006), p. 672.

Prodi, R., 'Stabilizzare l'Europa e rafforzare la sua presenza a livello mondiale', *Appunti di cultura e di politica* 26, no. 5 (2004), pp. 1–3.

Prüfer, S., *Sozialismus statt Religion. Die deutsche Sozialdemokratie vor der religiösen Frage 1863–1890* (Göttingen: Vanderhoeck & Ruprecht, 2002).
Punzo, M., 'Il dibattito sulla revisione del Concordato. I socialisti', *Civitas*, series four, 3, no. 1 (2006), pp. 45–64.
Quagliariello, G., *Cattolici, pacifisti, teocon. Chiesa e politica in Italia dopo la caduta del muro* (Milan: Mondadori, 2006).
Ramos-Rigidor, J. and A. Gecchelin, eds, *Cristiani per il socialismo* (Milan: Arnoldo Mondadori, 1977).
Ranchetti, M., *Gli ultimi preti. Figure del cattolicesimo contemporaneo* (Fiesole: ECP, 1997).
Rapone, L., *Cinque anni che paiono secoli. Antonio Gramsci dal socialismo al comunismo* (Rome: Carocci, 2011).
Rapone, L., *Da Turati a Nenni. Il socialismo italiano negli anni del fascismo* (Milan, 1992).
Relazioni della commissione parlamentare d'inchiesta sulla strage di via Fani, sul sequestro e assassinio di Aldo Moro e sul terrorismo in Italia, 2 vol. (Rome, 1993).
Raponi, N., *Tommaso Gallarati Scotti tra politica e cultura* (Milan: Vita e Pensiero, 1971).
Rensi, G., 'Socialismo e cristianesimo', *Critica sociale* 18, nos 23–24 (1908), pp. 52–53.
Riccardi, A., *Governo carismatico. Venticinque anni di pontificato* (Brescia: Morcelliana, 2003).
Riccardi, A., *Il 'partito romano'. Politica italiana, Chiesa cattolica e Curia romana da Pio XII a Paolo VI* (Brescia, 2007).
Riccardi, A., *L'inverno più lungo (1943–1944): Pio XII, gli ebrei e i nazisti a Roma* (Rome: Laterza, 2008).
Richard, P., *Origen y desarrollo del movimiento Cristianos per el Socialismo: Chile 1970–1973* (Paris: Centre Lebret Foi et développement, 1975).
Rinaldi, R., *Don Zeno, Turoldo, Nomadelfia. Era semplicemente Vangelo* (Bologna: Dehoniane, 1998).
Ristuccia, S., ed., *Intellettuali cattolici tra riformismo e dissenso* (Milan: Edizioni di Comunità, 1975).
Rocca, G., *Donne religiose. Contributo ad una storia della condizione femminile nei secoli XIX–XX* (Rome: Edizioni Paoline, 1992).
Ricolfi, L., 'Elezioni e mass-media. Quanti voti ha spostato la Tv', *Il Mulino* 98, no. 6 (1994), pp. 1031–1046.
Rodano, F., *Questione democristiana e compromesso storico* (Rome: Editori Riuniti, 1977).
Rodano, M., *Diario minimo del mutare dei tempi. L'età dell'inconsapevolezza, il tempo della speranza (1921–1948)*, vol. 1 (Rome: Memori, 2008).
Roncalli, M., *Giovanni XXIII. Angelo Giuseppe Roncalli, una vita nella storia* (Milan: Lindau, 2006).
Roper Vidler, A., *A Variety of Catholic Modernism* (London: Cambridge University Press, 1970).

Rossi, M. G., *Francesco Luigi Ferrari. Dalle leghe bianche al Partito popolare* (Modena: Riccardo Franco Levi Editore, 1977).
Rossi, M., *I giorni dell'onnipotenza* (Rome: Coines, 1975).
Rossi, M., *La terra dei vivi* (Rome: Ave, 1954).
Rossini, G., ed., *L'impegno e i compiti dei cattolici nel tempo nuovo della cristianità* (Rome: Ave, 1967).
Rossini, G., ed., *Modernismo fascismo, comunismo. Aspetti e figure della cultura e della politica dei cattolici nel '900* (Bologna: Il Mulino, 1972).
Rossini, G., ed., *Romolo Murri nella storia politica e religiosa del suo tempo* (Rome: Cinque lune, 1972).
Ruffilli, R. and P. Scoppola, eds, *Giuseppe Donati tra impegno politico e problema religioso* (Milan: Vita e Pensiero, 1983).
Rusconi, G. E., 'Discorso pubblico e discorso teologico', *Il Mulino* 56, no. 5 (2007), pp. 771–780.
Sale, G., *La Chiesa di Mussolini. I rapporti tra fascismo e religione* (Milan: Rizzoli, 2011).
Salvatorelli, L. and G. Mira, *Storia d'Italia nel periodo fascista* (Turin: Einaudi, 1962).
Santagata, A., *La contestazione cattolica. Movimenti, cultura e politica dal Vaticano II al '68* (Florence: Viella, 2016).
Santarelli, E., *Storia critica della Repubblica. L'Italia dal 1945 al 1994* (Milan: Feltrinelli, 1996).
Santese, A., *La pace atomica. Ronald Reagan e il movimento antinucleare (1979–1987)* (Florence: Le Monnier, 2016).
Saresella, D., 'Angelo Crespi collaboratore di Coenobium e la crisi religiosa di inizio Novecento', in F. Panzera and D. Saresella, eds, *Spiritualità e utopia: la rivista Coenobium* (Milan: Cisalpino, 2007), 297–320.
Saresella, D., 'The Battle for Divorce in Italy and Opposition from the Catholic World (1861–1974)', *Journal of Family History* 42, no. 4 (2017), pp. 401–418.
Saresella, D., *Cattolicesimo italiano e sfida americana* (Brescia: Morcelliana, 2001).
Saresella, D., *Cattolici a sinistra. Dal modernismo ai giorni nostri* (Rome: Laterza, 2011).
Saresella, D., 'Christianity and Socialism in Italy in the Early Twentieth Century', *Church History* 84, no. 3 (September 2015), pp. 585–607.
Saresella, D., *Dal Concilio alla contestazione. Riviste cattoliche negli anni del cambiamento* (Brescia: Morcelliana, 2005).
Saresella, D., *David Maria Turoldo, Camillo De Piaz e la Corsia dei Servi di Milano* (Brescia: Morcelliana, 2008).
Saresella, D., 'The Dialogue between Catholics and Communists in 1960s Italy', *Journal of History of Ideas* 75, no. 3 (2014), pp. 493–512.
Saresella, D., 'Ecclesial Dissent in Italy in the Sixties', *Catholic Historical Review* 102, no. 1 (Winter 2016), pp. 46–68.
Saresella, D., 'Giorgio La Piana and the Religious Crisis in Italy at the Beginning of the 20th Century', *Harvard Theological Review* 110, no. 1 (2017), pp. 75–99.
Saresella, D., 'I cattolici democratici e la fine dell'unità politica dei cattolici', in S. Colarizi, A. Giovagnoli and P. Pombeni, eds, *L'Italia contemporanea dagli anni Ottanta ad oggi*, vol. 3, *Istituzioni e politica* (Rome: Carocci, 2014), pp. 205–225.

Saresella, D., 'I Cristiani per il Socialismo in Italia', *Studi Storici* 59, no. 2 (2018), pp. 525–549.

Saresella, D., 'Il movimento socialista, il modernismo e la questione religiosa (1898–1907)', in A. Botti and R. Cerrato, eds, *Il modernismo tra cristianità e secolarizzazione* (Urbino: Quattro Venti, 2000), pp. 145–159.

Saresella, D., 'La Chiesa contemporanea tra modernità e tradizione', *Passato e presente* 87 (2012), pp. 139–153.

Saresella, D., 'O modernismo italiano entre história e historiografia', *OPSIS* 17, no. 2 (2017), pp. 194–215.

Saresella, D., *Romolo Murri e il movimento socialista (1891–1907)* (Urbino: Quattro Venti, 1994).

Saresella, D., 'The Vietnam War, the Church, the Christian Democratic Party and the Italian Left Catholics', *Social Sciences* 7, no. 55 (3 April 2018), pp. 1–12.

Saresella, D., ed., 'Romolo Murri dalla democrazia cristiana al fascismo', special issue, *Modernism* 1, no. 1 (2015).

Saresella, D. and G. Vecchio, eds, *Mazzolari e il cattolicesimo italiano prima del Concilio Vaticano II* (Brescia: Morcelliana, 2012).

Sartiaux, F., *Joseph Turmel: prêtre historien des dogmes* (Paris: Les Éditions Rieder, 1931).

Sassoon, D., *One Hundred Years of Socialism. The West European Left in the Twentieth Century* (New York: Tauris, 2010).

Sassoon, D., *Togliatti e il partito di massa. Il Pci dal 1944 al 1964* (Rome: Castelvecchi, 2014).

Scappini, E. and D. Tuorto, 'I risultati difformi del voto alla Camera e al Senato', *Il Mulino* 55, no. 3 (2006), pp. 461–464.

Schirripa, V., *Giovani sulla frontiera. Guide e scout cattolici nell'Italia repubblicana* (Rome: Srudium, 2006).

Schultenover, D. G., *A View from Rome. On the eve of the Modernist Crisis* (New York: Fordham University Press, 1993).

Scirè, G., *Gli indipendenti di sinistra. Una storia italiana dal Sessantotto a Tangentopoli* (Rome, 2012).

Scirè, G., *Il divorzio in Italia: partiti, Chiesa, società civile dalla legge al referendum (1965–1974)* (Milan: Bruno Mondadori, 2007).

Scirè, G., *L'aborto in Italia. Storia di una legge* (Milan: Bruno Mondadori, 2008).

Scoppola, P., *25 aprile. Liberazione* (Turin: Einaudi, 1995).

Scoppola, P., *Coscienza religiosa e democrazia nell'Italia contemporanea* (Bologna: Il Mulino, 1966).

Scoppola, P., *Crisi modernista e rinnovamento cattolico in Italia* (Bologna: Il Mulino, 1963).

Scoppola, P., 'Il detonatore Craxi', *Appunti di cultura e di politica* 1, no. 6 (1978), pp. 8–11.

Scoppola, P., 'Ipotesi per la presenza politica dei cattolici', *Aggiornamenti sociali* 45, no. 1 (1994), pp. 53–62.

Scoppola, P., 'L'Ulivo non può attendere', *Appunti di cultura e politica* 26, no. 4 (2003), pp. 5-8.
Scoppola, P., *La coscienza e il potere* (Rome: Laterza, 2007).
Scoppola, P., 'La Democrazia cristiana', in G. Pasquino, ed., *La politica italiana. Dizionario critico 1945-1995* (Rome: Laterza, 1995), pp. 228-229.
Scoppola, P., 'La fine del bipolarismo', *Appunti di cultura e di politica* 10, no. 5 (June 1987), pp. 15-17.
Scoppola, P., 'La fine del partito cristiano', in F. Traniello and G. Campanini, eds, *Dizionario storico del movimento cattolico. Aggiornamento 1980-1995* (Genoa: Marietti, 1997), 155.
Scoppola, P., *'La nuova cristianità' perduta* (Rome: Studium, 1985).
Scoppola, P., *La repubblica dei partiti: evoluzione e crisi di un sistema politico (1945-1996)* (Bologna: Il Mulino, 1991).
Scoppola, P., 'Quanti partiti per i cattolici?', *Micromega*, no. 2 (1990), pp. 7-15.
Scoppola, P., 'Qualche storica ragione per respingere il presidenzialismo', *Il Mulino* 40, no. 335 (May-June 1991), pp. 442-455.
Scoppola, P., *Un cattolico a modo suo* (Brescia: Morcelliana, 2008).
Scoppola, P., 'Un Patto per la riforma', *Appunti di cultura e di politica* 15, no. 2 (February 1992), pp. 1-3.
Scoppola, P., 'Votare per l'Ulivo e non solo contro Berlusconi', *Appunti di cultura e di politica* 24, no. 2 (2001), pp. 8-11.
Scoppola, P. and F. Traniello, eds, *I cattolici tra fascismo e democrazia* (Bologna: IL Mulino, 1975).
Scornajenghi, A., *L'alleanza difficile. Liberali e popolari tra massimalismo socialista e reazione fascista (1919-1921)* (Rome: Studium, 2006).
Segatti, P., 'Cattolici e voto', in R. Mannheimer and P. Natale, eds, *L'Italia a metà. Dietro il voto del paese diviso* (Milan: Cairo Editore, 2006), pp. 84-96.
Segatti, P., 'L'offerta politica e i candidati della Lega alle elezioni amministrative del 1990', *Polis*, no. 6 (1992), p. 257.
Sereni, E., *Il capitalismo nelle campagne* (Turin: Einaudi, 1947).
Siccardi, S., 'Cuori di pace e venti di guerra', *Testimonianze* 46, no. 427 (2003), pp. 5-10.
Saccardi, S., 'Dopo l'Iraq', *Testimonianze* 46, no. 428 (2003), pp. 5-7.
Smith, B. H., *The Church and Politics in Chile: Challenges to Modern Catholicism* (Princeton, NJ: Princeton University Press, 2014).
Socci, A. and R. Fontolan, *Tredici anni della nostra storia* (Milan: Editoriale italiana, 1988).
Socialismo e religione (Rome: Libreria Editrice Romana, 1911).
Sorel, G., 'Le illusioni del progresso', in G. Sorel, *Scritti politici*, ed. R. Vivarelli (Turin: Unione Tipografica Torinese, 1963), 678.
Sorel, G., *Lettere a Benedetto Croce*, ed. Salvatore Onufrio (Bari: De Donato, 1980).
Sorge, B., 'Guerra preventiva all'Iraq?' *Popoli. Mensile internazionale di cultura e informazione missionaria della Compagnia di Gesù*, no. 1 (2003), p. 1.

Sorge, B., 'Manifesto per la costituente cattolica', *Micromega*, no. 2 (1990), pp. 16–23.
Sorge, B., 'Ripartire dalla Costituzione', *Aggiornamenti sociali* 57, no. 6 (2006), pp. 461–466.
Sorge, B., *Uscire da tempio. Intervista autobiografica* (Genoa: Marietti, 1989).
Sorge, B., 'Valutare con sapienza i programmi', *Aggiornamenti sociali* 57, no. 3 (2006), pp. 193–198.
Spadoni, D., 'Dal cristianesimo al socialismo', *Critica sociale* 18, nos 23–24 (1908), pp. 365–367.
Spini, G., *Italia liberale e protestanti* (Turin: Claudiana, 2002).
Spriano, P., *Gramsci e Gobetti. Introduzione alla vita e alle opere* (Turin: Einaudi, 1977).
Spriano, P., *Storia del Partito comunista*, vol. 1, *Da Bordiga a Gramsci* (Turin: Einaudi, 1967).
Spriano, P., *Storia del Partito comunista*, vol. 2, *Gli anni della clandestinità* (Turin: Einaudi, 1969)
Spriano, P., *Storia del Partito comunista*, vol. 3, *I Fronti popolari* (Turin: Einaudi, 1970).
Spriano, P., *Storia del Partito comunista*, vol. 4, *La fine del fascismo* (Turin: Einaudi, 1973).
Spriano, P., *Storia del Partito comunista*, vol. 5, *La Resistenza: Togliatti e il partito nuovo* (Turin: Einaudi, 1975).
Sturzo, L. and G. Salvemini, *Carteggio (1925–1957)*, ed. G. Grasso (Soveria Mannelli: Rubbettino, 2009).
Sturzo, L. and A. De Gasperi, *Carteggio (1920–1953)*, ed. G. Antonazzi (Brescia: Morcelliana, 1999).
Tassani, G., 'Nuovi movimenti e politica in area cattolica', in F. Traniello and G. Campanini, eds, *Dizionario storico del Movimento cattolico. Aggiornamento 1980–1995* (Genoa: Marietti, 1997), 176–178.
Teodori, M., *Laici. L'imbroglio italiano* (Venice: Marsilio, 2006).
Tissier de Mallerais, B., *Marcel Lefebvre: une vie* (Paris: Clovis, 2002).
Togliatti, P., *Comunisti e cattolici* (Rome: Editori Riuniti, 1966).
[Togliatti, P.], 'Il caso della "Sinistra cristiana"', *Rinascita* 2, no. 1 (January 1945), pp. 16–17.
Togliatti, P., *Opere*, vol. 1, *1917–1926*, ed. L. Gruppi (Rome: Editori Riuniti, 1967).
Togliatti, P., *Opere*, vol. 2, *1926–1929*, ed. L. Gruppi (Rome: Editori Riuniti, 1972).
Togliatti, P., *Opere*, vol. 3, *1929–1935*, ed. L. Gruppi (Rome: Editori Riuniti, 1973).
Togliatti, P., *Opere*, vol. 4, *1935–1944*, ed. L. Gruppi (Rome: Editori Riuniti, 1979).
Togliatti, P., *Opere*, vol. 5, *1944–1955*, ed. L. Gruppi (Rome: Editori Riuniti, 1984).
Togliatti, P., *Opere*, vol. 6, *1956–1964*, ed. L. Gruppi (Rome: Editori Riuniti, 1984).
Torchiani, F., *L'oltretevere da oltreoceano* (Rome: Donzelli, 2015).
Toscani, F., 'Come pensare l'Europa', *Testimonianze* 46, no. 427 (2003), pp. 33–45.
Traniello, F., *Religione cattolica e stato nazionale. Dal Risorgimento al secondo dopoguerra* (Bologna, 2007).
Traniello, F., 'Verso un nuovo profilo dei rapporti tra Stato e Chiesa in Italia', in F. Traniello, F. Bolgiani and F. M. Broglio, *Stato e Chiesa in Italia. Le radici di una svolta* (Bologna: Il Mulino, 2009), 13–52.

Tranvouez, Y., *Catholicisme et société dans la France du XX siècle* (Paris: Karthala, 2011).

Tranvouez, Y., *Catholiques et communistes. La crise du progressisme chrétien 1950–1955* (Paris: Cerf, 2000).

Treves, C., 'I popolari e la proprietà', *Critica sociale*, no. 8 (16–30 April 1920), p. 113.

Treves, C., 'La Chiesa e il nuovo assetto europeo', *Critica sociale*, no. 23 (1–15 December 1919), p. 336.

Treves, P., *Scritti novecenteschi*, eds A. Cavaglion and S. Gerbi (Bologna: Il Mulino, 2006).

Trinchese, S., 'Giordani Igino', in *Dizionario biografico degli italiani*, vol. 55 (Rome: Istituto dell'Enciclopedia Italiana, 2000), pp. 207–212.

Trionfini, P., *Francesco Luigi Ferrari. Accompagnò i cattolici al senso dello Stato* (Milan: Cantro ambrosiano, 1997).

Trionfini, P., 'I cattolici italiani, la seconda guerra mondiale, la resistenza: una bibliografia', *Bollettino dell'Archivio per la storia del movimento sociale cattolico in Italia* 31, no. 1 (1996), pp. 35–184.

Trionfini, P., *'L'antifascismo cattolico' di Gioacchino Malavasi* (Rome: Edizioni Lavoro, 2004).

Trionfini, P., *La laicità della CISL. Autonomia e unità sindacale negli anni Sessanta* (Brescia: Morcelliana, 2014).

Trotta, G., *Giuseppe Dossetti. La rivoluzione nello Stato* (Florence: Camunia, 1996).

Turati, F., 'Possono i socialisti cristiani iscriversi nel nostro partito?', *Critica sociale* 18, no. 8 (1 August 1908), pp. 227–228.

Turoldo, D. M., 'Meditazione sul voto del 18 aprile', *Cronache sociali* 2, no. 8 (1948), pp. 1–2.

Turoldo, D. M., 'Presentazione', in *Gli estremisti di centro. Il neo-integralismo cattolico degli anni '70: Comunione e Liberazione* (Rimini: Guaraldi, 1975).

'Un dibattito su Gramsci e la storia d'Italia', *Studi storici* 8, no. 3 (July–September 1967), pp. 637–649.

Vacca, G., *L'Italia contesa. Comunisti e democristiani nel lungo dopoguerra* (Venice, 2018).

Vacca, G., *Modernità alternative. Il Novecento di Antonio Gramsci* (Turin: Einaudi, 2017).

Vacca, G., *Vita e pensieri di Antonio Gramsci (1926–1937)* (Turin: Einaudi, 2012).

Vaccaro, L. and M. Vergottini, eds, *Modernismo. Un secolo dopo* (Brescia: Morcelliana, 2010).

Valente, G., 'Dall'Action française agli atei devoti', in A. Riccardi, ed., *Le Chiese e gli altri. Culture, religioni, ideologie e Chiese cristiane nel Novecento* (Milan: Guerini e associati, 2008), pp. 411–428.

Valle, A., 'Dieci anni di Libera? Annuncio e denuncia', *Jesus* 26, no. 6 (2004), pp. 10–12.

Valle, A., *Parole opere e omissioni. La Chiesa nell'Italia degli anni di piombo* (Milan: Rizzoli, 2008).

Vecchio, G., *Alla ricerca del partito. Cultura politica ed esperienze dei cattolici italiani nel primo Novecento* (Brescia: Morcelliana, 1987).

Vecchio, G., 'I cattolici milanesi e la locale Camera del lavoro (1889–1896)', *Bollettino dell'archivio per la storia del movimento sociale cattolico in Italia* 12, no. 1 (1977), pp. 151–179.

Vecchio, G., *I cattolici milanesi e la politica* (Milan: Vita e Pensiero, 1982).

Vecchio, G., *Lombardia 1940–1945. Vescovi, preti e società alla prova della guerra* (Brescia: Morcelliana, 2005).

Vecchio, G., *Luigi Sturzo. Il prete che portò i cattolici alla politica* (Milan: Centro Ambrosiano, 1997).

Vecchio, G., *Pacifisti e obiettori nell'Italia di De Gasperi (1948–1953)* (Rome: Studium, 1993).

Vecchio, G., D. Saresella and P. Trionfini, *Storia dell'Italia contemporanea* (Bologna: Monduzzi, 2002).

Ventrone, A., *Vogliamo tutto. Perché due generazioni hanno creduto nella rivoluzione 1960–1988* (Rome: Laterza, 2012).

Vercesi, E., *Democrazia cristiana in Italia* (Milan: Tipografia e Libreria dell'Unione, 1910).

Vercesi, E., *I papi del secolo XIX*, vol. I, *Pio VII* (Milan: Società Editrice internazionale, 1932).

Vercesi, E., *Storia del movimento cattolico in Italia (1870–1922)* (Florence: Edizioni de La Voce, 1923).

Versace, E., *Montini e l'apertura a sinistra. Il falso mito del 'vescovo progressista'* (Milan: Guerini e associati, 2007).

Verucci, G., *L'eresia del Novecento. La Chiesa e la repressione del modernismo in Italia* (Turin: Einaudi, 2010).

Verucci, G., *La Chiesa nella società contemporanea* (Rome: Laterza, 1988).

Villa, R., *A un anno dalla scomparsa di Dossetti. La testimonianza profetica nella Chiesa del Concilio Vaticano* (Portogruaro: Nuova dimensione, 1997).

Vimercati, D., *I lombardi alla nuova crociata. Il 'fenomeno Lega' dall'esordio al trionfo* (Milan: Mursia, 1990).

Vinay, V., *Storia dei Valdesi*, vol. 3 (Turin: Claudiana, 1980).

Vinci, P. [E. Buonaiuti], 'Polemiche. Socialismo cristiano', *Nova et vetera* 1, no. 11 (1908), pp. 88–89.

Vittoria, A., *Storia del Pci (1921–1991)* (Rome: Carocci, 2006).

Vittoria, A., *Togliatti e gli intellettuali. La politica culturale dei comunisti (1944–1964)* (Rome, 2014).

Von Balthasar, H. U., 'Madre Teresa, san Francesco e frate Boff', *Il Sabato* 9, no. 10 (1986), p. 11.

Voulgaris, Y., *L'Italia del centro-sinistra (1960–1968)* (Rome: Carocci, 1998).

Wattebled, R., *Stratégies catholiques en monde ouvrier dans la France d'après-guerre* (Paris: Ed. Ouvrières, 1990).

Wicks, J., 'More Light on Vatican II', *Catholic Historical Review* 94, no. 1 (2008), pp. 75–101.

Wolf, H., *Papst und Teufel. Die Archive des Vatikan und das Dritte Reich* (Munich: Verlag, 2008).

Wolf, H. and J. Schepers, eds, *In wilder zügelloser Jagd nach Neuem. 100 Jahre Modernismus und Antimodernismus in der katholischen Kirche* (Paderborn: Ferdinand Schöningh, 2009).

Wolff, R. J., *Between Pope and Duce: Catholic Students in Fascist Italy* (New York: Peter Lang, 1990).

Wynants, E. G. E. P., ed., *Histoire du mouvement ouvrier chrétien en Belgique* (Leuven: Leuven University Press, 1994).

Zagari, M., 'Domani è troppo tardi', *Politica* 4, no. 2 (1958), p. 3.

Zambarbieri, A., *Il cattolicesimo tra crisi e rinnovamento, Ernesto Buonaiuti ed Enrico Rosa nella prima fase della polemica modernista* (Brescia: Morcelliana, 1979).

Zambarbieri, A., 'La Koinonìa di Ernesto Buonaiuti', *Humanitas*, no. 56 (2001), pp. 213–230.

Zambarbieri, A., 'La ricerca e la disciplina. Ernesto Buonaiuti e la condanna della Rivista storico critica delle scienze teologiche', in M. Guasco, A. Monticone and P. Stella, eds, *Fede e libertà. Scritti in onore di p. Giacomo Martina* (Brescia: Morcelliana, 1998), pp. 423–481.

Zanchettin, C., 'La Chiesa e l'aborto. Intervista a Jaques-Marie Pohier', *Il Regno* 18, no. 258 (1973), pp. 15–18.

Zangrandi, R., *Il lungo viaggio attraverso il fascismo. Contributo alla storia di una generazione* (Milan: Feltrinelli, 1962).

Zanini, P., *David Maria Turoldo: nella storia religiosa e politica del Novecento* (Milan: Paoline, 2013).

Zanini, P., *La rivista Il gallo: dalla tradizione al dialogo (1946–1965)* (Milan: Biblioteca Francescana, 2012).

Zavoli, A., 'Gerardo Bruni e i cristiano-sociali', *Discorsi e immagini* 2, no. 9 (1981), pp. 8–21.

Zene, C., 'I subalterni nel mondo: tipologie e nesso con le differenti forme dell'esperienza religiosa', *International Gramsci Journal* 1, no. 4 (June 2015), pp. 66–82.

Zerbi, P., 'Per una biografia di Ezio Franceschini (1906–1983). Letture, ricordi, documenti', *Aevum* 61 (1987), pp. 521–564.

Zizola, G., 'La democrazia nella Chiesa', *Il Mulino* 57, no. 4 (2008), pp. 674–687.

Zúquete, J. P., 'Populism and Religion', in C. R. Kaltwasser, P. Taggart, P. Ochoa Espejo and P. Ostiguy, eds, *The Oxford Handbook of Populism* (Oxford: Oxford University Press, 2017).

Index

Abbà, Maurizio 168
Abune, Paulos 123
Acquaviva, Gennaro 127
Adam Heinrich Müller 7
Adjubei, Aleksei 78
Adjubei, Rada 78
Adornato, Ferdinando 163
Agnes, Mario 114
Agnoletto, Vittorio 158
Alberigo, Giuseppe 85
Albertario, Davide 12
Albondi, Alberto 113
Alessandrini, Ada 75–76
Alicata, Mario 62, 64
Allende, Salvador 107
Alvaro, Corrado 38
Amato, Giuliano 141, 152
Ambrosini, Maurizio 169
Amin, Samir 91
Andreatta, Beniamino (Nino) 140
Andreotti, Giulio 114, 116, 129, 133
Anselmi, Tina 140
anti-fascism 3, 23–32, 34–37, 39, 41, 44, 47, 52–57, 60–64, 68–69, 79, 82
Antiseri, Dario 164
Antoniazzi, Sandro 95
Apollonio, Mario 73
Aratasi, Rodolfo 32
Ardigò, Achille 83, 116
Arrupe, Pedro 119
Avolio, Giovanni 18

Bachelet, Alfonso 124
Bachelet, Vittorio 95, 97, 115, 124
Bagarella, Leoluca 142, 150
Balabanoff, Angelica 21
Balasuriya, Tissa 165
Balbo, Felice 61–63, 67–68, 70
Balducci, Ernesto 5, 72, 78, 86, 92, 100, 110, 114–115, 121, 123–124, 128, 175
Balduzzi, Renato 172
Balthasar, Hans Urs von 120

Banzer, Hugo 94
Barbagallo, Corrado 38
Barbaini, Piero 128
Barca, Luciano 61
Barsotti, Divo 78
Barth, Karl 101
Bartoletti, Enrico 78
Basile, Carlo Emanuele 82
Bassetti, Maurizio 170
Basso, Lelio 35, 81
Battaini, Domenico 22
Bazoli, Luigi 116
Bedeschi, Lorenzo 49, 56, 72, 92, 101, 109
Bellavite, Vittorio 128
Bello, Antonio (Tonino) 157
Benedict XV, pope (Giacomo Della Chiesa) 36
Benedict XVI, pope (Ratzinger, Joseph Aloisius) 6, 148
Benevolo, Leonardo 133, 153
Benigni, Umberto 11
Berlinguer, Enrico 4, 107–108, 112–115, 127–129, 176
Berlusconi, Silvio 143, 145, 151–155, 157, 160–161, 170
Bernanos, Georges 87
Bernareggi, Adriano 66
Bertezzolo, Paolo 138
Bertini, Giovanni 24
Betori, Giuseppe 172
Bettazzi, Luigi 110–114
Beveridge, William 77
Bianchi Bandinelli, Ranuccio 69
Bianchi, Enzo 165, 170
Bianchi, Giovanni 143
Bianchi, Stefano 60
Bianco, Gerardo 146
Bidawid, Raphael 160
Biffi, Giacomo 151, 153, 163
Bigalli, Andrea 170
Bignami, Enrico 22
Bindi, Rosy 157, 165, 171–172

Binetti, Paola 172
Bloch, Ernst 104
Bo, Carlo 70, 75, 101, 109
Bo, Giorgio 82
Boato, Marco 90
Bobbio, Norberto 141
Bocca, Giorgio 94
Bocenina, Nina 97
Bodrato, Guido 140
Boff, Leonardo 165
Boldori Attilio 25
Boldrini, Arrigo 56
Bolgiani, Franco 116
Bonino, Emma 171
Boniolo, Giovanni 171
Bonomelli, Geremia 32
Bonomi, Ivanoe 20
Bontadini, Gustavo 73
Bontempelli, Massimo 38
Bordiga, Amedeo 23
Borghese, Junio Valerio 107
Borsellino, Paolo 130, 133, 141, 150
Bossi, Umberto 137, 139, 145, 151
Branca, Vittore 88
Brancia, Umberto 165
Bravo, Anna 163
Brezzi, Paolo 112
Brunelli, Gianfranco 140, 156, 157
Bruni, Gerardo 65, 69
Bufalini, Paolo 62
Buonaiuti, Ernesto 3, 5, 19–22
Buscetta, Tommaso 130
Bush, George W. 160, 166
Bussu, Salvatore 123
Busti, Mario 54
Buttiglione, Rocco 145

Cabrini, Francesca Saverio 12
Cacciaguerra, Eligio 50
Caffè, Federico 78
Cagol, Mara 94
Calamandrei, Piero 69
Cantono Alessandro 32
Caponnetto, Antonino 130, 142
Caprio, Giuseppe 114
Cardinal, Ernesto 125
Carretto, Carlo 74
Carrin, Jay 1
Casaroli, Agostino 127
Casati, Alessandro 19

Casini, Pier Ferdinando 144
Castagnetti, Pierluigi 153
Castro Ruz, Fidel Alejandro 91
Catholic Associations
    Association of Italian Catholic Workers
        (ACLI) 53, 95, 114–115, 120–121,
        127, 134, 143, 158
    Catholic Action (AC) 24, 34–35, 42,
        59, 62, 64, 72–74, 86, 94, 97, 115,
        119, 120, 130, 144, 145, 162
    Federation of Catholic University
        Students (FUCI) 34–35, 60, 62, 135,
        150, 172
    Italian Confederation of Workers
        (CISL) 95
Catholic fundamentalism and integralism
    24, 49–51, 95–102, 109, 111,
    115–117, 120, 151, 171
Catholic political unity 4–6, 24–31, 69,
    71–72, 74–79, 134–137
Cavazzoni, Stefano 24
Cazzamali, Luigi 11
Cazzani, Giovanni 34
Cecchi, Alberto 100
Cerrato, Rocco 104
Cervellati, Pier Luigi 133
Cervesato, Arnaldo 22
Chenu, Dominique 114
Chiesa, Mario 140
Chiesa, Romualdo 61
Chinnici, Rocco 130
Christianity and Marxism 2–8, 33–34,
    38–39, 40–51, 52, 56, 60–69, 76–79,
    99–105, 125–126, 175
Ciampi, Carlo Azelio 152
Cianciari, Marisa 61
Ciancimino, Vito 129, 130, 133
Ciotti, Luigi 138, 150
Cocchi, Romano 26, 67
Codignola, Tristano 81
Colella, Pasquale 70, 128
Colmegna, Virginio 169
Colombo, Giovanni 153
Communion and Liberation (CL) 95, 97,
    109, 111, 115–117, 120
Concordat (Lateran Treaty) 3, 27–28, 31,
    34, 37, 41, 68, 71, 93, 98, 127–128,
    148
Congar, Yves 87
Contorno, Salvatore (Tutuccio) 130

Cordova, Agostino 141
Cordovani, Mariano 64–65
Corghi, Corrado 93–94, 101
Cossutta, Armando 137
Costa, Andrea 49
Cotta, Sergio 88
Council Vatican II 5, 51, 69–70, 73, 77, 85–89, 95–96, 102, 104, 109, 134, 148, 151, 166, 168
Crainz, Guido 120
Craxi, Benedetto (Bettino) 115, 127–129, 132, 139–140, 143
Crespi, Angelo 21, 22, 29
Croce, Benedetto 3, 14, 40, 47, 49, 50–51, 60–62, 176, 177
Cuminetti, Mario 89, 123
Curci, Carlo Maria 10
Curcio, Renato 94
Curiel, Eugenio 73
Curran, Charles 165

D'Alema, Massimo 145, 152, 154, 161
D'Amico, Lele 61
D'Escoto Brockmann, Miguel 125
Dalla Chiesa, Carlo Alberto 94, 130–131, 136
Dalla Chiesa, Fernando (Nando) 131, 136
Dalla Chiesa, Rita 131
Daniélou, Jean 87
D'Annunzio, Gabriele 23
De Bono, Emilio 47
De Giorgi, Fulvio 172
De Lubac, Henri-Marie 87
De Marsanich, Augusto 80
De Matteo, Aldo 121
De Mita, Ciriaco 127, 132–134, 145
De Piaz 5, 72–73, 109, 123, 128, 175
De Rosa, Gabriele 41, 88
De Rosa, Giuseppe 140
De Ruggiero, Guido 37
Debray, Régis 94
Del Bo, Dino 73
Del Noce, Augusto 97, 125
Del Turco, Ottaviano 144
Della Sala, Vitaliano 157, 158
Delogu, Ignazio 100
Di Lello, Giuseppe 130
Di Marco, Salvatore 100
Do, Michele 168
Donati, Giuseppe 26–32, 47, 60

Donini, Ambrogio 37–38, 52, 101
Dorigo, Vladimiro 87
Dossetti, Giuseppe 5, 55, 68, 77–79, 86, 91, 117, 175–176
Duggan, Christopher 1
Dunnage, Jonathan 1
Dupuis, Jacques 165

Early Christianity 1–2, 7–8, 11, 17, 19, 20, 32, 36–38, 40–51, 85–86
Elia, Leopoldo 140
Endrici, Celestino 30
Engels, Friedrich 7–8
Englaro, Eluana 173
Escobar, Roberto 164
ethical issues
    abortion 109–112
    civil rights 6, 170–173
    divorce 108–110
    euthanasia 170–173
    same-sex unions 6, 170–173

Fabro, Nando 69, 100, 178
Falck, Giorgio Enrico 53
Falcone, Giovanni 130–131, 141, 150
Fallaci, Oriana 162
Fanfani, Amintore 77, 80–83, 86, 112
Farinacci, Roberto 25, 34
Ferrara, Giuliano 163
Ferrari, Francesco Luigi 26–28, 31, 60
Ferri, Enrico 32, 49
Feuerbach, Ludwig Andreas 21
Fiore, Carlo 101
Fioroni, Giuseppe 171
Florit, Ermenegildo 96
Fogazzaro, Antonio 60
Follini, Marco 139
Fontolan, Roberto 117
Foot, John 1
Forlani, Arnaldo 133, 144
Forlenza, Rosario 1
Formiconi, Bernardino 125
Formigoni, Guido 1, 162, 169
Franceschini, Alberto 94
Franceschini, Dario 157
Franceschini, Ezio 90
Francis I, Pope (Bergoglio, Jorge Mario) 148, 173–174
Franco, Massimo 138
Franco, Vittoria 171

François-Noël Babeuf 7
Franz von Baader 7
Franzoni, Giovanni 109, 111, 161, 172
Frédéric Ozanam 7
Frei, Betto (Carlos Alberto Libânio Christo) 94
French Revolution 2, 7, 9, 12

Gabrielli, David 166
Gaiotti, Paola 138, 140
Galasso, Giuseppe 46
Gallarati Scotti, Tommaso 15, 19, 60
Galli, Giorgio 114
Gallo, Andrea 69, 94, 96, 101, 123, 161, 170, 173
Galloni, Giovanni 127
Gambescia, Paolo 141
Gangale Giuseppe 22
Garaudy, Roger 5, 99
Garavini, Sergio 137
Garibotti, Giuseppe 29
Gasparri, Pietro 127
Gasperini, Oreste 65
Gazzola, Pietro 32
Gedda, Luigi 74, 97
Gemelli, Agostino 36
Gentile, Giovanni 51
Gentiloni, Filippo 154, 160, 166–167, 171–172
Gervasio, Giuseppe 144
Ghisleri, Arcangelo 22
Giacomelli, Antonietta 60
Gioacchino da Fiore 37, 120
Giolitti, Giovanni 46
Giordani, Igino 30
Giovagnoli, Agostino 1, 115
Girardi, Giulio 100–102, 104–105, 125, 178
Girotto, Silvano 94
Giudici, Giovanni 38
Giuliani, Carlo 15
Giussani, Luigi 96
Gobetti, Piero 27, 44, 62
Gonçalvez, Beira 122–123
Gorbačëv, Michail 137
Goria, Giovanni 132
Gorrieri, Ermanno 138
Gozzini, Giuseppe 124
Gozzini, Mario 78, 99, 100, 110–112, 124, 128, 178

Gramsci, Antonio 3, 23, 25, 27, 40–51, 97, 104
Grandi, Achille 24
Gronchi, Giovanni 81
Grosoli Pironi, Giovanni 24
Gruppi, Luciano 100, 178
Guareschi, Giovanni 72
Guarnotta, Leonardo 130
Guevara, Ernesto (Che) 85, 94
Guglielmino, Salvatore 143
Gunder Frank, André 91
Gutiérrez, Gustavo 103

Hegel, Georg Wilhelm Friedrich 21
Hitler, Adolf 3, 53, 54
Hobsbwan, Eric. J. 85
Holy See 3–4, 7, 9, 12–13, 15–16, 29, 33, 36–37, 42, 45, 47, 52–53, 59, 66, 70–72, 76, 85–88, 91–96, 113, 128, 146–148, 150–151, 156, 160, 165–167, 170–174, 176
Horn, Gerd-Rainer 1
Hügel, Friedrich von 22
Hussein, Saddam 159

Iaccarino, Rosario 169
Impastato, Giuseppe (Peppino) 130
Ingrao, Pietro 62, 137
Insolera, Italo 133
Italian Episcopal Commettee (CEI) 88, 146, 151, 167, 170–172

Jacini, Stefano 19
Jemolo, Carlo Arturo 37, 70, 72
John Paul II, pope (Karol Wojtyla) 6, 105, 119, 125, 146, 152, 160–161, 165–166, 174
John XXIII, pope (Angelo Roncalli) 78, 85, 86–87, 99, 122, 151, 158, 167
Jotti, Nilde 71

Kautsky, Karl 8
Keynes, Maynard 77
Kolakowski, Leszek 104
Küng, Hans 165
Kutter, Hermann 101

La Farge, John 59
La Malfa, Ugo 35

La Piana, Giorgio 38–39
La Pira, Giorgio 5, 77–79, 81, 83, 87, 101, 175
La Torre, Pio 130
La Valle, Raniero 88, 100, 109–110, 112, 114, 128, 132, 138, 140, 161
Labor, Livio 134
Labriola, Antonio 4, 13–14, 40, 60, 104
Labriola, Arturo 14
Lamennais, Hugues-Félicité Robert de 4
Lazzati, Giuseppe 5, 55, 77–79, 88, 97, 117, 135, 164, 175
Ledóchowski, Wlodzimierz 52
Lefebvre, Marcel François 96, 151, 167
left-wing parties
    Communist Refoundation Party 137, 139, 150, 153–155, 158
    Italian Communist Party (PCI) 3–6, 25–26, 30, 39–40, 42–51, 60–69, 74–76, 80–82, 86–87, 93, 97–98, 104, 107–108, 110–117, 127–134, 149–150, 152, 175–178
    Italian Democratic Party (PD) 6, 152, 155–156, 157
    Italian Democratic Party of the Left 137–140, 144, 152, 153, 157, 170
    Italian Social Democratic Party (PSDI) 79, 111, 127, 131, 133
    Italian Socialist Party (PSI) 1–6, 9–14, 18–21, 23–26, 30, 32, 40, 45–46, 77–78, 86–87, 107–108, 114, 125, 127–134, 140–141, 143–144, 175–178
    Margherita 155, 157, 170, 172
    Proletarian Democracy (DP) 121, 133, 137, 158
Leo XIII 9, 49, 70
Lercaro, Giacomo 79, 86, 91, 96
Letta, Enrico 117
Levi della Vida, Giorgio 37
Levoni, Rodrigo 18
Libertini, Lucio 137
Lima, Salvo 129, 130, 133
Loisy, Alfred 49
Lombardo Radice, Lucio 62, 101, 104, 110, 178
Longinotti, Giovanni 24
Longo, Luigi 71–72
Luda, Maria 32

Lumia, Giuseppe 130
Luperini, Cesare 100

Mafia 114, 123, 129–131, 133, 135–136, 140–142, 150
Maggi, Maria 75–76
Maggiolini, Alessandro 151, 163
Maglione, Luigi 64
Malatesta, Alberto 21
Malavasi, Gioacchino 34–35
Malvestiti, Piero 34–35, 54
Mancuso, Vito 164, 172–173
Mangano, Alberto 133
Manuel II Palaeologus 167
Mao Tze Tung 85
Marcel, Gabriel 87
Marchesi, Concetto 37, 178
Marcora, Giovanni 124
Marcuse, Hebert 90
Margiotta Broglio, Francesco 127
Marighella, Carlos 94
Marini, Franco 153
Maritain, Jacques 4, 59, 68, 71, 78, 87, 92, 117
Marquardt Friedrich Wilhelm 101
Marras, Vincenzo 161
Martinazzoli, Mino 144
Martini, Carlo Maria 124, 146–148, 151, 154, 159
Martire, Egilberto 60
Marx, Karl 7–8
Marxism 4, 7–9, 13–14, 20–21, 40–51, 60–69, 76–80, 100–105, 125–126, 175–178
Mastella, Clemente 144, 157
Mattarella, Piersanti 130–131, 134
Mattarella, Sergio 132
Matteotti, Giacomo 23, 29, 47
Matteotti, Matteo 81
Mauri, Angelo 11, 24
Mazzantini, Jacopo 156
Mazzi, Enzo 91, 128
Mazzolari, Primo 5, 32–34, 56, 72, 74–77, 87, 175
McLeod, Hugh 1
Meda, Filippo 11
Meille, Giovanni Enrico 11, 19
Melandri, Eugenio 121
Melloni, Alberto 167

Menapace, Lidia 93
Messineo, Antonio 81
Metz, Johann Baptist 100
Meucci, Gianpaolo 100
Meynier, Enrico 11
Miccoli, Giovanni 36
Miglioli, Guido 24–26, 28–29
Milani, Lorenzo 72, 90, 96, 124
Minzoni, Giovanni 32, 34
Mirabilia, Felice 64
Missiroli, Mario 51
Modernism (Catholic) 2–4, 11, 19–22, 23, 33, 42, 45, 47, 49, 51–52, 56, 60, 89
Molinari, Pompilio 62
Moltmann, Jürgen 114
Monaco, Franco 139, 145
Monni, Giuseppe 114
Montagnana, Rita 71
Montesi, Mario 75–76
Montesi, Pio 65, 67
Monticone, Alberto 140, 156
Montini, Giovanni Battista 35, 52–53, 64, 66, 88
Morghen, Raffaello 37
Moro, Aldo 81, 83, 86, 107–108, 111, 113–114, 116–117, 124, 146
Moro, Carlo Alfredo 124
Moruzzi, Paolo 60
Motta, Mario 67
Mounier, Emmanuel 4, 59, 68, 87
Murri, Romolo 2, 13–18, 24, 26–28
Mussolini, Benito 3, 16, 23–25, 29, 32–34, 46–47, 53–54, 64, 127, 176

Napoleoni, Claudio 126
Naro, Cataldo 142
Nasseef, Adbullah Omar 123
Natta, Alessandro 129, 137
Nenni, Pietro 27
Newman, John Henry 171
Niccoli, Mario 37, 38
Nicoletti, Michele 135
Noce, Teresa 71
Novelli, Diego 136

Occhetto, Achille 137, 145
Olivelli, Teresio 55
Olivetti, Adriano 69
Orfei, Ruggiero 87, 100, 102, 178

Orlando, Leoluca 131, 133–134, 136–138, 143
Ossicini, Adriano 3, 4, 60–64, 67, 97, 126
Ottaviani, Alfredo 64, 71

Paggi, Mario 35
Pallante, Antonio 70
Pansa, Giampaolo 140, 142
Paoloni, Francesco 10
Pappalardo, Salvatore 137
Parri, Ferruccio 70
Pastore, Giulio 82
Pecoraro, Paolo 61–62
Pedrazzi, Luigi 117
Pellegrino, Giovanni 110
Pelletier, Denis 1
Pepi, Giovanni 141
Pera, Marcello 162–164, 166
Perroni, Felice 20, 21
Piana, Giannino 165
Piastrelli, Luigi 34
Pignedoli, Sergio 66
Pincherle, Alberto 37–38
Pinochet, Augusto 172
Pintacuda, Ennio 130, 134, 137
Pioli, Giovanni 60
Piovanelli, Silvano 159
Pius IX, pope (Giovanni Maria Mastai Ferretti) 9
Pius V, pope (Antonio Ghislieri) 168
Pius X, pope (Giuseppe Melchiorre Sarto) 3, 13–16, 38, 60, 89
Pius XI, pope (Achille Ratti) 3, 27, 34, 36, 47, 52, 53, 59
Pius XII, Pope (Eugenio Pacelli) 16, 52–53, 70, 72, 85, 87, 99
Pohier, Jacque-Marie 110
Pollard, John 1
Pollastrini, Barbara 171
Pollichino, Salvatore 131
Pombeni, Paolo 31, 79
Pope 96, 102, 105, 109, 114
Popper, Karl 164
Prampolini, Camillo 10, 17, 41, 49
Pratesi, Piero 87, 112
Prezzolini, Giuseppe 28, 51
Prodi, Paolo 116, 138
Prodi, Romano 6, 116, 117, 134, 146, 152, 154–156, 169–172, 177

Protestant culture (or groups) 10, 11, 18, 19, 22, 37, 93, 101, 158
Puecher, Giancarlo 55
Puglisi, Giuseppe (Pino) 142, 150
Puljic, Vinko 160

Quadrotta, Guglielmo 20–22
Quagliariello, Gaetano 163
Quarello, Gioachino 32

Raffaelli, Mario 123
Ragaz, Leonhard 101
Rahner, Karl 100–101
Rampolla del Tindaro, Mariano 52
Rapelli, Giuseppe 32
Ratzinger, Joseph Aloisius 6, 148
Ravaglia, Giovanni 50
Reagan, Ronald 121
Rensi, Giuseppe 2, 14, 20–22
Riboldi, Antonio 123
Ricard, Jean-Pierre 168
Riccardi, Andrea 122–123
Ricolfi, Luca 145
Ridolfi, Ferdinaldo 34
right-wing parties
    Forza Italia (FI) 142–143, 145, 153, 154–155
    House of freedom 154–155
    Italian Social Movement (MSI) 80, 108
    National Alliance (AN) 145, 154
    Northern League 137–139, 145, 150–151, 153–155
Riina, Salvatore (Totò) 130
Rinaldi, Claudio 145
Rinaldini, Luigi 56
Riva, Clemente 113
Rizzo, Francesco Paolo 135
Rocco, Alfredo 46
Rodano, Franco 3, 4, 60–64, 67–68, 97, 105, 114, 176
Romani, Mario 95
Romanò, Angelo 112
Romero, Oscar 166
Romolo Murri 2, 12–18, 20, 22, 24, 26–28, 32, 48, 50, 60, 89, 177
Rosati, Domenico 114, 120, 140
Rosmini, Antonio 60, 79
Rossi, Anastasio 11
Rossi, Manlio Mario 19
Rossi, Mario 74
Ruffini, Ernesto 96
Ruini, Camillo 146, 151, 154, 166, 171–172
Rumor, Mariano 93
Rusconi, Gian Enrico 91, 168
Russo Jervolino, Rosa 145
Rutelli, Francesco 154, 161, 171

Sabbah, Michel 160
Sacchetti, Otello 76
Sacconi, Filippo 61
Sala, Giuseppe 54
Saltini, Zeno 72, 73
Salvatorelli, Luigi 27
Salvemini, Gaetano 27, 31
Santini, Alceste 101
Saraceno, Chiara 91
Saraceno, Pasquale 83, 91
Sartiaux, Félix 49
Sassoon, Donald 1
Scalfaro, Oscar Luigi 152
Scaraffia, Lucietta 163
Schaff, Adam 5, 99, 178
Schillebeeckx, Edward Cornelis Florentius Alfonsus 165
Schuster, Ildefonso 53–54
Sciascia, Leonardo 133
Scoppola, Pietro 12, 86, 109, 111, 116–117, 126, 132, 135–136, 139, 143, 148, 153–155, 164, 171
Sebregondi, Giorgio 61
Secular Parties
    Italian Liberal Party 79, 111, 127, 131, 133
    Italian Radical Party 108–112, 171–173
    Italian Republican Party (PRI) 79, 111, 127, 131, 133
Segapeli, Urbano 18
Segni, Antonio 81
Segni, Mario 138, 139, 144–145
Sereni, Emilio 52
Serrati, Giacinto 23
Setti Carraro, Emanuela 130
Severi, Ennio 61
Siccardi, Sergio 160, 162
Siri, Giuseppe 96
Socci, Antonio 117
Sorel, George 14, 40–41, 47–49

Sorge, Bartolomeo 117, 130–131, 134, 136–137, 155, 161
Sorza, Carlo 31
Spadolini, Giovanni 115
Spadoni, Domenico 21
Speranzini, Giuseppe 26
Starabba Di Rudinì, Antonio 12
Stragliati, Giuseppe 30–31
Sturzo, Luigi 24, 28–31
Suenens, Leon-Joseph 86
Sullo, Fiorentino 82

Tagliabue, Aristide 11
Tambroni, Ferdinando 82
Tardini, Domenico 64
Tatò, Antonio (Tonino) 61, 114
Tedesco, Giglia 61
Teilhard de Chardin, Pierre 62, 87, 101, 110
Teodori, Massimo 164
Tettamanzi, Dionigi 159, 166–167
Thatcher, Margaret 120
Thomassen, Bjørn 1
Thorez, Maurice 52
Ticozzi, Giovanni 56
Tiliacos, Nicoletta 163
Togliatti, Palmiro 4, 23, 39, 63, 66, 68, 70–72, 80, 97–98, 108, 176
Toniolo, Giuseppe 89
Torres, Camilo 85, 91, 94, 125
Tortonese, Mario 19
Toscani, Franco 169
Traniello, Francesco 117
Tranvouez, Yvon 1
Trentin Silvio 31

Turati, Filippo 12–14, 18, 20, 23, 27, 28–29, 31, 46
Turchi, Nicola 19
Turmel, Joseph 49–50
Turoldo, David Maria 5, 72–73, 96, 109, 114–115, 123, 175
Tyrrell, George 19

Vandervelde, Emile 47
Veltroni, Walter 152, 157
Vendola, Nicola (Nichi) 150
Vercesi, Ernesto 42
Verucci, Guido 89
Vittorini, Elio 38, 69–70
Vivaldi, Mario 61
Von Balthasar, Hans Urs 120
Vorgrimler, Hebert 101

Welby, Piergiorgio 172–173
Wilhelm Emmanuel von Ketteler 7–8
Workers Union 11, 25–27, 32, 45–46, 49–50, 53, 78, 95, 115, 120–121, 127–129, 134, 143, 158

Zaccagnini, Benigno 112
Zagari, Mario 81
Zagrebelsky, Gustavo 171
Zanchettin, Claudio 110
Zanetti, Armando 31
Zanotelli, Alex 121, 148, 161
Zhakka I Ywas 123
Zizola, Giancarlo 168
Zoli, Graziano 121
Zolo, Danilo 100
Zuppi, Matteo 122

www.ingramcontent.com/pod-product-compliance
Lightning Source LLC
Chambersburg PA
CBHW070026010526
44117CB00011B/1721